Native American Drinking

Native American Drinking

Life Styles, Alcohol Use, Drunken Comportment,
Problem Drinking, and the Peyote Religion

Thomas W Hill PhD

New University Press LLC

www.NewUniversityPress.com

Los Angeles   Las Vegas

Printed in the United States of America
First Edition

Cover design by Siena Holland. Cover formatting by
Trescela Samson.

The cover design is based on a traditional Woodland Indian
image of a Thunderbird taken from a woven bag of nettle
fiber and wool. The Thunderbird is an Other-Than-Human
Person who possesses great power that can be shared with
humans through a blessing.

For information about permission to reproduce selections
from this book, or about bulk discounts for classroom use,
contact www.NewUniversityPress.com.

ISBN: 978-0-9829219-1-3

Library of Congress Control Number: 2013930478

This book is dedicated to:

the memory of my mother, Grayce Easton Hill, who taught me to value the lessons that books have to teach and who sacrificed so that I might have an education,

the memory of my uncle, Thomas Hanks Easton, who showed his ten children and me that becoming an uncommon human being has more to do with generosity of spirit, intelligence, and hard work than with one's starting station in life,

Paula who knows that anthropology is a demanding mistress, but still continues to live with me, and

the Indians of Sioux City without whose friendship and help this study would have been impossible.

TABLE OF CONTENTS

PREFACE

Alcohol consumption among Native Americans has been a topic of interest to lay-people, governmental administrators, religious leaders, scientific observers, and Indians themselves almost since the beginning of contact between Native American and European societies. Unfortunately, this long attention has not resulted in a single, coherent view of the subject. Disagreements exist not only on the extent to which drinking is a problem for Native Americans, but also on the manner in which the topic should be approached. From which perspective should it be viewed—from a macro, societal vantage point or from that of an individual drinker? How should the research questions be posed—in terms of the prevalence and incidence of "alcoholism," "alcohol addiction," "alcohol use disorder," or "problem drinking?" Which methods should be used to collect relevant information—questionnaires with predetermined, multiple-choice options or more open-ended interviews conducted within the context of an ethnographic field study? What kinds of explanations best account for the drinking patterns observed—genetic predispositions, psychological traits, or sociocultural and economic conditions? Which form of textual representation best conveys the truths of these matters—fictional prose that carries readers into the minds and hearts of imagined actors or solemn, scholarly words that strive to describe and analyze with some degree of precision? This unsettling state is disheartening to those who turn to the social and biomedical sciences, optimistically expecting established facts and ready answers to troubling problems. Such facts and easy answers, alas, are not the way of the world. As a result, the only course open to concerned individuals is to critically read a variety of studies on the topic, to think through the issues involved, and to come to their own conclusions.

This book represents my attempts to grapple with some of these issues over the course of many years starting as an undergraduate student with my participation in an ethnographic field school directed by Bill Bittle. The school was conducted with the Kiowa-Apache of Oklahoma, and I focused my research on their peyote use. As a graduate student I became involved in a study of skid row alcoholics in Seattle, Washington conducted by James Spradley at the University of Washington. The goal of that inquiry was to see the men's drinking experiences and their interactions with the police-court-jail-treatment systems from their point of view. Following that experience, I conducted a year-long ethnographic field study focusing on the alcohol use of the Santee Dakota and Winnebago Indians of Sioux City, Iowa. That research allowed me to see their drinking practices during one slice of time, but led to other questions related to how the patterns had changed over time. As a result, I started conducting historical research in archives around the country in an attempt to identify the forces that affected the ebb and flow of drinking and drinking-related problems among the Nebraska Winnebago. Drawing on these experiences and the data collected, I published a number of articles and chapters scattered over a variety of journals and books, but never pulled them together to present a more unified view of the issues. Reprinting the previously published works together with new materials in this book, hopefully, will rectify that situation. Although the fieldwork data were collected many years ago, sadly, the situation they depict has not changed dramatically, and I would argue, the analyses offered are still valid and have current relevance. Although three chapters, One, Two, and Six are reprinted with only minor changes, Chapters Four, Five, Eight, and Nine have been extensively augmented with additional ethnographic details and discussions, and Chapters Three, Seven, Ten are new. I also have condensed and cut certain sections of the previously published material to reduce unnecessary repetition from one chapter to the next.

I describe the content and arrangement of the chapters below in order to frame the discussions that follow for the readers. Chapter One serves as an introduction to the book by considering how anthropologists have looked at heavy drinking among non-Western populations in situations of acculturation (the process of sociocultural change that occurs when two societies come into contact). I briefly outline the development of one of the most effective methodological approaches used by anthropologists and historians to study non-Western societies: ethnohistory. I then identify three major models developed by researchers to account for heavy drinking in acculturation contexts and evaluate them in light of recent theoretical and methodological developments. The discussion draws on case studies to exemplify these developments.

Chapter Two continues the focus on anthropology's approach to alcohol use. Robin Room, a long-time sociological researcher on alcohol use, wrote an article entitled "Alcohol and Ethnography: A Case of Problem Deflation?" in the journal *Current Anthropology* in which he argued that the ethnographic methods used by anthropologists and the theoretical assumptions underlying their studies lead to underestimating the problems associated with alcohol consumption. After describing his view, I argue that he misjudges the ethnographic approach and that in his theoretical criticisms he falls into "presentism" by failing to adequately place the anthropological studies he considers in their historical contexts. I have reprinted (with permission) his response to my comments.

Chapter Three serves as an introduction for the ethnographic chapters that follow by describing the location of my research and highlighting some of the social and economic characteristics of the Sioux City Indians. I also discuss the factors that influenced the type of research I conducted and examine the manner in which I interacted with my native consultants. In an attempt to see drinking activities in terms of the Indians' cultural systems, an intensive research strategy was coupled with a methodology that included extensive participant observation.

Chapter Four describes the major life styles of the "everyday" Winnebago and Santee Dakota of Sioux City. The role that drinking plays in these life styles is identified, and the forces influencing the adoption of particular life styles are discussed.

Chapter Five focuses on drinking standards and the factors that constrain unacceptable drinking over the course of the life cycle. One man's transition from hell-raiser to family man is used as a case study to illustrate the changes that occur and the forces that can affect the success or failure of such developments. In contrast to some researchers who argue that a single set of drinking standards or norms is shared across ethnic and class lines in the United States, I show that multiple sets are used by the Indians of Sioux City and that some forms of heavy and frequent drinking are defined as acceptable behavior.

Chapter Six looks at drinking from the perspective of drunken comportment. How do the pharmacological properties of alcohol interact with social and psychological variables to produce behavior? The discussion is framed in relation to the "time-out" model—one of the most influential social views proposed. It is compared to the more traditional "disinhibition" model and is evaluated in relation to two key activities of Sioux City Indians: "raising hell" and "visiting." As we will see, although the time-out model accounts more adequately for drunken behavior than the disinhibition view, it does not consider situational factors as fully as necessary and overestimates the extent to which drunken comportment is treated as time out. As a result, I suggest that a "new games" characterization is more accurate.

Chapter Seven examines heavy and problem drinking from several perspectives by starting with the drinking patterns followed by specific Sioux City Indians. The discussion progresses from a consideration of the sociopsychological forces at work and moves into an examination of biochemical and physiological factors. The concepts of tolerance and physical dependence are introduced, and critical questions are addressed including whether Native Americans metabolize alcohol differently and are at greater risk genetically than other populations. This discussion sets the stage for an informed consideration of the controversy over "alcoholism" as a disease or bad habit.

Chapter Eight returns to an ethnohistorical approach by examining the development of heavy drinking among the Nebraska Winnebago in the 1800s and the reactions that developed in response to the increased drinking. The ethnohistorical view allows us to see that a society's—in this case, the Winnebago's—particular pattern and level of drinking are not necessarily unchanging, but can, in fact, alter in response to a variety of forces. One of the major developments that occurred during the early 1900s was the widespread adoption of the Peyote religion (today, often also called the Native American Church). This religion helped many Winnebago reorient their lives and control their drinking.

Chapter Nine continues the ethnohistorical perspective and raises a thorny set of questions related to developing effective treatment and prevention programs for heavy and problem drinking. Using the description of the Peyote religion reviewed in the previous chapter, I focus specifically on the religion from the perspective of a therapeutic system to identify the elements that made it successful and to compare it to other systems. I argue that a common set of principles underlies all effective treatments. In addition to having sound treatment principles, however, their implementation must be compatible with the cultural tradition of the population served while at the same time accommodating the unique needs of each client.

In the closing chapter, I return to the basic point that human behavior legitimately can be described and analyzed from many perspectives. One significant difference among studies of Native American drinking is the degree to which intrasocietal diversity is recognized and the manner in which it is handled theoretically. Do researchers assume that all Indian problem drinkers are produced by the same forces and share the same biopsychological characteristics? Or do they consider that problem drinkers may constitute a variety of biopsychological types shaped by multiple sociocultural factors acting in diverse ways? I explicitly indicate the position that underlies the interpretations offered in this work and briefly discuss the focus that this study places on understanding individual reactions to larger sociocultural forces.

Throughout my ethnographic writing I always have tried to let my consultants describe their experiences in their own words, believing that their direct and vivid speech best conveys an accurate and sensitive picture of their situation. In turn, I hope they find that the manner in which I have framed and interpreted their statements and actions does justice to their beliefs and will help make their drinking patterns and lives more understandable to the larger society.

ACKNOWLEDGEMENTS

Because I had the opportunity to participate in a number of academic programs and attend several first-class schools, I was exposed to many scholars and teachers who shaped my outlook on life and my views of anthropology. Wilfred Husted of the Smithsonian Institution taught me archaeology along the rugged and beautiful banks of the Big Horn River in Montana. Bill Bittle at the University of Oklahoma introduced me to ethnographic fieldwork one summer with a wonderful group of Kiowa-Apache who often answered questions of "Could a Kiowa-Apache do X?" with the telling response: "It's up to the person!" At the University of Wisconsin, one of the country's great public universities where I did my undergraduate studies, I was exposed to insightful scholars and caring teachers across many disciplines. I owe much to Walter Agard, Harvey Goldberg, Herbert Howe, Eugene Kaelin, Paul MacKendrick, George Mosse, and Lawrence Veysey. In anthropology, David Baerreis, Leonard Glick, and Catherine McClellan set the standard for scholars who worked hard to be excellent teachers. They became the models for my own teaching. At the University of Pennsylvania, Ward Goodenough, Dell Hymes, Anthony Wallace, and John Wittoff had a profound influence on my view of anthropology. During a year-long program at the University of Washington intended to introduce anthropologists to the field of mental health, Mansell Pattison, who appreciated multi-disciplinary approaches, guided my introduction into the world of psychiatry, and James Spradley let me join him in his research with skid row tramps. When I wanted to increase my competency in biomedical anthropology, Sol Katz provided knowledgeable direction and help in a postdoctoral program at the University of Pennsylvania.

Of equal importance, of course, to my development were my fellow graduate students who became my friends and shared the excitement of learning while also challenging and shaping my views. My thanks to Mike Foster, Jay Noricks, James Stokes, and John Van Ness for their invaluable friendship.

Although I had not intended to stay long at my first academic job, I soon discovered how lucky I was to find a department at the University of Northern Iowa filled with individuals determined to create a democratic and humane niche that allowed for the proper mix of teaching, research, and service; I never left. My interactions and conversations with Doug Brintnall, James Chadney, John Cole, Jeff Ehrenreich, Catherine Farris, Doug Foley (who passed through briefly), Mark Grey, Eric Henderson, Julie Lowell, Gene Lutz, Ron Roberts, Kent Sandstrom, Michael Shott, Jerry Stockdale, and Anne Woodrick have left their imprint on my work.

I was fortunate to find students who were just as interested as I in Native American culture and history and who had a keen curiosity about the role that anthropology could play in understanding contemporary issues. I benefited greatly from their probing, thoughtful approach to our classes.

My family has always been a source of encouragement and support. My sister, Penny Stoudt, many years ago after reading a high-school paper I had written, gave me the good advice that my writing would be much improved if I included verbs in my sentences. I have tried to follow that useful suggestion ever since. My cousin, Jean Easton Starr, put my wife and me up while I rummaged around in the National Archives one summer and offered enthusiastic encouragement. Jeanette Rehahn and Mark Evanoff, my sister-in-law and brother-in-law, provided warm hospitality and a quiet retreat for writing, while Cisco, their Australian Heeler, became my loyal companion. My beloved wife, Paula, has kept my life interesting and has served as a sounding board and perceptive critic. Although she has not been enthusiastic about this last project, she has graciously stopped yelling "Bah, Humbug!" whenever it is mentioned. Out of such accommodations lasting marriages are made.

I want to thank the Board of Directors and the staff of the Sioux City American Indian Center and the staff of the Iowa Comprehensive Treatment Program for Indian Problem Drinkers for their cooperation throughout my period of field research. I especially want to thank Reva Barta, Fay Whitebeaver Brown, Arlene Hoffman, Leonard Mackey, Theordora Means, LeRoy Pelkey, Richard Rattray, and Winona Thomas. Their friendship and help were indispensable to my study. Although they must remain anonymous to protect their privacy, I want to acknowledge the deep appreciation and affection that I feel for the individuals who worked with me as my consultants. Without their willingness to share their experiences and lives with me, there would have been no study.

I also would like to thank William Anderson, former Superintendent of Schools, Sioux City, Iowa; Alfred Du Bray, former Superintendent of the Winnebago Indian Agency; and William Hansen, former Chief of Police, Sioux City, Iowa for making relevant records available to me during my field research.

Special thanks must go to my friend and general editor, Jay Noricks, who first suggested this book and offered much encouragement; to Darciann Samples, my sharp-eyed copy-editor; and to Siena Holland, who designed the book's cover.

Finally, I also must acknowledge the contributions of Lily, Bounder, and Daisy without whose furry presence on my lap, books, papers, and keyboard, I would have completed this project years ago, but then, the writing would not have been nearly as much fun.

CHAPTER 1
ALCOHOL USE, NATIVE PEOPLES, AND ANTHROPOLOGISTS[1]

Introduction

Anthropologists have described and commented on the use of alcohol by native peoples for many years, but until the 1940s, most of their observations and comments were made secondarily to their major research goals. Since then, anthropologists have increasingly focused specifically on drinking patterns and have applied a variety of theoretical perspectives and methodological approaches to the topic.[2] During this period, however, ethnohistorical approaches have been relatively neglected by anthropologists and other social scientists in the study of alcohol use. This neglect is unfortunate, because ethnohistory provides a perspective that contributes substantially to the understanding of a society's drinking patterns.

Ethnohistory developed in the United States and Canada as cultural anthropologists and archaeologists began using written documents as additional sources of data in their studies of Native American cultures. Although the use of documents by anthropologists is an old practice, extending back at least to the early 1900s,[3] it was not until after World War II that many anthropologists became interested in the approach and that the term itself became widely used. During the 1950s and early 1960s, many researchers viewed ethnohistory as the application of historical techniques in the study of populations usually studied by anthropologists—non-Western, nonindustrialized, or nonliterate peoples. Richard Dorson, a folklorist, expressed this view in 1960 at the first symposium held on the concept of ethnohistory: "Ethnohistory employs the chronological and documentary method of conventional history, but directs its attention to the ethnic groups relegated to the shadows in the White man's views of history" (1961: 16). As researchers critically examined the approach, however, some became increasingly aware that more was involved than just adding the use of conventional historical techniques to studies of non-Western societies. American historians had been using documents for years in their research on Native Americans, but had not produced the kind of understanding for which ethnohistorians were striving (Axtell 1978, Trigger 1985: 3-49). The difference, as Nancy Lurie (1961a: 79) put it, at the same symposium in 1960, is that "ethnohistory involves the special use of documents." The ability to make that "special use" of documents comes from the experience of field work and familiarity with anthropological concepts and theories. Because of this background, Lurie noted, "the ethnologist usually brings to bear special knowledge of the group, linguistic insights, and understanding of cultural phenomena which allow him to utilize the [documentary] data more fully than would the average historian." William Fenton (1966: 75), writing a few years later, expressed a similar view:

> The essence of the ethnohistorical method is distilled from concepts arrived at in working with the cultures of living societies in the field. These concepts . . . derive from the living culture and originate with ethnology or social anthropology as disciplines. . . . [E]thnohistory differs from history proper in that it adds a new dimension—the critical use of ethnological concepts and materials in the examination and use of historical source materials. The model of my concept of ethnohistory is field-oriented, having reciprocal lines running to the museum, on the one hand, and to the library and archive on the other.

Such a view of ethnohistory does not tie ethnohistorical techniques to any particular type of society, and the approach has been applied to a variety of Western societies. A number of researchers have adopted this position. James Axtell, for example, defines ethnohistory as "the use of historical and ethnological methods and materials to gain knowledge of the nature and causes of change in a culture defined by ethnological concepts and categories."[4] Other researchers, while accepting the importance of a particular methodology, still make a focus on specific groups a defining element. Washburn and Trigger, for example, argue, "It is now generally agreed that ethnohistory is not a discipline but a corpus of analytical techniques that scholars from different disciplines can use to study the history of nonliterate peoples."[5] The nature of the society is critical, according to Trigger, because "studying the history of nonliterate peoples relying mainly upon written materials produced by an alien creature is different from writing the history of a literate people who have abundantly documented their own activities."[6] Others remained unconvinced and argue, as Shepard Krech, does that "if ethnohistory continues to be used for the history of *ethnoi* that have been and currently are of anthropological focus, it will never be consistently or logically applied."[7] He suggests more accurate terms might be "anthropological history" or "historical anthropology." As he says: "if *ethnos* disappears from the criterion of meaningfulness, then it should be a fairly straightforward matter to decide that an anthropological analysis is also historical or a historical one also anthropological."[8]

In addition to varying definitions of ethnohistory, other differences in style and orientation can be discerned when specific ethnohistorical studies are examined. These differences reflect the disciplinary and subdisciplinary backgrounds of the ethnohistorians as well as the type of problem, society, and time period investigated and the extent to which the researcher adopts an idealist or positivist approach to history.[9]

When the focus is on alcohol use, I would suggest that the following features characterize an ethnohistorical approach: 1) a diachronic view of the drinking patterns and sociocultural system is taken; 2) all available data sources—written and pictorial sources, archaeological data, linguistic data, oral traditions, ethnographic reports, biological information—are utilized, even though the major reliance may be placed on written documents; 3) an explicit attempt is made to understand the drinking patterns and events described from the participants' perspectives, i.e., the goal is to achieve an "insider's" or "emic" view of the society;[10] 4) the drinking patterns and relevant activities are examined analytically in relation to the broader sociocultural and environmental contexts. Because ethnohistory represents a set of methodological techniques, rather than a particular theoretical orientation, no single view or interpretation of drinking activities emerges from ethnohistorical studies, nor is any set of topics or problems excluded on theoretical grounds.

I have organized the following discussion of ethnohistory and alcohol studies around one of the major topics found in the ethnohistorical and historical literature: the analysis of heavy drinking in an acculturation context. Acculturation is the process of sociocultural change that occurs when two societies come into contact. Rather than offering an exhaustive compilation of citations, I have tried to present a representative sample of works available in English and to provide a perspective with which to view them.

Heavy Drinking and Acculturation

When the European nations embarked on their discovery and colonialization of the rest of the world, alcohol was one of the items they carried with them and for which they attempted to induce the natives to trade. The Europeans were ultimately successful in this endeavor, and even in areas where native societies had not used alcoholic beverages before contact,[11] liquor became an important trade item.[12] What impact did this aspect of Western contact have on the indigenous peoples? The conventional answer has been that it was at least highly disruptive, if not catastrophic. The negative view has a long history. Belmont (1952: 45), writing about the Indians of New France at the end of the 1600s or early 1700s, observed that "insobriety among the Savages is quite a different vice than what it is among other peoples. . . . The Savages drink only for the purpose of becoming inebriated and become so only to do evil." The comments of Otto Frederikson published in (1932: 5-6) represent a more recent and florid version of the same view:

When alcoholic drink came into the red man's possession, he at once became obsessed with the idea of intoxication. Then he flung aside all restraint and became a fool, a madman, or a murderer as chance and his own unbridled nature might direct. . . . While they were under the influence of liquor, their passions controlled them absolutely. At first they might be moved to joyous songs and dancing, but these manifestations would soon be succeeded by frightful yells and roars. Gradually every good quality would be extinguished, until the Indians no longer resembled men. Disputes would follow, and then as they hurled themselves upon one another, the knives and tomahawks would come out to add mutilation or murder to the gruesome drama of fighting, running, howling, screaming, crying, groaning, and vomiting. . . . Safety among the drunken Indians was non-existent, and even the wretched children were obliged to seek protection in the brush, in fear of violence from their own parents.

Although this negative image has been developed strongly in relation to North American Indians,[13] similar views have been expressed about native societies around the world.[14]

Explanatory Models

Drinking as a Response to Sociocultural Disorganization.
When American anthropology turned its attention to studies of acculturation in the 1930s,[15] it adopted many elements of this negative view, often seeing heavy drinking as a sign of disruption and maladjustment. The interpretations given to heavy drinking in an acculturation context were shaped by the manner in which individuals were believed to be related to their culture. Early "culture and personality" anthropologists, like Ruth Benedict and Margaret Mead, were particularly influential. Because these anthropologists were intent on demonstrating the importance of "culture" and the malleability of human nature, any explanation of drinking problems that relied on "racial" differences[16] was seen as unwarranted. Instead of looking to biological factors to explain

behavior, one looked to social and cultural influences.[17] Each aboriginal culture was seen as possessing its own configuration or organization, and the majority of individuals raised within a given society were shaped into the appropriate type of person. Genetic variation within the population was assumed, but genetic coding was seen as being so plastic that most people would conform to the dominant pattern of the society. The small minority of individuals who were genetically or constitutionally incapable of being molded to their culture's particular configuration became the "abnormals" or "deviants" of the society.[18] Although Benedict (1934b: 223-230) recognized that not all cultures were completely integrated and that the amount of integration could change through time, in practice many researchers operated on the assumption that unacculturated societies would be fairly integrated and homogeneous.

As a result of these assumptions, when a researcher observed behavioral patterns like heavy drinking that appeared to be disruptive and maladaptive, he often thought that they must be due to sociocultural disorganization brought on by culture contact and change. One of the first American studies focusing on people's reactions to culture change adopted this perspective. Margaret Mead spent the summer of 1930 investigating the women's changing roles among the Omaha Indians in Nebraska. Mead found the Omaha culture highly disintegrated. In explaining the dramatic rise in the number of delinquent or "loose women" in the tribe during the last 50 years, Mead pointed to the breakdown of the old cultural tradition; instead of "a coherent social fabric[,] it [Omaha society] has been replaced by a series of discontinuous, non-comparable disunited . . . homes" (1960: 202). No single set of social standards identifying appropriate behavior existed within the tribe; parents and children often had conflicting values and beliefs; and many parents' behavior violated their own ideals. As part of the social dislocation, the old mechanisms of social control had broken down without new ones evolving. In addition, "economic dislocations" and "bad economic conditions" made positive adjustments even more difficult, particularly for the men. Mead (1960: 222) concluded that individuals caught within disintegrating societies like the Omaha's developed "formless uncoordinated characters" and were "left floundering in a heterogeneous welter of meaningless uncoordinated and disintegrating institutions." With variations, this model continues to be used to explain heavy drinking. In a disorganized situation, drinking activities may be seen as allowing the participants to achieve momentary feelings of power, to express hostility without anxiety, to satisfy dependency needs, or to cope with high levels of anxiety and psychological stress.[19]

Drinking as a Response to Deprivation. A second approach, which shares the view of heavy drinking as a sign of social strain, was more heavily influenced by Durkheim and the work of sociologists such as Robert Merton[20] than by early culture and personality workers. With this perspective, the causes of drinking are attributed less to the disruptive effects of acculturation *per se* and more to a lack of access to valued goals and means of achieving them. The emphasis is often placed on economic deprivation, but other forms are also recognized. Some authors see untoward activities such as heavy drinking developing spontaneously under conditions of deprivation; that is, they arise *de novo* each generation. With this view, the role that learning plays in sustaining these behaviors can be ignored or at least treated as secondary. The behaviors in question are expected to continue only as long as the deprivation lasts. When sufficient opportunities have been provided, the behavior should be eliminated.[21] Other researchers, although granting that activities such as heavy drinking may have originated in response to forms of deprivation, argue that once they come into existence, they may become normative and self-perpetuating. With this view, the transmission process by which these patterns are passed from one generation to another is a primary cause maintaining the behaviors. As a result, the activities may continue even though the conditions that originally led to their development are eliminated or changed.[22]

Drinking as an Expression of Traditional Values and Activities. Although the disorganization and deprivation models differ in a number of ways, both regard heavy drinking as a sign of social strain and psychological maladjustment. In contrast, a third approach which developed out of the culture and personality tradition, places less stress on disruptive and escapist functions of alcohol consumption and emphasizes the ways in which alcohol use contributes to the maintenance of a sociocultural system. This perspective recognizes that native societies have changed through time, but focuses on the manner in which traditional and foreign elements have been incorporated into new, viable patterns. Even though some forms of heavy drinking may be perceived as deviant and disruptive, others are seen as normative and may be interpreted as modified expressions of traditional values and activities.[23]

Another approach should be mentioned. This one recognizes that native societies have been adopting patterns of Western societies and argues that features of natives' drinking activities, such as the type of drunken comportment, have been learned from segments of the contacting society.[24] Although this perspective can be considered a distinct model, it does not by itself account for the origin of the patterns or explain why they are borrowed and maintained through time. As a result, it is often linked to one of the other models already discussed.

The three major approached are not, of course, mutually exclusive, and as indicated, some of the studies cited as examples of one orientation also utilize elements of the others. Nonetheless, such a classification helps highlight significant differences among explanatory models.

Critical Perspectives

In the 80 years that have elapsed since anthropologists first turned their attention to the study of heavy drinking in acculturation contexts, a number of theoretical and methodological insights have been gained and can be used to evaluate both ethnohistorical and field studies of drinking.

Diachronic Views. Although a historical perspective is required by the nature of the problem—drinking in a context of contact and change—a number of the studies cited above did not utilize ethnohistorical or historical procedures. A central factor accounting for a researcher's exclusive reliance on a synchronic approach has been the endurance of a perspective developed during an earlier period of American anthropology in which an emphasis was placed on brands of functionalism and structuralism that saw history as "unscientific" and "unnecessary."[25] As Mary Helms put it: "Emphasis on fieldwork, on patterns of culture traits, and on culture areas generally encouraged synchronic and functionalist perspectives more than historical-temporal ones" (1978: 4). These perspectives foster the misleading assumption "that investigation of the present in terms of the present is not only necessary, *but also sufficient* [her emphasis] for understanding both the present and the preconditioning past" (1978: 6). Such antihistorical or ahistorical views and the research procedures that flow from them fail to provide the data needed to evaluate fully the synchronic analyses produced by these studies. As Fenton (1952), Eggan (1954), Evans-Pritchard (1962a, 1962b), Lewis (1968), and others have pointed out, tracking the changes in a given institution or activity through time in a single society offers an excellent test for any synchronic analysis made of the institution or activity. As the situation and variables change through time, do the hypothesized relationships hold? Because the researcher is dealing with a single society, more variables are held constant than would be the case if he compared the "same" institution in two different societies.

The lack of an ethnohistorical perspective in alcohol studies has led to a variety of misconceptions concerning the development of drinking patterns among native peoples. A popular view, for example, holds that North American Indians quickly fell victim to the ravages of drink as soon as liquor was offered to them. William Macleod encouraged such an interpretation when he asserted: "Immediately upon experiencing the delights of liquor the North American Indians evinced an insatiable craving for them" (1928: 33). This generalization is not borne out by the historical record. Many groups were not particularly interested in alcohol when it first became available.[26]

Without a careful, ethnohistorical description and analysis of drinking activities and their sociocultural contexts, the relationships that exist between sociocultural change and heavy drinking are likely to be misread. The appearance of heavy drinking does not, by itself, necessarily indicate social disorganization and psychological maladjustment. Nor does the continuation of traditional behavioral patterns necessarily signal a well-adjusted population. The ethnohistorical studies of Anthony Wallace (1959, 1970a, 1978) of the Seneca and Handsome Lake's religion illustrate these points. The last decades of the 18th century brought significant changes in the fortunes of the tribes of that formed the Iroquois Confederacy.[27] Since the beginning of the American Revolution, the tribes of the confederacy had lost about 50% of their population through warfare, famine, exposure, and disease. The political structure of the old league was no longer intact. Most of the Iroquois land had been lost to the Americans, with the Iroquois remaining in New York settled on 11 reservations. Cornplanter and his band of Seneca, which included Handsome Lake, were living on Cornplanter's own land on the Allegheny River just below the northern boundary of Pennsylvania and the Allegany Reservation in New York. Their town consisted of about 40 houses and had a population of about 400 people. Despite the profound changes that had occurred, in many ways their "traditional" life style appeared to be intact. According to Wallace: "The several hundred survivors of the wars, the epidemics, the famines who now made up the Allegany band of Seneca were able to maintain the ancient marriage customs, the old religious rituals, the traditional economy from year to year with only marginal change" (1970a: 193).

But the series of events since the American Revolution had imposed a significant psychological toll on them: they had lost their self-esteem and self-confidence and were uncertain as to the value of their culture and their abilities to survive as a people. Wallace sees their psychological difficulties reflected in increased drinking, drunken violence, frequent witchcraft accusations, depression, and suicides. In discussing their alcohol use, Wallace notes that the people would spend whole nights in group singing, dancing, drumming, and quarreling. Sometimes violence accompanied the drunkenness: "The prevailing mood of drunken Indians was an explosive, indiscriminate hostility that vented itself in fighting even within the family" (1970a: 200). Although the Iroquois had engaged in periodic drinking sprees in earlier periods, these had been of relatively brief duration and had not been regarded by the Iroquois as such a serious problem.[28] Until this period, according to Wallace (1970a: 26, 27, 199), chronic individual drinking had been rare.

It was in this context that Handsome Lake began to experience his prophetic visions in the summer of 1799 and started to proclaim the religious and secular steps that the Iroquois must follow if they were to achieve redemption and social regeneration. An important element in Handsome Lake's Code, even from his first vision, was the condemnation of drinking.[29] As the people began to implement Handsome Lake's social gospel, many reservations experienced a renaissance. Wallace (1970a: 310) notes that although the temperance demand was not uniformly successful, alcohol use on the New York reservations declined dramatically between 1800 and 1810.

The psychotherapeutic techniques used in the Iroquois religious rituals changed over time from cathartic to control strategies. Wallace (1959) relates these changes to the increases that occurred in behavioral disorders throughout the 1700s and that peaked after the Revolutionary War. From the 1600s into the 1700s, when the Iroquois' sociocultural systems were relatively well organized, they relied heavily on expressive, cathartic techniques to deal with psychological distress. These procedures were integral elements in the cult of dreams, the medicine societies, and the condolence rituals and allowed troubled individuals to express and gratify their repressed or suppressed desires. Wallace feels that given the Iroquois emphasis on emotional control, autonomy, and independence in their identity ideals, these desires often centered on passivity, dependence, and self-indulgence. To the extent that intoxication allowed individuals to act out their desires in a socially acceptable fashion,[30] alcohol use functioned as a cathartic technique. Kelbert and Hale (1965: 18), in their study of alcohol use in Iroquois societies, comment on the similarity between intoxication and ritual license:

> When drunk, it was not necessary for the Iroquois to curb their emotions. They could exact revenge, they could indulge in unnatural behavior, all without fear of being punished or thought responsible for these acts. The license allowed an Indian while drunk was rather similar to the respect offered a person who was having a vision or taking part in the dream festival.

However, as Iroquois sociocultural disorganization and drunkenness increased throughout the 1700s, individuals no longer needed opportunities to act out psychological desires; they had too many occasions to do so. Instead, according to Wallace, they needed "control, order, organization: the image of a coherent, predictable world, and of [themselves] as . . . self-controlled, responsible, respected actor[s] in it" (1970a: 90). This kind of structure and the control strategies of psychotherapy to support it were offered by the Handsome Lake religion.

Wallace (1959: 94) uses the data from the Iroquois experience to offer the general hypothesis:

> that in a highly organized sociocultural system, the psychotherapeutic needs of individuals will tend to center in catharsis (the expression of suppressed or repressed wishes in a socially nondisturbing ritual situation); and that in a relatively poorly organized system, the psychotherapeutic needs will tend to center in control (the development of a coherent image of self-and-world and the repression of incongruent motives and beliefs).

Although Wallace does not develop this view in relation to changing functions of alcohol use within a society, it is, or course, highly relevant.

Intrasocietal Diversity. Another major theoretical realization, developing since the 1950s, has been that the amount of biological, psychological, and sociocultural diversity within a society is much greater than early culture and personality workers imagined.[31] A society is not a homogeneous collection of individuals all sharing one or two personality types; instead, it is an organization of diversity (Wallace 1970b). If a researcher looks closely at a society, he is likely to find a great deal of variation in the attitudes held toward alcohol use, the frequency and manner with which individuals participate in drinking-related activities, and the functions served by those activities. Drinking episodes that initially appear to be instances of the same type, such as "heavy drinking," on closer examination may turn out to represent a number of patterns, each having different origins and effects.

Given the nature of documentary evidence, adequately describing the range of variation in drinking patterns and separating similar-appearing practices are not always easy tasks. In many cases, little information on drinking is available for a given period, and when it is, the patterns described are frequently only the most visible or dramatic ones. Kelbert and Hale (1965: 4), who trace the introduction of alcohol into the tribes of the Iroquois Confederacy, comment on their source difficulties: "Although the sources are numerous, they are only fragments; a chronological account is not possible as there is no adequate step by step account. It is difficult to summarize the material as the sources do not agree on the data recorded or in the interpretation." In attempting to describe the drinking patterns in the 1700s, they remark: "It is almost impossible to form any complete picture of just who drank and who did not" (1965: 15).

Despite the difficulties, ethnohistorical and field research have demonstrated significant diversity in drinking practices within a variety of societies. Striking differences between the sexes have been documented. For example, with the exception of Gilbertese and Yap women, the societies of Micronesia have restricted drinking to males since liquor was introduced (Marshall and Marshall 1975). For either sex, typical variations may occur as individuals move through the stages of the life cycle. In a number of societies, fairly dramatic changes in drinking and drunken comportment may occur as young people become older and take on new social responsibilities.[32] For a given sex and stage of life, significant differences may exist among social positions. Taylor, in his study of colonial Mexico, found that peasants who held offices in village political structures appeared to be more susceptible to problem drinking because of their ritual drinking requirements (1979: 63-64). Within similar social positions, there may be great individual variation. Thus, Marshall (1979: 66-68) notes, even though young men on Truk are expected to drink and are considered "abnormal" if they abstain, a few, for a variety of reasons, do not drink. Another example is provided by Belmont in discussing the intoxication of Indians of New France. He notes that drunkenness does not occur among all the Indians and then details several of the significant exceptions: First, "almost all the old people and women do not drink. Secondly, the important personages or captains who have the management of affairs are given to sobriety. Also, there are a great number whose naturally noble character and great modesty would allow them to pass anywhere as excellent people"(1952: 48-49). For a given individual, drinking practices may vary greatly depending on the particular activity in which he engages and the social circumstances that surround him. A Native American in Sioux City, Iowa, drinks and behaves very differently when he goes out "raising hell" than he does if he is "just visiting" with family and friends (Hill 1978). Such intrasocietal diversity in drinking patterns suggests a number of theoretical and methodological implications, but a central one is that ethnohistorical and field researchers should assume that there will be important variations within any given society and attempt to describe them. In addition, such diversity should make us highly suspicious of any explanatory model that relies on a single cause to explain all forms of drinking or heavy drinking. Monocausal models do not adequately account for the diversity that abounds in drinking patterns.

Inherent Sociocultural Tensions.   A third theoretical insight relating to both the diversity of a society's population and the need for a historical perspective, is the growing recognition that social scientists have overdrawn the extent to which societies are well-integrated systems that, if left undisturbed by outside forces, will maintain, through the processes of socialization and social control, a social equilibrium with little deviance. Given the enormous amounts of biological, psychological, and sociocultural variations within any society and the extent to which ambiguity and contradictions are found in any society's rules or norms, a more realistic model recognizes that tension and conflict are present in all sociocultural systems. The specific types of tensions, their causes, their manifestations, and their impact will vary from one society to another, but all will have them. In contrast to an equilibrium model that sees deviant behavior as rare or occurring only in response to forces outside the system, a tension–management model assumes that deviance occurs in all societies and may arise from many sources, including changes originating within the system.[33] The particular types of deviance generated and their rates of occurrence are expected to vary from one society to another, reflecting their specific organizations and tensions. Such a perspective applied to heavy drinking does not allow an investigator to assume that its presence in a non-Western society is necessarily a recent phenomenon responding to acculturative pressures (for a development of this position in relation to Native American populations in the Southwest, see Levy and Kunitz 1971, 1974). What is required is a detailed study of the developments of the drinking patterns and a close examination of their sociocultural contexts.

The work of Mac Marshall represents such an approach. Marshall has conducted both ethnographic and ethnohistorical studies in Oceania, often focusing his research on alcohol use.[34] As part of a study on contemporary Trukese drinking behavior, he traced the historical development of their drinking patterns (1979).

The islands of Truk (now called Chuuk) are part of the eastern Caroline Islands of Micronesia. The first known European contact was made by a Spanish ship in 1565, although the next European visit did not occur until 1814. The islands subsequently underwent Spanish, German, Japanese, and American administrative control. Because of the Trukese's fearsome reputation as warlike and Truk's relative lack of fresh water, available women, and diversified crops, foreigners stayed away from Truk for most of the 1800s. As a result, Truk did not receive alcohol until after 1888 when traders began to move into the islands bringing alcohol and guns. Consumption of alcoholic beverages increased at about the time the Trukese gave up firearms and ended traditional warfare in the early 1900s.

Since the introduction of liquor, drinking has been a male prerogative. Although a few women do drink today, they are viewed negatively. Young men begin to drink on a regular basis around the age of 18, and this behavior, along with tobacco-smoking, is taken as a sign that they are "young men" and not "boys." In the village of Peniyesene on the island of Moen, where Marshall conducted his field research, most of the men between the ages of 18 and 30 drink and often become intoxicated. Their drunken comportment involves flamboyant, swaggering behavior that demonstrates that they possess the valued traits of bravery and strong thought. Such identity displays often involve them in physical altercations, typically with individuals outside their own lineages. These fights can be quite violent, sometimes causing serious injury or death. This form of drunken comportment, however, is not sociopathic; rather, it is expected and related to the "young man" stage of the life cycle. When they become "mature adult males" in their 30s, their drunken comportment becomes more subdued and less public. Marshall (1979: 65-66) notes that after reaching the age of about 50, most men rarely even drink.

Although the Trukese have obviously experienced much acculturation, Marshall does not believe that the heavy drinking and drunken comportment of the young men are due to acculturative pressures: "Trukese young men continue to do as young men their age have always done in these islands. Public drunkenness is not a major new problem afflicting youth in Truk, rather it is merely the present-day mode of doing what young men have always done as they progress along the path to full-fledged manhood" (1979: 125). Their behavior is a response to tensions inherent in the Trukese sociocultural system. The social positions of young men, traditionally and today, have been the most stressful ones in the society. A number of sociocultural factors contribute to this stress, including, according to Marshall (1979: 125), "the combination of character traits believed to make up a good person, the emphasis on *machismo,* and the relative powerlessness of young men vis-à-vis their elders." In addition, Trukese have great difficulty expressing aggression. Before the introduction of alcohol into Truk, young men were able to deal with their stresses and establish valued identities through warfare and traditional dancing. After these activities were eliminated, alcohol use offered similar possibilities; today, Marshall says, "young men simultaneously are able to work toward establishing the culturally valued identities of competence, true bravery, and manliness and to express aggression against others in socially permissible ways" (1979: 127). As indicated earlier, given the prominence assigned to economic deprivation by some theorists, it is important to note that Marshall found no relationship between unemployment in Peniyesene and the young men's drinking behavior.[35]

An Insider's Perspective.   Although the need to achieve an insider's view of a culture has always been a basic element in an ethnohistorical approach, this insight was given added emphasis in alcohol studies by the development of ethnoscience (see endnote 10). Describing drinking behaviors from an insider's perspective is difficult when working with living native consultants; it is even harder using documents written by outsiders whose understanding of the culture in question may be quite limited. The descriptions and evaluations of drinking activities given by outsiders are strongly influenced by their own standards. Although this is true of most activities, alcohol use often takes on a heavy symbolic loading that further distorts unbiased reporting. T. O. Beidelman, for example, in his study of the Church Missionary Society in Tanzania, reports that these missionaries took a very negative view of alcohol use: "Drink was considered not only synonymous with pagan ritual but a sign of absorption in physical pleasure and lack of control which were repellent to the C.M.S." (1982: 130). As a result of such attitudes, the missionaries "never recognized that alcohol and dancing were essential for completion of Kagura ritual . . ." (1982: 137). R. C. Dailey (1968: 54) has pointed out that for the Jesuits in New France: "Liquor came to symbolize white contact and its demoralizing effects. . . . For them, liquor became the scapegoat. Drunkenness was the catch-all category that was to blame for any vices or disorder that occurred." Attitudes and beliefs such as these strongly influenced not only the missionaries' perceptions of native life, but also their interactions with other people. Mac and Leslie Marshall (1976) have discussed the tensions that developed among the missionaries, other groups of foreigners (such as beachcombers, traders, whalers, and colonial administrators), and native leaders over drinking practices in eastern Micronesia. Alcohol use became one of the important symbols indicating a person's set of values and life style (also see Marshall and Marshall 1980 and Miller 1979; for parallel views and reactions among Protestant missionaries working with North American Indian groups, see Berkhofer 1965). Although such attitudes among missionary groups[36] may not surprise today's researchers, similar distortions are also found among other agents of contact. Saum (1965: 210), for example, in his study of fur traders and Indians, observes: "Though they did not always state it explicitly, traders believed that liquor was the symbol of the red man's fall at the touch of civilization." Stein (1974) describes similar views among European travelers in America during the first half of the 19th century.

Unless an ethnohistorian looks for such biases in his sources and uses them critically, his description and analysis of native drinking practices will be hopelessly misleading. William Taylor, a social historian, has produced an outstanding example of the manner in which documents can be used carefully to illuminate drinking activities. Taylor (1979) draws on many data sources—Indian codices, writings of Spanish colonists and chroniclers, trial records, and other administrative documents—to examine drinking, homicides, and community uprisings in rural villages of central Mexico and Oaxaca during the colonial period. Taylor (1979: 33-34) observes that although a number of drinking practices developed before Spanish contact, two major configurations can be identified in these regions:

> drinking only by the nobility, with harsh sanctions imposed on violators; and popular drinking on ritual occasions with milder punishment for violations. These two types follow a rough regional division. Ideal patterns of sumptuary drinking by the nobility and severe rules against drunkenness usually occur in communities controlled by warrior overlords, especially those in or near the Valley of Mexico that were under direct administrative control of the Triple Alliance [the "Aztec Empire"]. Religious rituals with drinking in this area seem to have been restricted to a select group of nobles, or at least ritual use by others was dictated by the nobility. . . . [M]ass drinking was more common outside the zones controlled by an entrenched warrior elite and perhaps is an old pattern in central Mexico that the Aztecs were attempting to suppress because of its association with rituals affirming the sanctity of the local community. Oaxaca provides strikingly more evidence of community drinking at the time of the conquest than does central Mexico. Within central Mexico, community drinking was apparently more common in regions that were independent or that may have paid tribute to the Triple Alliance but were not ruled from Tenochtitlan. . . .

Ritual use and periodic heavy drinking were central elements in both these patterns.

How did the drinking patterns change as these regions experienced epidemic disease, population decline, forced

resettlements, and various tribute and labor demands? Several lines
of evidence point to increased drinking during the early colonial
period. In areas where only nobles could drink before the conquest,
there are reports of commoners drinking. Spanish wines and
brandies were imported and sold in villages during the 1500s.
Business was good enough so that the Crown attempted to control
the trade. Pulque began to be produced for household consumption,
and inns and taverns were established in towns along the major
routes in the 1500s. Although commercialization of pulque and
mezcal did occur in Oaxaca before 1700, it was on a relatively
modest scale compared to the area surrounding Mexico City. Mexico
City not only became an important market for pulque, but also
served as a favorite place for visiting peasants to drink.

Although there was clearly an increase in secular drinking
during the early colonial period, the use of pulque in various ritual
contexts continued. Drinking rites accompanied marriages and
annual celebrations, and in some cases, these drinking feasts were set
according to the Christian calendar. Protection from new Spanish
diseases was sought through animal sacrifices coupled with
community drinking. In addition, pulque was also used symbolically
to affirm social responsibilities and duties and had strong
associations with agricultural ceremonies and life crises.

Taylor points out that much of the data on the Indians' drinking
behavior in the early colonial period comes from officials and priests.
They generally decried what they considered to be excessive
drinking and attributed many of the social problems they perceived,
such as marital infidelity, violence, and idolatry, to the consumption
of alcohol. Although conceding some truth to these assertions,
Taylor argues that these judgments were based on Spanish views of
moderate drinking and their beliefs concerning Indian abilities. In
general, Spaniards believed in limiting the amount of liquor
consumed so that a person would be able to remain conscious and
maintain his dignity. Indians, in contrast, were traditionally more
concerned with the occasions at which alcohol could be consumed
and with the social position of the person doing the drinking. Heavy

drinking and extreme intoxication within the appropriate ceremonial context were acceptable behavior. The Spaniards tended to see the Indians as children (*niños con barbas* —children with beards), morally weak and incapable of exercising judgment. As a result, Indians were not expected to be able to drink in "moderation." In addition, the Spanish also believed that alcohol released the baser, animal instincts in man. All these preconceptions helped shape the Spanish view of Indian drinking and led them to exaggerate the problems associated with alcohol consumption. Apart from general, negative statements concerning destructive drinking, such drinking is difficult to document. Using a daybook in which an alcalde mayor recorded all the individuals he encountered in municipal jails on his trips through the Mixteca Alta for over two years in the early 1600s, Taylor finds little evidence that alcohol caused serious social problems in these peasant communities. In weighing all the evidence, Taylor (1979: 45) concludes:

> that the principal difference between pre-Hispanic and postconquest drinking patterns after the initial adjustments of the sixteenth century seems to be one of shading and degree rather than radical change. A sharp increase in the scale of alcohol consumption took place, rather than a change in its use pattern. Chronic problems of individual alcoholism and drinking by women must have been greater after the conquest, but ritualized, periodically excessive drinking was common in both periods. It is ill-advised, I think, to assume that evidence of more drinking is somehow sufficient evidence of continuous, socially destructive drinking.

Discussion

Although our understanding of alcohol use in contexts of acculturation has increased since anthropologists and ethnohistorians turned their attention to the topic, no single theoretical perspective or explanatory model of heavy drinking has won unanimous support. Ethnohistorical studies like those of Taylor in Mexico, Marshall in Oceania, and Dumett (1974) in Africa indicate that the conventional view that sees heavy drinking in native societies as exclusively or predominately produced, singularly or in combination, by sociocultural disorganization, economic deprivation, or psychological maladjustment is often overdrawn, if not flatly inaccurate. The inadequacies in many of these studies can often be attributed to the failure of the researcher to appreciate one or more of the theoretical insights discussed. A revisionist view, however, should not obscure the possibility, as Wallace's study of the Seneca demonstrates, that heavy drinking can be used to cope with psychological difficulties caused or exacerbated by sociocultural change and that heavy drinking itself can lead to a variety of physical, psychological, and social problems. It is also clear that even though a society's drinking patterns can be stable for long periods, dramatic changes can occur fairly rapidly. In some cases, the direction of change is toward an increase in the extent of problem drinking, but in others, as among the Seneca following the adoption of Handsome Lake's Code, it is toward a decrease.

Intrasocietal diversity figures importantly in the consideration of drinking and acculturation in two major ways. First, the diversity observed within a society's drinking practices suggests that drinking—even heavy drinking—can serve many social, psychological, and biological functions within a single society. These functions may not only vary across categories of people and stages of the life cycle, but also change for the same individual from one drinking situation to another. Thus, while some forms of heavy drinking within a society may be seen as deviant and be disruptive, other forms may be normative and related to "traditional" values and activities.[37] Second, as our ethnographic examples have shown, acculturation can produce a variety of effects within a society depending on the nature of the two sociocultural systems in contact and the types of relationships that develop between them. It is clear that even rapid sociocultural change does not necessarily lead to psychological maladjustment.[38] The critical consideration, of course, is the manner in which the changes affect the members of the society physically and psychologically. Does the quality of their life decline? How is their health affected? Are new economic opportunities created? Do they aspire to new identities, or do they retain "traditional" identity ideals? Because populations seldom react socially and psychologically in a uniform manner to culture contact and change, the intrasocietal diversity that develops along these dimensions can be great.

A researcher dealing with drinking in an acculturation context faces a very complicated problem, then, for he must identify the numerous and complex linkages that exist among sociocultural changes, biopsychological factors, and drinking behaviors. Due to the large number of variables involved and the great differences that exist between societies undergoing acculturation, none of the basic explanatory models can be categorically accepted or dismissed out of hand; that is to say, our conclusions regarding 20th-century Trukese drinking patterns may not hold for the Seneca's in the late 1700s. As a result, a researcher must evaluate the merits of any explanation in relation to a given society within a particular time period. Such an evaluation, of course, involves a detailed examination of the data bearing on the topic, and this, in turn, inexorably leads a researcher to ethnohistory.

As indicated at the beginning of this chapter, one of the essential features of ethnohistory is the ongoing interaction between field and archival research. It is this interaction that has led to the development of a more accurate and complex view of heavy drinking in acculturation situations. And it is this interaction that ensures that ethnohistory provides the best set of methodological procedures and theoretical perspectives with which to study the past uses of alcohol.

Concluding Comment

Even though an enormous historical literature exists on the topic of alcohol use and acculturation, the number of societies for which we have adequate ethnohistorical studies is small. The comments of Dumett (1974: 95) regarding Africa can stand, with slight modifications, for most of the world: "Whereas the board range of issues connected with social and cultural change in the African colonial situation has been the subject of numerous books and articles, drinking practices within this context have not yet been studied in detail." Marshall (1976), reviewing the research conducted in Oceania, stresses how little we know about the past and present uses of alcohol in Pacific societies. In comparison, the topic has received more attention in Native American studies, but many of these works either are not ethnohistorical in nature or do not focus on drinking practices in detail. As a result, many of the conventional views regarding alcohol use among North and South American Indians need to be reexamined. Without minimizing the significant value of the previous research, it is safe to predict that the greatest contributions of ethnohistory to alcohol studies are yet to come.

Endnotes for Chapter 1

[1] This chapter was originally published as "Ethnohistory and Alcohol Studies" in *Recent Developments in Alcoholism, Vol. 2*, edited by Marc Galanter, 1984, Plenum Publishing Corporation. It is reprinted with the kind permission from Springer Science + Business Media BV. I would like to thank Jay Noricks for comments on an earlier draft of this chapter. I have not made major changes in the body of text. I revisited the competing definitions of ethnohistory, but I believe the discussion of the major approaches taken by anthropologists and historians to the use of alcohol by native peoples is still accurate. The theoretical and methodological weaknesses identified remain as relevant as ever. I added new references to a few topics such as the continuing discussion over the nature of ethnohistory (*see* endnote 9) and pointed out that the researcher of one of the case studies reviewed (*see* endnote 35) has changed his view (Marshall 1990a) on the extent to which drinking is problematic on Truk (now called Chuuk).

[2] For reviews and bibliographies *see* Bacon (1976), Barry (1982), Bennett (1988), Bennett and Ames (1985), Bennett and Cook (1990), Dietler (2006), Douglas (1987), Fox and MacAvoy (2011), Freund and Marshall (1977), Gordon (1984), Heath (1976a, 1976b, 1983, 1984, 1987a, 1987b, 1988, 1989, 1993, 2000), Heath and Cooper (1981), Heidenreich (1976), Leland (1976, 1981), Mail and McDonald (1981), Mancall (1995a: 245-259), Marshall (1974, 1976), Marshall, Ames, and Bennett (2001), Verhey (1991).

[3] Baerreis (1961), Hudson (1973), Hultkranz (1967), Schwerin (1976), Sturtevant (1966).

[4] Axtell (1979: 2), in the original the entire quotation is italicized. Also *see* Axtell (1997: 4), Carmack (1972: 234), Euler (1972), Hickerson (1970: 6), Spores (1980: 575-576).

[5] Washburn and Trigger (1996: 101); also *see* Trigger (1985: 164-172).

[6] Trigger (1982: 9).

[7] Krech (1991: 364).

[8] Krech (1991: 365).

[9] For additional discussions of ethnohistory, anthropology, and history *see* Adams (1962), Axtell (1981), Barrows and Room (1991), Calloway (2011), Cohn (1968, 1980), Crozier (1965), Darnell (2011), Deloria (2002), Dobyns (1972, 1978), Edmunds (2008), Eggan (1961), Ewers (1961), Fenton (1952, 1962), Fixico (1997), Fogelson (1974, 1989), Helms (1978), Krech (2006),

---

Leacock (1961), Martin (1987), Nabokov (2002), Sahlins (1981, 1985, 2005), Shoemaker (2002), Spores (1978), Valentine (1961), Walker (1970), Washburn (1961), Wunder (2007). Two major developments have occurred in ethnohistory since the 1960s. One has been the dramatic increase in the variety of topics addressed. As John Wunder (2007: 602) observed in relation to studies of Native Americans: "Questions of agency, voice, sovereignty, nationhood, marriage, status, class, intercultural connections, diplomatic mergers, race, and culture change abound." The second has been increased calls for what Raymond Fogelson (1974, 1989), only half-humorously, referred to as "ethno-ethno-ethnohistory," that is, for Native Americans to produce their own historical studies from their perspectives (*see* Nabokov 2002 for a review and discussion of Indian-centered approaches to history). Some writers (such as Calvin Martin 1987a, 1987b, 1987c) adopt an extreme position on this issue and argue that the worldviews of Native American and Western societies were so different that Western scientific and historical approaches cannot adequately describe or understand them.

[10] Since the 1950s, this emphasis on achieving an insider's view has frequently been associated with a set of theoretical and methodological approaches labeled "ethnoscience" and more recently called "cognitive anthropology" (*see* Black 1973; Casson 1981; D'Andrade 1995; Goodenough 1970; Hymes 1977; Kronenfeld et al. 2011; Spradley 1972b, 1979; Tyler 1969; Werner 1972; Werner and Fenton 1970 for discussion of this perspective) and (Brown 1980; Hill 1974, 1978, 1980a; Leland 1975, 1978; Spradley 1970, 1972a; Spradley and McCurdy 1975; Topper 1974, 1976, 1980, 1981; Waddell 1975, 1980a; Everett 1980) for applications to the study of drinking patterns. Such a goal, however, is not necessarily restricted to any single theoretical or methodological approach and can be seen as an essential element of 20th-century social and cultural anthropology (*see*, for example, Geertz 1977, Hallowell 1955, Malinowski 1961: 25, Waddell 1981).

[11] Societies in Oceania and those north of Mexico and the American Southwest lacked alcoholic drinks before European contacts (Bruman 1940, Cooper 1949, Marshall and Marshall 1975, Marshall 1980, Driver 1969, Waddell 1980b). Indian groups in the American Southeast may have made fermented beverages from such plants as the honey locust and persimmon before European contact, but this has not been clearly established (Driver 1969, Carr 1947, Hudson 1976).

[12] *See* Berthrong (1963: 89-92), Dumett (1974: 70-71), Howay (1942), Marshall and Marshall (1975), Morrell (1960: 58-60, 282), Pan (1975), Phillips (1961, vol. 1: 109), Ray (1974: 85-87, 148-155), Ray (1975: 144, 155, 179), Ray and Freeman (1978: 128-144), Taylor (1979).

[13] *See* Bailey (1969: 66-74), Berkhofer (1978: 37-38), Jacobs (1950: 53-55), (1972: 33, 39), Jaenen (1976: 110-116, 196), Jenness (1963: 253-254), Macleod (1928), Mancall (1995a, 1995b), Phillips (1961: 213), Sheehan (1973: 232-242), Stein (1974), Unrau (1996).

[14] *See* Buell (1928: 851-853), Gibson (1964: 150, 409), Gongora (1975: 141), Leenhardt (1937: 206, *cited in* Howe 1977: 152), Lugard (1965: 597-605), Macleod (1928: 31), Phelan (1959: 158), Price (1950: 118-121, 152-153, 165, 196-197), Thompson and Adloff (1971: 11, 211-213, 285, 359, 490), Ward (1978: 135-136).

[15] Redfield, Linton, Herskovits (1936), Bee (1974).

[16] Macleod (1928: 33), for example, attributed the Indians' difficulties with alcohol to a "constitutional weakness."

[17] These views were so influential that it was not until the 1970s that anthropologists seriously began considering the role of biological factors in drinking patterns (Hanna 1976, Schaefer 1981).

[18] Benedict (1934a, 1934b); Mead (1928), (1959: 201-212).

[19] *See* Carpenter (1959); Curley (1967); Dailey (1964); Du Toit (1964); Hammer (1965); Harrod (1971: 41-44, 56-57); Hutchinson (1961); Jaenen (1976); R. Levy (1966: 306-308), (1973: 408-413); Lomnitz (1976: 185-185); Mohatt (1972: 264-266); Wallace (1959, 1970a, 1978); Whittaker (1963: 87).

[20] Merton (1938) and (1957: 161-194).

[21] Dozier (1966), Graves (1970), Hurt (1961-1962), Hurt and Brown (1965: 222), Jessor, Graves, and Hanson (1968), Jorgensen (1972), Millar and Leung (1971: 95), Mohatt (1972: 267-268), Schlesier (1979), White (1970).

[22] White (1970), Lewis (1966a, 1966b).

[23] Bunzel (1940); Carpenter (1959); Dailey (ms., 1964, 1968); Devereux (1948); Honigmann and Honigman (1945, 1965); Hurt and Brown (1965: 222-224); Ishii (2008: 15-16, 32-36); James (1961); Kelbert and Hale (1965); Lemert (1954a: 26), (1954b), (1958: 91, 98-99); R. Levy (1966: 308-319), (1973: 413-426); Levy and Kunitz (1971, 1974); Lomnitz (1976); Lurie (1971); Mancall (1995a: 68-79), (1995b: 430-431); Marshall (1979); Ray (1975: 252); Taylor (1979); Waddell (1975, 1980a); Wallace (1959, 1970a).

[24] James (1961), Lemert (1958: 96), MacAndrew and Edgerton (1969), Marshall (1979), Taylor (1979), Unrau (1996: 116), White (1970).

[25] Fenton (1952), Helms (1978), Herskovits (1960), Hudson (1973), Hultkranz (1967).

[26] *See* Frederikson (1932), Howay (1942), MacAndrew and Edgerton (1969: 90-115), Phillips (vol. 1: 109), Saum (1965: 213-214), Trigger (1976: 433). Waddell (1985: 264), for example, after examining the fur trade journal of Francois Malhoit, who wintered among the Chippewa, concluded, "the Chippewa of 1804-05 were no more or no less abusive in their uses of alcohol, when it was periodically available, than any other population— including Malhoit's own workers, under similar circumstance. To argue that these Indians craved or were slaves to rum is wrong."

[27] *See* the appropriate articles in Trigger (1978) for a discussion of, and literature on, the tribes of the confederacy.

[28] Trelease (1960) and Norton (1974) discuss the development of the fur trade with the Iroquois Confederacy and liquor's role in the trade. *See* Carpenter (1959) and Kelbert and Hale (1965) for discussions of alcohol use in the earlier period.

[29] Such a view was not uncommon in other North American Indian revitalization movements, *see* Amoss (1978), Barnett (1957), Cave (2006), Dowd (1992), Forsyth (1911), Herring (1988), Slotkin (1956).

[30] *See* Carpenter (1959), Dailey (ms., 1964, 1968), Kelbert and Hale (1965), MacAndrew and Edgerton (1969).

[31] Bock (1980: 131-138), Lewontin (1974), Lindesmith and Strauss (1950), Pelto and Pelto (1975), Wallace (1970b), Williams (1956, 1974).

[32] *See*, for example, Hill (1974, 1980); Leland (1978); R. Levy (1966), (1973: 422-424); Lemert (1962); Waddell (1980c).

[33] Edgerton (1976, 1978), Moore (1974), Lloyd (1968).

[34] Marshall and Marshall (1975, 1976, 1980), Marshall (1975, 1979).

[35] Although my review of Marshall's 1979 study in this chapter does not stress the unproblematic nature of Trukese drinking (in fact, it appeared to me on the basis of his description that there were a number of potential problems associated with drinking), he now feels that he presented it as essentially nonproblematic. As he said, "I underplayed the extent of alcohol-related problems in Truk because I did not find evidence for much 'alcoholism' of the sort discussed under the rubric of the disease model of alcoholism" (1990a: 363). He now believes "that excessive drinking has led

to many kinds of problems in Truk—social, economic, and political as well as physical . . . . This change in my perspective results both from changes in me . . . and changes in Trukese society" (1990a: 364-365; also see Marshall and Marshall 1990 and Marshall 1990b). During his earlier fieldwork, he apparently failed to realize than an individual does not have to be an alcoholic to experience or cause a variety of problems through heavy drinking and failed to discover the women's view of drinking. As a result, he was surprised that a prohibition law took effect in Moen Municipality in 1978 and that women were the moving force behind the prohibition movement. This case demonstrates that even with a good researcher, any method (ethnohistorical, ethnographic fieldwork, or survey) is only as good as its execution. Marshall, as he acknowledges, did not adequately identify and describe the intrasocietal diversity regarding the perceptions and evaluations of heavy drinking. A 1985 survey confirmed that there was no relationship between employment status and alcohol use (Marshall 1990b).

[36] As Beidelman (1982: 9-11) points out, although there has been a tendency in acculturation studies to treat all missionaries as though they represented a unitary category, significant differences in attitudes toward such behaviors as drinking, dancing, and smoking existed among them, reflecting differences in their ethnicity, class, and education. *See* Gunson (1966) for a discussion of the changing views on the use of alcohol among English-speaking missionaries in the Pacific during the 1800s and Ronda and Axtell (1978) for a critical bibliography on Indian missions among North American Indians.

[37] This is not to suggest that traditional, nondeviant, heavy drinking is unrelated to problem drinking. Although many factors contribute to problem drinking, individuals who regularly drink heavily increase their risks of developing drinking problems.

[38] *See* Chance (1960, 1965, 1966) for a case study and Wallace (1970b: 165-206), Berry (1980), Goodenough (1963), and Spicer (1961: 517-544) for overviews.

CHAPTER 2
DO ANTHROPOLOGISTS DEFLATE PROBLEM DRINKING?[1]

Robin Room's article "Anthropology and Ethnography: A Case of Problem Deflation?," the accompanying comments, and his reply to those comments in the journal *Current Anthropology* present several substantive and methodological issues that deserve further discussion. Room presents at least two major arguments. On the one hand, he argues narrowly that anthropologists who dealt with alcohol use among "tribal" and "village" societies before the 1970s underestimated the problems associated with alcohol consumption as a result of their ethnographic methodology: "Ethnographic methods, in short, may underestimate the problems related to drinking because they are better attuned to measuring the pleasure than the problems of drinking" (Room 1984: 172). On the other hand, he charges, more generally, that "systematic" problem deflation can be found in the anthropological literature dealing with alcohol use. This deflation he attributes not only to "methodological error" but also to theoretical assumptions and emphases. Arguing that ethnographic methods *per se* lead to problem deflation is very different from asserting that *some* ethnographic descriptions have underestimated problems related to alcohol use because of the theoretical orientation and sociocultural milieu of the researchers. Many anthropologists would dispute the first charge and accept the second but assert that such a generalization is trivial and can be applied with equal validity to any discipline or methodological approach.

On the basis of his use of Heath's description (1984: 172), it seems that Room views an "ethnographic approach" as consisting of a combination of participant observation and informant interviewing. How do these procedures specifically lead to problem deflation? We are never told or shown with reference to specific studies; instead, Room shifts the issue to the manner in which these procedures *might* be applied. He has the mistaken view that these techniques are designed primarily to study "everyday" events and to "focus on public and collective behavior" (1984: 172-73). Although it is true that ethnographers generalizing about a society's behavioral patterns may emphasize commonly occurring events and describe what Goodenough (1971) has called the "public culture" of a community, this does not mean that the procedures used to collect data are necessarily limited to these tasks or that ethnographers have exclusively couched their description in terms of public culture. If an anthropologist is interested in the "private pain" associated with drinking or in the cognitive and behavioral diversity found in drinking-related practices, ethnographic procedures allow him to study these topics. Room never demonstrates how "ethnography," when considered narrowly as a set of methods, leads to problem deflation

Room's handling of the "interpretive" aspects of ethnography in relation to problem deflation is weakened by the adoption of the perspective and methodology of "presentism" (Stocking 1965). Although he frames the issue as a historical one, the major sources of data upon which he tries to establish the existence of problem deflation are the results of two recent conferences, a collection of readings, and several review articles. As several commentators noted, this is a very weak foundation upon which to establish the central contention of the article. Irrespective of the quality of the collected readings and review articles, such works are composed for particular audiences and with specific goals in mind that relate only tangentially to Room's major thesis. By not directly examining ethnographic studies within their historical contexts, Room is led to an incomplete and misleading view of ethnographic studies of alcohol use. He suggests that a number of factors—including functionalist assumptions, culture-bound concepts of "alcoholism," the middle-class liberal background of ethnographers, and reactions against colonial administrative and missionary perspectives—have influenced anthropological studies dealing with alcohol use. However, he fails to show how these factors actually affected specific researchers or studies through detailed historical analysis. Failing to adopt a thoroughgoing perspective of "historicism" and to delineate what Hollinger (1979) calls "communities of discourse" in relation to the issues or questions surrounding each of his proposed factors, Room does not demonstrate any of his suggested connections. His treatment of the development of anthropological research during the 20th century is superficial, and as a result, his view of the manner in which anthropologists have dealt with alcohol use is distorted.

Room's discussion of functionalism in anthropology demonstrates his truncated historical view. He accurately notes that since about 1930 many anthropologists have been concerned to show how various elements of a sociocultural system fit together into a functioning whole but then he argues that "the deemphasis of the problematic side of drinking is not only a matter of oversight, but rather tends to be inherent in a functionalist perspective" (1984: 171). His treatment disregards the manner in which "functionalist" concerns related to two of the major research interests that occupied cultural anthropologists during the 1930s and 1940s: "culture and personality" and "acculturation." For American anthropology, the early works of Ruth Benedict and Margaret Mead, which developed a number of themes within the Boasian tradition, became points of departure for later research. While their approaches did assume that unacculturated societies would tend to be homogenous and well-integrated,[2] every society was also viewed as possessing a number of individuals who were seen by the society as being abnormal or deviant because their personality types did not articulate with the prevailing cultural configuration.[3] In addition, acculturating societies that experience conflict, disorganization, and deprivation were expected to show high rates of psychic distress and behavioral problems (Mead 1932; 1972: 490-92). Although their studies were criticized on a number of points[4] and even though alternative theoretical and methodological approaches developed,[5] many researchers of the 1930s and 1940s continued to share the assumptions that many members of an unacculturated society, with the exception of a few deviants, would be psychologically similar and that heavy acculturation and sociocultural disorganization would adversely affect the mental health and behavior of individuals experiencing the changes.[6] This general perspective offered researchers who dealt with drinking practices several theoretical options. If a researcher focused upon the negative, escapist aspects of alcohol use, drinking could be attributed to sociocultural disorganization and deprivation. If, on the other hand, a researcher focused on the positive, normative aspects of drinking, an attempt could be made to demonstrate how drinking-related activities fit into the cultural configuration of the society. This second approach could be taken even with societies that lacked alcoholic beverages prior to white contact by showing the manner in which "foreign" elements, including the use of alcohol, had been incorporated into the society to maintain a new social equilibrium. Even though a given researcher might stress either the positive or the negative side of drinking activities, this theoretical perspective allowed for the acknowledgment and description of both aspects. One can find the full range of treatments in ethnographic literature appearing since 1930.[7]

Room admits (1984: 171), citing Heath again, and in response to Levy's comments (1984: 188), that anthropologists have noted problems associated with drinking, but he argues that because these studies often placed the source of the problems outside the society, he does not need to consider them in relation to his contention of systematic problem deflation. In the context of Room's argument, whether the causes are attributed to sources outside or inside the society or even whether the causes are accurately identified or not, is beside the point: there is a large body of ethnographic literature that clearly describes the negative aspects of drinking practices and that cannot be seen as contributing to problem deflation. If one focused exclusively on these studies, in fact, a case could be made that anthropological studies have been guilty of problem inflation. But to focus on only one end of the continuum of approaches taken to drinking is to distort the historical record.

I readily concede that some anthropological studies of alcohol use have suffered from a variety of methodological and theoretical weaknesses (Hill 1984), but these weaknesses have not always operated in the same direction in relation to the treatment of drinking problems: in some studies they have led to problem deflation but in others to problem inflation. I applaud Room's attempt to identify the biases and defects in ethnographic studies, but the approaches taken to alcohol use are embedded in, and represent expressions of, particular research traditions (Laudan 1977) and strategies. To evaluate and understand particular studies of drinking, we much determine the manner in which they relate to prevailing research traditions and strategies and delineate the ways in which both the ethnographers and the traditions reflected other social and cultural influences. To do so requires careful historical study. Veysey's (1979: 23) admonition to intellectual historians applies with equal force to historical sociologists and anthropologists: "Generalizations . . . to be credible, must be extremely hard earned. They require far more arduous preparation, far more careful spadework, far closer attention to logic, than many of our predecessors a generation ago were aware."

Reply
by Robin Room

Hill's complaint that my article adopted "the perspective and methodology of 'presentism'" seems related to the fact that it started from concerns oriented to the present—from concerns about how anthropological evidence on drinking in tribal and village societies is cumulated and summarized in the recent literature. This starting point quickly led into historical considerations, since synoptic and cross-cultural analyses of the ethnographic literature are necessarily unusually dependent on rather old studies. The systematic sampling approach of hologeistic studies pushes this to extremes: thus, for the underlying studies concerning the average society in Schaefer's sample, the mean time since publication was 40 years (see p. 174 of my article). The article nevertheless remained rooted in present-day concerns, and this seems to me a legitimate perspective, although one quite different from the thoroughgoing historical studies Hill calls for. I would welcome the historical studies, examining the past in its own terms and without "the enormous condescension of posterity" (Thompson 1964), but the separate question of how we got where we find ourselves also seems worth trying to answer.

Hill's discussion of the historical and ideological context of functionalism in anthropology is a welcome elaboration, but we seem to end up with much the same conclusion: that in a functionalist account, where drinking was seen as "bad" it tended to be attributed to outside causes and influences, while "good" drinking was seen as integrated into the cultural configuration of the society. Contrary to Hill's assertion, I did not argue that studies acknowledging problems but placing their source outside the society can be ignored in considering problem deflation. My argument was not that drinking problems are unrepresented in the ethnographic literature but rather that on balance the "continuum of approaches" has been biased against the representation of problems. The "anomie" interpretations, acknowledging drinking problems, are overbalanced by what Leland calls the "reverse firewater hypothesis" and belittled in synoptic statements that "in cross-cultural perspective, 'problem drinking' is very rare" (Heath 1975: 57).

It should be acknowledged that my discussion of ethnographic methodology is the view of an interested outsider. My concern was with what seemed to have happened in fact in the literature, not with the theoretical capabilities of the methods. Ethnographic methods may not necessarily lead to problem deflation, but they seem in practice to have lent themselves to it. While the case of "cultural negativity towards alcohol" among poor Mexicans (1984: 172) certainly exemplified this issue for me, the discussion also adduced the testimony of a number of ethnographers on the issue (see Levy 1984: 172, 182; Honigmann 1984: 177-78; Beckett 1984: 179).

Endnotes for Chapter 2

[1] This chapter was originally published as "On Alcohol and Ethnography: A Problem in the History of Anthropology" in *Current Anthropology*, 1985, Vol. 26, No. 2, pages 282-284. It, along with Robin Room's reply, is reprinted with the permission of the University of Chicago Press. The copyright for these materials is 1985 by the Wenner-Gren Foundation for Anthropological Research. All rights reserved. Since Room published his article an ongoing debate developed between Dwight Heath and Room concerning the relative merits of a sociocultural model versus a distribution-of-consumption model (and the quality of the data for each) in relation to the nature of alcohol control policies (*see* Marshall 1990a for a discussion and references, also *see* Heath 1992, 2007 and Room and Hall 2011). Neither that discussion nor the fact that Marshall acknowledges he was guilty of "problem deflation" on Truk or Chuuk in his earlier fieldwork (see endnote 35 in Chapter 1) alters my views as expressed in this chapter.

[2] Benedict (1930, 1935a); Mead (1961 [1928]: 1-13; 1959: 201-12). Benedict (1934a: 223-30) realized, however, that cultures differed in their degrees of integration and that a culture's integration could change through time.

[3] Benedict (1930, 1934a); Mead (1961 [1928]: 1-13; 1959: 201-12).

[4] *See*, for example, Bennett (1946); Goldfrank (1945; 1978: 38-39, 127, 171); Li (1937); Radin (1933: 41-60, 115-16, 176-82); Winston (1934).

[5] *See* Barnouw (1979), Bock (1980), Herskovits (1938), Keesing (1953), and Wallace (1970b) for critical overviews of these developments.

[6] Devereux (1942), Devereux and Loeb (1943), Macgregor (1946), Mekeel (1937), Hallowell (1950). In the 1950s and early 1960s, under the force of growing criticism, culture-and-personality studies underwent a fundamental reorientation (Lindesmith and Strauss 1950; Orlansky 1949; Wallace 1961, 1962.) The theoretical and methodological approaches associated with these changes have had a significant impact on anthropological studies of alcohol use.

[7] *See* Bunzel (1940, 1976); Elkin (1940); Erikson (1937); Goldfrank (1943); Hallowell (1946, 1950); Honigmann and Honigmann (1945); Joseph, Spicer, and Chesky (1949: 77, 86, 108, 129, 162, 198, 238-40); Kluckhohn (1967 [1944]: 88-95, 126); Kluckhohn and Leighton (1946: 113-14,162, 226, 236-39); Leighton and Kluckhohn (1948: 89); Lemert (1954); Lurie (1952: 190-251); Slotkin (1953); Speck (1933); Vogt (1951: 47-70, 105-7, 128-33, 162-66);

Wallace (1951). I am not suggesting that all these studies took the same theoretical and methodological approach to drinking or that they all adopted Benedict's and Mead's positions. Bunzel's (1940) seminal study of drinking, for example, was influenced by her work with Kardiner and others on topics related to culture and personality at Columbia University during the late 1930s (see Bunzel 1976; Goldfrank 1978: 111-12, 125; Kardinar 1939). Keeping to the period under discussion, I have cited only examples of studies from the 1930s through the early 1950s; the same general treatments of drinking, including an interest in drinking problems, have continued into the present.

CHAPTER 3
RESEARCH SETTING AND THEORETICAL APPROACH[1]

> Ethnography is to social
> science as jazz is to music.
>
> Michael Agar

In order to provide the reader with a fuller context for the following chapters, I will briefly describe the Sioux City setting, my research approach, and the nature of my interactions with my native consultants.

Indian Population and Indian Social Service Agencies in Sioux City

Sioux City is located in the western part of Iowa on the bank of the Missouri River. The town of South Sioux City lies directly across the Missouri River in the state of Nebraska. West of Sioux City the Big Sioux River flows into the Missouri River and separates Iowa from South Dakota. The small town of North Sioux City is located in South Dakota on the west bank of the Big Sioux River. European and American settlement in the Sioux City vicinity began in the late 1840s. The town itself was platted in the winter of 1854-55 and was incorporated in 1857 (Allen 1927: 134-159, Clark et al. 1890-91: 50-60). The 1970 census lists the total population of the Sioux City Iowa-Nebraska Standard Metropolitan Statistical Area (henceforth SMSA)[2] as 116,189.[3]

The Indian population of the Sioux City SMSA was given by the 1970 census as 865,[4] but others would place their number as high as 2,000 (Rattray n.d.: 4). It is difficult to accurately determine the number of Indians living in Sioux City because many Indians are relatively mobile, not only moving frequently within the Sioux City area, but also traveling from one city to another. Although a core of Indians has resided in Sioux City for long periods, the more mobile and transient portion is not apt to be picked up by the census. In addition, since a number of reservations[5] are relatively close to Sioux City, Indians who list their residence elsewhere spend a great deal of time—both working and engaging in recreational activities—in Sioux City. As a result, the number of Indians actually in Sioux City was probably greater than the census figure. Conservatively, I would estimate the number to be at least 1,000 in 1970. Although the Indian population is composed of many tribal groups, the largest numbers come from the Santee Dakota, Winnebago,[6] Omaha, and Yankton tribes.

Linguistically, almost all the Sioux City Indians spoke English (the exceptions being a few elderly individuals), and for the vast majority, English was their first and only language. A sense of the linguistic situation can be gained from the 1980 census data on the three major reservation communities in Nebraska.[7] The reservation populations are linguistically more conservative than their urban counterparts in Sioux City, but even here only 19% to 31% of persons over five years of age spoke a language other than English at home (19% for the Santee, 22.6% for the Winnebago, and 30.5% for the Omaha). In 1970, the American Indian Center offered native language classes for interested young people but dropped them due to lack of participation.[8]

Social and Economic Characteristics of the Indian Population

Some idea of the Indians' social and economic conditions can be gained from the special tabulation of the 1970 census data. Although these figures are based on sample data and are subject to sampling variability, they provide the best statistical picture available for the Indian population in 1970. The following figures and percentages are based on a sample figure of 852 Indians in the Sioux City SMSA.[9]

Age. Over half of the Indian sample was under 18 years, while only 3.5% were 65 years or older. (In the general SMSA population, 3.5% were under 18 years, and 12% were 65 years or older.)

Education. Forty-nine percent of Indians 25 years or older had at least a high school education, and 13% had one year or more of college. (In the general population, 59% of those 25 years or older had completed high school, and 21% had at least one year of college.)

Employment. Of the available civilian labor force (persons 16 years and older), 15% of Indian males and 14% of females were unemployed. (In the general population, 4% were unemployed.)

Income. The median family income for Indians was $4,630, and the mean $8,303. Only five Indian families had incomes over $25,000. The poverty line for a family of four was $3,700. Thirty-eight percent of Indian families lived in poverty. (In the general population, median income for all families was $8,971, and 9% of families lived in poverty.)

Housing. Forty-three percent of Indian households were owner occupied, while 57% were renter occupied. (In the general population, 70% of households were owner occupied, while 30% were renter occupied.)

Prevalence of Heavy Drinking

Although no attempt was made to measure the prevalence of heavy or problem drinking within the Indian population, some indications can be obtained. The Indian Project, which will be described below, was an organization that dealt with Indian problem drinkers. It served a total of 135 Indian clients (87 males and 48 females) from October 1968 through June 1971. This is a large number given the population size.

I also compiled data on arrests and dispositions from the Sioux City Police Department. Arrest records must be used with caution because numerous factors in addition to the state of intoxication can influence arrests. As a result, contrary to the assumptions made by some researchers (for example, Graves 1970), not all Indians who drink heavily run the same risks of being arrested. The risk varies in relation to the life style and drinking pattern, with drinkers who are on the street with no permanent place to stay having the greatest chances of being picked up. Nonetheless, arrest records can offer one kind of measure of the extent of heavy drinking, but it can not be assumed that the person arrested necessarily sees his or her drunkenness as a problem.

During 1970, the total number of arrests for intoxication of individuals eighteen years or older in Sioux City was 2,446. Indians accounted for 1,028 of these arrests or 42%.[10] However, a large percentage of these arrests is attributable to a relatively few individuals who were arrested repeatedly. Eight men, in fact, were responsible for 30% of the total Indian arrests. Nonetheless, 43 Indians (39 males and 4 females) were arrested five or more times, and a startling 287 Indians (211 males and 76 females) were arrested at least once for intoxication.[11] Although this figure includes people who resided outside Sioux City, given the estimate that only 413 Indians were 18 years or older in the Sioux City SMSA (U.S. Bureau of the Census n.d.: A: 2), this is a large number. Such data suggest that many Indians in the Sioux City area drank heavily at least on occasion, supporting the statements consistently made by local Indians when they cited drinking as a major problem confronting the Native American population. Additional corroborating information can be seen in the high age-adjusted alcoholism death rate of 138.6 per 100,000 during the years of 1985-87 at the Omaha-Winnebago Hospital in Winnebago, Nebraska. The U.S. rate for all races was 6.0 per 100,000 (Aberdeen Area Indian Health Service 1990: 57).

Indian Social Service Agencies

At the time of my research in 1970, Sioux City had two major social service agencies specifically focused on the Indian population: the Sioux City American Indian Center and the Iowa Comprehensive Treatment Program for Indian Problem Drinkers. The second program was referred to as the "Indian Project" by the people of Sioux City, and I will also use that label for brevity's sake. The Indian Center was organized in 1967 with the aid of a grant from the Episcopal Church. When I began my research the Center had a full-time staff of four: an executive director, two community workers, and a secretary. During the 12 months I was in Sioux City, several staff changes occurred, including the addition of a librarian aide in

1971. The staff was responsible to a twelve-member board, which was elected by the Indians of the city. All of the staff and all members of the board, with one exception, were Indians.

The Center offered a variety of programs and services to the Indians of the city, including classes on arts and crafts, a day care center for preschool children, food classes, a tutoring program for Indian students, a library center and reading program, and other educational and recreational activities. In addition, the staff provided counseling and referral services. Troubled individuals could come to the Center and discuss their difficulties with a staff member. When necessary, the staff member would refer the individuals to another program or service in the area and would work to insure that the entitled benefits and services were received. Board and staff members also represented the Indian population in discussions with other agencies such as the Bureau of Indian Affairs, Sioux City Police Department, and the Sioux City School Board.

The second major program, the Indian Project, was initiated in October 1968. It was conducted by the Office of the Governor of Iowa and was financed in part by the Social and Rehabilitation Services, Department of Health, Education, and Welfare. The general goal of the project was "to determine the effects of a coordination of community resources in reducing problem drinking among members of Indian tribes located in the Tama and Sioux City areas of Iowa" (Rattray n.d.: 10).[12] A local field office was maintained in each area. The Sioux City office was located in the Goodwill Industries' building and was staffed by a community coordinator, a counselor, and a secretary. In some cases the secretary also functioned as a counselor. Indians filled these positions during most of my research period.

The Project's programs were open to any Indian who had a problem with drinking. The major tasks of the Project's staff were to evaluate the needs of a problem drinker, refer the person to the appropriate treatment program(s) or service(s), and follow the individual through the various stages of the treatment program, assisting in any manner possible. The Indian Project drew upon a large number of agencies and programs in the Sioux City area including Alcoholics Anonymous, Winnebago Public Health, Sioux City Mission, St. Joseph Hospital, Salvation Army, Halfway House (Western Iowa Men's Residence), and Sioux City Police (Rattray n.d.: 22).

Research Strategy and Methodology

Although a number of considerations influence the type of research an investigator conducts, a central factor is his general theoretical orientation. As will be apparent in following chapters, I share the view of cognitive theorists who believe that the effect an event will have upon the behavior of an organism depends on how the event is represented in the organism's picture of itself and its universe. From this perspective any correlation between stimulation and response must be mediated by an internal system of concepts and relations. The internal representation or model of the universe in humans has been referred to by such terms as cognitive maps, schemas, propriospects, or mazeways.[13] For an anthropologist who adopts this point of view, one goal of the study becomes, as A. I. Hallowell (1955: 88) put it, "to apprehend in an integral fashion the most significant and meaningful aspects of the world of the individual as experienced by him and in terms of which he thinks, is motivated to act, and satisfies his needs."[14]

Such a concern has important consequences for the selection of the research strategy[15] and methodology. Identifying the significance and meanings that any single area or domain of the world has for even one individual is a difficult task requiring a great deal of intensive work. Such a perspective does not lend itself readily, at least initially, to either a research strategy that involves the study of a large number of people or a methodology that places heavy reliance on questionnaires and predetermined response categories. As a result, my general theoretical orientation led me to employ an intensive research strategy (working with a relatively few individuals, but considering them in relation to many variables) combined with a methodology that would allow me to examine drinking behaviors in detail.

Another factor influencing the choice of the research strategy and methodology is the amount and type of research previously conducted by others on the problem. At the time I conducted my research (1970-71), studies on urban Indians and those dealing specifically with their drinking patterns or psychological adjustments were relatively few in number. Although we have learned more about Indian drinking patterns in the intervening years,[16] studies on the drinking of urban Indians have lagged behind. Moran, who reviewed studies on urban Indians and alcohol use concluded, "As it stands, we do not know very much about alcohol use, treatment, or prevention among American Indians who live in urban areas" (2002: 289). Although there were some exceptions, many of the relevant studies at the time of my research employed an extensive research strategy (looking at large numbers of people while examining either a few or many variables) and relied heavily upon questionnaires, psychological tests, and the records of various agencies to obtain their data.[17] These studies often assumed that certain easily obtainable data, such as arrest rates for drunkenness, could be used to measure the occurrence of drunken behavior and the types of adjustment made. The higher an individual's arrest rate, the greater his extent of drunkenness and the poorer his adjustment. The studies frequently attempted to correlate such measures of adjustment with other variables such as gender, age, tribal affiliation, and marital status. The methodologies used seldom brought the researcher and subjects into extensive contact outside the interview or test situation, and in some cases, even this contact was only one or two interviews. As a result, the researchers often did not attempt to validate their measures or their interpretations through extensive participant observation and failed to obtain an *insider's* view of drinking activities. It appeared to me that an intensive ethnographic study was needed to confirm or modify the work that had previously been conducted.

Thus, on the basis of my general theoretical orientation and the amount and kind of research previously conducted, I decided to work intensively with a limited number of individuals in an attempt to see alcohol consumption from their perspectives and to relate their views to my own observations. The methodology used included direct observation and participation in selected activities,[18] informal interviews, focused interviews, several card-sorting techniques, collection of data from records of various agencies, and analysis of written documents.

Although I adopted an intensive research strategy, I am not arguing that it is always superior to an extensive one, for both strategies ideally need to be used. Each has advantages and disadvantages. One of the major weaknesses plaguing an intensive approach is the problem of sampling. Most anthropologists conducting ethnographic research rely upon the type of nonprobability sampling that Honigmann (1970) aptly calls "opportunistic sampling." That is to say, ethnographers frequently interview "whoever turns up and shows a readiness and ability to provide information" (1970: 268). The difficulty with this approach— which I also used—is that the researcher can not be certain his findings will hold for the entire population. In an attempt to overcome any sampling bias, however, I worked with people who differed in age, gender, and marital status. In addition, I engaged in the type of nonprobability sampling that Honigmann calls "judgment sampling." With this form of sampling, an "ethnographer uses his prior knowledge of the universe to draw representatives from it who possess distinctive qualifications" (Honigmann 1970: 268). As I learned more about the different life styles found among the "everyday" Indians of the city (in contrast to the "somebodies," both to be defined below), I formally interviewed and worked intensively with persons from each one. By "formal interview," I mean I either took notes during the discussion or tape recorded it. Although I formally interviewed only eighteen native consultants,[19] during the year I was in the city I observed and informally interviewed[20] many people in a variety of settings. The information gathered through these encounters was of great value and has been used in my study. Nonetheless, even though I interviewed—both formally and informally—Indians from tribal groups other than the Santee and Winnebago, my sampling was not randomly conducted and most of my formal interviewing was conducted with Santee and Winnebago. As a result, my statements should be taken as applying only to individuals from these two tribes even though for ease of reference I speak of the Indians of Sioux City without further tribal qualifications.

Fieldwork Situation

Few elements are as critical to the quality of a study as the type of relationship that exists between the researcher and the people studied. Many factors affect this relationship, some beyond the control of the anthropologist. In areas where other researchers have already worked, for example, the impressions they made on the people—for better or worse—influence the people's reactions to later workers. With the publication of books like *Custer Died for Your Sins* by Vine Deloria, Jr. (1969) and the release of singer Floyd Westermen's record album by the same title (both of which took a critical view of anthropological research), American Indians who never had any personal contact with researchers may hold rather strong feelings concerning anthropologists and anthropological research.

Another important variable determining people's reactions to an anthropologist is the type of study conducted and their understanding of its purpose. In the past, a research project whose contribution could be appreciated only by academicians might have been accepted uncritically by the group being studied. Today, the tolerance or cooperation of people will frequently be given only if a large percentage of the population or its leaders feel that the study has some relevance to the major concerns and needs of the people. If individuals can see few benefits deriving from an investigation, they may decide not to participate.[21]

The personality of the researcher is also important in determining the type of relationship he has with the group being studied. Elicitation of information is in many instances based upon a feeling of trust between a researcher and his native consultants. If a consultant cannot be honest with the researcher when reporting feelings or events because of fears that the information will later find its way into the community, valid data are difficult to obtain. Even if the researcher is viewed as dependable and trustworthy, he will still face great difficulties in finding individuals with whom to work if he makes people feel uncomfortable.

Before describing my entrance into Sioux City, I should briefly outline the academic experiences that led me to choose Sioux City as my research site and the type of research that I conducted. Although I have always been attracted to the intellectual freedom and comprehensiveness offered by the cross-cultural and holistic perspective of anthropology, like many anthropology students of the 1960s, I felt that anthropology could be of help in solving the practical problems facing contemporary societies. Thus, I sought a research topic that was both theoretically interesting as well as socially beneficial. Partly as a result of such applied interests, I spent a year of my graduate training in a psychiatric field and research training program at the University of Washington. The program was directed by Mansell Pattison, a psychiatrist, and was intended to introduce anthropologists to the field of mental health. As part of that program, I worked with James Spradley, an anthropologist, who was conducting research with "tramps" (often labeled "skid row alcoholics" by outsiders) at an alcoholic treatment center. Spradley was interested in developing an "emic" or "insider's" view[22] of tramp subculture through the use of "ethnoscientific" methodology.[23] His general theoretical position was one that I had adopted while at the University of Pennsylvania, so I jumped at the chance to work with him in experimenting with methodological techniques and collecting information at the alcoholic treatment center. Following my year in Seattle, I returned to the University of Pennsylvania to prepare for my doctoral research. I had decided by this time to work with an urban population of Native Americans, focusing on their social and psychological adjustments to city life. I then began collecting information on potential sites for my study. I contacted Indian organizations located in urban settings and researchers who were familiar with particular populations. The Sioux City American Indian Center was one that responded to my request for information, and what I learned about the city seemed encouraging. Following further communication with the Center, I traveled to Sioux City to visit the Indian Center and the Indian Project. There I discussed the problems the Indians faced in the city, the possible contributions that my study could make in solving some of them, and the feasibility of conducting research in the city. The type of research in which I was interested was seen as useful, and the agencies agreed to cooperate with me in my study.

I moved to Sioux City in July 1970 and remained there for one year. As Rosalie Wax (1971: 16) observes, many anthropologists in conducting their fieldwork pass through three stages:

> First, there is the stage of initiation, or resocialization, when the fieldworker tries to involve himself in the kinds of relationships which will enable him to do his fieldwork—the period during which he and his hosts work out or develop the kinds and varieties of roles which he and they will play. Second, there is the stage during which the fieldworker, having become involved in a variety of relationships, is able to concentrate on and do his fieldwork. Third, there is the post-field stage, when the fieldworker finishes his report and tries to get back in step with, or reattach himself to, his own people.

The first stage of research can be of critical importance because the anthropologist often establishes an identity that remains with him throughout his time in the field. In addition, the social contacts he makes during this phase can have a profound impact not only on his subsequent contacts, but also on the kinds of data he obtains. If, for example, he develops strong ties to an unpopular and isolated faction within the community, he may have difficulties establishing relationships with, and obtaining information from, other factions.

During my first two months in Sioux City, I worked as a full-time volunteer at the Indian Center. The tasks in which I engaged were varied and included acting as a substitute driver in transporting day care children; accompanying community workers on various tasks, such as placing a man in a nursing home; helping set up a rummage sale for the Center; answering the phone; and providing transportation for individuals who needed rides to various agencies. The Indian Project cooperated with the Center, and if they needed help transporting clients to an agency, I sometimes drove them. While I was working at the Center, I always tried, without being obtrusive, to identify myself as a graduate student in anthropology and to briefly share my ultimate goal, namely, to conduct research dealing with the kinds of problems the Indians were facing. I did this to make certain that people were not misled by my ties to the Center. My work and affiliation with the Center proved to be an invaluable introduction to the Indian community. Three features of this experience deserve comment.

First, the Indians of the city viewed the Center in a positive light and approached it if they thought the staff could help them. This is not to say that there was no political activity, and sometimes even turmoil, occurring in relation to the Center and its staff. Loose factions or alliances existed within the Indian population, and if a policy of the Center or one of its staff members upset one of these factions, the Center could become the focus of community discussion, and a group of concerned individuals might lobby with board members, circulate petitions, or present their grievances at a board of directors' meeting. However, the Indian Center (and the Indian project) was considered, on the whole, to be trustworthy and of benefit to the Indians. As a result, my ties to the Center helped overcome the suspicion with which I otherwise would initially have been viewed by the Indians of the city. If I had attempted to conduct a study simply by moving into Sioux City and working without any connection to the Indian Center or Indian Project, my chances of successfully completing my research would have been greatly reduced.

Second, through my work at the Center, I had an opportunity to see Indian life from a unique perspective. I was exposed to the broad range of problems with which the Center dealt. By observing the staff's efforts, and in some cases trying to solve the problems myself, I saw firsthand the difficulties that troubled individuals and the Indian agencies faced in dealing with them. In addition, because the staffs of the Indian Center and Indian Project were very open, generously sharing their experiences and knowledge with me, I was able to see how they viewed the problems of Sioux City Indians and the manner in which their agencies articulated with other social service agencies.

Third, while working at the Center I was able to meet many people ranging from influential local leaders to destitute transients. During my interactions with these individuals, I was often able to talk to them about their life styles and experiences. These encounters not only added to my knowledge of Indian life, but also established social connections on which I could later follow up.

By the end of the second month I felt comfortable working at the Center. I liked the staff members; I was meeting a good cross-section of the Indian community; I had numerous opportunities to interview people informally; and I was beginning to participate in and observe various activities in the Indian community. I could have continued in this fashion for the entire year. The drawback with such an approach was that I had reached a plateau of sorts. Following my regular routine at the Indian Center and using the procedures I have outlined to obtain information, I was not learning much that was new. Instead, I was obtaining the same kind of data on recurring incidents.[24] In spite of all that I had learned up to this point, my knowledge and my relationships with Indians, other than the staffs of the Indian agencies, were still relatively superficial. What I had not yet attempted was to examine systematically and in depth selected individuals' behaviors and views. Without this kind of detailed probing and the information that results from it, I could not achieve the type of understanding I sought.

As a result, I stopped working full-time at the Center during my third month in the city. I maintained close ties to the Center and Indian Project, however, frequently dropping by to visit with the staffs and engaging in many of the same activities I had before, such as giving rides to people, but on a more limited basis. Based on my knowledge of the community and suggestions offered by the staffs of the Indian agencies, I began approaching individuals who I thought would make good consultants, asking them if they would be willing to work with me. Before I interviewed anyone, I explained the nature of the study, the manner in which we would work together, and the uses to which the information might be put. Every individual was assured that anything he/she told me would not be repeated to other people in the community and that no real names would be used in any publications. When I first began interviewing, I had no money available to pay my consultants, and they participated without reimbursement. Later, funds became available, and I was able to pay them $1.00 an hour (not much even by the standards of 1970). I always made it clear that I was paying them for their time and not buying information. Several individuals did not wish to be paid for helping me, but I insisted that they take the money. I am quite certain that the small amount I was able to give people was not sufficiently rewarding to induce anyone to work with me. Although my consultants appreciated the money, in retrospect I think its greatest value was in helping *me* feel more comfortable. One of the hardest aspects of fieldwork for me is overcoming my reluctance to impose upon people. Thus, by giving my consultants an immediate and tangible reward, however small, I felt better about taking their time.

I do not mean to imply that my consultants viewed our work together as arduous or unpleasant. On the contrary, most—if not all—enjoyed our sessions. In addition, my relationship with most of the people I interviewed extended beyond the interview situation. I viewed these people as my friends and interacted with them on that basis. I visited them in their homes, ate with them, went to ball games and pow-wows with them, drank with them, attended AA meetings with them,[25] trying—as most anthropologists do—to become a participant in many of their activities. After I started developing these kinds of relationships with my consultants, my research entered the second phase of fieldwork that Rosalie Wax described, the heart of the ethnographic endeavor. After anthropologists establish relationships like these, their research activities have become embedded in, and part of, non-research activities. Although the role of researcher is never completely forgotten either by the anthropologist or his consultants, in many contexts and with many activities, that element of the relationship is not very salient. As a result, an ethnographer is often operating on two levels simultaneously. On one level, he is behaving in the manner that he thinks is appropriate to the relationship and situation—whether it be responding to a request for a ride or a loan, or engaging in conversation over a beer. On another level, he is viewing, and later reviewing, the behavioral stream analytically, matching the people and behavioral patterns against his understanding of them. Why did this incident happen the way it did? How was individual A's behavior affected by his relationship with his mother? Why did she use that term to describe that kind of behavior?

This kind of participation is central to ethnographic research. First, by interacting with and observing the anthropologist outside the interview situation, the consultants have opportunities to get to know him. If he proves to be relatively mature, trustworthy, sympathetic, and tolerant, they are apt to be less suspicious and guarded during formal interviews. Second, in a similar fashion, these same experiences allow the anthropologist to see his consultants in a variety of settings and to evaluate their performances as consultants. Does the person report events accurately? How perceptive are his judgments of other people? How do other community members evaluate and respond to him? Third, the events witnessed by the ethnographer become both phenomena to be explained and tests against which his growing understanding of the culture can be measured. When unexpected or puzzling incidents occur, he can explore these in detail with his consultants. Whenever the anthropologist ventures out to observe and participate in his consultants' world, he is evaluating the data he is obtaining from his formal sessions and testing the models or hypotheses he is generating about the society. Because ethnographic research is composed of multiple approaches or procedures, it allows an anthropologist to see a research problem from many different perspectives and to offer richly textured descriptions that do justice to the true complexities of human behavior.

Behavioral Diversity and Life Styles in Sioux City

Because each Indian in Sioux City followed a unique behavioral pattern, I faced the problem of trying to organize that behavioral diversity into a manageable and meaningful overview without distorting individual behaviors. To handle this difficulty, I organized the data around the major life styles of the Indians. Such an approach has the advantage of allowing me to use the data derived from my formal interviews as well as the information collected through my observations and informal interviews with Indians other than my consultants. The difficulty with this approach is deciding how many life styles to distinguish and on what basis. Applying white, middle-class standards or conceptions could easily lead to an ethnocentric and misleading description. One way of minimizing such ethnocentric distortion is to see how the Indians themselves categorize the diversity.[26] Identifying these categories is a difficult task, however, for the Indians of Sioux City, like people everywhere, can classify individuals numerous ways depending upon the purpose of the classification and the sociocultural context within which the categorization process occurs. They can generate categories on the basis of physical traits, overt behavioral characteristics, covert characteristics (such as beliefs or attitudes), or on the basis of some combination of all these traits. Theoretically, they can create as many different categories for people as there are ways of combining the relevant attributes.

As a result, I supplemented my interviews and observations with three other techniques that involved having the consultants sort cards bearing the names of individuals well known to them (each card bore one name).[27] All three sorting tasks required the consultant to draw upon his knowledge of the people under consideration, to compare their attributes, and to categorize them on the basis of those comparisons. These tasks elicited many salient terms and categories that my consultants used in other settings.

Although my consultants frequently categorized people at a level of generality similar to that of a life style in their daily activities, they seldom, if ever, were called upon to generate a comprehensive, all-purpose, and rigorous classification of every Indian in the city. As a result, it is hardly surprising to learn that they did not all produce the same number or kinds of categories. This diversity does not create great difficulties in their daily activities, for any differences or ambiguities that exist between two interacting individuals can be resolved, or at least reduced, through ad hoc communication.[28] The manner in which a researcher handles this diversity depends, in part, on his goals. If the individual variations are of theoretical or practical concern, the classification of each consultant may be used. If, on the other hand, the researcher's major concern is developing a descriptive overview—as mine was—he may follow Ward Goodenough's suggestion that one way to determine the adequacy of a description is to see if it produces behavior that would be judged as appropriate by authoritative consultants. Thus, using Truk (now called Chuuk) as an example, Goodenough (1970: 99) argues: "If operating according to the standards I attribute to the people of Truk results in behavior within the range of variance they accept as properly Trukese, then a description of those standards satisfactorily represents what we may call Trukese culture."

This is the approach I used in the chapters that follow. The classification described in Chapter Four is a composite, drawing upon the distinctions and categories regarded as relevant by many of my consultants. Although the various card sorting tasks were valuable, I was also guided by the distinctions made during the course of their daily activities. Variations existed, but broad agreement was expressed by my consultants on the areas relevant to considering life styles: an individual's working habits, drinking patterns, degree of family orientation, and extent of "hell-raising."

Life-style categories organize the behavioral diversity of a population at a useful level, but we must be aware that they distort the true variation in several ways. At one level of generality a category may be treated as unitary, but at a lower level other significant distinctions may be made. Thus, even though three men may be described as "liking to raise hell," it may be recognized that each performs a given activity differently. For example, in terms of aggression, the first man frequently looks for fights; the second, while not prone to starting fights, will fight if he is provoked in any way; and the third man fights only if he is seriously insulted. In addition, a given individual may be categorized in relation to a domain because he has a tendency to behave in a certain manner. On occasion, however, he may perform in an uncharacteristic fashion. If we keep such variations in mind, the use of life-style categories should not overly distort the behavioral diversity exhibited by the Indians of Sioux City.

Endnotes for Chapter 3

[1] I would like to thank Eric Henderson, Gene Lutz, Jay Noricks, Jerry Stockdale, and James Stokes for comments on an earlier draft of this chapter.

[2] The SMSA is comprised by Woodbury County, Iowa and Dakota County, Nebraska.

[3] U.S. Bureau of the Census 1973: 17-76.

[4] U.S. Bureau of the Census 1973: 17-76. The 2010 Census lists the total population for the Sioux City IA-NE-SD metropolitan area as 143,577 and the non-Hispanic American Indian population as 2,354 (http://diversitydata.sph.harvard.edu/Data/Profiles/Show.aspx?loc=1292).

[5] The Winnebago and Omaha reservations, which are contiguous to each other, are located 23 and 33 miles, respectively, south of Sioux City in Nebraska. The Santee reservation lies about 90 miles west of Sioux City in Knox County, Nebraska. The Yankton reservation is located in Charles Mix County, South Dakota about 120 miles west of Sioux City.

[6] The Wisconsin Winnebago and some individuals from Nebraska prefer to identify themselves as Ho-Chunk, *see* the discussion in Chapter 8. As my consultants and most of the literature that I will cite use the term Winnebago, that is the term I will use in this book. I believe that individual tribal members have the right to identify themselves and their tribe with whatever term they desire and that researchers ideally should follow that request.

[7] U.S. Bureau of the Census 1983a: 29-355.

[8] The linguistic situation in Sioux City provided the background for a humorous incident that occurred during my fieldwork. The Indian Center needed to hire a community worker and advertised locally. The Center's Board of Directors received a number of applications from both Indians and non-Indians and proceeded to conduct job interviews as part of the process of selecting the best candidate. Although several of the non-Indians were sincerely interested in the position, they did not possess much knowledge of the Indian population and their cultural traditions. One of the Indian board members politely asked an applicant how he, speaking only English, could effectively deal with the Indian population. After the board member asked the question, he looked over to the side of the room where I was observing the process and winked at me. Everyone in the room, except the applicant, knew that the board member spoke only English and that the

problem seldom confronted a community worker. Except for the wink, which the applicant did not see, nobody gave any indication that a clever — and telling — joke had been made. The board later hired a well-qualified, local Indian (who spoke only English).

[9] The information is drawn from U.S. Bureau of the Census n.d. A: 2, 9, 14-16; B: 3-6.

[10] These figures are taken from the official tabulation of the Sioux City Police Department in their annual report. The more detailed breakdown, which follows, comes from my own tabulation of the arrest records. My figures are based on a higher count of total Indian arrests for intoxication (1,103 versus the official number of 1,028). The variations come from differences in the classification of individuals into the official "racial" or ethnic categories. In some cases, I noticed inconsistencies in the classification of a given individual from one arrest to another and corrected those errors. In addition, a substantial number of people are of mixed heritage and could be classified as either "Indian," "White," or "Negro." When I knew the background of the persons in question and knew that they were seen as "Indians" by the Indian population, I counted them irrespective of the official police designation.

[11] Indian women accounted for 13% of all the Indian arrests for intoxication.

[12] Tama is a small community some 200 miles east of Sioux City. Over 400 Mesquaki Indians lived in the Tama area in the 1970s (U.S. Department of Commerce 1971: 134). For a penetrating study of Mesquaki life *see* Foley (1995).

[13] *See* Bandura (1986, 2001); Bruner (1990); D'Andrade (1995); Dougherty (1985); Gardner (1985); Goodenough (1963, 1971); Hallowell (1955); Kronenfeld, Bennardo, de Munck, and Fischer (2011); Miller, Galanter, and Pribram (1960); Neissser (1976); and Wallace (1970b) for discussions of this perspective.

[14] Ward Goodenough (1989: 31-32) argues that an ethnographic researcher faces two major tasks: "One . . . pertains to describing the criteria people under study use to discriminate among things and how they respond to them and assign them meaning, including everything in their physical, behavioral, and social environments. This is the task of cultural description. The other task is to describe these same environments and the effects of people's behavior on them, not in terms of how the people perceive them, but in terms appropriate to the questions under investigation." One might

add the ethnographer must also choose a representational style with which to convey his results to his readers. As John Van Maanen (1987: 4) put it: "Ethnography is the result of fieldwork, but it is the written report that must represent the culture, not the fieldwork itself. Ethnography as a written product, then has a degree of independence (how culture is portrayed) from the fieldwork on which it is based (how culture is known)."

[15] John Galtung (1967) suggests that the research strategy of a study be considered the ordered pair (m, n), where "m" equals the number of units studied (the units for anthropologists are often people) and "n" equals the number of dimensions along which the units are examined. Thus, a researcher could adopt an extensive research strategy (many, few) in which a large number of people are examined in terms of a few dimensions, or an intensive strategy (few, many) in which a few individuals are studied, but in relation to a large number of variables.

[16] Heavy drinking constitutes a major health problem for *some* Indian communities in the United States and is associated with a variety of other problems including accidents, suicides, unemployment, assaults, legal difficulties, and marital strife; for discussions and bibliographies, *see* Deters et al. (2006); Heath (1989a); Kelso and DuBay (1989); Lex (1985); Mail and Walker (2002); May, McCloskey, and Gossage (2002); Oetting and Beauvais (1989); Rieckmann et al. (2012); Weibel-Orlando (1989a); Welty (2002); Whitesell et al. (2009, 2012a); Zahnd et al. (2002). For an overview of the negative impacts of the liquor trade on Indian societies in Eastern North America from the 1650s to the American Revolution *see* Mancall (1995a: 85-129). What many people fail to realize, however, is that great inter- and intra-tribal variations preclude any simple generalizations about Indian drinking and undercut the stereotype of the drunken Indian. For example, the Indian Health Service calculated that the age-adjusted alcohol-related death rate for their Indian populations (divided into 12 service areas) for the period 1996 – 2001 was 43.2 per 100,000. The U.S. rate for all races was 6.9 for the year 2000. The Indian rate is 6 times higher. The Indian rates varied, however, from a high of 86.4 in the Aberdeen service area to a low of 18.3 in the Nashville service area. The Aberdeen service area includes the Indian health facilities in North and South Dakota, Nebraska, and Iowa (Indian Health Service 2008: 62). Survey research on Native American drinking has also found that heavy drinking varies greatly among and within tribal groups. Philip May (1996), for example, in a review of the

literature on the epidemiology of drinking found that some tribal groups had only 30% drinking adults, whereas others had from 37% to 84% (also *see* Beals et al. 2003; Beauvais et al. 2004; Jessor et al. 1968: 182-184; Kunitz and Levy 1994, 2000; Levy and Kunitz 1974; May and Gossage 2001; Spicer et al. 2003; U.S. Dept. of Health & Human Services 2007; Whitesell et al. 2007, 2012b; Wu et al. 2011).

[17] *See*, for example, Graves (1970), Graves and Van Arsdale (1966), Martin (1964), Price (1968), Snyder (1968), and Weppner (1968). Qualitative research continues to be underutilized. Jim Orford (2008b), for example, in his critique of the prevailing approaches used in the study of addiction treatment calls for greater use of qualitative research and an increased focus on the users' perspectives.

[18] In a strict sense this is participant observation, but I agree with other researchers who would use the term as a label for the combination of techniques that make up ethnographic research, i.e., direct observation, informant interviewing (asking an individual to report on events and behavior that the researcher did not witness), respondent interviewing (asking an individual to report on his own behaviors and thoughts), document analysis and direct participation (*see*, for example, Agar 1980: 114, McCall and Simmons 1969: 1-5, Zelditch 1962).

[19] Traditionally the individuals who work closely with an anthropologist have been called "informants." Because of the unfortunate pejorative quality the term has acquired from other fields, I will not use it in this book.

[20] Agar (1980: 90) suggests that three elements distinguish an informal ethnographic interview: 1) the ethnographer does not have an existing list of questions to ask the informant, 2) the ethnographer does not adopt the formal role of interrogator, and 3) the interview occurs in a variety of situations. As he puts it: "The general idea distinguishing formal from informal interviews, is again, the idea of control. In the informal, everything is negotiable" (1980: 90).

[21] For discussions of the nature of the relationship between anthropologists and Native Americans and the types of ethnographic studies conducted *see* Biolsi (2004), Biolsi and Zimmerman (1997), Clifton (1990), Hymes (1969), and Strong (2005).

[22] The term "emic" (which comes from the word "phonemic" and stands in contrast to "etic" from the word "phonetic") is often defined as referring to an insider's view of a given culture. This gloss can be misleading if an insider's view is taken to mean that the native participants will be conscious

of their emic systems and will be able to accurately articulate them. Native speakers of a language are not able to offer a phonemic analysis of their sound system or to describe the grammatical rules they follow in speaking. As Dell Hymes points out: "Emic analysis is simply analysis of the units and relations of a system, where the functional relevance of the units and relations within the system is validated. It means the difference between discovering the principles that actually underlie the choice of residence of members of a community . . . and classifying the observed facts of residence according to a preconceived scheme" (Hymes 1983 [1970]: 181). An emic description of a culture, then, like a phonemic description of a language, implies that the distinctions made, the units or categories used, and the relationships that hold among the distinctions and categories within the frame of analysis are those of the people studied, whether or not they are consciously aware of them or are able to formulate them. These stand in contrast to the etic distinctions, units, relationships, and frames of analysis that are distinguished by the outside investigator and that are used to help identify the emic systems. Kenneth Pike, who originally coined the terms in 1954, more recently defined an emic unit as "a physical or mental item or system treated by insiders as relevant to their system of behavior and as the same emic unit in spite of etic variability" (1990: 28). *See* Goodenough (1970: 104-130), Hymes (1983 [1970]), and the papers collected in the volume edited by Headland, Pike, and Harris (1990) for additional discussions of emics and etics.

[23] The "cognitive revolution" in the human sciences occurred in the 1950s, and anthropology was a major disciplinary player. As I pointed out in Chapter One, a strong current in the anthropological movement was the set of methodological and theoretical approaches often labeled "ethnoscience" (or "ethnosemantics" or "the new ethnography") during the 1960s and 1970s (*see* Black 1973; Casson 1981; Goodenough 1970, 1981; Hymes 1977; Spradley 1972b, 1979; Tyler 1969; Werner 1972; and Werner and Fenton 1970 for discussions of this perspective). James Spradley (1970, 1972a) was among the first to apply an ethnoscientific approach to the study of drinking patterns; also *see* Brown (1980), Everett (1980), Leland (1975, 1978), Siverts (1973), Spradley and McCurdy (1975: 599-641), Topper (1974, 1976, 1980, 1981), and Waddell (1975, 1980A). For recent developments in what is now called cognitive anthropology, *see* D'Andrade (1990, 1992, 1995); D'Andrade and Strauss (1992); Doughterty (1985); Holland and Quinn (1987); Kronenfeld, Bennardo, de Munck, and Fischer (2011).

[24] The situation is similar to what Glaser and Strauss (1967: 61) call "theoretical saturation." They use the term in relation to particular conceptual categories: "Saturation means that no additional data are being found whereby the sociologist can develop properties of the category. As he sees similar instances over and over again, the researcher becomes empirically confident that a category is saturated." Once a category is saturated relative to a particular group, the researcher either needs to move on to new groups or to utilize different kinds of data.

[25] During the year I was in Sioux City, the Indians reactivated an Indian Chapter of AA and invited me to attend with them. The meetings were run informally, more like a sociable gathering with food than a formal meeting. People were free to raise an issue concerning their alcohol use if they wished and that might be discussed, but there was no emphasis on identifying themselves as "alcoholics."

[26] The distinctions and categories used by an individual in his day-to-day activities are significant to anthropologists because they are in large part dependent upon the individual's sociocultural systems. As Bruner, Goodnow, and Austin (1956: 10) put it many years ago: "The categories in terms of which man sorts out and responds to the world around him reflects deeply the culture into which he is born. The language, the way of life, the religion and science of a people; all of these mold the way in which a man experiences the events out of which his own history is fashioned. In this sense, his personal history comes to reflect the traditions and thought-ways of his culture, for the events that make it up are filtered through the categorical systems he has learned."

[27] These sorting techniques are derived from the work of psychologists (see Kelly 1955, Bannister and Mair 1968) and anthropologists (see Romney and D'Andrade 1964, Spradley 1970).

[28] See Wallace (1970b: 111).

CHAPTER 4
LIFE STYLES AND DRINKING PATTERNS OF URBAN INDIANS[1]

> First, I was a boy, running around playing. Then all of a sudden, overnight, I discovered there was something else: running around at night, raising hell, fightin', drinkin'—that went on for a long time. Then all of a sudden I realized—woke up and said, "Well, there's nothin' to runnin' around, drinkin', raisin' hell. . . ." You mellow, you start associating with older people, even when you drink. Sit down and talk with them. Even started talking with L.T. over here about the tribe.
>
> Sioux City Indian

Introduction

Every social system is based upon a set of social identities and their associated roles. In mainstream America, waitresses, policemen, bartenders, plumbers, professors, and students are people who have acquired particular cultural identities and have learned to play the roles related to them. Though some identity categories such as female and daughter tend to be lifelong; others are temporary, we assume them for a time and then lay them aside as we move on to new identities. Because identities are differentially evaluated, some are intentionally sought and claimed with pride, while others, being viewed negatively, are feared and avoided. In order to understand the roles that alcohol use plays among Sioux City Indians, we must know something about the activities and contexts in which drinking occurs and how identities relate to these activities. In this chapter, an overview of the major life styles followed by the Sioux City Indians is presented; the drinking patterns that figure in the life styles are described, and the forces that shape the development of individual life styles are discussed.

Somebodies and Everyday People

The individuals participating in my study distinguish a category of people whom they call the "somebodies" or the "professionals." This category is usually contrasted with the "everyday" or "common people." Somebodies are described as Indians who have "gone out and done something with their lives." Typically, these individuals have at least a high school education and perhaps further training or college. Somebodies hold skilled jobs and are well known not only among Indians but also in the larger community. Non-Indians frequently assume, sometimes incorrectly, that the somebodies are always the leaders of the Indian community. Although my consultants feel that the somebodies do not socialize extensively with the everyday people, they do attend Indian events such as powwows and often take leading roles in Indian organizations.

Most of the people included in my study consider themselves "everyday people." As a result, I will have little to say about the somebodies. By focusing on the everyday people I am not implying that the somebodies are of any less practical or theoretical interest. With a limited amount of time, it is difficult to work with all segments of the population. Although I will not attempt to estimate the number of Indians following each of the life styles delineated, it is important to note that when I did my field research the somebodies represented a small percentage of those who identified themselves as Indians and participated in the Indian affairs of the city.

People Who Like to Raise Hell

Another distinction is made between people who "like to raise hell" or "get into trouble" and those who do not. "Raising hell" refers to engaging in activities that carry a risk of encountering trouble or adversity. These difficulties include not only physical dangers but also legal entanglements. Despite the hazards, hell-raising activities are generally viewed by their participants as enjoyable, exciting, or fun. People who like to raise hell (henceforth called "hell-raisers") typically are in their teens or twenties and single. Girls and women are sometimes described as "raising hell," but are more frequently characterized as "running around." Although similarities exist between males who raise hell and females who run around, I have limited my discussion to males.[2] This section of the chapter focuses on the younger hell-raisers (teens and early twenties) who reside more or less permanently with their parents or other relatives. The life styles of the other hell-raisers are described in a subsequent section of this chapter entitled "People on the Street."

Raising hell is not incompatible with work. Some young hell-raisers either work steadily or on a part-time basis. Although those who are economically independent may rent apartments or houses by themselves, many young hell-raisers live with their parents or other relatives and are partially or completely supported by them. Money for alcohol, however, is seldom provided by parents. As a result, children must either work part-time, rely on friends for their alcohol, or obtain it through illegal endeavors. Illegal hell-raising activities range in severity from curfew violations and shoplifting to armed robbery. In order to obtain beer and cigarettes, young hell-raisers sometimes break into small corner groceries. The burglaries may be rather bold; one individual breaks the glass in a door or window and slips inside while another keeps watch outside. In addition to providing the items they desire, this kind of activity affords them an opportunity to display their bravery and burglary skills.

Individuals who are identified as hell-raisers do not raise hell all of the time, but during their leisure hours they tend to look for "the action" which is often found in bars and at drinking parties. When hell-raisers are in these settings they have a tendency to put on strong identity displays that assert that they are "tough." These displays may lead to an identity struggle with another individual, and in turn, may develop into a fight. Following Wallace and Fogelson (1965), I will use the phrase "identity struggle" to refer to those arguments (verbal and nonverbal) between two or more persons over the possession or nonpossession of identity features.[3]

Such struggles may result from the manner in which two individuals interact.[4] As long as two participants in an encounter accept the identity features claimed by the other as legitimate and as long as each behaves in an acceptable manner, the interaction proceeds reasonably well. If, however, one individual offends another by violating a rule of the encounter that the offended person feels should be followed in deference to these identity features, an identity struggle may develop. Not all violations of a person's rights lead to identity struggles, however. One participant may fail to give another the proper deference for a variety of reasons, including accidental oversight. Violations may be corrected through "remedial work," which Goffman (1971: 109) describes as functioning "to change the meaning that otherwise might be given an act, transforming what could be seen as offensive into what can be seen as acceptable."[5] Thus, if one individual maintains eye contact with another longer than the second individual deems acceptable, the offended person might respond with a mild challenge, perhaps by returning the stare or by asking, "What do you think you're looking at?" If the offender provoked the individual accidentally, he could remedy the offense by responding to the first challenge by averting his eyes, and by answering the second challenge with, "Nothing, sorry." If the offender refuses to remedy the offense, a "show-down" and an identity struggle might result.

As indicated, when an individual goes out raising hell, he will frequently put on strong identity displays that assert he is "tough" and possesses the necessary qualities for effective fighting: strength, speed, co-ordination, and mastery of fighting techniques. These identity features are claimed through both nonaggressive and aggressive behaviors. A nonaggressive display does not involve a direct violation of other individuals' rights or a direct challenge to their identities. Such a display might involve: 1) making verbal claims that assert the possession of positively valued traits; 2) telling of past exploits that demonstrate the possession of positively valued features; 3) making verbal or nonverbal threats as to what corrective actions would be taken *if* somebody should violate one's rights; 4) reacting with strong verbal or nonverbal challenges to minor and accidental violations of one's rights; or 5) using "strong" body movements, stances, and gestures. Through such nonaggressive techniques an individual can put on a fairly strong identity display and at the same time minimize the chance that he will be involved in a "run-in." In contrast, when an individual puts on an aggressive display, he does so either by violating other individuals' rights (thereby assuming greater prerogatives than other people feel he is entitled, while at the same time not giving them the deference to which they feel they are entitled), or by directly attacking or challenging their identities. To a certain extent even the aggressive techniques can be ranked according to their seriousness. Some, such as talking too loud or speaking longer than appropriate, infringe upon the rights of others present, but do not involve flagrant violations of their rights. A more serious violation occurs when an individual begins "acting smart," "cute," or "good" (i.e., tough) with other people. Even though these techniques involve an open identity attack or violation of rights, they can still be corrected, at least theoretically, with the appropriate remedial work. Thus, for example, if one individual makes a "smart" comment to, or about, another person, the offense might be corrected if the offender said he was "just kidding" and did not mean anything by it.

The following incidents exemplify the ways that identity displays and struggles can develop into fights. One individual describes a fight that arose over who was the better fighter:

> Some white guy was with my cousin, Tom R. An' Tom was goin' around tellin' everybody that, you know, he knocked the shit out of me up on Virginia Street. Knocked the hell out of me. Me and Bill said, "We're gonna have to see about that," you know. So we went and got all tanked up, drunked up, this and that. And we got feelin' pretty cocky, bouncin' around, you know. Went down there [to the Fourth Street area], and I seen him. "Tom," I said, "I hear you said you knocked the hell out of me." He said, "Who did you hear that

from?" About the time he said that, I hit him. I just hit him with my fist, and I cut the whole side of his face open. I must have hit him so hard, just right. Anyway, he went to the hospital, and he got him[self] sewed. We was still on Fourth Street. This was about, oh, two o'clock. Him and this guy come walkin' again. And right then he wanted to go again. I said, "Didn't you have enough?" He said, "No." So we was bouncing around, and I was knocking the hell out of him again. I had him down, kickin' him. The other guy was gonna sneak around and hit me with them [brass] knuckles. . . . And about that time Bill went around and hit him. Knocked him right off that curb. That guy just laid there. Then the cops pulled up, and we took off up the alley.

Another person provides an example of a dispute over the right of one group to keep beer purchased with money provided by a second group:

This is what started it all. Some friends come up to me, "Hey, Bob! Some guys over here just stole our beer. We give them some money to go get beer." Well, I figured I'm gonna get some of that beer. I walked over to these guys, "Hey, you guys. My friends want their beer back, either that or their money." They told me, "Well fuck off." They asked me who I thought I was. "I know who I am, and I want my friends' beer." One guy looked at me and said, "You better find out who you're messin' with." I said, "I don't give a shit who I'm a—look you guys, this is my friends' beer here. We can start a damn big fight here. . . ." It was a just a scuffle I should never have gotten into, because I was in no position to mess with nobody. . . . My little brother Peter would have beat the shit out of me that night. . . . This one certain guy got out of the car. They all got out of the car. This one certain guy comes up to me. I was takin' off my jacket, had a real nice jacket on. . . . I wasn't looking for fights, I was looking for pussy. You could tell by the way I was dressed. I should never done that, man, walked up to those guys and started all that shit. The next thing I know I was taking my coat off and got it down to here, just around my deal. The next thing I know something hit me. I was down on the ground. What chance have you got then? . . . He won it fair and square. I mean, I, I don't think he should have hit me with my arms binded, you know. Knocked me down. Some other dude, a couple of other dudes tried to kick me, you know, but this guy, "Naw, I'll do it myself." He knew he had me beat. That's the only reason he said that, otherwise he knew I could have got up, and I knew I would have got ganged. Maybe that would have been worse, maybe it was better that I stayed. I couldn't get up anyway—what the hell. I'm glad I only come out with this. I got cut across [shows the cut on his face]. . . . He hit me many times. I can remember him hitting me in the face. . . . I remember saying this, "Don't ever let me get up, I'll kill you." I remember saying that. He kept on telling me to apologize for coming up to his car. I kept tellin' him, "Don't you ever let me get up, I'll kill you."

When Bob attempted to intercede and retrieve the beer on behalf of his friends, those with the beer made no attempt to justify their possession of it. Their claim to the beer was based solely on their claimed ability to hold it, by force if necessary. Unfortunately, Bob did not have the fighting ability to back up his demand for the beer's return. He did demonstrate his courage, however, in attempting to retrieve it and his gameness by indicating that, even though he was beaten, he would still "kill" his opponent if he ever got to his feet.

One man who had been a hell-raiser in his younger days reported that he and his friends would occasionally go to the Fourth Street area looking for a fight. As he says, "We used to go downtown just smashing people up for nothing. . . . We always [knew] we were gonna get in a fight down there." Another individual's brother did the same sort of thing:

Phil likes to go out on a street on a Friday night and just bust up, you know, just for fun. Bang a local white boy in the head, or something, you know. One night he even caught a colored guy down here and started callin' him "nigger" and everything. The colored guy was with five or six white boys in the car. Phil started calling him "Uncle Tom," "nigger nose." The colored guy wouldn't do anything. Phil's gonna get himself in trouble by doing all that shit.

Fights or challenges of this sort frequently appear to be directed against individuals who are members of an "outgroup." The criteria used to define these outgroups vary from situation to situation and do not always include racial or ethnic characteristics. In some cases, the area of town an individual is from is the most important criterion: a west side group of Indians, Blacks and whites may be aligned against a group from the north side or against a group from out of town.

Although fighting ability is generally admired by hell-raisers, individuals who attempt to settle too many kinds of disputes with violence or who use weapons unnecessarily in fights are viewed as difficult or dangerous and are treated accordingly. One young man describes such a person:

Jim is very, very dangerous. I never did trust this guy and never will. . . . I wouldn't hang around with him at all. . . . I mistrust and fear Jim . . . for what he'd do to me: shoot me or something, stab me. He's stabbed a few guys, cut a few guys up. . . . Jim would kill a guy.

Drinking is an activity in which hell-raisers frequently engage. Although drinking serves many functions and figures in the pursuit of many goals, at times the state of intoxication appears to be valued for its own sake. Thus, individuals will drink on occasion just to become drunk.[6] In addition to alcohol, some hell-raisers also use other drugs, including amphetamines, tranquilizers, hallucinogens, marijuana, and a solution that is made from an inhaler and injected into the bloodstream. Glue and gasoline sniffing also occur.[7] One former hell-raiser, who was introduced to many drugs by older members of his peer group, describes the first time he took the inhaler solution:

> I was scared the first time, you know. I heard 'em talking about bubbles, you know. Man, I started thinkin'. I was about to chicken out the first time, you know. An' they knew it was my first time, B.W. and them. They said, "Don't worry man; you ain't gonna get no bubble." An' I, I tried to act brave and I said, "I'm not sweatin' it. Go ahead and shoot." An' soon as it all goes in, boy, your head, just—I don't know, just a real good feelin'. To me it was.

Hell-raisers drink in a variety of settings including bars, homes, and cars. If a young hell-raiser has his own apartment or house, he will hold parties there. In some cases the parents of minors[8] allow their children to have parties in their home as long they do not have to furnish all the alcohol. If a house is unavailable and a minor has a car, he and his friends will ride around drinking. If the weather is warm, they might have a party outdoors in a secluded spot. Minors who have money seldom face difficulties obtaining alcohol because they can always find someone of legal age to purchase it for them.

Although the search for action may take dramatic forms, hell-raisers also engage in less spectacular activities. They spend much time talking and joking with their friends. Because females also frequent scenes of action, these setting are used to pursue sexual liaisons. Hell-raisers admire sexual prowess and approve of premarital sexual behavior. As one man put it:

> I don't feel it's wrong to sleep with a woman if I'm not married to her. I don't feel that way. Just as these people in Polynesia, they don't feel it's wrong to run around without things on their breasts. It's somebody else that feels that it's wrong, see. If I go down here and sleep with a woman it doesn't bother me. Why should it? That's—it's as natural as drinkin' a glass of water.

Individuals Who Don't Think of Trouble

Not all young Indians like to raise hell or get into trouble. Individuals who do not are variously described as "trying to do good," "don't think of trouble," "won't get into trouble," and as being "good people," "nice people," "clean-cut," and so on. Generally these individuals do not "hang with" others who regularly get into trouble, nor do they usually attend the same parties or patronize the same bars as hell-raisers. Even though they may admire physical prowess and fighting ability, they are less likely than hell-raisers to look for fights or to resort to physical violence in settling disputes. They are also less likely to engage in illegal activities such as shoplifting or breaking and entering. Their drinking patterns are diverse; in general, they start drinking later in life than hell-raisers (often in their late teens as opposed to the early teens of many hell-raisers), and they do not drink as heavily, though some drink fairly often.

Some of these individuals felt that to avoid engaging in hell-raising activities they had to stop interacting with Indians of their age group. One young person who had been a hell-raiser in his mid-teens discusses this:

> I just sort of lost interest in my own, you know, own people. I just didn't hang around with the guys, probably because they started getting into—they were too much for me. I wasn't made to be that kind of guy, you know. Just go off and get drunk every night, break into places, beat people up. That wasn't my bag so I just jumped in with other . . . guys. . . . It's not because I don't want to be Indian, I mean you as an individual got to, to find people, other individuals that are attractive to you. And if your own, a, type of skin isn't attractive then don't hang around with it. Well hell, if this guy don't, doesn't want to do nothing but booze, get drunk, break in, all this child shit, don't do it man. I don't hang around with these guys. That's the only reason.

Other individuals have less difficulty finding Indian companions who share their behavioral standards.

Family Men and Homebodies

Although young people may adopt several life styles as they grow older, the one viewed as socially desirable and part of the ideal life cycle, is the one in which men become "family men" and women become "homebodies." When a man marries, he is expected to settle down and fulfill his familial roles by becoming a good husband, father, and provider. Even men in their thirties and still raising hell may claim they eventually want to get married and settle down, but are not yet ready to do so. Others indicate that they have not yet met the right woman, but as soon as they do, they will settle down. Although this ideal is espoused, some men never become successful family men. It should be noted in this context that a man and a woman may live together without viewing their relationship as a permanent one and that, in addition, not all co-habiting couples see their relationship as the first step in settling-down. This view is apparent in the following quote in which a man briefly describes his working and drinking patterns when he was in his twenties and living in Chicago:

> I worked, you know, out of daily pay offices in Chicago. I really didn't care whether I was making big money or not. I was just boozing anyway. . . . I didn't work every day; I think I worked enough to pay my rent, and the rest of the time I boozed up with the boys. I was getting in pretty heavy with this Indian girl that I met over there. She urged me to go to work steady, but I didn't really care. I didn't care to get married either. I didn't want to get productive and real stable all of a sudden.

Another man discusses the manner in which his relationship with his wife, Betty, changed through time:

> [When you started staying with Betty did you intend to stay with her?] No, no. Hell, no. Just like them other girls [he mentioned earlier]. I just thought to myself, I'll just stick around here for awhile and then take off. I don't know what

in the hell held me there. I didn't want her land; I didn't want—you know. And I didn't care for her at all, just a shack-up. But I stuck around there till, till I took off, maybe— I was with her about four years, and then I took off, and I went on that railroad [i.e., he worked on a railroad crew]. But I always, I don't know, I couldn't forget her. I was always thinking about coming home. Until she sent me a telegram, she said that Nancy [their daughter] was born. Well, then I knew I had to. But I guess you think different when you're a kid. As you grow older, you know, you think about settling down.

As the quote indicates, the birth of a child is frequently seen as an event signaling the need to reassess one's life and to make the appropriate changes in behavior. Another man describes the circumstances under which he learned that his girl friend was going to have a baby and the impact that the information had on him. At the time, they were staying in Chicago:

I was drinking heavy, heavy, and Shirley would, was afraid of this. She would get scared, but I never did touch her [that is, hit her], you know. . . . But she was still afraid. After we moved a couple of times, and she tried to keep my friends [who all drank] out of the house, she found that she couldn't do it. She left. She left me once, but she was already pregnant by then.

So, for awhile I thought, "Well, I can get along without her." But as the days went on, I found that I couldn't. So I started callin' her. Call her at home [in Iowa]. . . . She told me, "Do you think you're ready? Do you think that you can stop drinking?" She waited. She waited for quite awhile. But I was still workin', see, day to day. I still worked on a day-to-day [basis]. And I stayed in Chicago for the rest of the winter. . . . I think that it was January or February, she finally told me. She said, "If you're gonna quit drinkin', you had better do it now." . . . "Cause," she says, "We're goin' to have a baby soon." That about knocked me down there. So, that's when I started makin' up my mind. I said, "Well, better slow down here and work and try to get back to Sioux City and straighten things out."

Even if a man is strongly committed to settling-down, his transition from hell-raiser to family man can be difficult if he has been deeply involved in hell-raising. His new identity requires significant changes in behavior for which his earlier life style has poorly prepared him. Thus, a hell-raiser may begin married life with little formal education, a police record, an erratic work record, and a history of heavy and frequent drinking. Each of these can affect an individual's ability to fulfill his duties as a family man. Similar difficulties face women who have "run around" when they attempt to settle-down and become homebodies. The extent to which an individual is able to overcome these liabilities varies greatly. One man who had been deeply involved in hell raising and had spent time in prison, for example, continued to have problems with heavy drinking. Nonetheless, he felt if he could control his drinking, he could find work and make a life for himself and his family: "I never had trouble gettin' a job, or, you know, keeping a job as long as I was sober. No, I can't say I drank because I was, a criticized, or antagonized or anything like that. I drank because I wanted to."

People on the Street

When the phrase "on the street" is applied to an individual, it carries at least two possible meanings. With the first, the prototypic meaning, it describes a person who does not have a house, apartment, or room in which to stay and must find a spot to "flop" or sleep each night. Although many kinds of people may face this situation, it is a fairly common one for the individuals referred to by terms such as "winos," "hopeless drunks," "bay rummers," and "bums." With the second meaning, the phrase describes an individual who has a place to stay, but who behaves in other ways like a "wino." Specifically, it indicates that a person goes on long drunks, lacks a steady job, manages to survive by using the techniques of street life, and/or frequently interacts with people who have no place to stay. Teenaged hell-raisers are generally not viewed as being on the street. Although they may hang around the downtown area of Sioux City, they are too young to go into bars, and their social cliques consist primarily of other teenagers. Older, working hell-raisers may be described as being on the street because they drink and hang out with winos and other hell-raisers who do not have a place to stay. Nonworking hell-raisers may be on the street in either sense of the phrase. In contrast to working hell-raisers, these individuals not only become intoxicated, they also often go on drinking binges. In contrast to the winos on the street, the nonworking hell-raisers get into fights more frequently and are more interested in sexual experiences. As they are generally younger and in better physical condition, they are also more likely to take temporary jobs that demand greater exertion and to engage in more serious illegal activities—such as breaking and entering, jack rolling (robbing an intoxicated person), and armed robbery—to obtain money.

While winos are on the street, their lives center on the acquisition of intoxicants (often a bottle of cheap wine or bay rum), shelter, and food. Because many of these individuals do not have steady incomes, much of their time is spent obtaining these goals. Some of the activities or techniques used to acquire intoxicants include borrowing, pawning, peddling (selling an item to other people), panhandling (begging or bumming), pooling (sharing money for a bottle), boosting (shoplifting or stealing small items), hustling or whoring by women, jack rolling, selling one's blood, and taking spot jobs (jobs that last only for a few hours or a few days). The particular technique selected depends upon a number of factors such as the length of time a person has been on the street, his physical condition, his knowledge of street life, and the resources (money, goods, and people) available to him.

Once individuals on the street have spent their cash on hand, they will borrow whenever they can. Their success depends on their prospects of, and reputations for, repaying their loans. For example, those who receive steady incomes independent of their own work efforts (such as land-lease or social-security payments) are good risks for a loan if they are trustworthy. Individuals who regularly alternate between street life and total abstinence are also good candidates for loans as they are known to have money when they "go on the wagon." In any case, even relatives and friends of a good risk are apt to set a limit on the amount of money they will loan him until he has repaid them. Some people on the street, however, have relatives who regularly give them money, calling it a "loan" even though both know that it is a gift and never will be repaid. One man I knew used to see his mother on her pay day, and she would give him $5. Both were aware that it would never be repaid, but the transaction was conducted in terms of a loan. Aside from such gifts, however, individuals who have been on the street for a while usually have borrowed all they can from friends and relatives and must rely on other techniques to obtain needed money. The sequence of techniques used by one of my consultants is discussed:

> [At what point during the last drunk did you start pawning things?] Well, that's when I can't borrow any money. Like I told you, I was borrowed out. I borrowed here and there and down there. [You borrowed first before you started pawning?] Oh yeah, I borrowed first. [Who did you borrow from?] Only the guys that I know, where I worked, like down at [name of the business]. Why I worked with them guys, some of them for over ten years, and they know me, see. I borrowed from them. Hell, I don't know, maybe from ten or fifteen guys down there. I was borrowed out. What I mean by borrowed out, I couldn't borrow any more. [Did you borrow from your relatives?] No, I don't fool around with them, not even my boy [i.e., his son]. I wouldn't get it from him anyway cause he knows what it's going for see, and he don't drink. After that, why, I started peddling my stuff.

Pawning and peddling are similar. When an individual pawns an item he takes it to a pawn shop and has an opportunity to repurchase it. In peddling, the object is sold outright to other people.

Pawning is generally not used by people who have been on the street for a long period since they have already parted with everything they wish to pawn. The technique is used frequently, however, by individuals who have been off the street for awhile and who have acquired material items. Peddling is used any time a person acquires something by boosting (shoplifting or stealing). Items obtained through boosting are not usually pawned for obvious reasons. Not all the items peddled, of course, are stolen. Some objects such as groceries may be acquired through a social agency. One man describes this: "Groceries, sometimes somebody will go over and get an order [food order] from Catholic Charities or Father Jones or Salvation Army. Go down and get all we can get and then go down and sell it to whoever wanted to buy it." The extent to which pawning and peddling items can be a major source of income for someone who has not been on the street for a while is illustrated in this description of a two-month drunk:

> When we first started drinking, Robert had everything, you know, in the house: Frigidaire, gas stove, heat, electricity, everything. When we got done we didn't have nothing. They turned the electricity off, gas off, no heat. He sold the stove, Frigidaire; they were pretty near new. I think he sold them for seven and a half. And little stuff like lamps and chairs, everything went. Pretty soon we had to move on the floor. Man, that's awful ain't it? . . . That was his house, his own. But they took it—well, might as well say he sold it, because he borrowed money on it, see. I know, some mornings I used to go with him to the lawyer, C.M. He used to go over there and get 25 or 30 dollars. Well, pretty soon he [the lawyer] said, "Well, I'm taking over the house." He said, "You guys will have to move out."

Panhandling or bumming is used frequently whenever a person is on the street. This technique consists of approaching someone and "performing" or "putting your story on him." It may be a simple request, "Can you spare a quarter?" or a more elaborate one, including the reason why the money is needed, "I'm hungry, haven't eaten all day" or "I need a drink real bad." Panhandling is generally conducted at the most profitable time and place. When there are few people out, an individual does not waste his time working the streets. Although most bars do not allow panhandling inside, it can be done surreptitiously.

The lower Fourth Street area of Sioux City assumes a special significance in the lives of people on the street because it contains many bars, a Gospel Mission, a pool hall or two, and a number of inexpensive hotels. Although a number of bars, including two which were "Indian bars" and "wino hangouts," went out of business prior to my research, enough still flourish to keep the area alive. The bars are important to winos not because they provide them with a place in which to drink, but rather because they attract people with money who come into the area to have a good time. This is not to say that winos do not go into bars, they do, but not for their "serious" drinking. As one individual put it: "A real wino is going to be a little hesitant about going into a bar and drinking. He might buy a glass of beer, a glass of beer you can nurse for hours. But he's doing that for a purpose too, somebody else might come in. That's the way we used to do it, by afternoon, everybody's usually out on the street." For these people the bars function as watering holes do for hunters, drawing drinking people with economic resources from the surrounding area and concentrating them where the people on the street can find them.

Although few men or women attempt to work regularly for any length of time while they are on the street, they may take temporary or spot jobs if their physical conditions allow it. There are several ways of obtaining such work. Certain firms in the city handle temporary jobs, and a person can register with them. The firm takes a percentage of the person's wage for setting up the job. To obtain employment in this manner an individual usually has to show up at the job office for several days to prove his dependability and desire. The state employment office also lists spot jobs, and individuals can go through their office. In addition, during the summer months people who need laborers often approach men on certain corners offering them employment. A man looking for work can hang around one of these corners in the morning and wait to be approached. Fairly stable relationships may develop between a given business and men on the street. For example, Indians often work for a sub-contractor who furnishes the manpower to move and load cattle hides. This man often has several crews or "hide gangs" working at one time, not only in the Sioux City vicinity, but also in other areas of the Midwest. Depending on the location, a job out of town may last as long as four or five days. The work is hard, and the pay is a penny a hide. A crew may move as many as 1800 hides a day, thus providing a daily wage of $18. Because the work is difficult and many of the crew drink, alcohol is often furnished as an incentive to get men to work on the hide gangs.[9] The number of crews sent out varies from day to day, so work is not always available. Individuals wanting work will seek out the sub-contractor. If he needs men, he sends recruiters out on the street to hire them or, in some cases, bails them out of jail. One woman whose husband often worked on the gang describes it:

> They drink, they drink on the way there, and they drink while they're there, and usually on the way home. . . . And [the sub-contractor] will just keep givin' 'em a little more at a time to keep, to keep 'em drunk, you might as well say. And they know that they can get that drink any time, so they'll go right back to work—no matter how drunk an' how sick. And if they get in jail, he gets 'em out. Because he knows that they'll go to work, an' he takes that $15 [for bail] out of what they earn. . . . My husband has always said, before he went back with him this time, he said he hated to go back with him, you know. An' he's gettin' too old for the work. And the way it is, an' the way I hear others talk, I think you almost have to be drunk to do it—to keep going—because it's terrible. . . . So I know he doesn't care to work for him, but he's just about to the point where there's no place else for him

to go or anything like that. He's applied different places, but, you know, I've always thought that the record he has, they probably hesitate to even give him a chance.

In addition to the activities already discussed, individuals on the street also engage in a number of illegal techniques to obtain their goals. Boosting, which has already been mentioned, is used frequently. Most of the items obtained in this manner are peddled to people who either are unaware of their stolen status or do not care. If the need arises, objects can be sold to a fence who specifically handles stolen goods.

Some individuals on the street will also "roll" or "jack-roll" people if they get a chance. In some cases, this involves taking any money that a drinking companion has on him after he falls asleep or passes out. In other cases, it involves robbing a likely looking person by force. The victim may be knocked unconscious or to the ground before taking his money. The type of person considered an appropriate target varies with the particular jack-roller, but individuals who appear to have more money than they need or are seen as wasting it are often treated as fair game. As a former jack-roller indicated:

> The man, or a woman, come in here [a bar] with a man hangin' on her arm and kids outside, see. Now, she's drinking her check up. She's boozin', and she'll keep hustlin' til next week—I mean til next month, until she gets that next check. She might pay her rent. She's hustlin' too. . . . [So she's fair game?] Sure, she's fair game. She ain't got no business drinking those kids' money. So if she's going to throw it away, we might as well get it. But, there are a lot of cases where you know where to draw your lines, you know. Somebody's fair game, and somebody isn't.

Occasionally a few individuals on the street engage in armed robbery or burglarize businesses to obtain money. As indicated earlier, the individuals engaging in these activities are often the hell-raisers on the streets who are in better shape physically than the older winos.

Women on the street are able to use their appeal as sex objects to obtain their goals. Men are often willing to buy them drinks in exchange for their company or sexual favors. Depending on their age and attractiveness, women usually have little difficulty finding a place to spend the night. In some cases, a woman will help support a man by "hustling" or "whoring" for him. Although a man may send a woman out hustling for him or allow a woman to support him through hustling, it appears to be fairly uncommon among the Indians of Sioux City for a man to "pimp" regularly for a woman.

Once an individual or group obtains enough money to buy a bottle of wine, a place to drink must be found. Drinking openly on the streets, particularly in the downtown area, invites arrest for intoxication or public drinking. The ideal spot to drink is in someone's house or apartment. Often those individuals on the street with places to stay will share their lodgings with people if their "guests" furnish the drinks. If a house or apartment can not be found, a secluded spot may be sought in the railroad yards, warehouse area, or on the river front. After the alcohol is consumed, the process begins again.

An individual on the street with no place to stay must find a spot to "flop" each night. During the summer, this situation does not present a serious problem, for one can sleep outdoors. However, during the winter greater care must be given to finding a reasonably warm place for the night. People with quarters of their own may sometimes permit others to spend the night. Lacking this, empty houses, abandoned cars, and favored spots such as those beneath loading docks will provide adequate shelter if a blanket or two has been stored there. In the colder months, individuals also rely more upon organizations such as missions for both shelter and food. In lieu of any other place, the city jail is always available.[10]

Although many Indians are fairly mobile, moving from one town or area to another, mobility is particularly characteristic of people on the street. These individuals, especially the hell-raisers, may set out "on the road" to seek excitement and adventure. This search frequently takes them to the cities of Chicago, Minneapolis-St. Paul, Denver, and Omaha as well as to other areas. One man describes how he began to travel:

> I came from Winnebago, a little town, and after being in the service, let's put it this way, you're in the service, you see a lot of excitement, a lot of people, this and that, and all of a sudden you go home. Maybe go to a movie once a week. The only place of entertainment is a bar. You start looking for other—first you start going to Sioux City, you know. Then you hit the road. . . . When I come out of the service, my brother wrote to me and told me he was living in Denver. I was working on a farm down there in Nebraska. You know, kind of daily pay deal. I decided I was just getting fed up with going home with the chickens, you know. Getting up early and going out into the fields, the sun coming up. But I made enough, I remember, that week I made enough, something like $40 or $50 in my pocket. Then I hit the road. I started hitch-hiking. I got my little suitcase and got on the highway. Said good-bye to my dad and this and that. I believe I was gone two years the first time.

While on the road, they continue the same patterns of raising hell and getting by using the techniques of street life. As they often have relatives in the cities to which they travel, they rely on them while becoming familiar with a new city.

Periodic Drunks

Another category distinguished by the people participating in my study was frequently called "periodic drunks." These individuals generally are in their thirties or older. Many view themselves as having a drinking problem and periodically go "on the wagon," abstaining completely. During the period of abstinence, they often obtain a job and work regularly, saving their money or buying desirable items such as televisions or used cars. Many avoid the downtown area while on the wagon, hoping to escape temptation and to minimize the amount of borrowing attempted by their former drinking partners still on the street. During this period, some attend Alcoholics Anonymous.

This pattern is followed for varying lengths of time, from several weeks to several months or even years. At some point they start drinking again. Once this occurs they either attempt to get back on the wagon or go on a long drunk. Often they continue drinking and quit or lose their jobs. They use whatever money they have saved to pay their rent and buy alcohol. After their savings are spent and they have borrowed, pawned, and peddled all they are able, they end up on the street with no place to stay. There they remain until deciding to go on the wagon and commencing the process again.

Developing a Life Style

As indicated in the discussion of life styles, the processes by which an individual evolves particular identities and life styles over the course of the life cycle are complex, varied, and difficult either to predict in advance or to reconstruct retrospectively.[11] While growing up, young Indians are exposed in varying degrees to a variety of identity models, including prototypic hell-raisers and family men. These models include not only the identity ideals they embody, but also assumptions and understandings concerning the nature of life and the manner in which these identities are related to the larger sociocultural system. Over the course of the life cycle, as each person interacts with the institutions of society and lives through the unique experiences that shape his life (viz., incidents of racism, poverty, benevolence, parental love, parental neglect, educational successes and failures), he draws upon these models and their related assumptions to construct his sense of identity and to explain to himself and to others who he is and why he acts as he does. Is a specific act of hell-raising reprehensible or valorizing? It depends entirely on the manner in which it is framed. An act of burglary, for example, when seen from the perspective of a man who feels he has been abandoned by his parents and victimized by a racist and uncaring society, represents a justifiable act of a man brave and resourceful enough to assert his worth by taking what society owes him. From the perspective of a hard-working family man, the act is an expression of a psychologically disturbed, immature person who is too lazy to get a job and earn what he wants.

It is difficult to generalize about the processes because each specific act of behavior has its own set of situational determinants and cognitive/motivational underpinnings. As a result, a set of similar behavioral acts (a number of burglaries, for example) by the same person may represent a series of unique incidents when considered from the person's sociopsychological perspective. Despite the diversity at this level of analysis, however, I was struck by the many situations in which hell-raising activities were presented by participants in terms of acquiring, claiming, or validating valued identity features. That is, irrespective of the mainstream view, these acts were often presented or interpreted by the participants as laudatory. This was true even though the acts could also be related to unfortunate or undesirable life circumstances of the individuals in question (viz., an assault might be attributed to a racist remark or a burglary to societal inequality).

Erving Goffman (1967), who examined various kinds of "action" in American society from his dramaturgical perspective, offered a clue to understanding the strong appeal that hell-raising activities hold for some people. Goffman suggested that settings of action provide an individual with an opportunity to behave under circumstances where his performance is both consequential and problematic. That is, the outcome of the performance is both uncertain and important to the individual. For example, if an individual becomes involved in a fight his performance is consequential because whether he wins or loses is significant to his well-being. It is also problematic; he does not know beforehand whether he will win or lose the fight. Goffman argued that a successful performance under these circumstances depends on two sets of individual attributes: "primary properties" and "character." Primary properties are the specific skills and knowledge needed to successfully perform the required activities. To be a victorious fighter, for example, it would be advantageous to possess traits such as strength, stamina, speed, and knowledge of specific fighting techniques. Character is the set of capacities, or lack of them, for standing correct and steady when faced by sudden pressures. Goffman distinguished several aspects of character including "courage," the capacity to envisage immediate danger and yet still proceed; "composure," the ability to carry out the activity with poise; and "gameness," staying with an activity and continuing to put all one's effort into it regardless of setbacks. Thus, when an individual performs successfully in a situation where the outcome is consequential and problematic, he has demonstrated that he possesses both the required primary properties as well as the necessary character attributes.

This perspective helps explain a hell-raiser's behaviors. By participating in hell-raising activities an individual can claim and validate valued identity features. He can demonstrate that he possesses primary properties such as strength, fighting ability, sexual prowess, and cleverness; and character attributes such as courage, defiance of authority, composure, and gameness. Even if an individual does not always participate in the action, he can at least watch the events and enjoy the action vicariously. Although many of these ideals are also found in mainstream models, their expressions through hell-raising activities—particularly in the illegal acts—clearly run counter to what is seen as acceptable behavior in middle-class society. Similar identity ideals or value systems have been reported among other contemporary groups with different cultural backgrounds.[12] This suggests that hell-raising values have developed, in part, as one type of response to the relatively deprived positions these groups have occupied in their national sociocultural systems. They form an alternative system of values through which participants can feel good about themselves.

Why would an Indian in Sioux City adopt these ideals and related behaviors if they do run counter to many mainstream ideals? To answer that question we need to consider the situational contexts of given individuals and the psychodynamic/cognitive processes driving the specific acts and leading the individuals to embrace these ideals.

Youths most likely to engage in hell-raising activities, and to adopt a valorizing version of the hell-raising ethic to explain their participation, are raised in troubled homes.[13] Given the kinds of educational programs in which these children participate and their background preparation, the teacher's approach may not lead to highly successful and personally satisfying academic performances.[14] Failure in terms of middle-class academic standards, however, does not necessarily mean that the children will view themselves as inferior. The children may embrace a set of standards that place worth on attributes such as physical prowess, toughness, artistic abilities, or verbal skills. Depending on the children's abilities, they may excel through legitimately recognized avenues within the school system that relate to those standards, such as athletics. The same ideals, however, may also lead the children to seek prestige outside the official system through hell-raising. Because these behaviors are generally treated as conflicting with adequate performances within the school framework, the Indian student who follows this path may drop out or be pushed out before graduating.[15] Sadly, the Sioux City school system at the time of my study did not deal effectively with Indian and other minority students (*see* Iowa State Department of Public Instruction 1971). The Superintendent of Schools, William Anderson, acknowledged that the Indian dropout rate was the highest in the city, running at about two-thirds.[16]

In addition to the psychosocial factors at work, neurobiological influences may also be involved, particularly in relation to alcohol and drug use. Children who experience early-life stress (childhood maltreatment—such as physical abuse and neglect, emotional abuse and neglect, or sexual abuse—or stressful life events—such as parental divorce, family violence, or economic deprivation) are at an increased risk of developing a variety of behavioral problems, including alcohol and drug dependence.[17] Because many people who are exposed to these early-life stressors do *not* go on to develop alcohol or drug addiction, genetic and environmental factors appear to play both predisposing *and* protective roles in the development of these problems (*see* Enoch 2011 and 2012 for discussions of these factors).

The experiences of Bob and his brothers exemplify this path from a troubled home into hell-raising activities and demonstrate the critical role of individual differences in these processes. Among Bob's earliest recollections of his family were those of parental drinking and abuse:

> All I know is that they used to go out and just get drunk. That's all I can remember, outstanding about the time I lived with them. They used to get drunk, and Dad, Dad had a bottle one time and cracked it over Mom's face one night, cut her eye. I can remember that I got scared. He used to whip us. We had to sleep on the floor and cover up with coats on the floor. [You didn't have any beds?] No, no beds. My mom and dad might have had a mattress. I remember sleeping on the floor there.

When he was about five years old, Bob and his siblings were removed from their home and sent to different institutions. Bob and two of his brothers were sent to a boarding school in Marty, South Dakota. He remained at Marty until he was sixteen before returning home. He lived with his parents even though they still drank. He continued to feel some hostility toward them:

> I hate to hold my parents accountable, but who else am I going to blame. . . . I got to hold my parents accountable for all the problems we got today. They're primarily responsible. I mean, if you bring up a kid, bring a kid into this world without an intention to take care of it, then your act of creating him was purely out of—putting your dick in a girl and getting a good screw. You know, what I mean, to say it bluntly. . . . You've got to be ready. That's what I'm going to do for my kids. I'm gonna love my kids. . . . I don't think I'll ever be able to do to my kids, what my mom and dad done to

us. I mean, we've, we've never been together as a family, not ever, ever, ever.

When he returned to Sioux City, he began to associate with young hell-raisers and to engage in a variety of hell-raising acts:

When I first got here, you know, everything was strange. Like when I first went to Marty. . . . I was in need of friendship. And I was moping over the friendships I just lost. . . . I bumped into a guy named R.T., the first guy I met in Sioux City. And from there I met B.W., and A.G. and all the other Indians, you know. And I started associating with them, going down to Prince Henry's, here, downtown. Started doing the things they do, you know, drinking, carrying on like that, you know. I just started smoking then, too, you know. It was about, I was about 16. . . . Right then I was exposed to every vice in the book: drinking, you know, screwing, smoking, all the bad stuff, you know. That's when all that stuff entered my life, right there. When I first come back to Sioux City. That's when I first became a hoodlum. That year, that summer, especially when my brothers got back, two of them had already gone to Eldora[18] for breaking and entering and car theft.

As he grew older, however, his standards began to change, and even though he no longer thought of himself as a hell-raiser he still felt pressure at times to engage in illegal activities. He offered the following observation on the pressures he thought helped drive hell-raising activities and provided an example of the conflicting standards he used to guide and evaluate his own behavior:

I don't think you realize, I don't think any middle-class white realizes, the urge you have to every now and then go out and get in a lot of trouble. Just go out and blow it, blow everything up. Any more, I more or less have suppressed it, I hope I have. Although when I got drunk, as recently as two months ago I tried to break into a place. Every now and then that urge comes up. [Why then? Why two months ago? What set you off?] I don't know; I just wanted something. . . . But I never did break in. I got to the door to see if it was locked; it was locked, so I walked away. I couldn't do it. . . . I guess, I guess when Jim and Jack come home, I felt so guilty about not having any money at all. You know, they come home, and they had all the money. . . . When Jack come home he spent all the money he had from the service on me. And I felt guilty. . . . [So you think that was the reason you felt like doing that?] Yeah, so I would have $30 or $40 so I could spend it on them the next day and make them feel good, you know. [What finally stopped you?] I couldn't do it. I was afraid what would happen if I got caught. Then everybody would look at me. That's completely adverse as to what you've been talking all your life, dreaming about. Something in me suppressed that urge to.

Although Bob was momentarily tempted by the situational pressures of his lack of money and the guilt he felt at not being able to reciprocate the generosity of his friends, he was sufficiently committed to an alternative set of ideals and a plan for his future that he ultimately did not allow himself to engage in the act of burglary.

In contrast, his brother Mark, reacting to a similar set of circumstances had made a different kind of long-term adjustment, one that reflected a different set of values. After returning from Marty, Mark had been sent to the Iowa Training School for Boys in Eldora, Iowa five times for breaking and entering, car theft, and parole violation. He was currently living at home with his parents, and although he would work occasionally, he did not hold any job for very long. Recently, he had been arrested for public intoxication. As Bob said:

You see, Mark feels that he's justified. See, he knows Mom and Dad have never done nothing for him, so what really does it mean that he would do anything like going out and getting a job? Does it mean anything to him? Mark doesn't want it. . . . Mom and Dad care, are concerned only for his own good. Sure Mom and Dad holler about, "Well, you don't give but God damn five dollars a week." And Mark takes that to be that, well, if he worked it would be only for them. But Mark doesn't realize that working, going to college, or something would be for his own good because he's got a long life ahead of him. [Do they ever threaten to throw him out?] Oh yeah. Many times, many times. They threaten not to feed him. And Mark feels guilty when he eats the food at our house. I can tell it. I used to feel the same way too. [Did you?] Yeah, and I imagine my other brothers have too. All of us have because of the way Dad rides us when he gets drunk. . . . I talked to him a hundred times. "Mark, you, you are 100% eligible for a loan to go to Haskell.[19] If you want to live in the past, Mark, Haskell will be another Marty. Same Indians, same girls. The same situation as Marty. . . . [What does Mark say when you say that?] He says he's going to Denver, before Christmas. I say, "On relocation?"[20] He says, "No, I'm going out there." "How? You ain't got no money. You won't work." He says, "Just shut up. Suck a dick." . . . In your attempt to help him, you think, I mean, he thinks that you're his enemy, his adversary. It's really hard to communicate with him.

As we discussed the differing reactions made by both of them to similar experiences, Bob said:

I can make a comparison between Mark and me. People have made me feel important. Well, ever since I was at Marty I started realizing when Meatball [a nickname for one of the teachers] would call me in his office and start telling me, "Bob, you've got potential." Right then I started to realize, "Well, if he says, maybe I do." Then I got out, and I realized how much Mom and Dad thought about me—as far as my going to college and stuff. And Dad used to sit there and all he'd do is brag about me. That'd make me feel important. . . .

I'd get to listening to him, and I'd get to believing it. And he says, "Yeah, I got a boy that's going to college and take up law. He'll be a Senator some day." I actually believed him. Because I felt that within myself that I got a capacity to do something, and I'm determined.

Bob's view of his brother's behavior corresponded to what Mark said about his own life. When Mark and I were talking, he mentioned that his parents frequently cussed him out, and I asked him if that bothered him. "Yeah, it did bother me a lot. Started holding grudges against them, I guess. When I get drunk, I cuss them out, and when they're drunk, they cuss me out, I guess. Even when they're sober, they cuss me out." He felt that he was being unfairly singled out for criticism:

I know I ain't no different from Bob. I know I'm his oldest brother, but, you know, they tell me to get out and work. My mom always tells me, you know, get out, go to Denver. . . . But my other brothers are still lying around the house. I can't say nothing about it, but she said something about it. What I say, they don't understand what—I mean they understand, but think I'm teasing them or something. . . . I don't even talk to them any more, because I know I ain't working now. If I tell them to get out and work, they tell me to get out and work.

When Mark engaged in burglary or shoplifting, he always had been drinking. "I get drunk, you know, when I want to break in. I go and break in." He felt that drinking increased his courage: "When a person drinks, that's the only time they get their nerve. . . . It's through the alcohol, they get their nerve. I noticed that about my brothers, I noticed that about all the Indian guys that drink. They're pretty quiet, you know. I know most the Indian guys around here. Once they start drinking, boy, they're loud."

One of the striking features of some of Mark's illegal acts was the lack of care with which he engaged in them. On more than one occasion he simply walked into a store and rather openly picked up beer and cigarettes. He behaved as if he did not care whether he was caught or not. When I asked him if that was the case, he said he thought he might be better off in prison. "You're always better off in jail or you are better off in Anamosa[21] or prison. I knew a lot of Indian boys that always thought that. I used to be one myself. I still think the same way. I think I'm better off in Anamosa or prison or something."

Both brothers grew up in similar circumstances and participated in a variety of hell-raising activities. Both men, when engaging in these acts, presented their behavior in positive, valorizing terms, attempting to claim and maintain a positive sense of identity. Each specific act, however, also developed out of a unique set of circumstances and carried other levels of meaning. Some of Bob's and Mark's cases of burglary developed out of situations in which they felt materially deprived. Some cases also carried elements of societal defiance and feelings of hostility, revenge, and self justification. Some of Mark's, however, also contained features of hopelessness and a desire to be removed from an unpleasant setting—even at the cost of incarceration. While Bob had moved beyond his earlier hell-raising ideals and was contemplating paths to take him beyond his present situation, Mark continued to hold on to his old models and was unchanged in his behavioral patterns.

Concluding Comment

The Indian population of Sioux City is not a homogeneous block of individuals sharing a single personality structure and single life style. Instead, they distinguish a number of life styles and recognize that even individuals adopting similar ways of life are psychologically diverse and capable of behaving in disparate ways. The values and identity ideals embodied in some of their life styles are indistinguishable from mainstream, middle-class ones. Others, notably those related to hell-raising and life on the street, can be seen as arising in response to, and in some cases in opposition to, middle-class values and ideals. People have a need to feel good about themselves, and if they can not do so by embodying official, mainstream ideals, they will turn to others. This does not mean that the adoption of identity ideals and one life style over another is foreordained or a simple process. On the contrary, growing up, individuals are exposed in varying degrees to a variety of prototypic identity models and the narratives relating them to life's circumstances. As we saw, manifold and complex processes shape a person's reaction to these models, and in some cases, can lead individuals from the same family to take different psychological and social paths.

Drinking standards and drinking behavior form critical elements in the life styles adopted and can have a significant impact on the course of a person's life. We turn to this set of issues in the next chapter.

Endnotes for Chapter 4

[1] This chapter was originally published in the *Journal of Drug Issues,* 1980, Spring, 257-272 and is reprinted with permission. Additional ethnographic details, examples, and discussion have been added. In this chapter and the three that follow, rather than changing the verbs to past tense, I followed the anthropological convention of presenting the data in the "ethnographic present." As long as the reader remembers the fieldwork was conducted in 1970-71 no confusion should result.

The research on which this chapter is based was supported by the Center for Urban Ethnography, University of Pennsylvania, and the National Institute of Mental Health, Public Health Grant 17,216.

I would like to express my appreciation to the Board of Directors and staff of the Sioux City American Indian Center, to the staff of the Iowa Comprehensive Treatment Program for Indian Problem Drinkers, and to the many Indians of Sioux City who were kind enough to share their experiences with me. Without the help and friendship of these people, the research would have been impossible.

I would like to thank Barbara Lex, Jay Noricks, Jerry Stockdale, James M. Stokes, and John Van Ness for comments on an earlier draft of this article or chapter.

[2] Although I interacted informally with young women of this category, because I was single, I thought it best not to work intensively with them. As a result, I have more complete data on the males.

[3] Wallace and Fogelson (1965: 380) define identity as "any image, or set of images, either conscious or unconscious, which an individual has of himself." They call an individual's full set of images his "total identity" and analytically distinguished real, ideal, feared, and claimed identities:

> Real identity is a subset of images which the person believes, privately to be a true present description of himself as he "really" is. Ideal identity is a subset of images which the person would like to be able to say was true but which he does not necessarily believe is true at present; the ideal subset of images often includes morally ideal components, but may also incorporate amoral or even, in relation to local conventions, immoral or "negative," in Erickson's sense, identities. . . . Feared identity is a subset of images which the person would not like to have to say was true of himself at present and which he does not necessarily believe is true; the feared subset

of images may include socially disvalued components, but it may also include identities which are, by some public convention, positive in value. Claimed identity is a subset of images which the person would like another party to believe is his real identity. Sometimes with respect to a given dimension of variation, the real, ideal, feared, and claimed identities can be construed as points on a linear continuum, such as a scale or a discrete continuous variable [1965: 380-381].

As the ideal identity is positively valued and the feared identity is negatively valued, a person is motivated to reduce the distance between his real and ideal identities and to increase the distance between his real and feared identities. The social and psychological processes through which individuals arrive at their ideal identity standards and attempt to embody them in particular situations are varied and complex. For additional discussions of the concepts of self and identity, *see* Fogelson (1982), Greenwald and Pratkanis (1984), Higgins (1987), Holland et al. (1998), Leary (2007), Linger (2005), Markus and Nurius (1986), Markus and Ruvolo (1989), Markus and Wurf (1986), Robbins (1973a), Schlenker (1985a), Sökefeld (1999), and Wallace (1967).

[4] As Goffman (1967: 241) put it:

When two persons are mutually present, the conduct of each can be read for the conception it expresses concerning himself and the other. Co-present behavior becomes mutual treatment. But mutual treatment itself tends to become socially legitimated, so that every act, whether substantive or ceremonial, becomes the obligation of the actor and the expectation of the other. Each of the two participants is transformed into a field in which the other necessarily practices good or bad conduct. Moreover, each will not only desire to receive his due, but find that he is obliged to exact it, obliged to police the interaction to make sure that justice is done him.

[5] Goffman (1971: 109) suggests that accounts, apologies, and requests are the major devices used to remedy offenses in our Western society.

[6] Although some individuals will drink alone, most drunkenness occurs in social situations and may serve latent functions of which the drinker is not clearly aware. This, however, should not obscure the point that at times the state of intoxications itself may be positively defined.

---

[7] The drug scene can change rapidly; when I returned for a visit in 1973, several young men and women who, during my field research, had only used alcohol, marijuana, and hallucinogens had started using heroin and had become dealers. They would buy $100 worth in Omaha and then cut the drug into nickel ($5) and dime ($10) bags for resale in Sioux City.

[8] At the time of my study (1970-71), the legal drinking age in Iowa was 21; in Nebraska it was 20; and in South Dakota it was 19 for 3.2 beer and 21 for other alcoholic substances.

[9] The use of alcohol to attract and pay off workers in certain occupations is an old custom in America (Rorabaugh 1979: 47, 132, 141). Needless to say, such practices may force an abstaining individual to choose between employment and sobriety.

[10] In some cases the relationship can become almost symbiotic. The Indian who was arrested most frequently for intoxication during 1970 was arrested over 70 times. Before I knew how frequently this individual, whom I will call Eric, was arrested, I was discussing his case with a relative of his, and I asked where Eric lived. The relative replied, "At the jail." Initially I thought he was joking, but later discovered this was no exaggeration. When I was collecting the arrest information, the Chief of Police kindly let me use an unoccupied desk in the room in which the records were located. The room, which was on the first floor of the court house, was fairly large with a counter running its length, separating the area for the public from the work area which contained desks, file cabinets, typewriters, and other equipment for the clerical workers who were all female. One day while I was examining the records at my desk, I looked up and to my amazement noticed that Eric—obviously very intoxicated—had come into the room. He knew all the women very well, joked with them, and asked to borrow some money. They all responded good-naturedly and bandied with him. In the course of their interaction, Eric came behind the counter into the work area and playfully danced one of the women around in a circle. She gave him some money, and as he left, they admonished him to go upstairs where the cells were located and turn himself in. It was apparent, however, even as they spoke that he had no intention of doing so. He wanted to drink some more. After he left, one of the women, obviously feeling a bit sheepish, walked over to my desk and told me that they tried to look after Eric. One of the women in the past had tried to discover why he drank so much. It was clear in the interaction I witnessed that Eric felt quite comfortable in the

setting, knew the clerical workers very well, and controlled the interaction to his benefit.

In other cases in Sioux City and in other cities, the relationship between heavy drinkers on the street and the local police-court-jail systems is less benign (*see* Spradley 1970 and endnote 8 in Chapter 5).

[11] *See* Cantor and Kihlstrom (1987: 190-243), Goodenough (1963: 215-251) and Rosenberg (1979: 195-255) for discussions of identity development and change.

[12] *See*, for example, Factor, Kawachi, and Williams (2011); Foley (1990); Gans (1962); Hannerz (1969); Liebow (1967); Miller (1958); Willis (1977).

[13] In a study of Native Americans incarcerated within the Nebraska Department of Corrections, Grobsmith (1989) found that the vast majority of her consultants came from troubled families: 89% stated that their parents drank or used drugs, only 24% were raised by their parents, and 47% had experienced physical abuse at the hands of parents or guardians. Also *see* Grobsmith (1994: 93-109). In a survey of 249 Indian men incarcerated in Canada, Waldram (1997: 46) found that 80% had at least one parent (or foster/adoptive parent) with alcohol or drug problems, and that 66% were raised in families where physical violence occurred. Thirty-five percent had experienced foster homes and 30% residential schools. In a study of 89 American Indian adolescents in a residential substance abuse treatment program, Deters et al. (2006) found that 98% had experienced at least one traumatic event in their lives and the average number of traumas reported was 4.1. Also *see* Koss et al. (2003), Robin et al. (1997), and Whitesell et al. (2009).

[14] I am not thinking primarily about teachers who are knowingly and overtly ethnocentric and biased in their interactions with Indian students, although they occur too frequently; rather, I am thinking more of those teachers like the one the Spindlers studied in a fifth grade class: "We found that the teacher was biased in his perception of relationships. The bias was consistently in the direction of positive appraisals for upper status and mainstream children. He was as consistently *negative* [their emphasis] in his appraisal of relationships for non-mainstream children as he was positive for others" (Spindler and Spindler 1990: 65). As they point out, this teacher was a kind and well-meaning person and strongly believed that he was giving every child in his classroom the same opportunities and attention.

His problem, however,

> was not so much disvaluing as ignoring. He simply did not interact in the same way or with the same intensity with children who did not match his own cultural experience and background. This process of selecting out certain children and certain behaviors for approval and reinforcement, and ignoring others, is potentially as damaging as the exercise of overt prejudice and hostility towards certain children [1990: 68].

[15] *See* Foley (1990, 1991, 1995: 55-83); Jacob and Jordan (1987); Labov (1972: 241-254); Ogbu (1990); Spindler and Spindler (1990); Trueba (1988); Trueba, Spindler, and Spindler (1990); Wax (1967); and Wortham (2006, 2008) for related discussions. Foley's conclusions regarding the silence of Mesquaki students in class are worth quoting as I believe they apply to Sioux City:

> Mesquaki silence has roots in a somewhat different speech style and in a long history of racial and political resistance. For many Mesquaki youth, sitting silently in white classrooms is also a political statement about racism. On the other hand, Mesquaki youth are still unique individuals. Some may be shy or have self-esteem problems. Others may be indifferent or rebellious. The silence of Mesquaki students is a complex form of self-expression and is always a product to unique cultural forces and of unique personalities. Professional researchers must stop feeding teachers monolithic explanations that emphasize only "speech styles," or "low self-esteem," or "rebellion" [1995: 68].

Collins (2009) reviews the changes since the 1960s in the theoretical and methodological approaches taken in the view that schools reproduce social inequality rather than generate social equality. He concludes that the generalization from Coleman's 1966 study "that differences among schools mattered much less than assumed and that family socioeconomic status was the strongest influence on a child's educational achievement and life chances" is still valid (2009: 41).

[16] *See* (Sioux City Journal 1973). In response to criticisms, the school system made several changes in their programs and initiated new ones in an attempt to better serve Indian students (Ricchiardi 1973). However, as will be detailed in Chapter 10, with the exception of Asian American students, other minority students (Native American, African American, and Hispanic) are still performing below white students in proficiency tests (Sioux City Community Schools District 2010).

[17] As Mary-Anne Enoch (2011: 17) notes in a comprehensive review, such stress "can result in permanent neurohormonal and hypothalamic-pituitary-adrenal axis changes, morphological changes in the brain, and gene expression changes in the mesolimbic dopamine reward pathways, all of which are implicated in the development of addiction." The roles of these neurobiological systems in problem drinking are discussed in Chapter 7. Also *see* Enoch (2012), Kreek (2011), Russo (2012), McEwen and Gianaros (2011), and McGowan (2012) for discussion of these systems. In addition to the role of early-life stress in addiction, a growing literature is exploring the links among lower socio-economic status, cumulative stress (referred to as "allostatic load"), and the toll on health (*see*, for examples, Hertzman and Boyce 2010, McEwen 2010, McEwen and Gianaros 2010, and Seeman et al. 2010). Also *see* endnote 13.

[18] He is referring to Eldora, Iowa, where the Iowa Training School for Boys is located.

[19] Haskell Indian Junior College located in Lawrence, Kansas.

[20] He is referring to a program developed by the Bureau of Indian Affairs in the 1950s to relocate Indians from reservations to cities like Chicago, Los Angeles, and Denver. In 1962 the name of the program was changed from Relocation Services to Employment Assistance. Although several related programs, including adult vocational training, were available to individuals, as Bob indicated, many Indians still referred to these options as the relocation program (*see* Fixico 2000, Officer 1971, and Prucha 1984: 1079 for discussions of the program).

[21] He is referring to Anamosa, Iowa, where the Anamosa State Penitentiary is located.

CHAPTER 5
FROM HELL-RAISER TO FAMILY MAN:
DRINKING NORMS AND CONSTRAINTS OVER
THE LIFE CYCLE[1]

> My folks were hollerin' at me and, you know, cussing at me and this and that, because she was p.g., and I wasn't trying to do anything about it, you know. I was still drinkin', raisin' hell.
>
> Frank Wolf, Sioux City Indian

> The only reason that he don't drink, is because he's scared of his mother, and he's scared of his sister, because she's not scared to talk to him, see. She'll tell him to either sober up or get out of there, because that's her home, see.
>
> Sioux City Indian

An individual's drinking norms[2] and behaviors are not static; they change not only from one social setting to another; they also change over the course of the life cycle. To better understand how they develop for Sioux City Indians and the manner in which various constraints operate to control heavy drinking, I will use the categories and stages of the life cycle introduced in the last chapter to organize the discussion, and I will examine one man's case history in detail.

Young People

I will begin the discussion of norms and constraints with the individuals in their teens or twenties who live in a household headed by their parents or other relatives. At this stage of the life cycle, their most important social contacts are generally with peers and household members. If the young persons are hell-raisers, their personal and peer standards of drinking are apt to be fairly liberal; that is, frequent intoxication is acceptable behavior. Their actual drinking patterns, however, are more conservative due to economic constraints and parental pressures. Although beer is frequently consumed, other forms of alcohol are also ingested. As indicated in Chapter Four, if a young hell-raiser does not work at least part-time, he will be unable to purchase alcohol and instead will have to rely upon the generosity of his parents and working friends or resort to illegal acts. The amount of money a young, working hell-raiser has available to spend on alcohol depends on the extent to which he helps meet the operating costs of the household. Even if an individual earns and retains ample money with which to drink, his parents may exert a restraining influence.

If the young people are "individuals who don't think of trouble," their personal and peer standards of drinking are generally more restrictive than those of young hell-raisers. Some individuals engage only in limited experimentation with alcohol during their early and mid-teens and do not become intoxicated. Others experience intoxication at this age but limit drinking to weekends or special occasions. A "nice girl" describes her smoking and drinking behavior during her late teens:

> My best friend lived next door. . . . I used to go over there. We used to play records, play cards, or just sit around. We used to go up to the laundromat and sit down there and smoke [cigarettes] and drink pop. [Did you drink when you were in high school?] No, oh, I tried it a couple of times, you know. My mother and them used to drink, and they used to go to bed. You know, a can of beer sitting there. I'd take a drink to see how it tastes. See, my brother took me one time, and he give me a can of beer one time. But otherwise he wouldn't let me drink. He wouldn't let me smoke. I used to sneak and smoke, and Judy [her friend] used to too. Her mother used to let me smoke. I could go over there and sit there and smoke. She wouldn't let Judy smoke. See that was

> after I got out of school that I used to go over there and drink
> with her [Judy's mother]. My mother, she wouldn't let me
> drink . . . but I could go to Judy's Mother's and drink. And
> Judy could go over to my house and sit there and smoke, but
> I couldn't, and she could drink too. My mother was real
> strict, if I went some place I'd tell her what time I'd be home,
> and I had to be home. It was after I got out of school my dad
> told me I could smoke. He told me I could smoke if I bought
> my own cigarettes. Then finally, it was . . . [when I reached
> the legal drinking age], that's when my dad went and offered
> me a beer once.

Even though both parents often drank, as her comments indicate,
they were strict with her. Another woman describes a similar
relationship between her father and his daughters:

> He felt that if we did drink, he didn't want us to do it in front
> of him. And I never did smoke or drink in front of him. He
> knew that I smoked, and one time I thought: well, I'm just
> going to, you know, light up the cigarette. An' I just felt so
> funny sittin' there; I didn't even feel like takin' a drag, you
> know. I thought any minute he might say something, so I just
> put it out, an' I walked out of the room. When my other
> sisters started smokin' in front of him, . . . I couldn't.

In general, drinking standards that parents apply to their
children vary in relation to the child's age, economic role in the
household, and gender. Even parents who frequently become
intoxicated themselves are not likely to knowingly approve of their
children's regular intoxication, especially if the children are in their
early to mid-teens. Depending on parental behavior, however,
children may be unsupervised for long periods, thereby escaping
effective control. Parents also feel their right to influence their
children's drinking behavior is directly proportional to the amount of
support provided the children. As a result, children who contribute
money for household costs enjoy greater freedom in determining
their level of drinking than do their nonworking siblings of the same

age and gender. A child's gender affects parental standards because parents generally hold more restrictive standards for their daughters' drinking than their sons'. As children reach their late teens and twenties, many parents begin applying standards of drinking to their children that are similar to their own personal standards.

During this period, most children have personal drinking standards equivalent to, or more liberal than, the standards their parents hold for them; however, some children's personal standards are more restrictive. In the cases with which I am familiar, one or both parents were heavy and frequent drinkers. The reasons the children gave for their more restrictive standards related to neglect or abuse they felt they had received from drinking parents. Although only one of these individuals abstained completely, the rest did have moderate standards.

If a child's drinking exceeds parental limits, the parents may apply a variety of corrective measures. Depending on the child's age, physical coercion may be used. For example, when one man was in his early teens, he and other young relatives would steal and drink his parents' beer. As he said, "My mother would get a hold of us and beat the hell out of us. Well, that sobers us up!" As children reach their middle to late teens, corporal punishment is applied less frequently. Verbal approaches are also taken in correcting children's behavior. Some of these practices are referred to as "preaching." One such technique uses negative examples in pointing out possible dangers of excessive drinking. One man recalled:

> My dad, he used to preach to me when I was smaller, you know. . . . I went to the store with him once. . . . We seen some winos walkin' in an alley. They reached in a garbage can full of green apples, rotten, you know. An' they started eatin' them. He said, "You keep your drinking up, an' you keep raisin' hell and this and that; that's the way you're going to be." He said, "I don't want to see you like that." He said, "I won't even talk to you . . . if I see you on the street like that."

In some cases, parents will also attack a child's identity by implying or stating that he already possesses negative attributes. A parent might, for example, accuse a child of being lazy or worthless because all he does is lie around the house and go out drinking. Depending on the child's economic contribution to the household, any of these techniques may be coupled with financial pressures.

When unacceptable behaviors and social control mechanisms are discussed, some writers assume that the unacceptable behaviors occur because social controls are lacking or are not applied. But as Erving Goffman (1971: 368) has pointed out in a discussion of social control within a family unit, the success of sanctions on a family member ultimately depends on his voluntary acceptance of the moral force of the sanctions and on his willingness to change his behavior. If he chooses to ignore the sanctions, the family has little else that it can do. It sometimes happens, in fact, that children are committed to their drinking standards strongly enough to risk rupturing family life. If the parents persist in attempting to change the child's behavior, he may move out temporarily or permanently. A woman describes such an incident that occurred when she was in her late teens, though the conflict in this case did not center solely on drinking:

> We [her mother and herself] were always on the outs, and she'd, you know, she'd kick me out, or I'd leave for about a month, two months. [Where would you go?] I'd stay with my . . . girlfriend. I used to stay down there all the time, and I'd go to work, go to work every day and stay there. The longest I was gone was about two months. They finally came after me. I was mad.

Family Men and Homebodies

As indicated in Chapter Four, although young people may adopt several life styles as they grow older, the one viewed as socially desirable and part of the ideal life cycle, is the one in which men become "family men" and women become "homebodies." Even though family men may patronize some of the same bars as hell-raisers after work and on weekends, they do so not to raise hell but to drink and socialize; they are not expected to fight or womanize. In addition, family men also drink in their homes or those of their relatives or friends. Beer is the common, but not the only, type of alcohol consumed. Their drinking patterns vary within the limits set by maintaining a steady job. When a man marries, his wife's drinking standards become of critical importance. If the husband and wife both drank heavily before marriage, their drinking standards may not change. Some couples drink every day and become intoxicated at least several nights during the week. On weekends they may begin drinking on Friday night and continue until Sunday when the husband must sober up for work on Monday. Other couples, however, feel that the changed circumstances of their life after marriage, particularly after having children, require them to adopt new, more restrictive standards. They may, for example, explicitly limit drinking to weekends. In other cases, if neither husband nor wife did much drinking before marriage, the same patterns continue. When a couple's standards differ, they may quarrel frequently over drinking until they reach a consensus. The agreement worked out may go either way: some couples adopt the more restrictive standards, but with others, the more conservative member gives in and starts drinking more frequently or heavily. If a couple never achieves agreement, drinking either becomes a chronic disruption or the union is dissolved.

Couples adopting liberal drinking standards vary in the extent to which they approximate the ideal roles of family man and homebody. Some couples are able to drink fairly heavily throughout the week and still maintain the family unit. The husband holds a steady job without missing many workdays. The couple's children, though not receiving as much attention as other children, are not neglected or left unsupervised. One individual raised in such a household describes it: "We never did go hungry because of our parents' drinking. They always bought groceries and bought what we needed before they drank. And they still do. . . . My father don't drink his whole pay check up; they pay their bills and buy groceries, and then they drink." Another woman describes the control her father exercised with his drinking:

> He would drink at this bar and come home in a cab. An' he would be, ah, you know, drunk, pretty full. An' if I was there, I always had to help, you know, get him to bed. An' if he'd want a sandwich or coffee, you know, an' then he'd be talkin' to me while I was doin' it—fixin' something to eat. An' then he'd go to bed, but I never did see him like sit and drink an' get drunk. . . . [As he got older, he would] keep a bottle of whiskey in the fridge. He'd come home from work, an' he'd maybe have a shot, you know. An' that would be all. But he didn't do that all the time either, so that's what made me think it must, that he sorta didn't feel good, but didn't want to say anything to us girls. But, [her other sisters] wouldn't get up an' fool with him, you know. [When he'd come back?] Yeah. So he'd just, you'd know, he'd be singing an' talkin', and he'd go in an' go to bed. But if he knew I was there, then he'd be hollerin' an' sayin' he wanted something to eat. He knew I'd do it, so. An' I'd listen to him. Pretty soon he'd pass out, and he'd be asleep, an' that was it. He wouldn't drink again for--see, they paid him every two weeks, an' he didn't always go out every two weeks. But it was probably, maybe a month or a month an' a half apart, he would go. . . . [Would he spend it all?] No, he wouldn't even take. I don't know what he would take, but I know he'd always hide his money some place. . . . He wouldn't spend money to make anybody go without.

Other individuals and couples, however, do not function as effectively, and the family unit is unstable with one or both parents absent from the home for long periods. The family may be supported through a combination of temporary jobs, unemployment compensation, and welfare programs. In some cases, the children are legally removed from the home and placed with other relatives or in foster homes, boarding schools, or correctional institutions. Among the first memories of a man who was born in the town of Winnebago are fights between his father and mother, both of whom drank heavily. His grandmother assumed the responsibility of raising him and his siblings until they were taken from her and placed in various institutions. In the following passage he describes his early years and recounts the time his grandmother, acting on a premonition that her grandchildren needed her, came to Sioux City from Winnebago:

It was blizzarding, snowing. My grandmother was out there on the farm [i.e., her allotment in Nebraska] by herself. And she had a feeling, you know, a premonition of danger or whatever you call it these days. She got up in the middle of the night; she put on her warm clothes and started walking. She walked into town. On her way to Sioux City a semi picked her up and brought her along into Sioux City. And we used to live on the East side. . . . She walked from where that truck driver let her off. She walked over to where Mom used to keep us. And she went to the house, and we were just little kids then, and we were alone. . . . There was no heat, nothing to eat, and she took us away. So I think after that she kept us. . . .

Now this was my grandmother on my dad's side. Now, she did her best to make a home for us by herself. Ah, what little money she had, she bought food, and then she raised a garden. And she was a bootlegger. And these early memories, I can remember a lot of people coming to our house, sitting out in the shade, an' a lot of people coming from Sioux City. At that time Indians couldn't buy beer, and they'd come over to grandmother's house and buy some brew. She made a pretty good dealer. I can always remember that there was, ah, a crop of brew on the back of the stove all the time. . . . Grandma got too old. She was in her 60's already. One day the government man came. This was in 1943 I believe. Government man said, "Ah, we'll have to take the children from ya; you're too old." Grandma didn't want to let us go, had no choice. But they sent us different places.

Frank Wolf's Transition to Family Man.[3]   To illustrate the manner in which drinking standards can change as a person moves through the stages of the life cycle and the role that social sanctions can play in shaping drinking behavior, I will briefly describe one man's transition to family man. The man, whom I will call Frank Wolf, had been a typical hell-raiser in his younger days. Both his parents were Santee and lived in Sioux City at the time Frank was born. When he was about three, his parents moved to Omaha, Nebraska, where they lived for three years before returning to Sioux City. Throughout Frank's early childhood, his father drank heavily, and the family was supported primarily by his mother. When Frank was around ten or eleven, his father was forced to give up drinking because of failing health. His father worked at least seasonally until he reached retirement.

Although Frank had some encounters with the law during his early childhood, his difficulties increased when he reached junior high school. He started drinking frequently at thirteen or fourteen years old and got into trouble repeatedly for such offenses as curfew violation, illegal possession of alcohol, breaking and entering, and assault. When he was fifteen he was sent to the Iowa Training School for Boys for less than a year. After he returned to Sioux City, he continued hell-raising and was placed on probation several times. He dropped out of school and began working at various jobs (such as construction, hide gang, and beef packing), but he continued to raise hell. During this time his parents attempted to curtail his participation in hell-raising activities but with little success. Frank recalled, "They would holler at me, and I'd just tell them to leave me alone." Eventually they "just plain give up."

Before Frank began working regularly, he faced the problem of obtaining money to use for drinking. His parents, particularly his mother, were reluctant to give him much spending money because, as his mother told him once, "All you do is . . . piss it out in the alley anyway." Frank's father, however, was more sympathetic and would occasionally slip him a few dollars along with a warning not to tell his mother. When Frank ran out of money he would break into grocery stores and bars to obtain alcohol and cigarettes. He said that he and his friends did this so often they were almost professionals.

Once Frank began working more regularly, he had less difficulty obtaining money and was able to drink as often as he desired and, in fact, drank quite heavily. He describes his drinking patterns during this period: "We used to drink every night, you know. I mean we never got wiped out or anything, but we got to feelin' pretty good. We'd still make it to work. . . . Weekends, we used to be drunk all weekend, never sober."

Frank's transition from hell-raiser to family man developed slowly. When he was in his late teens he started going with an Indian girl named Sharon. Sharon was a "nice girl" who had not run around very much. Frank and Sharon began living together, and within a year she became pregnant. They eventually began to view their relationship as a permanent one. They moved several times within the Sioux City area and once to a large city in another state. At the time of my study Frank was twenty-two and Sharon was twenty-three. They had been living together for four years and had two children. Both Frank and Sharon had seasonal jobs. While they were at work the children were cared for by their grandparents.

Settling down began when Sharon moved in with Frank. The changes in Frank's behavior did not, however, occur immediately as he continued to go out and raise hell. Social pressures to continue the previous behavioral patterns still came from his old friends. Frank would see some of them at work and would occasionally go out with them. When this happened, Frank said, "Sharon'd be madder than hell at me." The social pressures to settle down came not only from Sharon but from Frank's parents as well: "My folks were hollerin' at me and, you know, cussing at me and this and that, because she was p.g., and I wasn't trying to do anything about it, you know. I was still drinkin', raisin' hell."

The social pressures to continue hell-raising decreased as many of Frank's friends either began to settle down themselves or leave town; some got married, several joined the armed services, and one went to prison. Even though some members of Frank's old peer group remained in Sioux City, the frequency of his interactions with them declined and at the time of my study he and Sharon seldom saw them socially. Frank and Sharon shared most of their leisure activities, socializing primarily with their relatives. They might, for example, go out for a night of bingo or spend the evening watching television at Frank's parents' home. Although they did not have a group of young, married couples with whom they regularly socialized, they would occasionally go out with another young couple.

Although Frank and Sharon had been together for four years, Frank still expressed some feeling of ambivalence about life as a family man. He wanted to visit such places as Colorado and California, and at times he felt like seeking new "adventures" on his own. Though he realized that it was difficult, if not impossible, to do these things as a family man, he was not planning on "taking off" for he also felt responsible for supporting and taking care of his wife and children. He dealt with his ambivalence philosophically: "I guess I had my fun so I have to let it end. . . . Them days are gone. Never find 'em again. You can't bring them back."

Frank's personal standards of behavior concerning illegal activities also changed considerably. He had begun, in fact, to reevaluate some of his hell-raising activities in light of his present situation, and he expressed a wish that he had "done good, not got in trouble or anything" in his earlier years. His feelings appeared to be based on pragmatic considerations; it was sometimes difficult for him to find a job because of his police record. His changed standards applied not only to more serious illegal activities, but also to less serious offenses like shoplifting. The changes in Frank's behavior had been so pervasive, at least as he viewed them, that he felt he was "scared to do anything." For example, he and Sharon had been in a department store looking at sunglasses, and he had wanted to steal a pair. But as Frank said: "I just didn't want to get caught and there I'd be. . . . I'd be embarrassed, an' she'd probably be embarrassed. My name would be in the papers. Pay in twenty-five dollars for stealin' a three-dollar pair of shades, you know (laughs). It'd be kind a funny, you know." A few years earlier Frank would not have hesitated to steal the sunglasses nor would he have felt much embarrassment if caught. At the time of the study, however, this type of behavior was no longer compatible with the identity features he was then claiming. Such behavior would have led to his embarrassment if knowledge of it had become public.

Although Frank's behavior in relation to many hell-raising activities had changed considerably, his drinking continued to create a problem with Sharon. At the time of my study, they could not agree on appropriate standards for drinking behavior. When Sharon started going with Frank her standards of drinking were closer to his. After they started living together and their children were born, she felt they were drinking too much. Frank was aware of the change in her attitude and felt that she was "like an old lady. Bitchin' all the time." Though Sharon did not object to them having a few drinks, she disapproved of them drinking throughout the entire weekend. She also resented remaining at home while Frank went out and drank by himself. She explained her attitude toward drinking as a result of childhood experiences with her parents. Both parents drank fairly frequently and heavily, and when her father drank, he sometimes beat her mother in front of the children. As she said, "I always had the feeling, you know, I wouldn't let my kids see that. I didn't want them to be neglected, you know, just for drinking."

Sharon attempted to influence Frank's drinking behavior in several ways. For example, she would tell him when she felt he had enough to drink if he did not appear ready to quit. If he went out drinking by himself, Sharon would sometimes go out by herself, "just to get back at him." If Frank persisted and continued to drink despite her objections, she would threaten to leave him. As she put it: "He has different ideas, like it's ok to go out once in awhile, you know. All these other husbands, they go out and drink by themselves, you know. I said, 'Well, I'm not like their wives.'. . . But I just told him, 'You can go and do it, but you remember,' I said, 'One of these days you're going to come back, and we're not going to be here.'" They had, in fact, "split up" twice over drinking.

One reason Frank and Sharon continued to advocate different standards of drinking was that each received some social reinforcement for their respective standards. Though Sharon received support from Frank's parents, her own parents still drank fairly frequently and heavily. As a result, her parents would side with Frank. One New Year's Eve, for example, Frank and Sharon attended a party at her parent's house and both drank. As the party continued, Sharon thought that Frank had had enough to drink and began to argue with him about it. Her mother sided with Frank and "threw" her out of the house while allowing Frank to remain. Sharon, however, went to her mother-in-law's where she received support for her actions at the party.

Several points should be made in relation to Frank Wolf's life history. His case demonstrates that active participation in some hell-raising activities may be limited to a particular phase in the person's life cycle.[4] This does not imply that all individuals who have been heavily involved in hell-raising activities in their youth will settle down as they grow older, but it does indicate that it can occur. Its occurrence depends upon the complex interplay among psychological, social, and background variables.

One psychological variable that affects the success of the transition is the extent to which an individual is motivated or committed to using the standards of behavior appropriate for a family man.[5] Frank Wolf, though clearly feeling some ambivalence toward his life style as a family man, gradually assumed his responsibilities and appeared to be reasonably committed to the family man standards. In other cases, even though a man has a family, he will not feel he is ready to settle down and will continue to raise hell. In addition, the degree to which an individual believes that he possesses the capacity to perform required activities successfully has been shown to affect the amount of effort expended and the length of time spent trying to achieve the goals in questions. This judgment of capacity has been called "perceived self-efficacy."[6] One of the major determinants of a person's evaluation of self-efficacy is past success or failure. If the individual has been successful, his self-efficacy increases; repeated failures lower it. As a result, if a hell-raiser has not been effective in the kinds of activities demanded of a family man, he may feel inadequate, underestimate his real potential, choose limiting and unchallenging jobs, create psychological difficulties for himself by focusing on his own assumed deficiencies and by making any hurdles encountered more daunting than they are, and abandon a course of action too easily when obstacles are encountered.[7]

A major social variable involved in determining the success of the transition is the kind of social contacts the individual has at the time of the transition. The individual who expects to settle down and become a family man may face a difficult transition if the other people in his social environment do not share his standards or positively reinforce his appropriate behaviors. Therefore, we would expect the hell-raiser who marries a woman who "runs around" to be less apt to make a successful transition to a family man life style than would a hell-raiser who marries a "nice girl" who does not run around. Similarly, if potential employers regard some of the hell-raiser's past experiences as signs of social or psychological unfitness, they may continue to treat him as a bad employment risk. Frank Wolf's transition ultimately involved withdrawing from his old peer group and establishing strong social ties with his wife and her relatives. These people, along with his parents, positively reinforced Frank's behavior as a family man and negatively sanctioned the behavior that was unacceptable. Drinking, the behavior which caused Frank and Sharon the greatest conflict, was an area in which their relatives disagreed about what constituted unacceptable behavior.

Other factors that can influence the success of the transition are the potential, or hidden, liabilities inherent in a hell-raising life style. An individual acquires certain attributes through hell-raising.

Although he may be proud of these when he is a hell-raiser, they may become liabilities when he attempts to become a family man. As I said earlier, a hell-raiser may begin married life with little formal education, a criminal record, an erratic work record, and a history of heavy and frequent drinking. Each of these background attributes can affect the person's ability to perform his duties as a family man successfully, even with a high level of motivation. In Frank Wolf's case, these factors were not insurmountable. In other cases, they have caused greater difficulties. The manner in which other people react to these background attributes may strongly influence a person's evaluation of his own potential to succeed. For example, if an individual is prevented from obtaining a well-paying, steady job because of his police or school record, he may begin to doubt his self-efficacy. This evaluation, in turn, may generalize to other areas of performance and may contribute to an unsuccessful transition to family man.

In relation to drinking, Frank's case shows how the drinking patterns of an individual at a given moment can be influenced by a variety of factors including the personal standards of the drinker, the standards that significant others hold for him, and the kinds of social pressures applied to him. It also illustrates the dynamic, consensual nature of drinking norms. Agreement as to what constitutes acceptable drinking for a given individual and situation may take time to develop. When I completed my study, Frank and Sharon had not yet reached that agreement. In some cases, the conflict is never resolved, and the marriage or relationship is ended.

People on the Street

If a young hell-raiser does not settle down as he grows older (the discussion also applies to women who run around), he may end up on the street. Depending upon his living situation and type of job (if he has one), his most significant social contacts are apt to be with other hell-raisers and winos on the street. Many of these individuals hold the most liberal personal standards of drinking in the population. They frequently drink to intoxication and remain intoxicated for long periods. Although some of these people view their own drinking as a problem, not all do. Some see it as one important element in having a good time. Such men are apt to claim worth in terms of hell-raising ideals. The older a man becomes, however, and the longer he actively participates in street life, the harder it becomes to sustain the full-blown, hell-raising way of life. Typically, his life begins centering more on the acquisition and consumption of intoxicants and less on chasing women, fighting, and seeking other forms of excitement which figure so prominently in the lives of younger hell-raisers. One man who had been a hell-raiser expressed the change: "You mellow; you start associating with older people, even when you drink. Sit down and talk with them. Even started talking with L.T. over here about the tribe. Whereas not too many years ago I was standing on the street waiting for the gang to come around I guess. Go look for a fight or something." The older hell-raiser finds it more difficult to stop drinking when he wishes. Life on the street becomes harder economically because he is unable to engage in the heavy labor demanded for some temporary jobs, and his health may begin to fail. People increasingly view him as a "wino," "bum," or "hopeless drunk."

These changes, of course, influence a man's sense of self-worth. Throughout his life on the street, he has been resisting the negative evaluations of his life style which "middle-class" representatives have always tried to press on him.[8] Because the values underlying hell-raising activities are admired, at least to some extent, by many Indians—whether hell-raisers or not—younger men are able to claim and validate their worth in relation to them despite middle-class evaluations. No one, however, admires a wino. As a man grows older, he is still apt to claim valued identity features on the basis of hell-raising ideals, but will show more ambivalence about his self-worth. At one time, he boasts of positive traits and attempts to validate these assertions by referring to deeds accomplished in his younger days. At another time, however, he also accepts stigmatized identity features and refers to himself as "nothing but an old drunk, no good for nothing." In general, the older the persons on the street grow, the harder it becomes to convince themselves that they are worthy of respect.

People who are on the street and have a place to stay either work fairly often, have a source of income independent of their own work efforts (such as social security, disability payments, or land-lease money), or are partially supported by their relatives. Persons maintaining places of their own for long periods obviously exercise enough restraint in their pursuit of intoxication to pay their rent. If an individual has sufficient money coming in regularly, he has relatively little difficulty obtaining alcohol, food, and a bed. Unless he runs out of money, he does not have to utilize the techniques of people on the street who have no regular income.

Those on the street, but staying with relatives, generally live with parents, spouses, consensual partners, or siblings. The kind and amount of support given varies a great deal. If a man is living with his mother or mate, the support may be extensive, including not only room and board, but money as well. In other cases, however, such as a man staying with his sister and her husband, the support may be limited to a place to sleep and an occasional meal. One man, after telling of his previous ability to stay at his sister's, recounted an incident that occurred on a recent drunk to demonstrate that he still could:

> Even today, you know, if I go over to Bill's [his sister's husband], they let me in. You know, when I was on this drinkin' streak, and two or three times I went up there. One night, it, it was raining real bad. . . . I was downtown, way downtown, an' it started to rain. An' Karen came by. She was with some guy. An' she said, "Get in here, get out of the rain." She said, "Where are you going?" I said, "I don't know." . . . She said, "Where can you go?" I said, "Well, I suppose I can go over to May's [his sister]. So I told her, "I'm looking for a drink; I'm trying to make a drink first, before I go home. So she said, "Well." And that guy she was with said, "I'll get him a drink."

> An' the bars were closed, and the liquor stores were closed.
> An' she took me over there to Sixth and Main—bootleg place.
> She got a bootleg jug for me, and then they took me to May's.
> It was really raining then. I knocked on the door, and Bill
> opened the door. And he said, "Haven't you got enough
> sense to get in out of the weather?"

It should be stressed that these individuals are not "locked" into one kind of situation, but may continually move from one place to another. A man, for example, quarrels with the woman supporting him and ends up on the street. After staying on the street for awhile, he moves in with his mother and later shifts to his sister's house.

If a person on the street stays with relatives, either temporarily or permanently, he becomes dependent on them in varying degrees. In some cases, relatives do not attempt to influence the individual's behavior and let him do as he wishes. In other cases, particularly when relatives hold more restrictive drinking standards for the person than he does for himself, they make vigorous attempts to curtail his drinking. If the person places great importance on the family's continued goodwill and support, they may be fairly successful. A man describes the effect of such efforts on a relative:

> The only reason that he don't drink, is because he's scared of
> his mother, and he's scared of his sister, because she's not
> scared to talk to him, see. She'll tell him to either sober up or
> get out of there, because that's her home, see. So he's scared;
> if it wasn't for them, he'd be drunk every damn day, and he
> won't go to work, see.

An individual in such a situation generally must limit his drinking to relatively short sprees, a day or two at most, and may not be able to drink at all in his relative's home. If the individual does not work often and his relatives do not give him any money, he must utilize the techniques of the street to obtain drinking money.

For those people on the street who are not restrained by relatives, the major constraints on drinking are apt to be related to their jobs, economic conditions, and health. If a hell-raiser works regularly, he must limit his heavy drinking to nonwork hours. A critical point is passed if a working hell-raiser decides to stop working steadily and begins to rely on spot jobs and the techniques of the street to get by. A man describes passing this point:

> I can remember when I worked in Omaha in '66. I can remember that I was saying to myself, "This is Sunday. You got to cool it. Tomorrow's Monday; you got to get back to work. You got rent to pay, food to buy, clothes to buy. Then next week you can go on another one [drinking spree]." And then after that it starts in: "To hell with it. I don't have to go to work. I got plenty of friends, and there's all kinds of guys who—like me—can get down here and hustle and chip in and this and that."

Once this shift is made, the only immediate constraints on the length of time a person remains intoxicated are apt to be economic and health factors. The influence of economic resources is illustrated in the following remark made by a man discussing an acquaintance then on a drinking spree: "This is his second week. I give him about two more weeks yet. He's still got a television, you know. He can still get $50 for that." A variety of physical ailments can plague hell-raisers and winos on the street. Some of these are due to assaults or accidents. In addition, a number of diseases result directly from the toxic effects of alcohol, while others are related to conditions of life on the street, such as malnutrition, which may accompany long periods of intoxication. As long as people are reasonably healthy, many find life on the street tolerable, if not completely desirable. But as one man said, "Once a person realizes he's ill on the streets, he looks for a place that can help him." At that point, the individual may go to a relative or social agency for aid. In some cases, in order to obtain agency help, individuals have to commit themselves to a hospital in Cherokee, Iowa which has an alcoholic treatment program. Some individuals commit themselves even though they have no intention of permanently abstaining from alcohol. As one person commented:

They want to go [to Cherokee] because they want—you might as well say they want to get fattened up. They're so damn run down, you know. When you're in Cherokee you get good eats, *good eats*. And you get vitamin pills all the time. . . . Inside of a month, you're up and a-rarin' to go, and you gain weight too. That's what they want. . . . They come back and start in drinkin' again.

Such people are not always as calculating as the quote might indicate, for some are honestly convinced when they commit themselves to treatment that they never want to drink again. However, as their physical condition improves, their evaluation of their options also changes.

Concluding Comments on Norms and Social Control

Some researchers who have studied drinking behaviors (such as Jessor et al. 1968), have argued that drinking norms or standards are widely shared across ethnic and class lines in America. With this view, what is deviant and unacceptable drinking for middle-class whites is also considered deviant and unacceptable by Native Americans. Such a position clearly does not apply to the Sioux City situation and, in my opinion, greatly underestimates the complexity of social life and the nature of norms. Within the Indian community of Sioux City multiple sets of drinking standards are found. Although there are a few people who are unalterably opposed to drinking in any form or amount, they represent a minority of the everyday people. Similarly, although there are some individuals who believe that nearly continuous intoxication for extended periods is acceptable, they too represent a minority. For most situations and significant relations (viz., spouse-spouse or parent-child), the majority of everyday people consider the range of acceptable drinking to lie between the two extremes of total abstinence and nearly continuous intoxication. The specific standard for a given individual within a particular relationship and situation is seldom set automatically, but rather is based on decisions reached through social interaction. That is, what is or is not acceptable drinking behavior must be negotiated. Further, these standards may also change as a person moves through the life cycle and as the circumstances of his life change. An acceptable drinking pattern for a young, single, hell-raising son may be unacceptable if that son is married and has two children. In some cases, all the people who have significant contacts with an individual agree upon standards which coincide with the individual's personal standards, and little attention is paid to the issue. In other cases, however, differences of opinion exist and the issue becomes a critical matter to everyone involved. Given the multiple sets of drinking standards, a researcher can not assume that all forms of heavy drinking necessarily represent deviant, unacceptable, or problem drinking.

Although some researchers have reported a general absence of negative sanctions directed toward heavy drinkers within Indian groups, this is not the case in Sioux City.[9] Drinking is a domain in which an individual is given a great deal of freedom by the general Indian population; strict conformity to a single, universal set of drinking norms is not demanded. Only the persons most directly involved or concerned with a given individual, such as his family, close friends, or employer, feel they have the right to openly question and negatively sanction his drinking. Let me stress that this does not imply that all drinking patterns are viewed as equally "right" or "moral;" value judgments are made and undesirable behaviors are covertly discussed. Negative value judgments may be subtly expressed to an offending person, but stronger informal sanctions are seldom applied by "uninvolved" people. If people have the right to apply corrective sanctions to an offending drinker, however, they generally do so. This is not to say, of course, that every person experiences the same degree of social control or that it is always effective. A single man on the street who has few relatives will not feel as much social pressure to control his drinking as will a married man who works regularly. And, as indicated earlier, even though negative sanctions are applied, they may not eliminate unacceptable drinking. In some cases a relative lack of informal social control mechanisms can contribute to problem drinking, but the Indian population does not suffer from a total or general lack of such mechanisms.

Endnotes for Chapter 5

[1] The research on which this chapter is based was supported by the Center for Urban Ethnography, University of Pennsylvania, and the National Institute of Mental Health, Public Grant 17,216.

I would like to express my appreciation to the Board of Directors and staff of the Sioux City American Indian Center, to the staff of the Iowa Comprehensive Treatment Program for Indian Problem Drinkers, and to the many Indians of Sioux City who were kind enough to share their experiences with me. Without the help, friendship, and trust of these people, this article would have been impossible.

I would also like to thank Jay Noricks, Jerry Stockdale, and James M. Stokes for detailed comments and criticisms of an earlier draft of this chapter.

[2] Although the concept of norms is frequently encountered in the writings of social scientists, a number of theoretical and methodological difficulties continue to be related to its use. As Jack Gibbs (1968: 208) observed, "despite the plethora of 'normative' explanations, the conceptual treatment of norms remains unsatisfactory. No particular generic definition of norms is widely accepted in the social sciences, and consensus is lacking as to the differentiation of types of norms." Hechter and Opp, summarizing the results of a series of multi-disciplinary workshops on the topic, commented that "where social scientists address normative phenomena they focus on some combination of behavioral regularities, oughtness, and punishment or reward" (2001: 404). Also *see* Gibbs (1981) and Horne (2001). Edgerton (1985) presents an informative discussion of rules from a cross-cultural perspective.

I will begin by defining a norm as a rule or standard used by an individual to guide his own behavior and/or to evaluate his own or other people's behavior. Although this definition serves to orient us, its problems become evident when we observe that in many behavioral domains an individual will have standards that will identify behavior in a variety of ways such as ideal, preferable, permissible, neutral, disliked, abhorrent, or unthinkable. The situation is further complicated because most standards are related in a complex fashion to situational variables; that is, how a given act will be evaluated will depend upon the circumstances surrounding it.

For present purposes, I am most interested in deviant/nondeviant behavior and acceptable/unacceptable behavior. Deviant behavior will be defined as behavior that does not conform to a given individual's evaluation of what is appropriate behavior in a given situation. Notice that deviant behavior is distinguished from unusual, unexpected, or unanticipated behavior. If a student in a classroom must communicate, due to a physical disability, with a teacher through written messages rather than orally, the behavior may be unexpected, but it is still appropriate. Unacceptable behavior will be defined as deviant behavior that elicits social control responses from an offended individual.

Sanctions are applied to the offending person 1) to make him aware that he has violated an assumed understanding of the rules of the encounter, and 2) to exert pressure on him to stop violating the rule and/or to correct the violation through remedial work. As defined here, unacceptable behavior is a subset of deviant behavior. Behavior may be seen as deviant by a given individual without that person overtly attempting to change the offending behavior. This may occur for a variety of reasons. For example, a person may not think the violation of the norm is sufficiently egregious, given the situation, to warrant the possibility of disrupting the social interaction. Or a person may fear reprisals from the offending individual and lets the deviant behavior go unchallenged.

The standards that a person uses to evaluate his own behavior will be called his personal standards or norms. As an individual who violates his own standards will not normally sanction himself, I will consider any behavior that leads to a negative self evaluation as unacceptable behavior. It is possible that a person can engage in behavior that he considers deviant, but not feel guilt or shame. For example, a person may believe that taking money from the communal coffee fund in the office is wrong, but will feel no shame or guilt if he takes some money surreptitiously on occasion.

Applying this perspective to drinking behavior, I will focus on the norms that identify the frequency with which an individual may drink and the amount he may consume. "Drinking standards" are defined as the norms that identify acceptable levels of drinking, both frequency and amount.

[3] This section draws heavily on a chapter originally published as "From Hell-Raiser to Family Man" in *Conformity and Conflict: Readings in Cultural Anthropology, 2nd Ed.* James P. Spradley and David W. McCurdy, Eds., 1974, Little, Brown, and Company.

[4] This has been found, of course, to be true for non-Indian populations as well as other Indian groups, *see*, for example, Foley (1995), Greenberg

(1985), Heath (2000: 79), Karacki and Toby (1962), Kunitz and Levy (1994), Levy and Kunitz (1974), Marshall (1979: 65-66), Matza and Sykes (1961), Moffitt (1993), Quintero (2000) and Siegal and Senna (1988: 51-53).

[5] *See* Bandura (1986: 477-482), Becker (1960), Janis and Mann (1977: 279-308) for discussions of commitment. The volume edited by D'Andrade and Strauss (1992) contains a series of papers considering the relationships that exist between cultural schemas and individual motivation.

[6] Bandura (1986: 391) defines perceived self-efficacy as "people's judgment of their capabilities to organize and execute courses of action required to attain designated types of performances. It is concerned not with the skills one has but with judgments of what one can do with whatever skills one possesses."

[7] *See* Bandura (1986: 390-453) and (1997) for discussions of self-efficacy.

[8] Spradley (1970) has described the "rituals of degradation" to which men on the street are subjected by law enforcement agencies. In Seattle, where Spradley did his research, these included such actions as insulting and threatening the men arrested, placing them in a crowded drunk tank with no bunks and only one toilet, and denying routine requests such as making a phone call. Although the sentence for public intoxication in Sioux City did not involve a sliding scale determined by a person's past record as it did in Seattle (the typical sentence was three days in Sioux City), Spradley's discussion of the symbolic message thrust upon these people by law enforcement agencies still applies to Sioux City. Also *see* Bahr's discussion (1973: 284-292).

[9] Although the absence of sanctions is widely regarded as empirically established (*see* Leland 1976: 58 for a list of investigations reporting such a situation), I think the data supporting such a view is inadequate. For example, J. O. Whittaker's article (1963) on the Standing Rock Sioux, in which he states, "social sanctions against the heavy drinker or alcoholic are virtually nonexistent" (1963: 90), is often cited uncritically as evidence for this position (*see*, for example, Grobsmith 1989, Littman 1970, Lurie 1971, MacAndrew and Edgerton 1969, Medicine 2007, Robbins 1973b, Weibel-Orlando 1989a: 270). Whittaker's conclusion regarding the virtual absence of social sanctions against the heavy drinker appears to be based primarily, if not exclusively, on his analysis of the responses given to six or seven questions out of 94 predetermined questions. Two basic criticisms can be made of his study: 1) many of his interpretations to the responses given to these questions are highly questionable, and 2) in any case, his data were

restricted to verbal responses, and the extent to which his respondents' sanctioning behavior actually corresponded to their descriptions of their behavior is an open question. As a result, his study hardly represents strong support for a general lack of sanctions against drunken violators.

CHAPTER 6
THE NATURE OF DRUNKEN COMPORTMENT: "TIME OUT" OR "NEW GAMES"?[1]

> You go out and talk loud, and you do have fun. There's a point where you have fun, laugh and joke, play pool, and dance, this and that. And then you start . . . to get drunk.
>
> Sioux City Indian

> Just for that period of time that I am drinking . . . I'm not really worrying and thinking about . . . everything. . . . You're not gonna worry about everything until you sober up an' start thinking again.
>
> Phyllis, Sioux City Indian

Introduction

Armed with the information presented in Chapters Four and Five, we are now in a position to consider in greater detail some of the meanings and functions of alcohol consumption.[2] My purpose is not to describe and catalog all the possible meanings and functions of drinking; rather, it is to develop a general perspective that will allow us to account for the diversity observed among Sioux City Indians. In addition, we will use the data to consider one of the most provocative models proposed to account for drunken behavior, the "time-out" model. This view, first formulated by Craig MacAndrew and Robert Edgerton, has displaced the "disinhibition" model as the conventional wisdom.[3] I will argue that the manner in which MacAndrew and Edgerton framed their model leads them to underestimate the importance of certain situational factors and to overestimate the extent to which drunken comportment functions as time-out behavior. A more appropriate view would see drunken comportment as "new-games" behavior.

Beliefs Concerning Drunken Comportment

Although alcohol consumption has many meanings to the Indians of Sioux City, I will focus upon the effects that drinking and intoxication are believed to have on behavior and the reasons given to explain participation in drinking activities. The effects that alcohol consumption has upon behavior were commonly felt to vary, at least to some extent, with the amount consumed and with the particular person doing the drinking. For example, one older individual who felt he had a drinking problem distinguished two major stages of intoxication. After a person begins to drink, he "feels good." At this stage: "You know what you are talking about and you feel like talking and all that. But after a while, maybe two or three hours of drinking, steady drinkin' — maybe two or three bottles of wine — now you're getting high, see. You're getting to where you don't know what you're talking about." When an individual is high, he is drunk. In addition to these two major stages this person also used the phrases "crazy drunk," "sloppy drunk," and "filthy drunk" to describe different states of drunkenness. Crazy drunk refers to acting in an extremely inappropriate manner. One time, for example, he encountered three men on a street in Sioux City singing loudly "in Indian." They wanted my friend to dance for them as they sang, but he made an excuse and continued on his way. In his view, these individuals were crazy drunk because they were making so much noise they were asking to be arrested. When an individual is sloppy drunk, he has lost much of his motor control and is unable to "help himself." Filthy drunk describes the state in which a person is so drunk he is unable to control his bladder or bowels or does not care whether he does so. Another man, who also had a history of heavy drinking, said he recognized a stage before drunkenness that he would describe as a "kind of happy glow." In this stage,

> some of the tension is gone. I guess that's when you start to forget. Then you're ready for some action. You say you want to have some fun. You go out and talk loud, and you do have fun. There's a point where you have fun, laugh and joke, play

pool, and dance, this and that. And then you start to—this is
another stage—then you start to get drunk.

As the preceding quotes suggest, many of the phrases used to
describe the stages of intoxication such as "getting a buzz on,"
"getting high," "feeling good," and "getting drunk" are also related, at
least in a general manner, to typical behavioral patterns. Thus, when
a person is "feeling good" or has that "happy glow" he is apt to be
talkative, outgoing, and amiable. His behavior changes, however, as
he continues to drink and becomes drunk. Although the behavior
can change in various ways, I was frequently told that people
become mean or violent. Unqualified statements of this type were
made when an individual tried to generalize about the effects that
alcohol consumption had on behavior. When drunken comportment
was discussed or examined in greater detail, it became clear that
most people recognized that the kind of drunken comportment
manifested depended upon the person getting drunk. Even
individuals who made strong, unqualified assertions that drunken
people become violent provided examples at other times that
contradicted an invariant connection between drunkenness and
violence or aggression. I think the people who made such overly
generalized statements were reacting to the fact that individuals who
initiate or become involved in arguments or fights have often been
drinking. In attempting to generalize, they tended to overlook the
other occasions when individuals interacted amiably without
conflict. One man provided an example of the variation that may be
seen in the drunken comportment of different persons when he
compared three friends:

I fear what Mike and Francis would do, because they'd do
anything when they get drunk. I got in a fight with Mike.
He's supposed to be my friend when he's sober. We fought
down at C.T.'s one night. But when Mike and Francis are
sober, they're completely different people. When they get
drunk, you can't trust them. They're rowdy as hell. Jack,

when he gets drunk, he just sits there sucking your ass all night, you know.

Another man observed that when people become drunk: "Some . . . become abusive and some . . . get real loud. Other people might go sit down, you know. Other people might want to start crying." Thus, although some individuals will make general statements declaring that drunkenness will involve increased aggression or violence, they do recognize on closer examination that other changes in behavior may occur.

The reasons people offered to explain their participation in drinking activities were frequently related to the effects believed to be obtained from alcohol consumption. These reasons included to get in the mood to have fun; to ease the tensions, worries, and anxieties felt; to obtain feelings of importance and worth; to obtain courage or the guts to engage in activities normally avoided; to feel more sexually inclined; to overcome various kinds of physical pains and symptoms; to socialize; to *show* people who did not want the individual to drink (that is, to spite those people); because there was nothing else to do; because everybody does it; because of alcohol addiction; and so on. Clearly, there was no single reason given for engaging in drinking activities.

If we take the meanings associated with alcohol consumption and intoxication at face value, it appears that alcohol consumption serves a variety of functions, some of which seem to be contradictory. People claim that alcohol puts them in the mood to have fun, while also asserting that it makes them mean or violent. How can this be? The contradiction occurs only if we assume that the effects of alcohol are solely pharmacologically determined and inevitably the same. Let us examine this issue further by considering the two dominant models of drunken comportment.

Models of Drunken Comportment

Disinhibition. Many individuals, scientists as well as laymen, believe that alcohol produces changes in the behavior of individuals by affecting or impairing the "higher brain functions." This impairment is felt to result in the loss of inhibitions, which, in turn, leads to a variety of behaviors that are normally held in check.[4] Craig MacAndrew and Robert Edgerton in their book *Drunken Comportment: A Social Explanation* criticize this analysis, arguing that:

> while there is indeed an abundance of solid evidence to confirm alcohol's causal role in the production of changes in at least certain sensorimotor capabilities, there is no corresponding body of hard documented evidence for the notion that alcohol plays a similar causal role in the production of changes in man's comportment [1969: 84].

In support of their claim, they cite numerous ethnographic examples to show there are societies whose members' drunken comportment either 1) fails to manifest anything that can be regarded as "disinhibited;" 2) has changed markedly through time; or 3) varies strikingly from one situation to another. They also point out that no societies exist in which drunken behavior does not remain within some culturally sanctioned limits. That is, there always remain some culturally defined inhibitions on behavior. Considerations such as these, they feel, raise serious questions about the adequacy of the disinhibition hypothesis.

Time-out. As an alternative interpretation, they argue that drunken comportment is essentially learned behavior. Individuals act when drunk as they have learned to act under these circumstances. In some societies, drunken comportment is expected to differ dramatically from sober behavior and does so. In other societies, an individual's behavior is not expected to change, and it does not. If a society imputes certain causal properties to the consumption of alcohol, such as an increase in aggression, people may interpret a person's behavior while intoxicated not as a function of his "moral character," but rather as a function of his intoxication. As a result, drunken individuals may avoid the sanctions that would otherwise be applied to their behavior. As MacAndrew and Edgerton put it, in such societies:

the state of drunkenness is a state of societally sanctioned freedom from the otherwise enforceable demands that persons comply with the conventional proprieties. For a while—but just for a while—the rules (or, more accurately, *some* of the rules) are set aside, and the drunkard finds himself, if not beyond good and evil, at least partially removed from the accountability nexus in which he normally operates. In a word, drunkenness in these societies takes on the flavor of "time-out" from many of the otherwise imperative demands of everyday life [1969: 89-90; their emphasis].

In an attempt to evaluate their model, MacAndrew and Edgerton apply it to the published literature on the drinking patterns of North American Indians and conclude that it accurately describes the Indians' drunken comportment:

Thus, by the first quarter of the nineteenth century, both drunkenness and the acceptance of the excuse conferred by drunkenness had spread over most of the continent. And in the following half century, a multitude of explorers, traders, trappers, missionaries, and soldiers would record— sometimes in passing, and sometimes in detail—that with few exceptions the Indians in every part of the continent had come to revel in drunkenness and to excuse the changes-for-the-worse that occurred at such times [1969: 151].

Although MacAndrew and Edgerton are primarily concerned with the North American Indians' drunken comportment prior to the establishment of reservations, they do argue that "drunken transgressions are almost everywhere a common feature of reservation life in both the United States and Canada . . ." (1969: 107) and that a time-out situation is found among at least some contemporary groups: "as the Indians were defeated and settled upon their many reservations, the state of drunkenness continued, as it does to this day, to be both claimed and honored as an excuse" (1969: 151-152).[5] MacAndrew and Edgerton's discussion contains at least three major propositions: 1) the way an individual behaves when drunk depends primarily upon what he has learned about drunken comportment; 2) drunkenness has frequently been used by the societies of the world to establish time-out periods; and 3) North American Indian groups currently, as well as historically, represent such societies because intoxication has been viewed as an acceptable excuse for norm violations (a few heinous acts such as murder or incest are exceptions).[6] Because I agree with MacAndrew and Edgerton that drunken comportment is primarily learned behavior,[7] I will focus on the second and third propositions in relation to the situation of the Sioux City Indians.

Drunken Comportment of Sioux City Indians

Let us begin by considering social encounters in general. During a social encounter, an individual's behavior may follow a number of lines depending upon the setting he is in and upon the circumstances, past and present, that surround him. These circumstances include such variables as the people with whom he is interacting, their identities, their past involvements with each other, and the kinds of activities being engaged in during the encounter. Each of these variables helps the participants to define the situation, or, to use Goffman's term (1974), to establish the "frame" for the on-going activities. This, in turn, enables the participants to behave acceptably and to anticipate the kind of treatment they are likely to receive from the other participants. What is acceptable behavior in one situation may well be unacceptable in another.

When our interest is the status of drunken comportment, we must ask, how does an actor's state of intoxication influence the reactions of others to his behavior? If drunkenness defines a time-out period, we would expect to find at least two elements present. First, we would expect intoxication to be offered as an account[8] for drunken norm violations. Second, we would expect this account to be accepted as valid or legitimate by the offended party and to eliminate or mitigate the sanctions that are normally applied to offenders of the norm in question. Unless both elements typically occur with drunken misconduct, I do not think we are justified in describing drunken comportment as time-out behavior.

It should be noted that I specified the offended party must accept the account as legitimate. This is of some importance as the rights and obligations to apply sanctions are not shared equally by the members of a society. They vary in relation to factors such as the norm violated, the people involved, and the circumstances surrounding the offense. A person may, for example, have no right and feel no obligation to sanction a stranger in a bar who is drinking more than the person feels appropriate; however, if his mother engages in similar behavior, it may be both his right and duty to apply a variety of sanctions to correct her behavior. As a result of these variations, people may respond to the same instance of misconduct in various ways and may maintain different attitudes toward any accounts offered for the offense. Individuals not directly involved with the misconduct may be willing to accept almost any account because they are more interested in moving onto other matters than they are in determining degree of culpability and administering punishment. On the other hand, the individual whose rights are violated probably will apply the most stringent criteria in evaluating the legitimacy of the account. If he accepts drunkenness as valid, we have strong evidence for time-out behavior. MacAndrew and Edgerton do not specifically discuss these issues in their general formulation, but it is obliquely raised when they attempt to explain why the time-out status of Indian drunkenness did not lead to mass slaughter by Native Americans (1969: 156-162). They feel that one of the elements which operated to control drunken violence was the presence of concerned relatives, who might have negatively sanctioned transgressions against their kinsmen regardless of the transgressor's state of intoxication. Although MacAndrew and Edgerton do not explore the implications of these cases, such instances clearly demonstrate the need to consider the responses which people make to drunken misconduct and any accounts offered in light of a variety of situational factors. By not considering adequately the role that these situational factors can play, they have overstated, I believe, the extent to which intoxication allows people to enjoy a time-out period.

In order to discuss these issues further, let us examine two sets of activities in which some Sioux City Indians engage.

Raising Hell. The first group of activities to be discussed is frequently referred to as "raising hell." As I pointed out in Chapter Four, when an individual goes out raising hell, he will frequently put on strong identity displays and may begin acting smart or cute with other people. Since we want to determine the manner in which the intoxication of a norm violator affects other people's reactions to the misconduct, we would ideally like to observe the same incident of misbehavior twice, holding all the variables of the situation constant except the offender's state of intoxication. In the first instance, he should be sober and in the second, drunk. Unfortunately, in field studies such ideal situations seldom present themselves, and the researcher must rely on the incidents he does observe, although this makes the task of analyzing the behavior much more difficult. One of the problems encountered with analysis of hell-raising activities (such as acting cute) is that drinking and drunkenness frequently occur as basic elements in the pattern. That is, one of the activities in which an individual usually engages when he raises hell is drinking.

As a result, it can be difficult to observe a case of acting cute in which the norm violator has not been drinking. One woman told me about such an incident, however, which occurred when she was in high school.

> We was out to phys-ed, and she kept war whooping, acting smart and everything. So I didn't know who it was. We was playing ball, and we went in, and this friend of mine, she was a white girl. She told me who it was. So I stopped and asked her about it. She made some remark, "What's it to you?" And she said, "I heard you were half white." I asked her what she meant by that. She said, "I heard you were a half-breed." So anyway, I told her off and kind of slapped her around a couple of times. Then after that, they never did bother me.

Although the context of this incident is very different from the one that will be described below, it does indicate that a person may apply negative sanctions if a sober individual begins acting smart or cute with him.

Another problem encountered in the analysis of drunken misconduct is that even though we may observe an encounter in which a drunken norm violator escapes negative sanctions, until we have discounted other factors that may have produced the same results, we do not know that the offender's drunkenness played a significant role in determining the outcome. For example, when one person offends another by acting cute, the offended individual may suspect that the offense was deliberate and realize that if he challenges the offender he may become involved in a showdown and possibly a fight. Depending upon the seriousness of the offense, the setting, and the people involved, the offended party may attempt to ignore the offense, feeling that greater damage might be done to his reputation by becoming involved in a fight or fearing defeat or injury if a fight should develop.[9] Needless to say, accurately determining and eliminating alternative interpretations of a given behavioral sequence can be extremely difficult.

In order to illustrate some of these points, I will relate an incident I witnessed at a powwow in a town several miles from Sioux City. As part of the proceedings, a softball game was played between a Sioux City team and a local team. The ball players were drinking beer while they played, but no one appeared intoxicated. The game was played with a great deal of good-natured teasing and joking. Following the game, a meal was provided for everyone attending the powwow. After the Sioux City ball players went through the food line, they began sitting together on the ground to eat. Two of the players, Robert and Bill, had a discussion with some of the other players concerning someone still in the food line. Robert asked who that big guy was. Nobody knew. Apparently, someone had said or done something that offended some of the Sioux City players, particularly Robert and Bill. Bill put his food down and started to go back to the line. Robert stopped him, saying in effect, "Let it go, we can take care of him later. This isn't the place to do it." The players sat down and began eating. Shortly thereafter, two young men, probably in their late teens, passed by me carrying their food. Both acted drunk, laughing and talking loudly. I was talking to a friend when they passed us. The taller one looked in our direction and said something that sounded like, "Take it easy there!" Neither of us made any response to his comment, partly because we were not sure he was addressing us and partly because we were not certain what he said. They continued on and as they started to pass the ball players sitting on the ground in a circle, the taller man said something to them and went through the motions of kicking Robert in his back, but stopped short of doing so. They continued past the group, but before they had gone very far, Robert jumped to his feet and grabbed the tall man around his neck from behind. In a single motion, Robert threw him down on his back. He appeared stunned and did not get up immediately. While this was happening, Bill jumped to his feet, came up to the prostrate individual, and kicked him in the back of his head. Robert then pushed Bill back. The companion of the prone man faced Robert and Bill and yelled: "What the hell do you think you're doing?" You didn't have to kick him. We were just kidding around!" Several older men who helped organize the powwow came over and asked what was going on. Bill said, "These guys were giving us a hard time in the food line and tried to kick Robert." Another Sioux City ball player spoke up and said, "You should have heard the language they were using in the food line, right in front of the women and children. I wouldn't even use language like that." A local ball player who was eating with the Sioux City team also made a comment about the taller man trying to kick Robert. The shorter man, who knew this individual, yelled, "Don't you lie, Henry! Don't you lie!" He also began shouting at the Sioux City ball players, particularly Robert and Bill: "If you want to fight, we'll get you sons of bitches. We'll get you. If you want to fight, why don't you fight my brother?" A woman who apparently knew the shorter man joined the older men, and they attempted to restrain him, positioning themselves between him and the Sioux City ball players. During this time, the taller man lay face up on the ground or doubled up on his side with his hands around his head. He appeared to be either unconscious or semiconscious. The older men finally got him to his feet and succeeded in getting the two men to leave the area. The Sioux City team talked for a while and decided to leave the area. They got into their cars and drove away. Several minutes after they left, the shorter man returned to the area with a hammer in his hand. He was accompanied by several other young men, one of whom had a sheathed bayonet stuck prominently in his belt. One of the organizers saw the hammer and attempted to take it from the man who resisted his efforts. Another older man joined the first, and they finally got the hammer, but only after wrestling the young man to the ground while he yelled such comments as, "You sons of bitches, leave me alone!" When they let him up, he attempted to get the bayonet from his companion, but the older men told his friends to get him away from the area, which they did.

Several interesting points stand out in this incident. The two men who precipitated the run-in clearly appeared to have been drinking and offended several people. If drunkenness were generally accepted as a legitimate account, we might have expected that no one in the food line would have taken the two men seriously. Several ball players, however, were offended and started to apply negative sanctions when Robert counseled restraint. We might also have expected Robert to argue for restraint on a similar basis; namely, the two men had been drinking and should not be taken seriously. He did not do this. Instead, he argued that the powwow was not the appropriate setting in which to seek redress for the offense. His view prevailed until the two young men again offended him in what he apparently considered to be a serious manner. Both he and Bill responded directly and rapidly. At no time during the altercation did any of the participants refer to the two young men's state of intoxication. Even when the young men discussed their behavior which provoked the fight, they did not say, "We were just drunk." Instead, they argued that their intentions had been misjudged. They were not really looking for trouble; they were "just kidding around."

After the incident, however, several observers were discussing the event. One of them commented that everybody involved had been drinking and implied that this was the cause of the run-in. I will discuss this last comment in a later section of the chapter.

I am arguing that the manner in which the norm violations were handled in this incident is fairly typical of the way they are handled in other cases of norm violations which occur as a result of hell-raising activities. In these activities, the norm violator's state of intoxication is only one variable that helps define the situation and determines the responses made by the offended person. In many cases, informal sanctions are applied to the drunken norm violators. That misconduct occurs in spite of the sanctions is not surprising in these cases because the offender acts as he does while realizing that there is a good chance the sanctions will be applied. Hell-raising activities would lose much of their appeal if the participants did not run the risk of penalties or negative sanctions. That is not to say, of course, that the probabilities of the sanctions being applied are constant; clearly they are not, because as I indicated earlier, they vary in relation to such factors as the seriousness of the offense, the setting, and people involved. These factors are considered by hell-raisers and influence their behavior. Part of the acting-cute-with-somebody game is to see how far a person can be pushed before he offers serious resistance. We can see these features in the powwow incident just described. Even though the two young men who initiated the run-in had offended some of the ball players in the food line, it is unlikely that overt sanctions would have been applied at the powwow if the two men had walked by the ball players as they sat on the ground without saying or doing anything else to offend them. The failure to sanction the men would have occurred not because they had been drinking, but because Robert knew that the application of corrective sanctions might lead to a fight and he was trying to observe the norm against openly fighting at an affair like a powwow.[10] The second offense, however, pushed him too far, and he did apply negative sanctions in spite of the no fighting norm. I think the two men expected to get away with their actions and were not prepared for Robert and Bill's responses. They miscalculated, but that was the risk they knowingly chose to run.

Just Visiting. Apart from cases such as raising hell in which the activities more or less clearly call for norm violations, there are others in which norm offenses are not a necessary part of the activities and yet occur when some individuals are drinking or are intoxicated. To consider how norm violations are handled in these cases, I will examine the interactions that are variously characterized as "just visiting," "socializing," or "just talking and laughing." I dropped by a home one afternoon and joined such a gathering. A group consisting of the couple who lived in the house, the wife's sister, a female friend of the wife, a male acquaintance of the husband, and several of the couple's children who wandered in and out of the setting were "just visiting." I joined the gathering around 2:00 p.m. and stayed for about two hours. We were drinking beer, but none of us were very intoxicated. The topics discussed while I was present included a recent incident in which a woman known to all the participants had been beaten up, a recent episode of glue sniffing by several young girls, a male relative of one of the participants who was drinking too much and was becoming a problem to his relatives, a fight in which a son of one of the participants had been involved, a sexual adventure of this man, the reasons people continue to drink when they know it will kill them, the reasons people drink in general, a story involving a participant's husband who had been caught trying to fool her by drinking wine out of a beer can, a neighborhood meeting called to discuss a summer youth program, and the existing social programs for Indians in Sioux City. These kinds of topics are typical for such a gathering.

The actual flow of conversation proceeded through a combination of declarative and interrogative interchanges. An individual would raise a topic, make his comments relating to it, and then yield to another participant who responded directly to what the previous speaker had said, adding his own comments relating to it, asking a question of the previous speaker, or introducing a new topic. A speaker would frequently make humorous comments, and other participants might interrupt the speaker with humorous remarks or asides of their own.

This type of interaction serves several functions. When the topic discussed is a recent incident of which some of the participants have no previous knowledge, such as the beating of the woman, information is shared. The comments made about such events, however, are seldom limited merely to the conveyance of factual information. The speaker often includes his analysis of the event—why it occurred as it did and his reaction to it. Discussions of this sort help the participants to understand the events and may either help formulate the appropriate stance to maintain in relation to it or reaffirm a stance already taken.

Events in which one or more of the participants were actors are frequently discussed in these gatherings. At times, these incidents are discussed to convey factual information or to illustrate some general point under consideration such as the treatment of Indians by the Bureau of Indian Affairs. At other times, the manner in which the speaker behaved, or should behave in the future, is the central topic discussed. In some cases, the individual's experiences may be presented as personal problems. When this occurs, the other participants may offer advice or behave in a supportive manner. Thus, even though a participant may not have any new suggestions regarding the problem, he may indicate the person did, or is doing, all anyone could reasonably do to cope with the difficulties.

As suggested, the participants are not just sharing information and suggestions on some subject during these interactions, they are also presenting or claiming particular kinds of identity features. Although this may be true of all of their behavior, it is particularly evident when the individuals discuss events in which they played an active role. At these times the participants will frequently present themselves in a positive light. This is not surprising, for as Erving Goffman (1959: 35) notes, "when the individual presents himself before others his performance will tend to incorporate and exemplify the officially accredited values of the society, more so, in fact, than does his behavior as a whole." In some cases, the identity features claimed by an individual do not correspond to the other participants' knowledge and evaluation of him. Even though this discrepancy may exist, the other participants may behave as if they accepted his evaluation of the situation and the identity features claimed. For example, a man may tell about a ball game in which he participated some years ago. In his version of the story he may cast himself as the hero of the game, going on to state how he could have played professional ball if he had so desired. Though other participants have heard other versions of the story or doubt some of the assertions made, they may well not openly disagree and, in fact, may help sustain his view by elaborating on the story or by commenting positively on the speaker's ball-playing abilities.

This kind of interaction involves what Goffman (1956) refers to as "presentational" and "avoidance rituals." Presentational rituals include "acts through which the individual makes specific attestations to recipients concerning how he regards them and how he will treat them in the on-coming interaction" (Goffman 1956: 485). Avoidance rituals, on the other hand, "refer to those forms of deference which lead the actor to keep at a distance from the recipient and not violate what Simmel (1950: 321) has called the 'ideal sphere' that lies around the recipient" (Goffman 1956: 481). Avoidance rituals deal with variables such as physical distance and physical contacts but also include "the verbal care that actors are obliged to exercise so as not to bring into discussion matters that might be painful, embarrassing, or humiliating to the recipient" (Goffman 1956: 482). People who interact in situations of sociability are presumably friends, or at least friendly acquaintances, and are allowed to claim positively valued identities and receive confirming information. In terms of the earlier discussion, an individual is allowed to make a nonaggressive identity display and to receive various kinds of supportive attestations. If a participant should present a less than desirable identity through the frank admission of a personal problem, he may still expect to receive support.[11]

Sociable interactions may develop along several lines. On some occasions, the prevailing orientation may be toward a "serious" discussion of the participants' personal problems. The people may be quite conscious of the therapeutic values of such encounters as one woman indicates:

> That woman that came with that case of beer Saturday. Well, she's got three kids, and they are really what I mean typical Indians, you know. She can't talk good English, and she doesn't have anybody, so I always—I know she's got problems, and she needs somebody to talk to. I, I tried it and think I'm helping her, but still maybe I'm not.

At other times the participants may not wish to share or discuss their personal problems and may instead attempt to keep away from serious topics and "just have fun." The woman quoted above, who could spend several hours drinking and discussing personal problems with her friends, was also capable of blocking out such difficulties on other occasions: "Just for that period of time that I am drinking . . . I'm not really worrying and thinking about, ah, everything. . . . You're not gonna worry about everything until you sober up an' start thinking again."

Although a single encounter may be dominated by one of these orientations, both may occur during the same encounter. That is, the participants may be laughing and joking for one sequence as if observing a rule against the introduction of serious topics and then in another sequence become serious and preoccupied with a participant's problems. Whether this serious aspect of a social encounter arises or whether a given participant wishes to share his problems undoubtedly depends upon a number of variables, including the number of people present, the kinds of relationships that exist among them, and the extent to which the individual is an "open" or "closed" person. Some individuals are quite open with their problems and will discuss them readily with almost anyone; others are guarded and will seldom talk openly about them. Individual differences in relation to these variables were illustrated at another social gathering that I attended. Jay, one of the participants, attempted to discuss a conflict that existed in another participant's family. The conflict revolved around the kinds of relationships that the other participant, Peter, had with his sister and mother. Jay was a good friend of Peter's sister and knew how she viewed the difficulties. When Jay started to discuss the issue, Peter appeared to become angry and said, "Don't you start talking about that. You can't even take care of your own problem!" and abruptly walked out of the house. Jay clearly felt the situation was an appropriate one in which to consider the problem, but Peter obviously disagreed.[12]

The discussion thus far has been based on social gatherings in which the participants have not been very intoxicated. What happens when they are fairly drunk? At such times, the same kinds of topics are apt to be discussed, and the interactions generally follow the same form. Some notable differences may occur, however, particularly in the kinds of identity displays presented. The most dramatic changes occur when a participant is fairly reserved and quiet on other occasions. To illustrate some of these changes in comportment, let us look at a man whom I will call John. His drunken comportment in sociable gatherings represents an extreme case. When John became intoxicated at these times, he frequently attempted to monopolize the conversation and engaged in extended monologues, a marked change from his sober demeanor. If sports came up as a topic, he might recount some of his past exploits. He would portray himself as a great athlete in his story and would state that he possessed certain desirable identity features. If the topic was local Indian affairs, he might tell what he thought was wrong with the way they were being handled and indicate what he would do to correct the situation if he were in charge. During his discussion he might stand up, wave his arms, and highlight his points by raising his voice or even shouting. In effect, John would put on a very strong identity display.

John could expect support for this kind of behavior as long as he remained within the norms of the encounter and confined his display to nonaggressive display techniques. His behavior, however, clearly included the use of some aggressive display techniques. His tendency to go on extended monologues, for example, violated the rule regulating the turn-of-speaking. His behavior implied that his identity features gave him the right to speak as long as he wished and thus infringed on the other participants' rights. A number of informal sanctions would be applied to correct his behavior. The kinds of sanctions used varied with the kind of relationship the participant had with John. Some individuals would try to ignore him by attempting to maintain a conversation with other participants; others might make humorous remarks about his behavior or his comments and at particularly trying moments tell him to "shut up." The individuals who took the strongest actions in attempting to correct his behavior were members of his family, particularly his wife. The sanctions appeared to have varying effects on his behavior. While the strongest would tend to quiet him somewhat and make him behave in a less disruptive manner, none seemed to correct his behavior completely or permanently. On some occasions, he would act as if he took no notice of the other people's reactions and would continue talking. This sometimes resulted in forcing him to talk to himself while the other participants continued to interact as if he were not present.

When John was drunk, he was also apt to openly attack the identities of other participants, usually the members of his family. His attacks often related to behavior or events that had occurred "outside" the encounter. He might, for example, accuse one of his sons of being lazy, not working, and never helping to provide food for the dinner table. John's wife describes his behavior toward his sons at these times:

> John gets on those kids as soon as he's drinking, you know. An', an' I don't know whether it's his guilty conscience that he knows he hasn't done anything, but he starts gettin' on them: Oh, they sleep all day, or they eat too much, an' you know. It's just all that. An' they get tired of listenin' to it, and I do too. Before you know it, why, we're arguin', and it's not right.

As the quote suggests, the sons would frequently answer their father's charges by attacking his identity, and their interactions would quickly develop into an identity struggle. John's wife tells of some of their sons' responses:

> The boys do talk back to him: "Well, you never raised us. You never did anything for us. Why are you hollering now?" and all that. . . . Jim has talked back to him, but it's never been like Ron. Ron's just ready to stand right up there and fight if he has to, and I hate to see that. Philip has hit him. Philip was fixing some sandwiches or something, and John did the same thing and was hollering to him about how much he eats and everything, so Philip just turned around and hit him right in the mouth and cut his lip. . . . It was a pretty bad cut, you know. He could have had a couple of stitches, but he wouldn't go. Philip, he doesn't argue so much, just like I say, that one time he hit him. He'll walk away and go up to his room. Just to get away from him because he knows that John goes on and on.

Clearly, John's identity attacks and the identity struggles that develop in response to them are not approved in these situations, but are viewed as occurrences to be avoided if possible. These kinds of arguments disrupt the household, cause psychological damage, and, on occasion, even lead to physical violence. Because the struggles are not carefully regulated, they do not lead to a resolution of the existing identity conflicts.[13]

John's drunken misconduct in sociable gatherings and the reactions made to it by other participants, both sober and intoxicated, demonstrate that negative sanctions are applied in these encounters to a variety of drunken norm violations. If my description and analysis are correct and negative sanctions are indeed generally applied to drunken misconduct, the question arises: why does the untoward behavior occur? As I pointed out earlier, this is not difficult to explain for some norm violations, such as those that develop when people are raising hell, because participation in such activities necessitates norm violations. In other cases, such as John's, the norm violations are more difficult to explain because the behaviors do not appear, on first glance, to lead to rewarding experiences for the norm violator. Let us consider this issue further in relation to John's case.

Wallace and Fogelson (1965: 383) suggest that two kinds of motives, often in combination, lead a person to initiate an identity struggle: 1) a manipulative motive to persuade or influence another individual to behave in a certain way toward one's self; and 2) a psychodynamically more complex motive of maintaining or restoring a positive identity in one's self. Although both motives were probably involved in John's behavior, the second would seem to be more important. This interpretation is also the one his family made of his behavior. John strongly felt the need to receive information that affirmed he was a person of worth because he was uncertain that he was such an individual or that other people saw him in such a manner. As a result, he felt compelled to put on strong identity displays in some sociable gatherings, even to the extent of violating the norms of the situation. When the confirmation or support he desired was not forthcoming, he reacted by attacking those who withheld their esteem. When he attacked his children's identities, he was essentially saying, because you children are not fulfilling your roles adequately you have no right to withhold your respect from me or to criticize my behavior. His attacks were both a defense against the attitudes and charges of his children and an attempt to force them to treat him in what he considered to be the appropriate manner. In addition, his behavior allowed him to cathartically vent any hostile or aggressive emotions he felt in a relatively safe context. As his behavior tended to follow the same pattern through time, it seems likely, though it is difficult to document, that in spite of the negative consequences that resulted from his aggressive identity displays, either the positive results outweighed the costs of the negative sanctions or he was unable to find a more suitable alternative response. That is, even though his behavior did not bring about the desired consequences, other than a cathartic release, he was unable to respond in a more appropriate or successful manner.

Discussion

In this chapter I have briefly considered two sets of activities that occur among some of the everyday Indians: raising hell and visiting or socializing. The drunken behavior that occurs during these activities may include norm violations, but it does not have a time-out quality to it because negative sanctions are applied to the violator by the offended party. This is not to say that intoxication is never offered as an account for misconduct. As I pointed out in the description of the powwow misconduct, it is encountered and with some frequency. It is typically accepted as valid, however, only by those individuals who have little reason to press for the worst possible interpretation of the misconduct. The people who accept intoxication as a legitimate or quasi-legitimate account are those already willing to overlook the lapse in behavior and to proceed with "regular" interaction. Thus, when a mother offers drunkenness to excuse her son's participation in a robbery, her friends accept it as valid. Under such circumstances if the offender had not been drinking or drunk, another account would have been offered and accepted. Similarly, after the powwow altercation when uninvolved bystanders were discussing the incident, one person suggested that the run-in may have occurred because the men had been drinking. No one in the circle of conversation found any reason to challenge the account. Cases such as these underline the need to carefully distinguish the various stances that different parties maintain in relation to specific norm violations. If we do not take these variables into account, we are very likely to misread the situations and to see drunken norm violations as time-out behaviors when they are not.

Beyond the empirical question, if the everyday Indians of Sioux City accept drunkenness as a valid account for drunken misconduct, there is another issue that I would like to raise concerning the appropriateness of MacAndrew and Edgerton's general model. Even though they stress that in all societies some norms remain in effect during drunken encounters, by using the phrase "time-out" to describe the drunken comportment of North American Indian groups, they suggest an image of behavior largely unguided or unregulated by norms. On the basis of my Sioux City data, the analogy used should not be one of an individual ceasing "to play the game" or calling "time out;" rather, it should be one of an individual commencing or playing a series of "new" or "different" games with the particular game played being determined by the circumstances. Such a view is more appropriate because it more adequately reflects the complexity of drunken behaviors—drinking and drunkenness are only one set of variables affecting the definition of a drunken encounter. As a result, the meaning given to drunken behavior seldom, if ever, derives solely from the state of intoxication. It is because of this that alcohol consumption may be used in many activities and settings with different results. In one situation it is viewed as helping to set the scene for a serious discussion of an individual's personal problems; at another time, it is believed to help block out such difficulties so that the person can have a good time. A hell-raiser may drink on one occasion to obtain courage and on another to feel more sexually inclined. At a general level of analysis it would seem that one of alcohol's major functions is to provide "framing cues" or "boundary markers" that help the actors to establish definitions of their situations. The specific kinds of situations that alcohol can help define in a given society will depend upon a series of factors such as the beliefs related to alcohol and its use, the types of activities in which drinking individuals engage, and the kinds of identity ideals maintained within the society. The point I would like to stress is that alcohol has the potential to help define a variety of situations within a single society. Although any substance which produces altered states of consciousness may provide potent framing cues, alcohol is particularly well suited for such a role because 1) alcohol produces changes in the sensorimotor capabilities of the drinker that are easily recognized by the drinker and others; 2) alcohol is reasonably fast acting once consumed; 3) the alterations produced in consciousness and behavior are not long lasting unless the drinker continues to imbibe; 4) the use of alcohol does not quickly result in obvious impairments in health; and 5) depending upon the amount consumed, the changes produced in the sensorimotor capabilities of the drinker are compatible with his participation in a variety of activities.[14]

Such a view seems to be, in some degree, implicit in MacAndrew and Edgerton's work. Instead of emphasizing alcohol's use as a nonspecific framing cue which can be used to help establish a variety of contextual definitions within a single society, however, they stress the possibility of a society viewing alcohol as a producer of moral incompetency. They then argue without enough critical care that many societies have used alcohol to define time-out periods. Although the extent to which the drunken comportment of Sioux City Indians is similar to that of other groups is an empirical question, I suspect that many of the societies which have been viewed as conferring a time-out status to drunken comportment will prove on closer examination to handle drunken comportment in a fashion very similar to the Sioux City Indians. There are several factors inherent in the use of alcohol that lead to such an expectation. Because the type of drunken behavior manifested by a person is influenced by many situational and psychological factors, unless a society restricts the use of alcohol to a limited number of people and/or kinds of social situations, a diversity of drunken behaviors are to be expected. The greater the diversity of drunken comportment shown in a society, the less likely it is that drunkenness will be accepted as a valid account by offended individuals. In societies with diverse drunken conduct, I would expect people to agree that the consumption of alcohol does influence behavior, but to be uncertain as to its exact effects. That is, although people know alcohol consumption can change an individual's behavior, they are presented with the difficult problem of accounting for the variations they can see in drunken comportment. Such a situation is unlikely to lead an offended party to accept drunkenness as a valid account for norm violations, but due to the ambiguities surrounding the effects of alcohol on behavior, intoxication could still serve as an acceptable account for those not attempting to push for the worst possible interpretation of the untoward behavior. This consideration suggests that intoxication would frequently be a useful account for "victimless" norm violations in which there are not specifically offended parties to press for the worst possible interpretation of the misconduct.

Endnotes for Chapter 6

[1] This chapter was originally published under the title of "Drunken Comportment of Urban Indians: 'Time-Out' Behavior?" in the *Journal of Anthropological Research,* 1978, Volume 34 Number 3, pages 442-467, and is reprinted with permission. Several minor changes have been made in the chapter.

The research on which this article is based was supported by the Center for Urban Ethnography, University of Pennsylvania, and the National Institute of Mental Health, Public Health Grant 17,216.

I would like to express my appreciation to the Board of Directors and staff of the Sioux City American Indian Center, to the staff of the Iowa Comprehensive Treatment Program for Indian Problem Drinkers, and to the many Indians of Sioux City, who were kind enough to share their experiences with me. Without the help and friendship of these people, the research would have been impossible.

I would like to thank Jay Noricks and James M. Stokes for detailed comments on an earlier draft of this article. Douglas Brintnall, Thomas Keefe, and John Van Ness also made helpful suggestions.

[2] Generally, the functions of an activity are taken to refer to the effects that the performance or nonperformance of that behavior have upon the individuals of a society and their environment. The functions of an activity are frequently distinguished from what Ward Goodenough (1963) has called the "meanings" of that activity. The meanings of a behavioral pattern for a people are the "several ways in which they associate it with their wants and felt needs and with various other features of what they regard as their life situation"(1963: 80). As Goodenough points out, the distinction between meanings and functions is similar to that made between manifest and latent functions (*see* Merton 1957: 63). The functions and meanings of a given activity may not be identical because people may not be aware of all the effects of the behavior, or they may mistakenly attribute consequences to the behavior which are, in fact, unrelated to it.

[3] For other treatments and discussions *see* Collins (1981), Fagan (1990), Fox and MacAvoy (2011) Gottheil et al. (1983); Heath (2000), Heinz et al. (2011), Lithman (1979), Lurie (1971), Mancall (1995a), Pernanen (1991, 1993), Room (2001), Room and Collins (1983).

[4] *See* Hallowell (1946) for an anthropological statement of this position.

---

[5] They cite (1969: 152) the following studies as evidence for this assertion: Curley (1967: 121-122); Hamer (1965: 293-298); Helm (1961: 105); Hurt and Brown (1965: 229); Lemert (1954b: 336-357, 1958: 101); and Whittaker (1963: 89). They also take care to point out (1969: 163) that their discussion is a general one:

> We do not suggest that this account of Indian drunkenness is in any sense definitive, nor even that it makes much sense (in this connection or in any other) to speak of the Indians of this continent as if they were all cast from the same mold, although for reasons of economy we have sometimes spoken as if this were the case. Rather, we have attempted to recommend the relevance of our formulation in a very general sense. . . . A truly *definitive* [their emphasis] application of our formulation, in contrast, would necessarily have been studiously time and tribe-specific and infinitely more attuned to the socially organized character of the participants' understandings of the circumstance in which they found themselves.

[6] They also advance the proposition that Indians learned what they knew about drunken comportment from the individuals who introduced alcohol to them: "It will be our contention that the Indians of this continent took as their exemplars of alcohol's effects on comportment the drunken doings of the very white men who introduced alcohol to them" (1969: 136). This issue extends beyond the scope of my research on the Santee Dakota and Winnebago for this book, but Peter Mancall (1995a), who undertook the most extensive review of the documents relating to Indian drinking in Eastern North America from 1650 to the American Revolution, questions their argument:

> I do not agree . . . that early American Indians learned how to drink from traders and adopted the traders' alleged intemperate ways. Liquor traders, after all, may have caroused with Indians, but the documentary record does not suggest that they left trading sessions impoverished, as their Indian trading partners did. On the contrary, traders my have been duplicitous in their dealings, and many certainly broke existing laws that prohibited the trade, but their use of alcohol rarely interfered with their economic goals. Further, to suggest that Indians used alcohol in the ways traders used alcohol does not fit a historical record that reveals that Indians

adapted colonial goods in ways that made sense in Indian villages. If they were not bound by colonists' views on how to use such goods as pots, there is no reason to presume that they intended to mimic colonists' drinking patterns either [1995a: 253].

[7] This is not to argue that alcohol does not produce a variety of physiological and biochemical effects, rather it is to assert that psychological and environmental factors play important roles in determining the kind of drunken comportment manifested. Much of the experimental data on the impact of ethanol on sexual behavior and aggression support this interpretation. A large number of studies have looked at the relationship between alcohol intoxication and aggression. In a recent review, Heinz et al. (2011) identified 13 theoretical models that tie various forms of cognitive disruption to intoxicated aggression and discuss in detail a model that sees alcohol affecting the serotonin system and GABA (gamma-aminobutyric acid) neurotransmission in ways that lead to impulsive aggression in genetically predisposed individuals. Even if these relationships are established, however, the expression of the aggression is shaped by the predisposed person's psychological understanding of his situation, and the responses others make to his actions are conditioned by the sociocultural context. Also see Adesso (1985), Carpernter and Armenti (1972), Foran and O'Leary (2008), Galanter (1997); Giancola (2004), Graham et al. (1998) Lang (1983), and Woods and Mansfield (1983).

[8] Marvin Scott and Stanford Lyman (1968: 46) define an account as "a statement made by a social actor to explain unanticipated or untoward behavior—whether that behavior is his own or that of others, and whether the proximate cause for the statement arises from the actor himself or from someone else." Also see Erving Goffman's discussion (1971: 108-118).

[9] It should perhaps be noted in passing that if the offended person decides not to engage in corrective actions he may feel he has to offer an account for his own behavior so that other people will not interpret his actions as signs of cowardice or fear.

[10] Had the two men walked quietly by the ball players the entire incident might have superficially appeared to support the time-out status of drunken comportment.

[11] See Hannerz (1969: 105-117) for a similar analysis of sociability within a Black population.

[12] Although none of the participants in this encounter were highly intoxicated, all had been drinking and yet Peter negatively sanctioned Jay when he thought Jay had violated his rights.

[13] Richard Robbins (1973b) has argued that among the Naskapi Indians of Schefferville, Quebec, drinking interactions represent what he calls "identity resolving forums." He feels that:

> when drinking a person is permitted to defend an identity that has been challenged, claim an identity he believes he is entitled to, or rectify an identity that has been spoiled by failure, and, that such interactions aim toward allowing the person to receive from others information which confirms the identity he is seeking [1973b: 110].

Robbins is arguing that during drinking interactions a person is permitted to make latent identity struggles manifest without experiencing negative sanctions as long as he does not physically injure other people (1973b: 109). Robbins believes that such interactions lead to the resolution of identity conflicts on a short-term basis even though he does indicate that a person in the process of restoring or defending his identity may threaten another individual who will feel compelled to resolve that conflict: "So while a person may resolve, at least temporarily, discrepancies in some of his social relationships, the whole process may lead to a steady spiral of identity struggles for the community at large, and hence lead to a steady increase in the frequency of those activities that serve as identity resolving forums" [1973b: 119].

In contrast to Robbins's description and analysis of the Naskapi drinking interactions, I am arguing that among the everyday Indians of Sioux City a person is entitled to put on an identity display in a sociable gathering and to receive supportive attestations from the other participants *only* as long as he limits his display to nonaggressive techniques. Once he begins to engage in aggressive displays he is violating the norms of the encounter and may be negatively sanctioned.

[14] MacAndrew and Edgerton (1969: 166-171) mention the first four properties along with some others in their attempt to explain why so many societies (on the basis of their interpretation of the ethnographic data) have relied on alcohol consumption to define time-out periods.

CHAPTER 7
PROBLEM DRINKING: BIOLOGY, BAD HABITS, AND ALCOHOLISM[1]

> When I'm drunk, I wake up halfway sober,
> but I'm so damn sick that I got to get out
> on the street and look for another drink.
> > Sioux City Indian

> Nothing ever seems to go right. Nothing is
> right, and before you know it, . . . you're
> just drinking, an' you're to the point where
> you don't care anyway.
> > Phyllis, Sioux City Indian

Introduction

To outsiders, one of the most puzzling aspects of the lives of Indians who drink heavily and suffer from a range of physical, psychological, and social problems related to their drinking is why the individuals do not simply stop drinking, or at least severely restrict their consumption. If your behavior is causing you difficulties, it should be relatively easy to change the way you act. Unfortunately, what appears to be obvious and easy from the psychological distance of an outsider becomes much more complicated and difficult as one assumes an insider's perspective and looks at the behavior in greater detail. In order to examine problem drinking[2] among Sioux City Indians, I will briefly describe the drinking patterns of several individuals selected to represent two major types of drinking and situations. "Phyllis" is a Santee who, while drinking heavily at times and seeing her behavior as a problem, attempts to maintain a home for her family and does not see herself as losing control of her drinking. In contrast, I will also look at several unnamed men (Santee and Winnebago) who consider themselves to be "periodic drunks." They feel they have lost control over their alcohol consumption and frequently find themselves on the street with no place to stay. Looking at the factors that influence the drinking patterns of these people will lead us into a consideration of the concepts of tolerance, physical dependence, and alcoholism and will raise several key questions: Do ethnic/racial differences play a role in the body's reaction to alcohol? Are Indians at greater risk genetically for developing problem drinking as the stereotypic view holds? Do neurobiological adaptations contribute to drinking difficulties? What psychological and social factors help produce episodes of problem drinking? Do we need the concept of alcoholism to explain heavy and destructive drinking?

Phyllis

Phyllis was born in Santee, Nebraska in the 1920s. She was the sixth child of eight. Her mother died when she was young, and the family moved in with her father's sister. While the family was in Santee, her father worked part-time for local farmers. In the early 1940s, the family moved to South Sioux City, Nebraska to improve her father's job opportunities. Phyllis briefly attended two Indian schools out of state before returning to help an older sister care for her new-born.

In 1945 Phyllis married a Santee who had just gotten out of the service. The couple moved several times during the early years of their marriage, including a short stay in Chicago. They eventually returned to Sioux City where her husband took several different jobs, including work at packing plants. They had eleven children. When she was first married, Phyllis only drank in social contexts for recreational purposes. Her husband drank heavily, and she tried to limit his consumption by not allowing him to drink at home. Her attempts proved unsuccessful; he continued drinking, but did so outside the home, frequently going away for weekends and occasionally for longer periods. Phyllis eventually relaxed her rules, allowing him to drink at home and began drinking with him. They began spending less time at home with the children and more time partying. Such behavior eventually resulted in the legal removal of several children from their home due to neglect. Over the course of their marriage, her husband spent several years in prison for such acts as robbery and parole violation.

At the time of my study, Phyllis was living with her husband and a number of their children. From this point in the chapter, I will shift to the ethnographic present and present tense. Both Phyllis and her husband drink quite frequently, but they try to limit their intoxication to short periods, several days generally being the maximum. The couple usually drinks beer and does almost all of their drinking at their own home or those of their friends'. Although they drink during the week, the weekends are the times of heaviest drinking, with acquaintances and friends dropping in to visit and drink. In the following passage, Phyllis describes the activity on such a weekend:

> Like last Saturday, we drank Friday, an' ah Saturday morning here come Jack. Well, we were still asleep, an' my husband took him in that old car, an' they went down to [name's the store] (laughs). And he bought some beer, and then my cousin came with her kids. An' she stayed there all day with 'em. . . . An' so then I had a beer, but you see I didn't ah get up an' eat anything, I just got up and started drinkin'. An' before you know it, here comes this other woman [that Phyllis had mentioned earlier]. She had a case of beer. An' I said, "Boy!" An' everybody was ah drinkin' by then. And my cousin, she'll take a beer anytime, but still she didn't drink all that much when the kids were there. And then Jack stayed for awhile, an' then he left, but this woman was still there. He came back by, then David come, an' then this William Tebrow come. And he, he's always after my cousin or else this other woman, so he went, and he got a case of beer. An' it's just ah, that's just the way it is.

Although Phyllis may remain intoxicated for short periods, like the weekends, she does not go on long drunks. As she says:

> I can just drink so much an' so long, an' then I don't want any more. . . . I just don't see how they [people who go on

long drunks] can do it, stay with it. Cause even if I drink, I've got to, I've got to stop. I really realize how messed up my place gets and everything. Then I'm thinkin' about the kids, an' I always wonder what they think. . . . I get to thinkin', "Well, I better quit." An' then I quit.

Phyllis maintains an ambivalent attitude toward her drinking. On one hand, she feels that she should not drink as much as she does and believes that drinking has contributed to her problems. On the other hand, she feels that it is difficult to stop drinking for a variety of reasons:

I think that if I didn't drink at all that I wouldn't have some of the problems that I got now. . . . I actually think that if, ah, if I didn't fall into the pattern of drinking that I could of avoided a lot of it, you know, myself. I should have. But, ah, you know, saying it and doing it are two different things, and then if you're living under that, those conditions, it's, it's just easy to take that drink and say, "Oh, the hell with it." You know. Nothing ever seems to go right. Nothing is right, and before you know it, you know, you're just drinking, an' you're to the point where you don't care anyway. Until I feel like I'm through drinking, then I don't. Then I don't want another drink.

As the quote suggests, Phyllis believes that drinking sometimes helps her to escape temporarily from her problems: "Just for that period of time that I am drinking, I'm not really worrying and thinking about, ah, everything. . . . You're not gonna worry about everything until you sober up and start thinking again." Although some of Phyllis's episodes of problem drinking occurred primarily in an attempt to deal with or escape from various personal problems, others developed when her initial intention was merely to "visit" or "socialize" with other people.

In the past Phyllis had attended some AA meetings and had attempted to abstain completely. At the time of my study, she was no longer trying to abstain, but rather wished to limit her drinking to acceptable amounts and periods. As she indicated, she was only partially successful. In addition to a need to find an occasional and temporary escape from her problems, she also encountered social pressure from her acquaintances, friends, and family which made it difficult for her to limit her drinking as much as she desired. In the following quote she comments on the pressure from her friends and the difficulty of avoiding it:

> I said to my daughter the other day, I said, "I don't care who I know," I said, "if I did want to go visiting somewhere, they're either drinking, or they're going to start. . .". An' naturally they know you drink. An' these people are funny. If you don't take a drink with 'em, they think: "Oh, well," you know, "she's too good," or "she thinks this an' all that."

In point of fact, there are nondrinking people, including some female relatives, who are potentially available to interact socially with Phyllis. But because Phyllis is known to drink, relations with these people are somewhat strained. One of Phyllis's relatives has refused to tell her where she lives. She occasionally will come to visit Phyllis and her family, but because she fears that Phyllis and her husband will come to her apartment asking for money and otherwise bothering her when they are drunk, she will not tell them her address or phone number. What happens over time is that individuals who drink heavily tend to interact on a social basis with other heavy drinkers. The net result, of course, is that different social networks maintain different standards of appropriate drinking. So when a person such as Phyllis desires to reduce or stop her drinking, it may not be easy to find nondrinking people with whom she can interact and feel comfortable. The contacts most readily available are with those who wish to continue drinking and who are apt to put pressure on old drinking friends to continue the established patterns. The continued interaction within given networks helps to perpetuate and reinforce the "correctness" of the individuals' drinking standards.

From within the home, the major social pressure to drink came from Phyllis's husband. Although he also felt, at least on occasion, that he had a drinking problem, Phyllis believed he was less concerned about controlling his drinking than she was: "He always says, 'If you quit, I'll quit.' An' I says, 'You know you're lying there. Cause,' I says, 'You're not going to quit for anybody.' I said, 'You never quit for the kids. You never quit because of me.' I says, 'You have to quit, because you want to quit yourself.'"

Phyllis tries to control her husband's drinking, but finds it difficult to do for as she said:

> I'm weak enough ta, ta drink, an', and he knows it. And it's just sort of like he says to me, "Well, *you* drink, you know. An' it's all right when *you* drink, but if you don't drink, you don't want nobody else to drink." Which is true, cause that's the way I feel. I mean, I don't want 'em around there drinkin'. An' he knows that, so most of the time, you know, he'll bring a beer home. An' if we get started, he, he knows (laughs)—that if he can get me started, you know, that I won't be all that cross.

Thus, although Phyllis views some of her drinking as unacceptable and expresses a desire to alter her behavior, her commitment and attempts to change can be outweighed by social and psychological pressures. In explaining her problem drinking, we do not need to refer to biological variables.

Periodic Drunks

Similar factors influence the behavior of the drinkers who are on the street. Unlike Phyllis, however, some of these individuals remain intoxicated for extended periods of time and state that they are unable to stop drinking voluntarily once they get started. This pattern is seen most dramatically in the behavior of the "periodic drunks." As described earlier, these people will alternate periods of complete abstinence with periods of extended intoxication. While the person is abstinent, he will frequently obtain a job, work steadily, and stay off the street. When drinking, he may lose or quit his job, drink up his savings, and end up on the street.

What factors interact to produce such a pattern? As in the case of Phyllis, an abstaining individual faces a number of social and psychological pressures to commence drinking. Since many Indians do drink and since alcohol consumption figures in many activities, it can be difficult for an abstaining person to completely avoid all contacts with alcohol and drinking. This represents a special problem for individuals who have been on the street, for many of their acquaintances are the heavy drinkers still on the street. An abstaining person may have relatives with whom he can stay, but they may drink themselves and may unintentionally, and in some cases intentionally, put social pressures on him to drink again. Or, if an individual has no family in the immediate area and few nondrinking friends, he must reconcile himself to being fairly lonely if he abstains. Many individuals who go on the wagon avoid the Fourth Street area where they are apt to encounter drinking acquaintances who attempt to borrow money or induce them to drink again. The pressure to drink may be overt, with the drinkers asking the abstainer such questions as: "What's the matter? Think you're too good to drink with us?" Or it may be subtle as it was in the following example:

I was walking around town. I had a little portable radio. . . . I ran into some of my friends, my so-called friends, you know. They wanted a drink, so I told them . . . , "I ain't got no money . . . , but I'll do the next best thing. I'll let you have my radio, and you can go down and hock it and see what you can get for it." Jim, . . . he's a good friend, he said, "I'll take it into my mother's." She gave us $3 for it. It wasn't an expensive one, you know. . . . Jim said, . . . "I'm not forcing you to drink, . . . but we'd like to have you drink with us, but you don't have to drink." So I said, "Oh hell!" . . . That's when I fell off the wagon and started [drinking again].

Another periodic drinker describes a different kind of pressure encountered when he ran into an old girl friend he had not seen in some time:

> I bought her some lunch. Then she kept on talking about drinking, see. So I figured maybe she wanted a drink. But I wanted to, you know, renew a friendship. [You had been drinking before this?] No, I never took a drink. But anyway, I talked to myself, "Well, hell, that's the only way I can be with her, is to drink with her." That's how come I got started.

In other cases, an individual begins to drink in response to various kinds of personal problems. One man, for example, who had been on the wagon for some time, was suffering from severe headaches and a stiffness of the body. At the same time, he was also quarreling with his wife. He began to drink again and later offered this description and analysis of his behavior:

> I was still getting headaches, and then at the same time I suppose I was looking for an excuse—to get myself a drink. [Were you and your wife having difficulties at this time?] Yeah, ah, but I suppose you could use anything for an excuse. . . . I remember I got up in the morning, you know. . . . I had a severe headache, temperature around 102. So I took my wife to work; . . . I didn't say anything to my wife. I just went down to the, went over to the liquor store and bought myself a pint of whiskey. [Now when you did that what were you thinking?] Well, I knew—I figured that I would take just one, but I knew in my heart that I wouldn't stop.

Situations and pressures such as these help account for the resumption of drinking, but they do not explain why the individuals continue to drink and remain intoxicated for long periods. Several possibilities exist. In some cases it is not difficult to explain, for once an individual has decided to drink again, he may intend to become intoxicated and to remain drunk for some time. This can be seen in the passage quoted above. The man knew he really did not intend to stop with one or two drinks.

In other cases, however, a person will indicate that he had no intention of going on a long drunk but was unable to stop. Many of the people with whom I worked believed that "alcoholics" crave alcohol and cannot commence drinking and stop; rather, they lose control. One man put it this way:

> Joe Blow over here, he can go out and get drunk tonight and come back in the morning. I just hate to admit that I'm one of these people that can't do that. I wish I could — I *wish* to *God* I could drink and in the morning say, "Well, I'm through. I got to go to work." But I can't. So it's just better not to have it at all.

Although such beliefs may be based on the individual's own experiences and observations, it is also the prevailing view of social workers, mental health personnel, medical workers, and members of Alcoholics Anonymous. People who drink heavily and frequently have learned through their contacts with these treatment workers that they view heavy drinkers as having the "disease" of alcoholism and expect alcoholics to crave alcohol and lose control. The influence of these professional workers can be seen in the following comments made by a periodic drinker who was discussing an acquaintance: "He's been sober going on four years. He's just one drink away from a big drunk again. He's an alcoholic as long as he lives. That's what they tell us in AA meetings, and they're right too." An individual who has such beliefs may begin acting to conform to the expected pattern. Even a drinker who does not initially subscribe to such beliefs may come to accept them as correct because professional workers continually press this interpretation. As a result, the professional dogma may become a self-fulfilling prophesy in some cases. Drinkers also know that if they desire help or aid from many social agencies, it is better for them to acknowledge that they have a drinking problem. Thus, even though an individual may not really see his drinking as a problem, in certain situations he may claim that it is and that he is unable to control himself because he is an alcoholic. Such cases help support the prevailing view.

Tolerance and Physical Dependence

In addition to these considerations, biochemical and physiological factors also can play a significant role in prolonging a drinking spree because alcohol can produce both tolerance and physical dependence. Tolerance involves a decreased responsiveness to a pharmacologic effect of alcohol or another drug due to prior exposure to the drug. Several types of tolerance are frequently distinguished. *Initial* tolerance refers to the amount of a drug required on first exposure to manifest a particular effect. *Acute* tolerance is used to describe the tolerance that develops following either a single exposure or a few exposures over a brief period. The tolerance that develops after numerous administrations of the drug over a longer period of time is called *chronic* tolerance. In addition, distinctions are made among dispositional, functional, and learned tolerance. *Dispositional* tolerance (which is also called *metabolic* or *pharmacokinetic* tolerance) refers to adaptations that increase the rate at which a drug is eliminated in the body and include changes in absorption, distribution, degradation, and excretion. These factors affect the degree of contact a drug has with its site(s) of action. *Functional* tolerance (also called *pharmacodynamic* or *cellular adaptive* tolerance) refers to the degree of sensitivity shown, usually by the central nervous system, to various effects of a drug. These adaptations may include such changes as the number of receptors or the efficiency of the receptors. As functional tolerance increases, the strength of the drug's effect decreases, although an increased dosage will reestablish the earlier response. *Learned* tolerance describes the compensatory responses a person acquires through past experiences with a drug and can be subdivided into behavioral and conditioned tolerance. With *behavioral* tolerance an individual learns to function under the drug's influence and adjusts to the drug's effects, such as learning to walk with less sway when intoxicated with alcohol. With *conditioned* tolerance a person associates environmental cues like sights, smells, or situations with administering a drug and begins to anticipate the drug's effects. These cues can produce adaptive responses, such as changes in blood pressure or heart rate, even before the drug reaches its sites of action.[3]

Dispositional, Metabolic, or Pharmacokinetic Tolerance. Of the factors that can contribute to dispositional tolerance, the rate of alcohol metabolism is the most significant. The liver serves as the primary site of alcohol metabolism, utilizing two major systems of enzymes: alcohol dehydrogenase (ADH) and cytochrome P450.[4] An enzyme is usually a protein that serves as a catalyst to induce chemical changes in other substances while remaining unchanged itself.[5] ADH is an enzyme that uses nicotinamide adenine dinucleotide (NAD) as a coenzyme to convert alcohol to acetaldehyde (*see* figure 1). A coenzyme or cofactor is a substance that enhances or is necessary for the action of an enzyme. At low to moderate blood levels of alcohol the ADH system accounts for most of the liver's oxidation of alcohol. At higher levels, the cytochrome P450 system of enzymes (but primarily cytochrome P4502E1),[6] which does not rely on NAD as a cofactor, contributes more substantially and can also be induced by chronic use of alcohol. Induction of cytochrome P450 enzymes can significantly increase the liver's metabolism of alcohol into acetaldehyde, contributing to the dispositional tolerance shown.[7] The acetaldehyde formed is converted in the liver to acetate primarily by the aldehyde dehydrogenase superfamily of enzymes (ALDH), which also uses the coenzyme NAD (*see* figure 1).[8] Most of the acetate formed passes into the blood stream and is metabolized in other tissues into carbon dioxide and water.

Figure 1 Ethanol and Acetaldehyde Metabolism

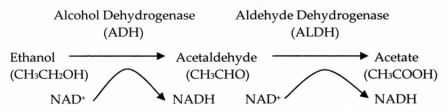

Alcohol Dehydrogenase (ADH)   Aldehyde Dehydrogenase (ALDH)

Ethanol $\longrightarrow$ Acetaldehyde $\longrightarrow$ Acetate
(CH_3CH_2OH)   (CH_3CHO)   (CH_3COOH)

NAD^+ NADH NAD^+ NADH

An average 150 pound person can metabolize approximately 7 – 10 grams of alcohol (the equivalent of a 10 ounce beer) per hour.[9] Metabolism rates, however, can vary greatly among individuals by up to about 400 percent.[10] A number of variables — including genetic factors, nutritional state, liver disease, gender, body mass, and previous drug use — can affect one's alcohol metabolism. With chronic use of alcohol (holding all other variables constant) the metabolism rate increases. However, as suggested, other factors can prevent the increase: if the nutritional state of the chronic drinker is poor or if the person has incurred liver damage, he may find that his capacity to metabolize alcohol has decreased in comparison to an earlier period in his drinking career. Following a period of abstinence, metabolic tolerance decays.[11]

Forms of Alcohol Dehydrogenase and Aldehyde Dehydrogenase. The relevance of these enzymes to alcohol use stems from the fact that both enzymes have variant forms that affect their biochemical actions. Seven different human alcohol dehydrogenases (ADHs) and three aldehyde dehydrogenases (ALDHs) have been identified as playing critical roles in the process of alcohol metabolism. As a result, the efficiency and rate with which these enzymes metabolize their respective substrates, namely alcohol in the case of (ADH) and acetaldehyde in the case of (ALDH), (*see* figure 1), can vary markedly. For example, people whose genetic makeup[12] encodes for the fastest-acting alcohol dehydrogenase enzymes will metabolize alcohol about eight times faster than a person with slower forms (Edenberg 2007). In a similar fashion, the two types of aldehyde dehydrogenase mainly responsible for metabolizing acetaldehyde to acetate in the liver are ALDH1 and ALDH2. ALDH1 is controlled by gene locus *ALDH1*,[13] and ALDH2 is governed by locus *ALDH2*. Variant alleles occur at each locus. At the *ALDH2* locus a mutant allele (called *ALDH2*2*) is partially dominant over the normal allele (called *ALDH2*1*) and lowers the ALDH2 activity in the liver. As a result, individuals who are either homozygous (*ALDH2*2/*2*) or heterozygous (*ALDH2*1/*2*) with the defective allele do not metabolize acetaldehyde as rapidly and have acetaldehyde build up in the blood stream. People who are homozygous with *ALDH2*1* alleles normally have no build up of acetaldehyde in the blood after consuming alcohol.

In addition, it has been discovered that the genes encoding for the various enzymes also vary in frequency among ethnic groups or gene pools. So for example, one of the genes (called *ADH1B*2*) that encodes for a faster acting type of ADH occurs frequently among Japanese and Chinese at about 75%.[14] It is rare to absent (less than 4%) in most Caucasians and African Americans. However, higher frequencies (20% - 32%) have been found in Jewish samples in both Israel and the U.S.[15] The gene has been found in Native Americans in southwestern California with a frequency of 7%.[16]

The defective *ALDH2*2* gene, encoding for the inactive form of aldehyde dehydrogenase, is relatively common among East Asians (at 12% to 41%),[17] but nearly absent among Europeans and Africans. Early studies of Native Americans using hair root analyses found the variant present.[18] The results of the hair root analyses must be viewed as questionable, however, since technical problems exist concerning the validity of the typing procedures.[19] More recent studies have found the gene rare or absent in both North and South American Indians.[20]

In the early 1970s, Peter Wolff (1972) discovered that Asians had a higher incidence of facial flushing than did American Caucasians following the consumption of alcohol (83% vs. 6%) and that many also experienced various unpleasant sensations such as heat in the stomach, increased heart rate, and sleepiness. In a later study (1973), he included 30 adult Cree Indians along with Caucasians and Asians in a similar experiment and found that about 80% of the Indians experienced flushing reactions. Wolff administered an ethanol solution by intravenous infusion into five of the Asians who had reacted to the alcoholic beverage with flushing and found a rapid vasomotor response. Wolff attributed the rapid onset of the flushing to genetic differences in the sensitivity of their autonomic nervous systems to alcohol. More recent studies, however, have conclusively linked the flushing and negative reactions in East Asians to the build-up of acetaldehyde in their blood and have shown this to be due primarily to the deficiency of ALDH2 in their livers.[21]

Although an ALDH2 deficiency is clearly the major cause of flushing and alcohol sensitivity in many East Asians, it may not be the only factor at work. Variations in the responses among individuals homozygous for the ALDH2*2 gene (i.e., who have two ALDH2*2 alleles) exist, including the speed with which the person flushes and the subjective reactions. Some evidence suggests that an unknown variant of an ADH1B*2 allele or variations in the sensitivity of vasoneuroreceptors may play a role.[22]

In a study that included 104 Native Americans (predominantly Sioux, Navajo, and Cheyenne), Deitrich et al. (1999) found that even though none of the Indian subjects carried the variant ALDH gene (i.e., all were homozygous with the normal ALDH2*1 alleles), 23% were flushers. Their flush reactions were milder and less unpleasant than those of Asians and had little effect on the frequency or amount of their drinking.[23] The evidence on flushing does not suggest any clear relationship to alcohol consumption among Native Americans. To the extent it influences drinking, it would be to reduce, rather than increase, alcohol consumption. There were no elevations in blood acetaldehyde levels in any Indian. As indicated, the underlying mechanisms causing the flushing reactions in Native Americans and Caucasians remain unknown.

Relationships to Problem Drinking. The differing genotypes and the related liver enzymes can have a profound impact on alcohol use and related disease risk. As we saw, those individuals who metabolize alcohol faster and thereby produce acetaldehyde at a faster rate, and/or who carry the defective gene (ALDH2*2) causing the ineffective conversion of acetaldehyde to acetate, experience a buildup of acetaldehyde in their blood.[24] Acetaldehyde is toxic and carcinogenic.[25] These people experience a variety of unpleasant symptoms including vasodilatation, lowered blood pressure, increased heart and respiration rates, nausea, and headaches.[26] As a result, such genetic traits help prevent these individuals from engaging in heavy drinking and developing alcohol dependence. For example, not one individual who carried two copies of the defective gene for aldehyde dehydrogenase (i.e., had two *ALDH2*2* genes) was discovered in a study of 1,300 alcohol-dependent, Japanese patients.[27] In addition, such individuals consume much less alcohol than do people with the normal genes (i.e., *ALDH2*1*), do not engage in binge drinking, and are at a lower risk for developing alcohol-related diseases like cirrhosis, pancreatitis, or esophageal cancer.[28]

Although the *ADH1B*2* allele occurs at low frequency outside East Asia and the Middle East, it has been found to protect European Americans from alcoholism[29] and Jewish populations from binge drinking[30] and alcoholism.[31] The *ADH1B*2* allele was also found in 7% of Native Americans in southwestern California, but was not associated with protection from alcohol dependence.[32]

The *ADH1B*3* allele reduces the risk for alcohol problems in African Americans,[33] Afro-Trinidadians,[34] and Native Americans in southwest California.[35] For example, in the studies of the southwestern California Indians, it was found that 6% carried the *ADH1B*3* allele making them about one-third less likely to develop alcohol dependence and to consume less alcohol in a 24-hour period.[36] In a recent study[37] with an expanded sample, 4% carried the *ADH1B*3* allele, and it protected against alcohol dependence. However, in another study with the same population, Gizer et al. (2011) found that variants in the *ADH1B* and *ADH4* genes protected against alcohol withdrawal symptoms, but did not confirm a relationship between allelic variants and alcohol dependence.[38]

As these studies and others not reviewed indicate, the *ADH* and *ALDH* genes are of great significance in understanding the development of problem drinking. Identifying their specific actions will be a rewarding if challenging task, as Edenberg and Bosron (2010: 125) commented in relation to *ADH* genes:

> The data demonstrating the role of *ADH* genes in affecting
> the risk for alcoholism is overwhelming, but the complexity
> of the association results, as well as the overlapping roles of
> many of the encoded enzymes in alcohol metabolism and the

strong linkage disequilibrium [i.e., nonrandom coinheritance of alleles] in this region make interpretation of the roles of specific SNPs [i.e., single nucleotide polymorphisms[39]] difficult.

The search for specific genetic variants and their relationships to alcohol-related problems is a dynamic and rapidly developing area of research among many populations.[40] Although further discoveries will undoubtedly continue, on the basis of the existing data, it is important to note *that no biological characteristics unique to North American Indians have been established that indicate they are at any greater risk of becoming problem drinkers than are Caucasian Americans.*

Functional or Pharmacodynamic Tolerance.   As indicated earlier, in contrast to dispositional tolerance, *functional* tolerance refers to changes in the sensitivity of the body to a given concentration of alcohol in the blood. Although the degree to which functional tolerance can develop to alcohol varies with the particular response measured, it has been demonstrated that tolerance can develop with a single exposure to alcohol. As Dora Goldstein (1983: 87) put it, "substantial [functional] tolerance can develop within a few weeks, days, or even hours." With daily intoxication, the developing tolerance tends to reach a plateau within three weeks. At that point, for both humans and animals, alcohol-influenced performances can have improved about 50% to 100%.[41] A genetic component in functional tolerance has been demonstrated in animal studies. Different strains of mice and rats have been bred to show varying neural sensitivities to alcohol.[42] Although functional tolerance involves different biochemical processes than metabolic tolerance, both types work in concert to allow an intoxicated individual to be affected less by a given amount of alcohol.

Physical Dependence. Physical dependence occurs when an organism needs the presence of a drug to perform its normal functions. The physical dependence is demonstrated when the drug is no longer present and the organism develops various pathophysiologic disturbances generally referred to as a withdrawal or abstinence syndrome.[43] A number of researchers have shown that the alcohol withdrawal syndrome is not a single, unitary set of symptoms, but rather consists of several sets which may occur separately or in combination. Heightened autonomic nervous system activation can cause rapid heartbeats, elevated blood pressure, excessive sweating, nausea, vomiting, and shaking or tremors. Excessive activity of the central nervous system can lead to motor seizures, hallucinations, and delirium tremens. Anxiety, irritability, agitation, dysphoria, and sleep disturbances are also present.

Although the degree and duration of drinking are clearly involved in the type of withdrawal symptoms manifest, the relationships are not simple ones. Nancy Mello[44] commented:

> The critical determinants of the onset of withdrawal symptoms are unclear since either a relative decrease in blood alcohol levels or abrupt cessation of drinking may precipitate the syndrome. . . . The severity and duration of withdrawal symptoms also do not appear to be directly related either to the volume of alcohol consumed or the duration of a drinking spree. We have concluded that the pattern of drinking may be more important than the duration of drinking in accounting for the expression of the alcohol syndrome (Mello and Mendelson, 1970).[45]

Heilig and his co-researchers[46] divided the withdrawal symptoms into three stages: 1) the acute phase, which in humans lasts up to about a week, 2) the early abstinence period, which continues for an additional three to six weeks, and 3) the protracted phase, which can extend beyond three months. The more severe physical symptoms, including tremors, seizures, and hallucinations, tend to abate within the first week. Anxiety, dysphoria, and disrupted sleep patterns continue into early abstinence. The period of protracted abstinence is marked by a shift in the negative emotional state and altered functions in the motivation systems. Repeated cycles of intoxication and withdrawal over time can lead to what has been called "kindling," a process that increases the sensitivity of the body to withdrawal and the severity of the withdrawal symptoms.[47]

Sioux City Indians who drink heavily for extended periods are acutely aware of the discomfort they experience due to their physical dependence on alcohol. One man who drank periodically describes how he sometimes felt on a drinking spree: "When I'm drunk, I wake up halfway sober, but I'm so damn sick that I got to get out on the street and look for another drink." Another man who also drank periodically describes it in this fashion: "When you start to get sick . . . you're not drinking just to be drinking to have fun, you're drinking . . . to keep your body under control, you know. Keep these illnesses out. You're drinking for survival, that's when it's bad, you know."

Neurobiological Views of Physical Dependence, Craving, Relapse, and Addiction. Although our knowledge of the development of tolerance and dependence has advanced greatly through research with animals and the development of new diagnostic and analytic procedures, including neuroimaging research in humans, we do not fully understand the cellular and molecular changes involved or the manner in which they relate to the development and maintenance of addiction. Studies of families, adoptions, and twins have shown that heritability of developing alcohol dependence or abuse ranges from about 50% to 60%, indicating that about half of the variability observed among individuals could be attributed to genetic factors.[48] A number of neurobiological models have been proposed.[49]

One influential view sees the development of addiction moving from reward-driven ("liking") to habit-driven ("wanting" or "relief-craving") behavior with the development of craving and relapse. This approach focuses less on the role of the physical symptoms of acute withdrawal and more on the changes in the motivational structure and psychological state. As Heilig and his co-workers put it, "a neuroadaptive view of alcoholism focuses on long-term plasticity that leads to a persistent negative affective state and altered function of key motivational systems as the proximal cause of relapse and excessive alcohol drinking" (Heilig et al. 2010a: 171).[50]

As indicated, although the increased anxiety observed during the period of early abstinence of withdrawal tends to dissipate after three to six weeks, there appears to be a shift in affective processes manifesting as difficulty experiencing pleasure (anhedonia), irritability, dysphoria, agitation, and sleep disturbances.[51] In addition, abstaining alcohol-dependent individuals are more sensitive to alcohol-related cues and stressors. These changes are believed to increase the likelihood of a relapse to drinking and continued consumption after relapsing. Some researchers have suggested the brain's reward and stress systems develop new set points.[52]

Understanding the neurobiological adaptations that lead to these states is a primary goal of research. The mesolimbic dopaminergic (DA) system and its connections play important roles in alcohol reinforcement, but its actions are complex.[53] Heilig and his co-workers argue that dopamine's major influence occurs in the early phases of the addiction cycle through its reward functions and its role in associative learning that increases the salience of environmental cues present during alcohol use. They suggest that to the extent dopaminergic systems play a central role in developing addiction, they do so indirectly "through a cascade that involves release of endogenous opioid peptides in the ventral tegmental area (VTA), resulting in disinhibition of DA neurons in this region."[54]

The symptoms related to the negative emotional states that predominate in the later stages of the addiction cycle may be connected to two neurochemical systems involved in stress-reactions: 1) the hypothalamic-pituitary-adrenal (HPA) axis, and 2) the brain stress/aversive system. Both are mediated by corticotropin-releasing factor (CRF). Withdrawal from chronic alcohol use activates both systems. When an individual is stressed, his brain's hypothalamus releases the hormone CRF. CRF causes the pituitary gland to release another hormone, adrenocorticotrophin (ACTH), which is carried in the blood stream to the adrenal glands located atop the kidneys.

They in turn release stress hormones (glucocorticoids) into the blood which act on target cells throughout the body. Coritsol is the major human stress hormone. The second stress system acts independently of the HPA. Neurons within the brain[55] also release CRF in response to stress. The belief is that during protracted abstinence the state of anxiety and dysphoria has returned to an earlier level, but the sensitivity of the systems has increased (i.e., developed new set points). As a result, a person will be more reactive to stress-provoking cues and more likely to relapse.

Blocking the CRF receptors in the brains of alcohol-dependent rats during prolonged abstinence prevented their return to seeking alcohol under conditions of stress. However, such action did not prevent the return to drinking when the animals were presented with alcohol-related cues or primed by giving them alcohol. Those behaviors were blocked with another drug,[56] but that drug did not affect the return to drinking under stress conditions. Such outcomes suggested that the two sets of responses (relapse under stress versus relapse in response to alcohol-related cues and alcohol priming) were influenced by different neurobiological mechanisms (Hielig et al. 2011: 677).

Although our knowledge about the neurobiological adaptations involved in addiction has increased dramatically in recent decades, much remains to be elucidated. Heilig and his co-workers (2010b: 340) summed up a prevalent view for many biologically-oriented researchers:

> [N]euroadaptations that occur after a prolonged history of alcohol dependence seem to persist long after brain alcohol exposure, and in some cases perhaps for the lifetime of the individual. . . . Long-term neuroadaptations in alcoholism drive escalation of voluntary alcohol intake, behavioral sensitization to stress, and a concomitant sensitivity to stress-induced relapse.

Psychosocial Views of Physical Dependence, Craving, Relapse, and Addiction. Given the data just reviewed, it might seem that some version of a biological perspective of addiction might be universally adopted by drug researchers, but such an approach is not without its critics. Some researchers like Harold Kalant (2009) argue that the approach by itself is too narrow. He reviewed the advances made by neurobiology in four areas: 1) intracellular signaling systems, 2) synaptic plasticity, 3) dopamine and the reward system, and 4) genetic factors. According to Kalant, the problem with all the advances is that while we increase our understanding of mechanisms involved in addictive processes, neurobiological studies will not identify the *cause* of the addiction. As he said with reference to synaptic plasticity, "Knowledge of these mechanisms can tell us *how* the change is brought about, but not *why*" (2009: 782, his emphasis). To understand the primary causes of addictive behavior we must employ an integrative or synthetic approach which ties these neurobiological processes to wider social and environmental contexts. As he commented, "it is inherently impossible to explain addiction by pursuing only the analytical study of drug interactions with the nervous system at ever-finer levels of molecular structure and function" (2009: 787). Kalant, of course, does not wish to denigrate the value of neurobiological understanding, pointing out, for example, that such knowledge may well lead to better pharmacological interventions to help individuals cope with increased vulnerability to drug problems and relapsing behavior. His major point is that a reductionist approach by itself will not lead to a full understanding of addiction.

Other critics point to the fact that much of the disease conception derives from a clinical perspective which is based on interaction and research with only a subset of the population with drinking problems. This subset is composed of the individuals who are the most severely impacted by alcohol-related problems and are the ones most apt to repeatedly relapse. These critics argue that an epidemiological or public health perspective produces a more accurate sense of alcohol-related problems than a clinical one. Arguing for such a view, Cunningham and McCambridge (2011: 7) summarized the results of a number of surveys:

> The majority of people who meet criteria for alcohol dependence at some point in their life: 1) do not seek treatment;[57] 2) resolve their alcohol dependence without any formal treatment or similar help;[58] and 3) do not relapse repeatedly to alcohol dependence.[59]

To take one study, for example, Dawson et al. (2005) published the results of a national survey of Americans 18 years and older examining the past-year status of people who met the criteria of alcohol dependence (from the Diagnostic and Statistical Manual IV) for earlier years (prior-to-past-year, PPY) dependence. The data were collected in 2001-2002 by personal interviews. Out of 43,093 individuals, 4,422 were identified as having been alcohol dependent PPY. Of these, 25% were still dependent in the past year, but nearly 50% were in full remission. Only 25.5% (1,205) of those with PPY dependence had ever been treated. Of those treated, 28% remained dependent. In contrast, only 24% of those *never* treated remained dependent. Even allowing for the possibility that individuals who sought treatment might be more severely dependent, the results are surprising to those who expect "alcoholics" to be able to improve only with help from professionals or 12-step organizations. In addition, the study also found that over 50% of the individuals in full recovery engaged in low-risk drinking.[60]

The issues involved in these alternative perspectives relate to the controversy of whether addiction or alcoholism is a "disease." Many elements in the "classic" or "traditional" view of alcoholism as a disease—notably that the condition is marked by progression from one stage to another, that it involves loss of control over drinking, and that its cure requires abstinence—can be seen in American thought from the end of the 18th century and the beginning of the 19th (Levine 1978). However, its contemporary form dates from the 1930s and 1940s when the Yale Center of Alcohol Studies, the National Council on Alcoholism, and Alcoholics Anonymous "rediscovered" this view. Discussing the disease concept of alcoholism can be frustrating because it is difficult to find a single, precise definition that includes all of its major facets. As Robin Room has observed, "the public presentation of the disease concept of alcoholism has been consistently vague or vacuous concerning the *content* of the concept" (1983: 54, his emphasis). Even though E. M. Jellinek is frequently seen as the ultimate authority for the disease concept, "Jellinek himself gave 'alcoholism' at least three quite different meanings in different periods of work (cf. Haggard and Jellinek, 1942, p. 151; Jellinek 1952, 1960) . . ." (Room 1983: 54). One way of handling such a situation is to identify the key elements from a number of authors who adopt the disease perspective. Using such an approach, Pattison, Sobell, and Sobell (1977) suggested that the traditional view of alcoholism as a disease consists of six related propositions:

1. There is a unitary phenomenon which can be identified as alcoholism.

2. Alcoholics and prealcoholics are essentially different from nonalcoholics.

3. Alcoholics may sometimes experience a seemingly irresistible physical craving for alcohol, or a strong psychological compulsion to drink.

4. Alcoholics gradually develop a process called "loss of control" over drinking, and possibly even an inability to stop drinking.

5. Alcoholism is a permanent and irreversible condition.

6. Alcoholism is a progressive disease which follows an inexorable development through a distinct series of phases.

Although each of these propositions has been challenged,[61] my concern at this point is the notion contained in the third and fourth propositions that some people ("alcoholics") experience an overpowering physical and/or psychological craving to drink that they find difficult to control. The concept of craving has been applied to both the *initial resumption* of drinking as well as to the *continuation* of drinking once alcohol is consumed. When used in this latter fashion, craving helps explain the loss of control of drinking; that is, the initial drink increases the craving, thereby causing the drinker to become intoxicated and to remain so for an extended period.

As I indicated earlier, many Sioux City Indians subscribe to propositions three and four of the traditional model. One man, for example, recounted an urge to drink even though he had been abstinent for over a year. "I was thirsty, you know, my mind was beginning to lose its defenses. My body was craving. Sometimes I wasn't even thinking about booze, and there it would be, right there in my mind. [What did you do when it came into your mind like that?] I'd do something else, like find something to do." When their beliefs are considered in light of the drinking patterns characteristic of "periodic drunks," we might easily conclude that the traditional model, in fact, is correct. However, the issues involved are more complicated than that. Since these beliefs are central to AA and many medically-oriented treatment facilities, Sioux City Indians may have adopted the official belief systems and begun to act on them. As suggested earlier, the institutional bodies that are responsible for educating and treating individuals with drinking problems may have created a counterproductive, self-fulfilling prophecy.

If we treat beliefs (or more accurately verbal statements of beliefs) as serving a variety of social and psychological functions in addition to those related to their "truth" or "falsity," we can see that the craving and loss of control ideas can play useful roles in a drinker's psychological system and social interactions. As many writers have noted, the reputed special nature of an alcoholic's craving and loss of control offer the drinker a helpful rationalization to explain his troubling behavior: "I don't drink in this fashion and cause various interpersonal problems because I have 'free choice;' I drink this way because I am an alcoholic and cannot control—or at least easily control—my behavior." As a result, any "blame" associated with the drinking is shifted, at least in principle, from the person to his "condition" or "disease."[62] One can easily see that even if the notions are not correct, powerful social and psychological forces—quite apart from any institutional influences such as AA or medically-oriented treatment programs—help maintain these beliefs in the community.

If "alcoholics" are not driven to their excessive drinking by a neurobiological disease which produces physical or psychological craving, what other explanatory model do we have? Jim Orford (1985, 2001), building on the work of a number of researchers, has developed what he calls a social-behavioral-cognitive-moral model to account for not only excessive drinking, but also for other forms of excessive "appetitive" behaviors such as gambling, eating, and sexual activity. Although Orford allows a role for biological variables, particularly in relation to excessive drug use, he explicitly disavows disease and biological models (2001: 344). He believes that psychological processes are of primary importance and sufficient to account for excessive behavior. Orford sees excessive patterns as strongly-developed, habitual behaviors about which the person feels great conflict. An individual's excessive appetitive behavior may have begun as "moderate" or "acceptable," but due to the interaction of a variety of psychological and social forces, the behavior in question becomes amplified:

> When the circumstances are right for the development of a strong habit—when incentives are strong and disincentives relatively weak—then there will be a tendency for discrimination to be eroded and for behavior to generalize to a range of additional stimuli or settings. The stronger the inclination to consume or approach under appropriate circumstances, the greater the tendency to do so under other circumstances also [1985: 188].

As a result, the behavior in question begins to be performed in a greater number of settings and serves an increasing number of functions for the person. As the "importance" of the behavior increases, the individual becomes more "committed" to it psychologically. This increased commitment or attachment, Orford feels is best viewed as a "strong appetite,"[63] and the excessive behavior becomes, in effect, an entrenched habit that can be very resistant to change.

Because the behavioral pattern is seen as "excessive" (either by the person's own definition or significant others'), conflict is generated by the behavior, and this component significantly changes the behavior. The person is caught in a classic approach/avoidance situation. On the one hand, the behavior is greatly desired, but on the other, it carries a variety of psychological and social costs. As a result, the person is apt to experience ambivalence and may manifest such traits as inconsistency, deviousness, and secrecy. When the individual experiences certain emotional-cognitive states (such as anxiety or increased arousal) or finds himself in particularly enticing situations, the strength of the desire to engage in the behavior will increase while the restraining forces weaken. If the person succumbs to the desire and performs the activity in question, he is likely to experience what Marlatt and his co-workers[64] have labeled the "abstinence violation effect": feeling dissonance about the relapse and evaluating himself negatively as weak-willed and a failure.[65] Such reactions make continued indulgence more likely, resulting in "loss of control." After an episode of indulgence, however, when the appetite is relatively sated and the negative consequences of the action have begun to mount, the balance of forces may shift again, this time in favor of restraint. The person begins another phase of moderation or abstinence. Under such conditions, as Orford says:

> The attraction of the terms "addiction" and "dependence" can be appreciated in light of the conflict model of excessive behaviour. . . . A process of increasing affective-behavioural-cognitive attachment to a particular form of behaviour produces an inclination sufficiently strong that behaviour is unresponsive to some of the normal restraints. Behaviour is apparently self-defeating and often as mysterious to the individual as to those around her. "Dependence" or "addiction" appears to provide an explanation of such behaviour. It represents an attempt to create a psychosocial disease out of excessive habitual behaviour, but in fact it explains nothing. . . . [I]t merely signifies conflict brought

about by a combination of strong inclination and strong restraint concerning a particular activity. The terms "dependency" and "addiction" are only used when both inclination and restraint are above a certain threshold. Until behaviour becomes harmful, or is subject to criticism or attempts at control, behaviour is never seriously referred to as "dependent" or "addictive" [1985: 238-239].

Integrative or Biopsychosocial View. Although alternative explanations or models such as Orford's are available to account for the behavioral patterns interpreted as "craving," "loss of control," and "relapse," our growing—yet incomplete—knowledge of the neurobiological changes involved in these processes offers compelling evidence of the importance of these factors in the behaviors. At one level, the differences between the views of alcoholism as "biologically based and driven" and alcoholism as a "bad habit" can be largely reconciled. In general, a sharp distinction between "psychological" and "biological" cannot be justified— psychological processes do not exist independently of neurobiological processes. As indicated earlier, it has been demonstrated that a component of tolerance is "psychological" in nature. Researchers have shown that particular situations are able to elicit compensatory, physiological adjustments in both animals and humans who were physically addicted to alcohol and other drugs, even when the test subjects had been abstinent for some time.[66] For example, one study[67] injected rhesus monkeys several times with morphine or methadone while exposing them to a set of stimuli that included taped music. One of the monkeys, after having been drug free for several months, reacted to the taped music with signs of withdrawal: restlessness, hair erection, yawning, urination, and a runny nose. Such findings imply that an abstinent individual experiencing certain biopsychological states, such as anxiety or stress-reactions, or being in particular social situations, can experience physiological signs and thoughts that he interprets as withdrawal symptoms. These symptoms, in turn, can trigger feelings of "craving" and a resumption of drinking. In addition, if one adopts, as I have done here, the view that drinking behavior is shaped by a variety of factors, some promoting and others inhibiting its occurrence, then withdrawal signs, subjective feelings of craving, or other neurobiological states—whatever their origins—become but one more set of variables influencing the occurrence of the behavior. Although individuals may find it increasingly difficult to stop drinking after they have repeatedly engaged in heavy consumption and suffered numerous episodes of withdrawal, some drinkers do stop.

It is clear that neurobiological adaptations occur in response to long term, heavy drinking and that these changes can affect the development, degree, and decay rate of both tolerance and physical dependence and may in fact permanently alter the set points of certain brain circuits in genetically predisposed individuals. It is also clear that while some people are able to control their drinking so as to minimize its untoward effects on their health and lives, at least *some* individuals find it increasingly difficult to limit or control their heavy drinking over time.[68] The relative roles played by genetic, biological, psychological, and social factors in these changes are difficult to determine. The fact that some "alcoholics" have been able to resume some types of drinking without loss of control or relapse does not necessarily argue against the importance of biochemical factors in other cases. Our ability to identify or discriminate different types of "problem drinkers," or even more narrowly, different types of "alcoholics," is not very good. Although abstinence clearly is not a necessary element for controlling all cases of problem drinking, it can be an effective technique for some individuals. The comment made by Damon Runyon applies: "The race is not always to the swift—nor the battle to the strong—but that's the way to bet." Similarly, although problem drinkers may be able keep their consumption within acceptable and nonproblematic limits while continuing to drink, abstaining unquestionably eliminates problem drinking. Abstainers may have to contend with other difficulties in their lives, but not those directly related to drinking. We will return to this question of abstaining in relation to treatment in Chapter Nine.

Concluding Remarks

At any single time many factors can contribute to an individual engaging in an episode of problem drinking: physical and social settings conducive to alcohol consumption; social pressures from acquaintances, friends, and family members; relaxation of social controls limiting drinking; various psychological motives and processes; and biochemical and physiological variables. The ways in which these factors interact through time to produce the episodes of problem drinking experienced by a given individual are enormously complex and varied. Although there is certainly no single route by which unacceptable drinking develops, those individuals who positively view and participate in heavy drinking increase their risks of experiencing drinking problems. If a person is genetically predisposed to develop problem drinking, adopting a style of heavy drinking would certainly allow its expression.

The range of problems that can develop is great. Heavy drinking puts additional pressures on what in some cases are already inadequate economic resources, causing some families to suffer materially. Job performance and attendance can also suffer. Heavy weekend drinking can lead to missed work days on Mondays. If jobs are lost, further economic hardship is created. Parental pursuit of drinking can lead to child neglect and the removal of the children from the home. As noted in Chapter Six, although I do not see alcohol as being the primary cause of the interpersonal conflicts, physical violence, or legal difficulties associated with activities such as "hell raising," heavy drinking individuals are more likely to interact with those who support and encourage participation in such activities. Over time a social and psychological dynamic operates that encourages people who view heavy drinking as acceptable to interact with each other. Concomitantly, the amount and significance of interaction with people who exert restraining influences on heavy drinking decrease. These developments can be seen as part of the "generalization" or "amplification" process of excessive behavior that Orford identified. So, even though alcohol consumption and drunkenness do not directly cause untoward events by themselves, they can be instrumental in placing a person in situations that increase the probability of being involved in such difficulties.

In addition to the economic, interpersonal, and legal problems associated with heavy drinking, such drinkers also run risks of developing multiple health problems. One of the unfortunate results of the development of metabolic and functional tolerance is that if a drinker consumes alcohol for its pharmacological effects, over time he will need to consume greater amounts to achieve them. If the damage done to an organ is related to the amount of alcohol consumed — and much evidence supports this — heavy drinkers who have developed tolerance will be at greater risk.[69] Chronic and heavy consumption — quite apart from nutritional deficiencies — can cause or play a facilitating role in a variety of diseases, including liver and gastrointestinal damage (e.g., alcoholic hepatitis, cirrhosis, gastritis), metabolic disorders (e.g., hypoglycemia, ketosis, gout), cardiovascular disorders (e.g., high blood pressure, cardiac arrhythmias, strokes), and fetal malformations.[70] Heavy drinking also adversely affects a person's immune system, increasing the likelihood of contracting a variety of diseases and exacerbating their course. In addition to pathological changes, other biochemical and physiological changes, such as those associated with the development of physical dependence or addiction, may play a role in increasing the amount consumed. Thus, some people may slowly drift into unacceptable drinking primarily on the basis of biological changes induced by their acceptable drinking. A heavy drinker also runs added risks if he encounters unusual stress. If he loses his job, a close relative dies, or his marriage breaks up, he may attempt to deal with the stress by increasing his alcohol consumption. Clearly not everyone so stressed will utilize heavy drinking as a coping mechanism, but because heavy drinking is already a habit, the chances that it will be used are increased.

The picture that emerges for many Sioux City Indians is that their sociocultural environment is structured in such a way so as to maximize the chances of developing a variety of drinking problems. Clearly, not all individuals are equally at risk—it varies with the life style adopted and a variety of individual factors—but for many people, particularly those who view heavy drinking as acceptable behavior, it is not surprising that they experience episodes of problem drinking. This is not to say, however, that there are no checks or restraints. When an individual's drinking has become unacceptable either to himself or to others in his social network, a variety of social and psychological processes come into play to correct and control that behavior. In some cases, these processes are completely successful and the excessive or problem drinking is limited to a single phase of the person's life and does not recur. In other cases, the control processes are not effective and the drinking reappears periodically throughout the life of the individual or becomes one element of a set that eventually leads to an altered life style and to the drinker's acceptance of a stigmatized identity such as "wino" or "hopeless drunk."

I will consider the implications of this kind of situation in terms of treatment and prevention in Chapter Nine. Before doing so, however, I want to place the development of problem drinking in a historical context by examining it evolution among the Winnebago in Nebraska.

Endnotes for Chapter 7

[1] The research on which this chapter is based was supported by the Center for Urban Ethnography, University of Pennsylvania, and the National Institute for Mental Health, Public Grant 17,216.

I would like to express my appreciation to the Board of Directors and staff of the Sioux City American Indian Center, to the staff of the Iowa Comprehensive Treatment Program for Indian Problem Drinkers, and to the many Indians of Sioux City who were kind enough to share their experiences with me. Without the help and friendship of these people, the research would have been impossible.

I would like to thank Jay Noricks, Ron Roberts, Jerry Stockdale, and James M. Stokes for comments on an earlier draft of this chapter.

[2] When we consider the concepts and terms to use in discussing the difficulties and problems associated with alcohol use, we encounter a wide array of choices, including "alcohol dependence," "alcoholism," "excessive drinking," and "problem drinking." "Alcohol dependence" is defined by the Diagnostic and Statistical Manual of Mental Disorders, 4th Edition (American Psychiatric Association 1994) as meeting at least four of the following criteria: drinking more alcohol than intended, unsuccessful efforts to reduce alcohol drinking, giving up other activities in favor of drinking alcohol, spending a great deal of time obtaining and drinking alcohol, continuing to drink alcohol in spite of adverse physical and social effects, and the development of alcohol tolerance.

Although all the individuals considered in this chapter would meet the criteria for alcohol dependence, problem drinking will be the key concept used in this chapter. T. F. Plaut has defined problem drinking as the "repetitive use of beverage alcohol causing physical, psychological, or social harm to the drinker or to others" (Plaut 1967: 37-38; in the original, the quoted passage appeared in italics). As Don Cahalan (1970: 13) pointed out: "One catch to Plaut's definition of problem drinking . . . is the difficulty of establishing causality in relation to problems. In any studies done at single points in time, when an association (or connection or correlation) is found between a problem and drinking, it is not a simple matter to determine which came first, the problem or the drinking." Another difficulty, which Cahalan does not mention, arises in attempting to specify what constitutes physiological, social, and psychological harm and from whose perspective that judgment should be made.

In Sioux City, the existence of multiple sets of drinking standards coupled with some sets defining forms of heavy drinking as acceptable behavior make the identification of problem drinking a complex task. We cannot assume automatically that heavy drinking is seen as problem drinking by all segments of the local community. And even if an investigator wishes to use "scientific" criteria foreign to the local community to define problem drinking, it is essential not to confuse those judgments with those made by the Indians themselves. To assume that a given drinking pattern exists within a community *in spite of* moral disapproval and the use of negative sanctions when in fact the drinking is treated as acceptable and nonproblematic behavior is to badly misread the situation. Even with an insider's perspective, because of the diversity of drinking standards, a given instance of drinking can be judged acceptable and nonproblematic or unacceptable and problematic depending upon whose perspective we adopt; for as we have seen, even within a given social network, conflicting views may be present.

One of the virtues of using the concept of problem drinking is its manifestly relativistic nature; that is, its use reminds us that labeling a given sequence of drinking as a "problem" involves a social judgment. We immediately need to ask *who* considers it a problem and *in what ways* is it seen as problematic? Such an approach—grounding the definition of problem drinking in the local community's standards—contrasts with some conceptualizations of "alcoholism" that attempt to define it as a "disease" and in such a way as to be culturally universal; that is, the defining attributes of "alcoholism" are expected to be the same irrespective of the cultural context in which they appear. If a researcher uses the concept of alcoholism, in most, if not all cases, "problem drinking" will be the more inclusive category with "alcoholism" composing a subset of problem drinking. One potential drawback that arises from using the concept of problem drinking defined by insider standards is the penchant of some heavy drinkers to deny the problems associated with their consumption. To handle such occurrences, problem drinking will be defined in this chapter as drinking so judged by the drinker himself and his family. If differing views are maintained within a family—as we encountered in Frank Wolf's case in Chapter 5—the variations will be noted.

After years of research among the Navajo, Kunitz and Levy (2000: 177) commented on the concept of alcoholism as a disease: "Although intermediate positions are possible, one extreme position is that people drink to excess because they are (psychologically) sick. The other is that people are sick because they drink to excess. The latter seems to us more consistent with the evidence from the vast majority of people who were part of this and previous studies." Also *see* O'Nell's and Mitchell's comments (1996).

[3] *See* Hug (1972); O'Brien (2011); Julien, Advokat, and Comaty (2011: 3-45, 446); and Kalant, LeBlanc, and Gibbins (1971) for discussions of tolerance.

[4] The enzyme catalase can also contribute, but plays a minor role (Lieber 2005).

[5] Several RNA molecules, called ribozymes, can function as catalysts and are exceptions to the generalization that all enzymes are proteins (Dresler and Potter 1991: 88).

[6] *See* Guengerich (2012) for a discussion of the cytochrome P450 system. Fifty-seven human P450s have been identified.

[7] This is the conventional explanation for the increased metabolism rate following chronic drinking (*see* Seitz and Mueller 2012 and Oneta et al. 2002). Haseba and coworkers (Haseba et al. 2012, 2005, 2003; Haseba and Ohno 2010) argue that chronic drinking and liver disease change the cytoplasmic solution hydrophobicity which enhances the catalytic efficiency of ADH5 for alcohol and is primarily responsible for the increase seen in metabolic tolerance. ADH5 is a type of alcohol dehydrogenase conventionally viewed as not metabolizing alcohol effectively. They suggest that it is these increases in ADH5 activity that allow patients with alcoholic liver cirrhosis to keep drinking. Also *see* Dam et al. (2009) and Keiding et al. (1983).

[8] *See* Vasiliou and Petersen (2010) for a discussion of aldehyde dehydrogenases.

[9] Masters (2009: 388).

[10] Ramchandani, Bosron, and Li (2001: 677); Hurley, Edenberg, and Li (2002:419).

[11] Lieber (2005). Oneta et al. (2002) found that the induction of cytochrome P4502E1 activity returned to normal levels after three days of withdrawal.

[12] Each human has 46 chromosomes which are found in 23 homologous pairs. Except for the X and Y chromosomes (the sex chromosomes), each homologous pair contains the same kinds of genes. An individual inherits two copies of each gene, one from each parent. Variants of the same gene are called alleles. If an individual inherits the same allele from each parent—such as the allele for brown eyes—he is called homozygous for that

trait. If he inherits different alleles from each parent—such as a blue-eyed allele from his mother and a brown-eyed allele from his father—he is called heterozygous for that trait.

[13] By convention the names of human genes (and their variant alleles) are capitalized and italicized. The acronyms of the proteins they encode are capitalized, but not italicized.

[14] Eng et al. (2007), Hurley and Edenberg (2012), and Li et al. (2007).

[15] Neumark et al. (2004), Hasain et al. (2002), Shea et al. (2001).

[16] Ehlers, Liang, and Gizer (2012).

[17] Hurley and Edenberg (2012), Li et al. (2009).

[18] See Goedde et al. (1986), Zeiner et al. (1984), Agarwal and Goedde (1991: 218), and Schwappach et al. (1986).

[19] Yin et al. (1988: 353) found that "the hair follicle was not a suitable peripheral tissue for genetic studies of ADH and ALDH isozymes. The difficulties encountered were rather low enzyme activities in hair roots and the freeze-thawing extraction procedure's greatly reducing enzyme activities." A. Yoshida, after carefully examining the procedures involved, concluded: "The observed absence of ALDH2 band [in hair root extracts] could be attributed to individual differences in extractability of hair root enzymes, poor development of hair roots due to environmental and/or hereditary background, and poor expression of mitochondrial enzymes due to environmental and/or hereditary background, not necessarily due to genetic abnormality of the ALDH2 locus" (Yoshida 1984: 298). Also see Yoshida (1991b: 172) and Santisteban et al. (1985).

[20] Chen et al. (1992), Deitrich et al. (1999), Novoradovsky et al. (1995), O'Dowd et al. (1990); Ehlers, Liang, and Gizer (2012). In an earlier study of Southwestern Indians based on autopsy liver samples rather than hair roots, Rex et al. (1985) found no Indians lacking ALDH2 activity, and a study by Bosron et al. (1988) on the Sioux also found no individuals lacking ALDH2 activity.

[21] Agarwal and Goedde (1991); Harada et al. (1980, 1981); Inoe et al. (1984); Mizoi et al. (1979, 1983, 1989, 1994); Yoshida (1991b).

[22] See Tasekshita et al. (1996 and 2001) and Yin and Peng (2005). Macgregor et al. (2009: 590) suggest the possibility that "this variant [ADH1B Arg48His] affects the steady-state concentration of acetaldehyde within the hepatocytes, which is where acetaldehyde is produced, and that this affects the release of vasoactive compounds into the circulation and causes alcohol-induced flushing." Linneberg et al. (2007) found that 14% of the adult

population in Denmark experienced hypersensitivity symptoms in the upper airways, lower airways, or skin following alcohol consumption. In a later study (Linneberg et al. 2009), they proposed that a plausible biological mechanism for these results might be a histamine-releasing effect of acetaldehyde.

[23] Only 8.7% of the flushers considered their reactions to be very unpleasant, and 60% said the reactions did not influence their drinking.

[24] Although physiological studies have not documented large increases in acetaldehyde in relation to the *ADH1B*2* allele, the conventional view is that it at least transiently raises the acetaldehyde levels in some tissues (Edenberg 2012: 337; Hurley and Edenberg 2012: 340).

[25] Seitz and Mueller (2012: 499), Seitz and Stickel (2007).

[26] Yin and Peng (2005).

[27] Yin and Peng (2005: 414).

[28] Hurley and Edenberg (2012); Li, Zhao, and Gelernter (2012a , 2012b); Takeshita and Morimoto (1999); Yin and Peng (2005).

[29] Bierut et al. (2012), Sherva et al. (2009).

[30] Luczak et al. (2002).

[31] Hasin et al. (2002).

[32] Ehlers, Liang, and Gizer (2012).

[33] Edenberg et al. (2006), Ehlers et al. (2001).

[34] Ehlers et al. (2007).

[35] Ehlers, Liang, and Gizer (2012); Wall et al. (2003).

[36] Ehlers (2007), Wall et al. (2003).

[37] Ehlers, Liang, and Gizer (2012).

[38] The failure to reproduce the findings of linkage with alcohol dependence may be due to different population samples and analytic procedures (Gizer et al. 2011).

[39] A SNP (pronounced "snip") is a single-base substitution of one nucleotide at a particular site in the DNA sequence. There are coding and non-coding SNPs. The coding SNPs are part of the gene that encodes for the corresponding protein. Non-coding SNPs occur outside the coding portions of a gene, but can still affect the expression of a gene. As Edenberg and Bosron (2010: 126) point out, noncoding variations in the *ADH* genes can play a significant role in the risks for alcoholism and alcohol-related diseases. About 240 SNPs have been discovered in the area of the chromosome that contains the seven *ADH* genes. An allele is polymorphic if it occurs in a population at a frequency above 1%. *See* Melke, Konigsberg,

and Relethford (2006) and Gluckman, Beedle, and Hanson (2009: 51-75) for discussions of genetic variations.

[40] For discussions of genetic variants and their potential relationships to problem drinking, *see* Agrawal and Bierut (2012); Borghese and Harris (2012); Buck, Milner, and Denmark, et al. (2012); Crews (2012); Cui, Seneviratne, Gu, et al. (2012); Dick and Kendler (2012); Edenberg (2007), (2011), (2012); Edenberg and Bosron (2010); Foroud and Phillips (2012); Gorwood, Le Strat, Ramoz, et al. (2012); Hurley and Edenberg (2012); Kimura and Higuchi (2011); Levran, Yuferov, and Kreek (2012); Long, Mail, and Thomasson (2002); Sarker (2012); Starkman, Sakharkar, Pandey (2012); Wolen and Miles (2012).

[41] Tabakoff and Rothstein (1983: 195).

[42] *See* Crabbe et al. (2006) and the other articles in the special issue of *Addiction Biology*, 2006, Vol. 11, No. 3/4 reviewing alcohol research with mice, rats, and non-human primates.

[43] Goldstein, Aronow, and Kalam (1968: 558).

[44] Mello (1972: 221).

[45]In another review of the literature on withdrawal symptoms, Gross, Lewis, and Hastey (1974: 198-199) commented as follows:

> Our findings [Gross et al. 1972a, 1972b, 1972c] demonstrated a progressive increase in many signs and symptoms of withdrawal starting early in the course of heavy drinking (as early as the second day). These data indicate that some of the signs and symptoms during the drinking period are manifestations of intoxication, while others are manifestations of partial withdrawal (Gross and Lewis 1973). Furthermore, as days of drinking continue, the effects of partial withdrawal increased.
>
> These experimental observations are consistent with such clinical data as those of Feuerlein (1967), who reported that 36% of the 268 case histories of delirium were "unprovoked", i.e., there was no evidence of reduction or cessation of alcohol intake or the onset of intercurrent physical illness as precipitation factors.

See Becker (2008), Finn and Crabbe (1997), Heilig, Egli, Crabbe, and Becker, henceforth Heilig et al. (2010a) and Saitz (1998), for discussions of withdrawal.

[46] Heilig et al. (2010a).

[47] *See* Ballenger and Post (1978), Breese, Overstreet, and Knapp (2005).

[48] *See* Schuckit (2011: 641) and (2009), Agrawal and Lynskey (2008).

[49] For reviews and discussions *see* Feltenstein and See (2008); Gardner and Wise (2009); Gardner (2011); Goldman (2008); Koob and Le Moal (2006, 2008); Nestler (2009); Robinson and Berridge (2003, 2008); Spanagel (2009); Volkow, Wang, Fowler, and Tomasi (2012).

[50] Also *see* Heinz et al. (2003); Breese, Overstreet, and Knapp (2005); Sinha and Li (2007); and Koob and Volknow (2010).

[51] Becker (2008).

[52] *See*, for example, Koob and Le Moal (2006, 2008). Koob and Le Moal (2008: 46) describe it this way: "the residual deviation from normal brain-reward threshold regulation is described as an allostatic state. This state represents a combination of chronic elevation of reward set point fueled by decreased function of reward circuits, recruitment of antireward systems, loss of executive control, and facilitation of stimulus-response associations, all of which lead to the compulsivity of drug seeking and drug taking . . . ."

[53] As Spanagel (2009: 661) said summarizing research on animals and humans: ". . . It may be postulated that neurochemical points of access directly modulating DAergic activity (e.g., GABA [gamma-aminobutyric acid], glutamate, serotonin, acetylcholine, glycine) must also play a crucial role in the acquisition of alcohol reinforcement."

[54] Heilig et al. (2010b: 336). *See* Spanagel (2009: 662-663) for a discussion of the possible role of endogenous opioids and endocannabinoids in the rewarding effects induced by alcohol.

[55] These areas include the hypothalamic paraventriculear nucleus (PVN), the central nucleus of the amygdala (CeA), the bed nucleus of stria terminalis (BNST), and the brainstem (Heilig et al. 2011: 676).

[56] This drug was naltrexone (an opioid antagonist, i.e., it blocks the actions of opioids), and the implications of its actions will be considered later in Chapter Nine when we examine treatment approaches.

[57] Cunningham and Breslin (2004), Dawson et al. (2005), Cohen et al. (2007), and Ko et al. (2010).

[58] Coehn et al. (2007), Dawson (1996), Cunnigham et al. (2000).

[59] Dawson et al. (2005), Dawson (1996), Dawson et al. (2007), de Bruijn et al. (2006).

[60] Also *see* Peele's (2007) discussion of these results.

[61] *See* Fingarette (1988); Peele (1989, 2007); and Pattison, Sobell, and Sobell (1977).

[62] Although a drinker may present the argument for reduced culpability,

whether or not significant people in his social network actually accept it is another question. Some research suggests that the medical model has not always helped alcoholics escape moral condemnation for their problems (*see* Room 1983: 69-73).

[63] Orford sees strong appetites as composed of at least three elements: affective attachment to the object of the appetite, behavior intention to consume or approach the object, and cognitive commitment to the object and its approach or consumption. The development of strong appetite can be attributed to the relative weight of incentives for appetitive behavior, or functions served by it, over the disincentives or restraints operating at each stage, plus the increasingly influential increment in attraction brought about by the powerful and complex learning and cognitive processes discussed [earlier] . . . [and] helped on by biological changes in the case of some drugs [1985: 207].

[64] Marlatt (1978); Cummings, Gordon, Marlatt (1980).

[65] In a reformulation of the abstinence violation effect (AVE), Marlatt (Marlatt and Gordon 1985: 179) argued that two elements comprise the AVE: "a cognitive attribution as to the perceived cause of the lapse coupled with an affective reaction to this attribution." In addition, "An increased AVE is postulated to occur when the individual attributes the cause of the lapse to internal, stable, and global factors that are perceived to be uncontrollable (e.g., lack of willpower and/or the emergence of the symptoms of an underlying addictive disease)."

[66] *See* Hinson (1985); Sherman, Jorenby, Baker (1988); Siegel (1983); Wikler (1977).

[67] Ternes (1977), cited in Hinson (1985: 114).

[68] *See* Marlett and Gordon (1985: 340-344); Sobell and Sobell (1995); Wilson (1988: 264-265, 273). Indeed, some studies report relapse rates in the 65% to 70% range within 90 days after treatment (Sinha 2011: 402).

[69] *See* Rehm et al. (2010) and Rehm (2011).

[70] *See* the relevant chapters in Preedy and Watson (2005) and Rehm (2011).

CHAPTER 8
ALCOHOL USE AMONG THE NEBRASKA WINNEBAGO: AN ETHNOHISTORICAL STUDY OF CHANGE AND ADJUSTMENT[1]

> I am a great man, I thought, and also a fleet runner. I was a good singer . . . . I was a sport and I wanted whiskey every day.
>> Big Winnebago before becoming a Peyotist

> All the evil that was in me I forgot. From that time to the present my actions have been quite different. . . . I am only working for what is good. . . .
>> Albert Hensley after becoming a Peyotist

Introduction

In the preceding chapters I have sketched a descriptive overview of, and offered analytic observations on, various facets of the life styles and drinking patterns of contemporary Sioux City Indians. The information presented was based primarily on my own observations of a sample of these individuals for one year and my consultants' comments on their own and other people's lives, both present and past. Although the focus tended to be on activities and events occurring during the period of my fieldwork, the implicit time frame was a bit longer, extending through at least the life spans of my consultants. A number of historical questions, however, remain unexplored: Have the drinking patterns observed always been present among the Indians? Did a hell-raising ethic only evolve in response to city life? When did drinking problems first occur among the tribes? If practices have changed, what forces shaped them? To answer these questions, we obviously need to add an ethnohistorical perspective. Although a complete ethnohistorical treatment of the tribes and their use of alcohol extend beyond the scope of this chapter, we can obtain a sense of the changing nature of the drinking patterns by examining their development among the Winnebago in Nebraska. It is primarily from this population that the Sioux City Winnebago derive. We shall discover that the extent of heavy drinking, in fact, has waxed and waned over time among the Winnebago and that the adoption and spread of the Peyote religion played a critical role in reorienting social life and controlling drinking during the early years of the 1900s. Our discussion of the Peyote religion will allow us to use the religion as a model in the next chapter to identify the social and psychological processes that can lead to successful treatments of problem drinking.

The Winnebago today are divided into two federally recognized entities: the *Ho-Chunk*[2] *Nation of Wisconsin* and the *Winnebago Tribe of Nebraska*. The division stems from the refusal of some Ho-Chunk to leave Wisconsin in spite of governmental efforts (including forced removal) to compel them to leave following treaties in 1832 and 1837. The Ho-Chunk who remained in, or continued to return to, Wisconsin became known as the disaffected bands, and eventually won official recognition from the government.[3] Nancy Lurie, an anthropologist who has studied the Ho-Chunk for many years, feels that those individuals who were more willing to adopt elements of the white man's life style moved out of Wisconsin. In the 1990s, the Winnebago in Wisconsin adopted the name of Ho-Chunk Nation, while those in Nebraska retained the name of the Winnebago Tribe of Nebraska. Because my consultants from this tribe preferred to call themselves Winnebago and most of the literature I cite uses that term that is the name I have used most frequently.

Before Nebraska

When first encountered by Europeans in the 1630s, the Winnebago were located in central and eastern Wisconsin subsisting by a mixture of horticulture, hunting, fishing, and gathering.[4] During the 1700s and early 1800s they spread along the drainages of the Fox,

Wisconsin, and Rock Rivers in Wisconsin and Illinois.[5] By 1860, while some 700 to 900 Winnebago remained in Wisconsin, the majority of the tribe had been settled on a reservation on the Blue Earth River in southern Minnesota. After the Sioux uprising of 1862, the settlers in Minnesota demanded that the Winnebago be removed from the state even though they had little to do with the uprising.[6] Under an act of Congress, the Winnebago were to be removed to a new reservation outside the boundaries of any existing state.[7] Consequently, in 1863 the majority of the Minnesota Winnebago (1,954 individuals) traveled to Crow Creek, Dakota Territory (South Dakota), where their new reservation was located.[8] The Winnebago were very unhappy with their new land. Brigadier General Sulley, who was temporarily located near Crow Creek, wrote a letter on their behalf to the Secretary of the Interior describing their land and situation:

> The land is poor; a low, sandy soil. I don't think you can depend on a crop of corn, even once in five years, as it seldom rains here in the summer. There is no hunting in their immediate vicinity, and the bands of Sioux near here are hostile to them. If they ever do procure anything worth stealing, they will be subject to depredations from small parties from the upper Indians without a military force is constantly kept here to guard them.

> They, the Winnebagoes, tell me they are friends of the Omahas, and speak nearly the same language. It is their wish to be united with them on the Omaha reservation, and, as they say, the Omahas are in favor of this also.[9]

The Winnebago did not wait for official approval and began leaving for the Omaha reservation. The difficulties endured during their migrations to the Omaha were severe. George Graff, a resident in Nebraska Territory, described the conditions of a party of over 500 Winnebago who were traveling downriver and landed near South Sioux City on their way to the Omaha: "Their plight was pitiable— children famishing and eleven have been buried from starvation."[10]

When the Indians finally arrived at the Omaha and other nearby agencies, the hard-pressed agents had to feed and care for them with their existing supplies and budgets. Although the agents were not able to provide all the materials the Winnebago needed, they prevented actual starvation. George Graff, who visited the Winnebago on the Omaha reservation in April 1864, reported: "They are now apparently comfortable—but have neither Robes, Blankets or a single Pony—They are subsisted by Agent Furnas—but it will be deplorable if they shall have no opportunity to raise corn before another year."[11] By September of 1864 Agent Furnas reported there were over 1,200 Winnebago on the Omaha reservation.[12]

A Reservation in Nebraska: the Early Period, 1865-1885

After providing enough care to prevent starvation, the government had to decide what to do with the Winnebago. Following several investigations of conditions at Crow Creek and the Omaha reservation, the Winnebago were allowed to remain in Nebraska Territory on land purchased from the Omaha. The Winnebago signed a treaty of March 8, 1865, that gave them a reservation of some 100,000 acres adjacent to the Omaha reservation and located about 23 miles south of Sioux City, Iowa. Under the terms of the treaty the government was obligated to erect a saw and grist mill; to break and fence 100 acres of land for each band; to provide the Indians with seed, livestock, and various kinds of equipment; and to construct several buildings including an agency building, a school house, and houses for various agency personnel and band chiefs.[13]

In the years following the signing of the treaty the Winnebago agents attempted to implement its terms and tried to make the Indians self-sufficient through farming. Both the Winnebago and their agents believed (although for different reasons) that it would be advantageous to allot some of the Winnebago land in severalty, i.e., to individuals. The Indians appear to have viewed this as a means of helping insure their possession of the land. The agents, in contrast, desired allotment primarily for its supposed "civilizing" effects, as

Agent Charles Mathewson indicated in a letter to E. B. Taylor, Superintendent of Indian Affairs, Northern Superintendency:

> The Winnebagoes are very desirous to have their land allotted to them so that they can live upon their own farms. If this could be done I think it would tend more to civilize them than any one act on the part of the Department—inasmuch as it would break up their banding together and spending their time in gambling and other vises. If this could be done they would be more industrious and many of them would become good farmers and with the stock which they now possess would be self sustaining [Mathewson 1866].

The government eventually agreed to the allotments, and the work of surveying the land began in the fall of 1869. Each head of a family was allotted 80 acres, and single males and females over 18 years without families received 40 acres. Over 400 allotments eventually were made.

Almost twenty years later, after the Dawes Severalty Act was passed in February 1887, another allotment was arranged because, as Agent Mathewson reported: "only about one-half of the original allottees could be found or identified. This was owing to the fact that English names were arbitrarily given them at the time of the first allotment and the failure to retain the English names also" (CIA-AR 1899: 231). Under the terms of the Dawes Act each head of a family was to receive 160 acres, single individuals over 18 years were to get 80 acres, and orphan children under 18 years 40 acres. Following these allotments, the President was empowered to negotiate with the tribe and purchase the remaining, unallotted Indian lands which could then, in turn, be opened to public sales.

During the 20 years that followed the first allotments the agents continued their attempts to "civilize" and make farmers of the Indians. Throughout this period Winnebago agricultural productivity and self-sufficiency did increase. The following figures comparing the Winnebago's situation at ten-year intervals give some measure of these changes:

Table 1 Winnebago Agricultural Productivity

	1869	1879	1889
Number of acres cultivated by the Winnebago:	300 acres	2,500 acres	4,300 acres
Bushels of wheat raised by the Winnebago:	200 bushels	9,300 bushels	2,000 bushels
Bushels of corn raised by the Winnebago:	6,000 bushels	25,200 bushels	125,000 bushels
Tons of hay cut by the Winnebago:	None	1,025 tons	4,000 tons
Number of houses occupied by the Winnebago:	23 frame houses	105 frame or log houses	198 houses[14]

Although some Winnebago were becoming successful farmers, others preferred to work for wages. In the summer of 1872, for example, about 200 men worked for white settlers in the area helping to bring in the harvest (CIA-AR 1872: 219). In 1879 their agent reported that "[t]heir services are in demand for all kinds of farm work and for cutting and hauling wood, &c., and in this way they earn thousands of dollars every year" (CIA-AR 1879: 107). Although such activities were beneficial in that they provided sources of income for the Indians and increased their contacts with, and knowledge of, white procedures, the agent also felt that they caused the Indians "to neglect the tillage and improvement of their own farms on the reservation" (CIA-AR 1879: 107). This tendency for some men to prefer wage labor over agricultural pursuits was noted by another agent five years later:

> Many of them are good farmers and occupy their farms at all seasons. Others occupy their farms during crop season and then put their children in school and take the remainder of

their family to the timber for the winter, where they engage in chopping and logging until seed time comes again. They fully understand the value of their labor and drive close bargains with their employers. They, as a tribe, prefer to be day laborers rather than farmers [CIA-AR 1884: 119].

The first day school for the Nebraska Winnebago was established in 1868 (CIA-AR 1868: 237). Later, an on-reservation boarding school and several off-reservation boarding schools also became available. The schools did not have much impact during this period because not all children attended and those who did, attended irregularly. The agent in 1878, for example, noted that there were 572 children between the ages of 6 and 17, and no more than one-fourth of these attended school during any part of the year (CIA-AR 1878: 101). Later, when attendance became more closely regulated, and as more students were sent to schools off the reservation, the traditional enculturation process—the pattern of fasting,[15] winter story-telling, formal lectures from older Winnebago, and informal observations and imitative play of adult life—became increasingly disrupted.[16] Religious changes also came slowly during these years. Although the Presbyterians had a missionary among the Nebraska Winnebago from 1881 into the 1900s, their proselytizing met with only limited success. The agent in 1884, for example, remarked that the Winnebago still "have more faith in the teachings of their medicine men than in Gospel teachings" (CIA-AR 1884: 119). And by the end of the 1880s their agent complained: "The medicine dance or lodge [a religious society] still holds the great body of these people firmly" (CIA-AR 1889: 240).

Drinking During the Early Period. In the years immediately preceding the Winnebago's removal from Minnesota in 1863, their agents and other governmental officials considered alcohol use to be a problem for the tribe (CIA-AR 1861: 706). Their agent in 1860 reported that a council of Winnebago, on their own accord (at least as the agent stated it), established a series of laws that prescribed punishment for particular offenses, including one month's confinement for drunkenness or bringing liquor onto reservation land (CIA-AR 1860: 297). Such data would suggest that at least some Winnebago felt drinking was enough of a problem to warrant defining drunkenness as a crime (or at least acquiescing to the agent's wishes to do so).

In contrast to the Winnebago's Minnesota experiences, alcohol use in Nebraska, from their arrival until the 1890s, does not appear to have been viewed as a major problem, although instances of drinking and intoxication occurred throughout this period. In 1868 the tribe accepted, by unanimous vote, a set of laws proposed by H. B. Denman, Superintendent of Indian Affairs, Northern Superintendency. The code made drinking a crime and also established a police force composed of seven members of the tribe: one captain, one lieutenant, and five privates. The force was paid by the tribe out of its annuity money and was supervised by the agent.[17] As a result of this action, the tribal council and Indian police became involved in controlling drinking. Offenders were brought before the tribal council of chiefs and the agent who determined the guilt of the offenders and passed sentences. Dr. Joseph Paxson, who served as the tribe's physician for one year (1869-70), reported a number of drinking violations in his diary but did not furnish many details. The following passage contains one of his longer descriptions of such a violation and provides details of the judicial process:

> Attended a trial during the afternoon. A number of the young men had been drinking to an excess. They have a 'Code of laws' among them, which makes drinking a great crime, and one that must be punished. The 'Chiefs' act as a jury and sometimes as the Judges. Nine out of the 14teen chiefs are required to constitute a quorum. The trials are usually held in a building known as the 'Council House,' but the day being pleasant it was held out under a tree. The 'Chiefs' seat themselves on the ground in the form of a circle, with the prisoner in the center. After an examination of the witnesses, by the agent, through the interpreter, or some one

for him, a chief will make a speech, as prosecuting attorney. The 'Chief of Police' or someone for him will act as district attorney. Sometimes the 'Chiefs' will act as a jury and select someone for the judge, in this case the subscriber acted as such. An examination of the witnesses found that whiskey had been bought, from the mate of a steamboat which was returning from up the river, and had stopped at the wood-yard for wood.

The Indians claimed that the law had [not?] been enforced on them before, hence they thought it would not now. Another said that he drank to test the law. Feeling that as this might now be a lesson to them, they were all discharged, with an earnest request to 'sin no more.' After this Little De Corii made a long speech, promising that each chief would look after his Band, and he then cautioned their young men that they must not drink, but be good men and not offend the great Father, meaning the President [Sellers 1946: 154-155].

Other offenders of the drinking law did not escape as lightly, for Paxson later indicated that two males were placed in the Winnebago's "jail" for 10 days and another man was sentenced to three months (Sellers 1946: 162). White men caught selling alcohol to the Indians were also prosecuted (Griffith 1869), and in one case the agent succeeded in obtaining enough evidence against a saloon keeper in Sioux City, Iowa to bring him to trial (CIA-AR 1872: 219).

In addition to these social control techniques developed and guided by the Indian agents, the tribe appears to have reestablished some of the police and disciplinary functions that traditionally had been vested in members of the Bear clan.[18] One of their duties consisted of controlling drunken individuals who disturbed the peace of a village. As the Winnebago established themselves in Nebraska, they settled into at least seven villages in the timbered, eastern part of their reservation. The distribution of the clans among the villages and the manner in which members of the Bear clan carried out their duties is not known in any detail, but when anthropologist Nancy Lurie conducted field research among the Nebraska Winnebago in the summer of 1950, some of her older consultants (born around 1870) remembered the social control actions of the Bear clan (Lurie 1952: 155-157). Exactly how long these kinds of traditional control techniques were used is unknown. It is possible that they played some role as long as the Winnebago remained in villages in the timbered part of the reservation. Although the Indian agents tried to induce the Winnebago to permanently move out of the timber onto their lands allotted in the western two-thirds of the reservation, they had little success. Families frequently would move out to their western lands for the summer, but return to the eastern timber for the winter.[19] It was only in the first decade of the 1900s that this pattern was completely broken.

How did the agents perceive Winnebago drinking during this period? In 1884 their agent, George Wilkinson, observed that they "are disposed to gamble and take a drink when occasion offers" (CIA-AR 1884: 119). Five years later, Agent Jesse Warner, while indicating that it was remarkable that there was so little crime among the Winnebago, also noted that he had to contend with a "few plain drunks" (CIA-AR 1889: 239). In general, observers during this period indicated that while heavy drinking and intoxication occurred among the tribe, such behaviors did not constitute a major problem; drunkenness was viewed as being no worse than among the same number of white Nebraskans.[20]

Years of Change

During the late 1880s and early 1890s two factors led to a reversal of Winnebago agricultural growth and to changes in their drinking patterns. One was the growth of the white population in areas bordering on the Winnebago reservation. The white population of the five counties bordering the reservation went from 21,000 in 1880 to 43,000 in 1890. By 1900 the white population in the five counties had risen to over 54,000.[21] As the number of settlers increased, attempts to use or obtain Indian land also increased. Some settlers, for example, would claim to have obtained a lease from an Indian which supposedly gave the settler the right to graze his cattle on the Indian's land. Although such leases were illegal until 1891, the agent faced a difficult time prosecuting the settlers. As the agent in 1889 complained:

> The statutes of the United States provide a penalty of $1 per head for each head of cattle driven upon the reservation but this is in the nature of a civil action and can not be brought except by order of the Department of Justice. Such action can not be brought to a successful termination during the herding season. The man under the cover of a pretended lease from one or more Indians has overrun all others near by, their crops are destroyed, and grass for hay eaten up. The fellow is gone, the cattle are distributed to their various owners. These herders are impecunious, and if a judgment is finally rendered it is not worth the paper upon which it is written. The next year a new set of herders repeat the farce of the preceding year, and so on [CIA-AR 1889: 239].

With new towns arising on the edges of the reservation, the Indians obtained increased opportunities to purchase alcohol. The agents attempted to prevent such sales, but it was difficult to do so. Even in those cases in which a guilty party was apprehended and a conviction was obtained, the punishment was frequently so light that it did not serve as a deterrent. In two cases brought to court in 1890, each defendant was fined one dollar and costs. The agent at the time observed: "Such slight punishment inspires no fear, and without the hearty co-operation of the Federal courts we can do little" (CIA-AR 1890: 138).

The second major event that shaped the lives of the Winnebago at this time was a legal one: on February 28, 1891 Congress passed an act that allowed Indians to lease their allotted lands to whites. The act was intended to help single women, aged or infirm males, and minor children who possessed land but were unable to farm it themselves. Until this act was passed, there was no legal way for such individuals to derive income from their lands. This was a serious problem; by 1890, at least 60 percent of the allotted land among the Winnebago belonged to people who were unable to work it themselves (CIA-AR 1890: 138). However, the act had unanticipated consequences: once a leasing option became available it became a frequent choice of able-bodied individuals not committed to an agricultural way of life. Many white settlers, of course, were pleased with the act and did whatever they could to secure leases from the Indians. One of the Indians' agents writing in 1892 commented on the settlers' reactions:

> The pressure which is brought to bear on those [Indians] who hold the most desirable lands, in the vicinity of the towns, is very great, and if the present condition continues, in a very short time, little if any of these lands will be in the hands of the allottees. Companies are formed whose sole business is in dealing in these leases. They have large interests at stake; they have the towns adjoining the reservation all working with them to the same end, that these lands may be gotten from the Indians, from under the control of the Government, to be occupied by the whites [CIA-AR 1892: 186].

The agent's comments proved to be prophetic, for by 1902 the Indians cultivated only some 3,500 acres and produced only 3,000 bushels of wheat, 10,000 bushels of corn, and 500 tons of hay (CIA-AR 1902: 654). The agent in that year described their situation as "decidedly gloomy" and offered this assessment and analysis:

> Little if any advance is being made, and in many particulars the reverse is true. Less land is being cultivated each year, and the character of the farming is poor. They are better clothed and fed than ever before in their history, but 'they toil not, neither do they spin.' The rentals from their leases supply all their wants. They have an abundance of land not leased, but they do not work it, and any rules in regard to the leasing of their lands or the payment of the rentals simply react on the aged men, women, and children. The

communistic spirit is so strong that if the able-bodied men are not allowed to lease their land or draw rentals, they will simply live off of the helpless class who may lease [CIA-AR 1903: 240-241].

The Spread of Heavy Drinking and Drinking-Related Activities

During this period when Winnebago agricultural interests and pursuits were waning, alcohol use rose dramatically. The increase appears to have developed throughout the 1890s and to have reached a high in the early 1900s. The agent in 1894, while indicating that heavy drinking was present, did not view it with great alarm: "The tribe as a whole is not addicted to drunkenness, and yet a number of them drink; some of them, at times become very intoxicated" (CIA-AR 1895: 189). In contrast, by 1904 drinking was regarded as a major problem. The Winnebago drinking patterns for this year can be described in greater detail thanks to an investigation that was held at the Winnebago reservation to examine the charges made by one Joseph Schell. He maintained in letters to the Commissioner of Indian Affairs and in newspaper articles that a variety of corrupt practices prevailed on the Winnebago reservation. A. O. Wright, Supervisor of Indian Schools for the Interior Department, was empowered by the Commissioner of Indian Affairs to investigate the charges and in so doing took sworn testimony from a variety of local individuals. The transcripts of the testimony provide important data on the drinking practices of the time. Although the Winnebago were able to purchase alcohol at a number of towns in the area, Homer, which was located north of the reservation on the road to Sioux City, Iowa, appears to have been the major spot where alcohol was obtained (T. Ashford 1904). The most detailed information regarding the number of Winnebago who drank fairly heavily came from three merchants of Homer who had traded with the Indians for many years and spoke at least some Winnebago. The following testimony is that of C. J. O'Connor (1904):

Q. Is drunkennes[s] prevalent among them?

A. Yes Sir.

Q. To about what extent did you say?

A. I suppose there are about 100 adult men and women who get drunk every once in a while.

Q. About how many women?

A. About 12 or 15 Indian women.

Q. About how many to your knowledge are total abstainers?

A. I know about 35 or 40 men and women who do not touch whisky and have never seen them drink liquor.

John Ashford (1904) testified:

Q. What are their general habits in regard to intemperance?

A. Well, that [sic] are about 1200 Indians on this reservation and I will say that there are in the neighborhood of 150 of those Indians who drink a good deal and probably about 20 habitual drunkards.

Q. How many of these Indians are women?

A. 10 or 12 women are habitual drunkards, and there are many Indians who very seldom leave the agency and come to town and cannot say as to their habits.

Q. How many adult Indian men and women you are reasonably sure that never drin[k] a drop?

A. I have no faith in an Indian who is exposed to liquor and there are a very few don't drink and I think there are probably half a dozen Indians on the reservation I have never seen drinking.

Q. Have you had a [sic] occasion to see numbers of these Indians drunk on the street of Homer?

A. Yes sir.

Thomas Ashford, Jr. (1904) made similar statements:

Q. About how many adult Indian women do you think are occasional drunkards and about how many habitual drunkards?

A. I have seen some Indians I would call drunkards. For a time they will sober up and say they have quite [*sic*] and in a few days later they would be drunk. There are about 10 or 12 who are habitual drunkards and some are women.

Q. How many occasional drunkards?

A. A large number of the adults in this tribe.

Q. About how many are total abstainers?

A. I can call to mind 5 or 6. These are men only. I do not know much about women.

Q. Have you frequently seen men and women drunk on the streets of Homer?

A. Yes.

Q. Have you seen many at one time?

A. On big days there would be a good many.

Other long-time residents in the area, while not indicating the range of drinking behaviors or estimating the number of different types of drinkers, did provide descriptions of those individuals who, at least on occasion, drank heavily. Mark Hunter, who was a justice of the peace for the Winnebago precinct in Thurston County, offered this account when asked to describe the "condition of the Winnebagoes in regard to the intemperance":

It is very bad. There is much drunkenness among them. One time I went to Homer with my wife and we counted forty-one drunken Indians on our way there, and often we had to drive on the bank as they would not give us a part of the road. They would call us names. Several different times I would meet from fifteen to thirty drunken Indians, both men and women [Hunter 1904].

A farmer who had lived in the area for about five years said:

The Indians would get their liquor in Homer, and some of them when they go home drive through my place which is not a public highway. I have seen from four or five to fifteen teams a day and there would be all the way from one to four Indians drunk in the wagon, women as well as men. I have seen them buy whisky from bootleggers every time I have been in Homer [Frum 1904].

Joseph Schell, the individual who precipitated the investigation, responded to a question asking him if he had ever seen any bad effects of liquor on the Indians:

I think when I see men and women and children laying pellmell in their wagons, one upon top of the other, without being able to take care of themselves or of their babies, moaning and groaning like wounded beasts; when I see women on the main street of Homer being so drunk that 2, 3 or 4 men have to come and pick them up like an inanimate object and throw them in the back end of their spring wagon, groaning and moaning, and drive them away, I think there can not be any other effect worse than that [Schell n.d.].

Although the testimony of these men may be suspect on some points, it does give us the broad outlines of the Winnebago drinking practices for 1904 and demonstrates that the patterns were complex. A fairly large number of Winnebago seem to have accepted the use of alcohol. Of this number perhaps 100 to 150 men and women (12 to 18 percent of the adult population) drank heavily at times with about 10 to 20 individuals doing so fairly frequently. It is also clear, however, that some tribal members seldom, if ever, drank.

An Insider's View. Although this information is the most detailed available on the number of individuals engaging in particular types of drinking, it still leaves many questions unanswered, the most important ones relating to the meanings and functions that these drinking practices had for the Winnebago. Under what circumstances did a person adopt a particular type of drinking? How were the various drinking practices evaluated by different segments of the tribe? How did the drinking activities relate to various phases of the life cycle? Although the unpublished documents are silent on these questions, some relevant and

suggestive information is provided by the autobiography of a
Wisconsin Ho-Chunk, "Big Winnebago" (also called Crashing
Thunder, Sam Blowsnake, or Sam Carley). Big Winnebago was born
in Wisconsin in 1875.[22] He gave his life history to anthropologist Paul
Radin who first published it in 1920 and then reissued it in a
different form in 1926.[23] Although Big Winnebago was raised among
the Wisconsin Ho-Chunk, he had relatives in Nebraska and visited
them several times.[24] On one visit to Nebraska, which probably
occurred in 1906, drinking figured prominently in his activities:

> I arrived in Nebraska in midsummer (celebration time). . . . I
> arrived very early in the morning and there I met a man
> whom I had once known. He used to go about with me.
> There were many people. We sat somewhat away from them
> and the man and his wife drank with me. . . . Then they took
> me to the place where they lived. They hauled my things for
> me.
>
> The next morning the Nebraska Winnebago were going to
> celebrate. They were coming together for a week. They had a
> large gathering. The people with whom I was staying went
> out and camped with those at the gathering. Two men
> arrived there. They recognized me and shook hands with
> me. They were riding in a buggy and I got in with them.
> They took me far away. On the road they stopped. We got
> out of the buggy and took out a jug containing four quarts of
> (whiskey). Then they had me drink with them. After that
> they brought me back to the gathering . . . .
>
> It was a large gathering and we danced every day. I got
> ready also and danced, and there I gave away my things. . . .
> After (the celebration) I remained there for a long time. I even
> got married there. I kept on drinking all the time. . . .
>
> Some time after that I went to visit an uncle of mine. . . . He
> said, 'Nephew, tomorrow they are going to have a Medicine
> Dance. Tonight they are going to have the trial dance. Your

aunt is going to buy provisions for the meal and you may go along with her.' So I went with her. When we got to town we drank. On the following day it was rumored that the woman and myself were missing. . . . The buggy we were riding in was broken up; my hat was gone and my trousers were torn open. I immediately went back to the place where I had come from, although the Medicine Dance was taking place. The woman, it was said, was still missing.[25]

Episodes like this one, and others in his life history, suggest that alcohol use was seen as an important element in having a good time. Drinking figured in socializing or visiting,[26] sexual encounters,[27] fighting,[28] robbery,[29] and work.[30] The positive or enjoyable evaluation of these activities can be seen in Big Winnebago's description of the events that occurred after the Ho-Chunk in Wisconsin received a payment of money from the government:

All who liked this kind of life, all who used to chase around for the fun of it, (would be there).There marriages would get badly mixed up, the stealing of one another's wives, fighting, robbery of one another's money. Even those married people who had been faithful to each other until then, would become unfaithful on this occasion. Many would be hurt here. And when the last payment was over, all those who had not spent their last cent on drink would begin gambling and the men and women would play poker. Only when our last cent was gone, would we stop and settle down. Many of us were generally left without enough money to go home . . . .[31]

These drinking-related activities, in addition to offering pleasure and excitement to the participants, were also compatible with some of the "traditional" values of Winnebago culture and could be used to claim or express a positive identity. Before Big Winnebago converted to the Peyote religion, he joined a group of Wisconsin Ho-Chunk during their midsummer ceremony. His description of his behavior clearly shows his positive view of himself at the time:

I went there and took part and I drank all the time. I considered myself a brave man and a medicine man and I also thought myself a holy man, a strong man, and a favorite with women . . . . I regarded myself as being in possession of many courting medicines. I am a great man, I thought, and also a fleet runner. I was a good singer of Brave Dance songs. I was a sport and I wanted whiskey every day.[32]

Although it appears that a good number of Winnebago regarded drinking and intoxication positively, as one element in having a good time, it is also clear that drinking occurred at times of stress and was used as a means of coping with unpleasant emotions. After Big Winnebago's older brother was killed, he began to drink more heavily. As he put it: "I wanted to die drinking, that is what I used to say, while I was drinking so heavily" (Radin 1963 [1920]: 26). This motivation for drinking soon changed, however: "After a while I became a confirmed drunkard. I had by this time quite forgotten that I wanted to die, and really enjoyed drinking very much."[33]

Implications. Big Winnebago's autobiography, then, indicates that alcohol was used in a variety of ways depending upon the circumstances surrounding the drinker. Given the diverse activities in which heavy drinking could play a part, it is apparent that whites unfamiliar with Winnebago life might easily misunderstand Winnebago drinking behaviors, focusing primarily on the use of alcohol and classifying all drinking-related behaviors as "drinking" or "drunkenness." As a result, they would miss much of the social and psychological diversity present in the origins and effects of the activities in question.

The diversity in drinking practices was not limited solely to overt behavior; it was also present in the standards used to evaluate drinking-related activities. Although many Winnebago approved of drinking, some did not, and if they had the right, would apply negative social sanctions to drunken individuals when they exceeded the limits of acceptable behavior. On one occasion, for example, Big Winnebago visited his family while he was drunk, and as he related:

"My relatives saw me and saw that I was drunk. They were sorry and an older sister of mine wept when she saw me. Then I made up my mind that I would not do it again."[34] Although Big Winnebago does not specify in what manner his relatives, other than his older sister, acted, it is clear that they communicated their displeasure with his behavior to him. Big Winnebago also provided an example in which negative sanctions were used to control particular kinds of drunken comportment. When Big Winnebago drank, he sometimes became belligerent and involved in fights; as a result, he often sobered up to find himself tied up.[35]

Based on Big Winnebago's autobiography and the observations of outside observers, it seems clear that differing sets of drinking standards existed among the Winnebago. However, the information is not rich enough to allow us to describe in any detail the manner in which a given individual's definition of "acceptable drinking" varied in relation to the person and situation considered. For a given set of circumstances, for example, what was seen as acceptable drinking for young, unmarried men, might not have been so considered for married women with children. Although we also are unable to determine how drinking standards related to stages of the life cycle, Big Winnebago does provide a suggestive statement. After pointing out that on one occasion he had four children by four different women, Big Winnebago added: "Nevertheless even after that I still courted women and kept drinking."[36] The implicit point being that having reached such a stage in life, a man ideally should not continue to behave as he did. If this is an accurate interpretation of his statement, it would be similar, as we have seen, to the views taken of "hell-raising" activities by contemporary Winnebago.[37]

The negative view of drinking among the Winnebago was not necessarily due to Christian or other religious influences.[38] Nancy Lurie (1961b: 130) has pointed out that Mountain Wolf Woman, a younger sister of Big Winnebago, was strongly against drinking. Her attitude developed before she became a Peyotist and was based on her own observations of the effects of drunkenness. In addition to any negative views of drinking that had developed within

Winnebago society on the basis of personal experiences, the "official" representatives of white America—Indian agents, teachers, missionaries—with whom the Winnebago had been in contact for many years, presented a critical attitude toward heavy drinking. As increasing numbers of Winnebago went to school, became Christians, and began adopting elements of white life styles, the "official" and negative view of heavy drinking had a greater influence on their own standards. Nonetheless, in contrast to this critical evaluation of drinking-related activities, many Winnebago not only tolerated, but positively viewed some of these activities. Similar views were also found among segments of the white population such as bootleggers, soldiers, and some settlers. Interaction with these people helped reinforce these attitudes among the Winnebago.[39]

Sociocultural Regeneration

Many drinking-related activities, although regarded as enjoyable by the participants, carried "hidden liabilities" that only became apparent over time. Thus, a man might engage in heavy drinking for a number of years and enjoy it very much, but as he became older, he might discover that he could no longer control his drinking. This was apparently the case with Big Winnebago's father.[40] As drinking-related activities increased throughout the late 1800s and early 1900s these liabilities, hidden and otherwise, which included erratic work performances, neglect of kinship obligations, marital and family instability, economic hardships, legal problems, and poor health, also increased. In response to a growing dissatisfaction with these aspects of Winnebago life, several social forces, both internal and external to Winnebago society, developed to correct them.

One of the most important internal developments was the adoption and spread of the Peyote religion.[41] Although some Winnebago appear to have had experience with peyote at least as early as the late 1880s,[42] its use was not widely accepted until about 1903 or 1904.[43] The Winnebago superintendent[44] made this comment in the 1906 Annual Report: "The use of the mescal bean [peyote] was introduced among the Winnebagoes within the past two years and many of the Indians have organized themselves into what is known as the Mescal Society. This is claimed by the members to be a religious organization and as there seems to be no law against the use of the mescal bean it is very hard to do anything with them" (CIA-AR 1907: 268). John Rave, the Winnebago regarded by other tribal members as the man responsible for introducing the Peyote religion to the tribe, underwent a dramatic change in life style following his conversion to the Peyote religion in Oklahoma during 1893-94. As he put it:

> Before that [conversion] my heart was filled with murderous thoughts. I wanted to kill my brother and sister. It seemed to me that my heart would not feel good until I killed one of them. All of my thoughts were fixed on the warpath. That is all I thought of. Now I know that it was because the evil spirit possessed me that I felt that way. I was suffering from a disease. I even desired to kill myself; I did not care to live. That feeling, too, was caused by this evil spirit living within me. Then I ate this medicine [peyote] and everything changed. The brother and sister I wanted to kill before[,] I became attached to and I wanted them to live. The medicine had accomplished this.[45]

Rave's view of his behavior before and after his conversion is supported by other Winnebago although some inconsistencies exist regarding the date of his change in behavior. Oliver Lamere, who was a member of the religion and served as an interpreter for Radin, for example, describes the introduction of the Peyote religion among the Winnebago in this fashion:

> Rave . . . was a bad man. He roamed from place to place. He participated in all the ceremonies of the Winnebago, the medicine dance alone excepted. He had been married many times. Up to 1901 he was a heavy drinker. In that year he went to Oklahoma and while there he ate the peyote. He then returned to the Winnebago and tried to introduce it among them, but none with the exception of a few relatives would

have anything to do with it. This did not in any way discourage him, however, and he continued using peyote, now and then getting a few more converts.

There was not very much religion connected with it in the beginning and the reason people drank it[46] was on account of the peculiar effects it had upon them. Nevertheless these Peyote people preached good things and gradually lost all desire for intoxicating drinks or for participating in the old Winnebago ceremonies. Then Rave began to do away with the old Indian customs. About four or five years ago the membership in the Peyote religion began to increase, for many people now noticed that those connected with the Peyote cult were the only people in the tribe leading a Christian life.[47]

What did it mean to become a Peyotist? First, of course, there was participation in the peyote ceremony performed during an all-night meeting and consisting of praying, meditating, singing, drumming, and eating peyote or drinking peyote tea. Because the peyote cactus (*Lophophora williamsii*) contains over 55 alkaloids, including mescaline and other psychoactive alkaloids, visions are sometimes produced.[48] Even though the religion obviously contained "traditional" Indian traits (but not necessarily Winnebago traits), the Winnebago Peyotists strongly viewed themselves as Christians—identifying Earthmaker (a traditional deity) with the Christian God, reading the Bible, confessing sins publicly, baptizing new converts, and singing peyote songs containing Christian ideas. Although other Winnebago also claimed to have introduced the Bible into the religion, there is no doubt that Albert Hensley was responsible for incorporating a number of Christian elements into the ceremony in the early 1900s.[49] The Winnebago Peyotists did not formally systematize or codify their religion's ethics in a written document, but their beliefs are apparent in their comments to Paul Radin during 1908-1913 when he was studying the tribe. It is clear that at least the leaders of the Peyotists were actively opposed to many traditional beliefs and ceremonies, such as those associated with war-bundles, the Medicine Lodge (a religious society),[50] and the use of traditional medicines.[51] After Big Winnebago had agreed to become a member, he gave up his "courting medicines." When he relinquished them his brother-in-law, a Peyotist, told him "that Earthmaker (God) alone was holy, that all the things (blessings and medicines) that I possessed, were false; that I had been fooled by the bad spirit (devil)."[52] Later, Big Winnebago himself said: "(It is false), this giving of (pagan) feasts, of holding (the old) things holy, the Medicine Dance, and all the Indian customs."[53] At the same time Big Winnebago gave up his courting medicines, he also had his long hair cut after his relatives showed him a passage in the Bible which said "that it was a shame for any man to wear long hair."[54]

Peyotists were expected to be legally married and to remain faithful to their spouses. Before Big Winnebago joined the religion he tried, in fact, to use this belief as an excuse for not eating peyote. In response to the urgings of his relatives to attend a meeting, Big Winnebago told his sister:

> I would be quite willing to eat this peyote (ordinarily), but I don't like the woman with whom I am living just now and I think I will leave her. That is why I do not want to join now, for I understand that when married people eat medicine (peyote) they will always have to stay together. Therefore I will join when I am married to some woman permanently.[55]

The use of liquor and tobacco were prohibited. When Big Winnebago's father described the behavior of the Peyotists he told Big Winnebago that they stopped drinking. In addition, "They also stop smoking and chewing tobacco. They stop giving feasts, and they stop making offerings of tobacco."[56]

Followers of the religion were expected to work regularly and to help one another in any manner they could. These expectations can be seen as Albert Hensley talked to Radin about his own life. Hensley returned to the Winnebago reservation in 1895 after six and a half years at Carlisle (a government boarding school in

Pennsylvania). He became a member of the religion around 1903 or 1904:

> After that [beginning to eat peyote] I married and now I have three children, and it would not have been right for me to continue in my wickedness. I resolved that thereafter I would behave as a grown-up man ought to behave. I resolved never to be idle again and to work so that I could supply my wife and children with food and necessities, that I would be ready to help them whenever they were in need.[57]

If an individual failed to live up to the religion's ethics, he was expected to repent. Public confession of these past sins was important, as Oliver Lamere indicated: "If a person eats peyote and does not repent openly, he has a guilty conscience, which leaves him as soon as the public repentance has been made."[58]

Appeal of Peyotism. Why did this religion spread so quickly among the Winnebago during the early 1900s? I believe its appeal was due to four major factors. First, peyote was seen as having the power to cure illness. Second, the new religion prohibited the consumption of alcohol. Third, Peyotism brought the promise of redemption for past failures and a moral code which provided a framework for future success. Fourth, because the consumption of peyote can produce visions and other states of altered consciousness, it provides empirical evidence of its power and, thereby, the truth of the religion. An additional factor concerning the Peyotists' method of recruitment should also be mentioned. In the early years, the religion spread through the tribe along family lines. As Radin noted: "As soon as an individual had become a peyote eater he devoted all his energies to converting other members of his family."[59] This is significant because it suggests that a person might be induced to try peyote and become a member even though he was not unhappy or dissatisfied with his life. Once he began participating, however, the experience of the ritual, the "power" of peyote, and the social interactions with other Peyotists may have made a "true believer" out of him. As we will see, this appears to be what happened to Big Winnebago.

That peyote was seen as having the power to cure is apparent in the claims made by many of the first converts.[60] Radin noted this himself:

> The first and foremost virtue predicated by Rave for the peyote was its curative power. He gives a number of instances in which hopeless venereal diseases and consumption were cured by its use; and this was the first thing one heard about it as late as 1913. In the early days of the Peyote cult it appears that Rave relied principally for new converts upon the knowledge of this great curative virtue of the peyote. The main point apparently was to induce people to try it. . . . [I]t is highly significant that all the old members of the Peyote cult speak of the diseases of which it cured them. Along this line lay unquestionably its appeal for the most converts.[61]

The power of peyote to cure illness would have been of great significance to the Winnebago at this time because they were suffering from variety of disorders. Venereal diseases, tuberculosis, and trachoma (an infectious disease of the cornea and conjunctiva) were prevalent. In 1903, Dr. Hart, the Winnebago's physician, estimated that probably forty percent were afflicted by venereal diseases (Hart 1903). As Hart noted, accurately determining the number of Winnebago infected was difficult because they rarely consulted a physician and these diseases were apt to go unobserved and unreported. His estimate was probably fairly correct, however, for later in 1915 a hospital was constructed in the town of Winnebago and examinations for venereal diseases became a routine practice. Between 1922 and 1925, a physician made over 500 examinations for venereal diseases and found 84 percent positive (Moore 1928). These cases were not, of course, randomly selected, but they indicate the magnitude of the problem and are in keeping with other observations and estimations made during this period. Although tuberculosis had been noted among the Winnebago by earlier observers, the most accurate determination of its prevalence was based on a study conducted by Margaret Koenig in 1919. On the basis of agency records and field investigation, she concluded that for the decade from 1909 to 1919 a conservative estimate would be "that at least one out of every eight Winnebago [was] suffering from some form of tuberculosis, either active or latent" (Koenig 1921: 21). In 1915, as a result of a special investigation, trachoma was estimated to afflict about 50 percent of the total population (Dewey 1915). This figure was based on the examination and treatment of over 400 individuals out of a total population of 1100.

Peyote ethics did not focus narrowly only on alcohol use, but offered a comprehensive plan for living. By maintaining a stable marital relationship, working hard, fulfilling kinship obligations, and refraining from untoward acts such as drinking, a Peyote convert could achieve success in terms that the dominant society would recognize.[62] As a result, Peyotism offered relief for a variety of physical and psychological problems and drew members from both the "traditional" or "conservative" segment of the tribe as well as from the younger individuals (like Albert Hensley and Oliver Lamere) who had been sent to government boarding schools off the reservation and who had missed the traditional Winnebago process of enculturation or socialization. Although the religion clearly could appeal to people who were suffering from guilt, anxiety, or self-doubt, others might participate in Peyote meetings simply to satisfy their curiosity or to honor a relative's request to visit a meeting, and in the process become deeply committed to the religion due to the same social, psychological, and pharmacological forces that helped troubled individuals.[63]

The importance of the moral code can be seen in the lives of the Peyotists. Many of them had "chased around" and had been heavy drinkers before joining the Peyote religion. I have already noted this in the case of John Rave. Albert Hensley had similar experiences. After returning from Carlisle, he began to drink. Hensley described his behavior:

At that time the Winnebago with whom I associated were heavy drinkers, and after a while they induced me to drink also. I became as wicked as they. I learned how to gamble and I worked for the devil all the time. I even taught the Winnebago how to be bad. [After joining the Peyote religion,] all the evil that was in me I forgot. From that time to the present my actions have been quite different from what they used to be. I am only working for what is good; not that I mean to say that I am good.[64]

Although the role of the psychoactive properties of peyote is more difficult to demonstrate, it clearly had a significant impact on the Peyotists. One of John Rave's early experiences with peyote in Oklahoma produced these results:

Then I looked again in another direction and I saw a man with horns and long claws and with a spear in his hand. He jumped for me and I threw myself on the ground. He missed me. Then I looked back and this time he started back, but it seemed to me that he was directing his spear at me. Again I threw myself on the ground and he missed me. Then suddenly it occurred to me, 'Perhaps it is this peyote that is doing this thing to me?' 'Help me, O medicine, help me! It is you who are doing this and you are holy! It is not these frightful visions that are causing this. I should have known that you were doing it. Help me!' Then my suffering stopped. 'As long as the earth shall last, that long will I make use of you, O medicine!'

Big Winnebago represents a particularly interesting case in relation to the importance of visions. In his younger years he had gone on vision quests in the traditional manner, but had not been successful. Under the influence of peyote, however, he experienced several visions that had a profound impact on him:

It was now late at night and I had eaten a lot of peyote and felt rather tired. I suffered considerably. After a while I looked at the peyote and there stood an eagle with outspread wings. It was as beautiful a sight as one could behold. Each of the feathers seemed to have a mark. The eagle stood looking at me. . . . Some time after this (I saw) a lion lying in the same place (where I had seen the eagle). I watched it very closely. It was alive and looking at me. I looked at it very closely and when I turned my eyes away just the least little bit, it disappeared. . . . Then I saw a small person (at the same place). He wore blue clothes and a shining brimmed cap. He had on a soldier's uniform. He was sitting on the arm of the person who was drumming, and he looked at every one. He was a little man, perfect (in all proportions). Finally I lost sight of him. I was very much surprised indeed. I sat very quietly. 'This is what it is.' I thought, 'this is what they all probably see and I am just beginning to find out.'

Then I prayed to Earthmaker (God): *'This, your ceremony, let me hereafter perform'* [his emphasis].[65]

As Radin observed in a note concerning Big Winnebago's conversion: "These three visions apparently gave him that sense of inward change for which he had looked in vain during his early fasts" (Radin 1963 [1920]: 58).

Mountain Wolf Woman, Big Winnebago's sister, after describing a vision in which she saw Jesus and became an angel, told Lurie (1961b: 42):

I knew when I ate peyote that they were using something holy. That way is directed toward God. Nothing else on earth is holy. If someone speaks about something holy he does not know what he is talking about. But if someone sees something holy at a peyote meeting, that is really true. They are able to understand things concerning God. I understood that this religion is holy. It is directed toward God. I even saw Jesus!

Because of these factors, Peyotism spread rapidly throughout the tribe after 1904. By 1908, it appears that at least half the tribe had tried peyote.[66] Following the first wave of enthusiastic adoptions in the first decade of the 1900s, however, Peyotism seems to have lost some of its appeal.[67] Nonetheless, it continued to attract from between one-third to one-half of the tribe into the 1920s. The superintendent in 1920, for example, reported: "Early in the calendar year 1919, a careful canvass of the population was made and it was found that about 40% of the tribe was addicted to the use of this drug" (Annual Report 1920: 9-10).[68] About one-third of the tribe were believed to be members of the Medicine Lodge (Annual Report 1920: 4).

Governmental Pressures. Although Peyotism was a very important social force among the Winnebago in the early 1900s, it was not the only one that was operating to redirect tribal life. A new superintendent, Albert Kneale, took charge of the Winnebago reservation in 1908 and embarked on a vigorous campaign to reduce the use of alcohol by the Indians. His description of the drinking problems he found corroborates some of the observations made earlier in the 1900s:

> I have said they [the Winnebago] were a drunken people. I mean that they were literally submerged in booze. A passenger train plied up and down the Burlington, going to Sioux City in the morning to return in the afternoon. The railroad people had found it advisable to provide a special car on this train for Indians, and the afternoon train was invariably delayed at Winnebago City, while the train crew emptied this coach. Some could stagger off under their own power, some must be assisted, and some must be carried off and dumped on the depot platform, where they remained, men and women, in drunken stupor, until, becoming sufficiently sober to realize where they were, they returned to their respective abodes. In the almost nine years of previous experience,[69] I had seen fewer than a half dozen drunk

Indians. Here, one was fortunate if he did not see from twenty-five to fifty every day. Apparently there had been no recent attempt to enforce the law [Kneale 1950: 206].

To counter this drunkenness, he initiated several plans. Although a state law prohibited the sale of liquor to Indians, it was not enforced. As a result, he began collecting evidence on guilty parties throughout the surrounding area and pushed to get convictions. He thought the impact of these activities was that: "Indians were no longer able to walk into a saloon and be served. Every dispenser of liquor in northeastern Nebraska, Sioux City, and Omaha had become aware of the existence of the law and every honest dispenser was on the alert to see that there was no violation in his establishment. The only remaining source was the bootlegger" (Kneale 1950: 209).

In addition to attacking the sources of alcohol, he also exerted pressures on the Indians to limit their drinking. He had the Indian police arrest Indians who were drunk on Indian land and had them confined for five days on bread and water in the agency jail for the first offense and ten days for each succeeding offense (Kneale 1909a). In 1909, he also induced the tribal council to identify the individuals who were responsible for "drunken brawls." Before these individuals could obtain their share of tribal annuities or lease payments they had to sign a pledge agreeing to abstain from alcohol for one year. If they violated the pledge they were to receive no annuity money the following year. In April of 1909, the council submitted the names of 90 individuals.[70] Although Kneale mentioned in his annual report for 1910 that all but one individual signed the pledge, I have been unable to find any indication of the effectiveness of this procedure or whether Kneale found any of the Indians in violation of their pledges and withheld their funds.[71]

Christianity. Christianity was another force with an impact during this period. Although Presbyterians had had a mission among the Nebraska Winnebago since 1881, their proselytizing produced only limited success, and they voluntarily turned their work with the Winnebago over to the Dutch Reformed Church in

1908. Although Winnebago acceptance of this church was not as swift or as widespread as the Peyote religion, it gained 155 converts by 1910 and became a force in attempting to change Winnebago life (Watermulder 1910).

Regeneration. By the beginning of the second decade of the 1900s, many of the trends so gloomily described by the agent in 1902 were starting to be reversed. These changes are apparent in the superintendent's comments made in 1910:

> The past year has seen the Winnebago Indians advance all along the line. Whereas last season probably not to exceed 3,000 acres of land was cultivated by Indians, and this in a very indifferent manner; they have under cultivation this season not less than 8,000 acres. Most of these 8,000 acres is in corn and is being fully as well cared for as the average white lessee cares for his crop. Drinking and drunkenness has [*sic*] become unpopular. There are possibly twenty habitual drunkards and outside these individuals there is little drinking. Several successful prosecutions in the County Court for statutory rape, adultery and fornication have done much toward clearing up the moral atmosphere. The complaints leading to these prosecutions were in nearly every instance brought by Indians. This shows a moral awakening among the people [Annual Report 1910].

The following year 174 Winnebago were engaged in farming, cultivating a total of 11,000 acres. By 1912 the number of Indians farming had increased to 181.[72]

Although identifying "causal" factors and determining their relative weight in historical events involves many philosophical and methodological difficulties,[73] a strong case can be made that the Peyote religion played an important role in the "regeneration" that occurred during this period. The testimonies that Radin collected from the Indians represent one type of persuasive evidence. Many of these claims can be corroborated with other data. Although many whites were actively opposed to the Peyote religion, some were not, and their statements concerning the religion are of great interest. Thomas Roddy,[74] for example, a white man who had extensive contact with Winnebago, wrote in 1909:

> I have attended several of the meetings, and have also experienced the eating and drinking of the 'peyote' medicine, with no bad effects. It is very surprising, the way Indians have become familiar with the Bible, and how closely they try to follow the teaching of Jesus. . . . Many members I have known twenty-five or thirty years, who formerly had been greatly addicted to the use of liquors and tobacco, and other vices; all have quit these habits and live for their religion. I cannot see wherein their minds have become impaired, as many talk and write, but I can see great improvements and advancement among the members. They are the best business men among this tribe, and their credit is good wherever they are known [Blair 1911: 283].

Special Officer W. Jacobs, after investigating conditions on the Winnebago and Omaha reservations, wrote in 1915:

> There is quite a sentiment I find on the Reservations, that they ought to be allowed to use it [peyote] in a religious way, to keep them from Drinking and doing things that are wrong, they tell me that there are a number of them that use it now that was the bad Drinkers, but since useing it they do not drink at all, and are good Citizens, and upon investigation i find that the Bad drinkers, are not Peyote, users. but would not attempt to say that this is the reason, for not Drinking [his errors, 1915].

Another indication of the impact of the religion is found on a list of Winnebago engaged in farming in 1910. The list was prepared by the expert farmer (Martin 1911) hired by the government to help the Winnebago with agricultural activities and was not drawn up in relation to religious practices. In addition to listing the 153 Winnebago who were engaged in farming, 43 of them were shown to be "doing well". By drawing upon other sources, I can identify among these 43 farmers 20 Peyotists, 6 Christians, 7 members of the Medicine Lodge, and 10 with unknown affiliations. The number of outstanding farmers who are Peyotists was high.[75]

Concluding Comments

When we compare the drinking patterns of the late 1800s and early 1900s with the contemporary ones, we see several similarities. Clearly, diversity characterizes both sets of patterns. Although diversity was present during the early period in Nebraska, it became more obvious, due in part to better documentation, during the 1890s and early 1900s. At this time important variations existed in the attitudes held toward alcohol use, in the frequency and manner with which individuals participated in drinking-related activities, and in the functions served by those activities. Some of these differences are reflected in the testimony given by whites during the 1904 investigation. They are even more apparent when the drinking patterns are viewed from the Winnebago perspective. Through Big Winnebago's autobiography and the statements of other Winnebago, we begin to approach an insider's view of the behavior. From this perspective, in addition to the other variations already noted, it seems fairly clear that 1) multiple sets of drinking norms or standards existed within the Winnebago population during the early 1900s and 2) some sets defined *some* forms of heavy drinking and intoxication as acceptable behavior.

The large number of activities that included alcohol consumption makes it difficult to accurately generalize about the nature of Winnebago drinking during this period. Thus, for example, although some of Big Winnebago's episodes of heavy drinking were stress related and escapist in function, many others appeared to be directed toward obtaining "traditional" Winnebago goals and related to achieving or expressing a positive identity in traditional terms: alcohol was used to help demonstrate, among other traits, generosity, friendship, sexual attractiveness, physical and spiritual power, and bravery. Given the argument presented in Chapter Six concerning alcohol's use in providing "framing cues" or "boundary markers" in social interaction, it is not surprising that alcohol played such diverse and seemingly contradictory roles.

On the basis of these considerations and given the availability of alcohol, the lack of a strong ethical interdiction against its use within traditional Winnebago culture,[76] ample amounts of leisure time, and a general sociocultural framework receptive to altered states of consciousness, alcohol's growing and widespread use at this time is understandable.[77] The fairly dramatic increase in drinking-related activities that began in the 1890s, then, does not necessarily indicate that the Winnebago population was experiencing a dysphoric reaction to massive sociocultural disorganization and deprivation. Rather, a substantial portion of the increase may have represented the outcome of "traditional" cultural standards in combination with a new external situation.[78]

To say that many drinking activities were related to "traditional" values and were considered as acceptable behavior by many Winnebago does not mean that all forms of drinking and drunken comportment were seen as acceptable or that all Winnebago held the same views of drinking activities. The earlier description of Winnebago drinking practices highlighted some of the variations apparent within the Winnebago population. Although the available documents do not allow us to delineate the limits that particular categories of individuals typically placed on other categories of people (e.g., what drinking standards fathers held for unmarried sons), it is clear that standards differed and that informal negative sanctions sometimes were applied to drunken individuals when they exceeded the limits of acceptable behavior. As we saw, some Winnebago opposed drinking on the basis of their own experiences. In addition, as the Winnebago came under the influence of Peyotism and Christianity, some acquired religious reasons for opposing drunkenness. Although passages in Big Winnebago's autobiography suggest the complex ways in which people used religious rationales to help control errant relatives, much of the subtlety that occurs when individuals manipulate various ideal codes of behavior and the pressure of real-life situations to influence others, or to rationalize aspects of their own behavior, is largely missing in the historical documents.

Even though forms of heavy drinking were viewed by many Winnebago as nondeviant behavior, this does not mean that drinking-related activities were free from negative consequences any more than they are among contemporary Indians. In the early period in Nebraska, when drinking activities were restricted to relatively infrequent episodes of brief duration due to a combination of limited financial resources, lack of easy access to alcohol, and the demands of daily activities, the adverse consequences were minimized and not regarded with special concern or alarm. However, as external circumstances changed, as the Winnebago obtained financial resources and increased leisure through their land leases and as they acquired ready access to alcohol through nearby white populations, the negative impact of these activities intensified and became of greater concern. Frequent and active participation in drinking-related activities in such a context can represent major problems themselves rather than being symptoms or expressions of other problems. In addition, given a population in which heavy drinking occurs frequently, if there are segments or categories of the society experiencing high levels of stress, anxiety, or a sense of aimlessness (as indeed some of the young people who were sent away to schools for long periods appear to have),[79] drinking and drinking-related activities can easily serve as short-term coping mechanisms. The desire to correct the negative features of drinking-related activities were partially satisfied during the early 1900s by adoption of the Peyote religion, conversion to Christianity, and a vigorous control program developed by Superintendent Kneale. These forces had a major impact, drawing many of the tribe toward acceptance of the Peyote and Christian moral codes and reducing, at least temporarily, the amount of drinking. Opposing sets of values or standards remained within the population, however, and as we will see in the next chapter, again grew to include a sizable portion of the population. What this episode of Winnebago history shows us, however, is that drinking standards and behaviors clearly can change over time in response to forces both internal and external to a society.

In the following chapter I will examine in greater detail the social, psychological, and pharmacological factors inherent in the Peyote religion that exerted moderating influences on problem drinking.

Endnotes for Chapter 8

[1] This chapter was originally published in *Contemporary Drug Problems*, Summer, 1985, pages 173-219 and is reprinted with permission from Federal Legal Publications, Inc. An earlier version was presented at the Social History of Alcohol Conference, January 2-5, 1984, Berkeley, California. The research on which this article is based was supported by Summer Research Fellowships, University of Northern Iowa, in 1977, 1980, and 1981. I would like to thank Jay Noricks, Omer Stewart, and James Stokes for comments on an earlier draft of this article. In addition, Dr. Stewart was kind enough to let me read, in manuscript form, the relevant chapters of his book, *Peyote Religion: A History.* I have made some changes in this chapter and added new data.

[2] Winnebago is a Siouan language closely related to the Chiwere language which was composed of three tribal dialects: Iowa, Otoe, and Missouria (Parks and Rankin 2001). The term "Ho-Chunk" is variously taken to mean "big voice" or "big fish" (Lurie 1978 and Lurie and Jung 2009).

[3] Lurie (1952: 119-127).

[4] Lurie (1978), Lurie and Jung (2009: 95-112), Spector (1974).

[5] Hall (1962, vols. 1 and 2), Jones (1974), Lurie (1952, 1978).

[6] Folwell (1924, vol. 2: 145-146, 255-256).

[7] Kappler (1904, vols. 1 and 2).

[8] Lass (1962-63), Lurie (1952).

[9] CIA-AR (1863: 442).

[10] Graff (1864a).

[11] Graff (1864b).

[12] Furnas (1864).

[13] Kappler (1904, vol. 2: 874).

[14] CIA-AR (1869: 789; 1874: 189; 1879: 236, 254-255; 1889: 504, 522-523).

[15] The Winnebago believed that young people had a duty to fast in order to obtain blessings from a spirit. Ideally, a spirit took pity on the fasters for undergoing the rigors of the fast and granted them specific powers to aid them in life, such as becoming outstanding warriors or productive hunters. Women were expected to fast during their menstrual periods (*see* Radin 1970 [1923]: 168-132, 229-232).

[16] *See* Radin (1970 [1923]), Lurie (1948), and Cloud (n.d.) for descriptions of the traditional enculturation process.

[17] Denman (1868a, 1868b), Winnebago Tribal Petitions (1868a, 1868b).

[18] Radin (1970 [1923]: 152, 177-180); Lurie (1978).

[19] *See*, for examples, CIA-AR (1891: 287-288; 1892: 304-305; 1897: 179); Watermulder (1912).

[20] *See*, for examples, B. White (n.d., volume 2: 235-237, 380-381); H. White (1872); CIA-AR (1869: 774; 1872: 219; 1878: 101; 1881: 130; 1887: 151).

[21] U.S. Bureau of the Census (1902: 547-548).

[22] Arndt (2012: 29).

[23] Radin (1983 [1926]). *See* Arnold Krupat's foreword and appendix to the 1926 edition (Radin 1983) and Krupat (1985: 75-106) for a discussion of the issues raised by the various versions and the inconsistencies present in Radin's publications. Also *see* Lurie's comments (Lurie 1961b: 96-98, 1972). I have used the 1920 edition (Radin 1963) exclusively. *See* Grant Arndt (2012) for an analysis and discussion of Big Winnebago's differing accounts of his role in the killing of a man in 1903 made during the course of the legal proceedings related to the murder and in his autobiography. *See* Jones et al. (2011: 110, 111) for photographs of Big Winnebago and (2011: 245) for a picture of his sister Stella Blowsnake Whitepine Stacy (i.e., Mountain Wolf Woman). The entire volume contains wonderful photographs of the Ho-Chunk in Wisconsin from 1879 to 1942.

[24] He later lived in Nebraska for about 25 years and worked for 13 years at a packing house in Sioux City, Iowa and for 6 years in Omaha, Nebraska at Nebraska Power Company (Blowsnake 1948).

[25] Radin (1963 [1920]: 38-39).

[26] Radin (1963 [1920]: 25, 34).

[27] Radin (1963 [1920]: 27, 34, 38-39).

[28] Radin (1963 [1920]: 27, 29, 33).

[29] Radin (1963 [1920]: 27, 34-35).

[30] Radin (1963 [1920]: 27).

[31] Radin (1963 [1920]: 34-35).

[32] Radin (1963 [1920]: 48).

[33] Radin (1963 [1920]: 26).

[34] Radin (1963 [1920]: 24); also *see* Lurie (1961: 35).

[35] Radin (1963 [1920]: 27); *see* Lurie (1961b: 49) for another instance in which physical restraint was used and Lurie (1961b: 65; 1952: 247) for comments on the use of silence as a negative sanction.

[36] Radin (1963 [1920]: 27).

[37] The lives of three of Nancy Lurie's Nebraska consultants would also appear to reflect this pattern, Lurie (1952: 363-364, 368). Also *see* her

comments (1952: 233-234, 285-286) and Hensley's in Radin (1970 [1923]: 350).

[38] In the early 1800s some Winnebago were influenced by Tenskwatawa, the Shawnee Prophet. One of his major pronouncements was that alcohol should be abjured. When Radin conducted his field research (1908-1913), he obtained a Peyotist's version of what the Prophet told the Winnebago. If the Prophet's teachings influenced Winnebago drinking standards at the end of the 1800s, or if they were used as a moral incentive to control drinking, one could justifiably argue that certain "traditional" Winnebago religious beliefs did interdict the use of alcohol. If this was the case, the question then becomes: what force did the teachings have and among which segments of the tribe? *See* Radin (1970 [1923]: 21-26); Jones (1974: 84-117); Forsyth in Blair (1911, volume 2: 273-279); Edmunds (1983).

[39] Robert Ashley, the agent in 1891, evaluates the state of morality among the Winnebago according to his ethnocentric standards and comments on the kind of examples set by local whites:

> As to the moral and religious life of this people I can not speak very encouragingly as a tribe. They have, or seem to have, but little conception of what morality really is, or true religion either. There are three very great drawbacks to progress, both morally and religiously. One is the medicine lodge and dance. Whisky is another, and is with them, as everywhere else, a great curse. Again, the customs practiced by white people living in towns near the reservation, who flock to see them dance, bringing horses for racing with them, and by their example undoing what a few are trying to do in the way of Sabbath observance. Until these hindrances can be controlled but little comparatively can be accomplished [CIA-AR 1891: 289].

Robert Berkhofer, in his study of Protestant missionaries, describes the influence of white settlers on the Indians and the reactions it engendered among the missionaries:

> Because of the proximity of these lower class whites to the Indians, the Indians assimilated many lower class habits to the disgust of the missionaries, who were usually middle class. Thus missionary attacks on Indian vices frequently reduced to the condemnation of the lower class habits in their own society. So pernicious did missionaries consider most white influence on Indian behavior that the majority of missionaries believed the less contact Indians had

with the white race the more favorable the prospects of missionary success [Berkhofer 1965: 100].

[40] Radin (1963 [1920]: 18).

[41] For discussions of the Peyote religion *see* Aberle (1982); Anderson (1996); Fikes (1996); Hertberg (1971: 239-284); La Barre (1975); Maroukis (2004, 2010); Radin (1914); Slotkin (1956); Smith and Snake (1996); Steinmetz (1990); Stewart (1948, 1974, 1980a, 1980b, 1987). *See* Wallace (1956) for the classic discussion of revitalization movements.

[42] Meeker (1896, 1898); Radin (1970 [1923]: 345). Omer Stewart (1987) discusses in detail the spread of the Peyote religion and compares the Peyote ceremonies of the Winnebago with those of other tribes. The Omaha, located contiguously to the Winnebago, learned of Peyotism at about the same time as the Winnebago, produced dedicated Peyotists, and followed a similar course in relation to Peyotism as the Winnebago (Stewart 1987: 162-165). In contrast, the Santee never became Peyotists (Stewart 1987: 174). *See* Maroukis (2004) for a discussion of the religion among the Yankton Sioux.

[43] Radin (1970 [1923]: 346).

[44] The position of "Indian agent" was abolished in 1903, but was replaced by that of "superintendent" (CIA-AR 1904: 204).

[45] Radin (1970 [1923]: 345-346).

[46] In addition to eating peyote buttons, participants sometimes drank a tea made from the buttons.

[47] Radin (1970 [1923]: 345-346).

[48] Anderson (1996: 92-102, 138-139), Furst (1976).

[49] Radin (1970 [1923]: 346, 372-373), Stewart (1987: 152-153).

[50] For descriptions of the Medicine Lodge or Dance *see* Radin (1911, 1945).

[51] Omer Stewart (personal communication) suggests that the Winnebago Peyotists did not perceive any conflict between the Peyote religion and "traditional" beliefs and practices (also *see* Stewart 1980a: 192-195). Although I suspect that not all Winnebago saw such a conflict, unless we completely discount Radin's views and the words of his Winnebago consultants, it would appear that during the period Radin conducted his field research (1908-1913), some Winnebago saw such a conflict. It should be remembered that Radin's attempts to obtain information on the secret ceremonies of the Medicine Lodge probably exacerbated tensions between the two groups (*see* Radin 1945: 35-49). How long such feelings remained in

the population is another question. Certainly by 1950 when Lurie conducted her field research among the Nebraska Winnebago, attitudes of antagonism and exclusivism had receded (Lurie 1952: 231-232). Also *see* endnote 67.

[52] Radin (1963 [1920]: 57).

[53] Radin (1963 [1920]: 67).

[54] Radin (1963 [1920]: 56).

[55] Radin (1963 [1920]: 51).

[56] Radin (1963 [1920]: 49), also *see* page 63 and Lurie (1961b: 130), Stewart (1987: 153-154). Stewart (1987: 154) says, "Radin described that Winnebago Crashing Thunder (Radin 1923: 409) took a vow of nonsmoking during his conversion about 1908. It is not clear whether it was Crashing Thunder's vow not to use tobacco which started Winnebago peyotists to prohibit tobacco in the peyote ceremony or whether his vow was simply an expression of a rule already established and seldom mentioned." But the quote in the body of the chapter stating that Peyotists stopped smoking and chewing tobacco was what Big Winnebago's father told him *before* he was converted (Radin 1970 [1923]: 353). (Also quoted in Radin 1963 [1920]: 49.) It seems clear that the rule prohibiting tobacco use was already established before Big Winnebago's conversion. Parenthetically, it might be noted that in Radin (1970 [1923]) the passage in question is titled "J.B's Peyote Experiences" although it is attributed to Sam Blowsnake (Big Winnebago) in his autobiography. This is an instance of the inconsistencies that occur among some of Radin's publications. (*See* endnote 23.)

[57] Radin (1970 [1923]: 350).

[58] Radin (1970 [1923]: 349).

[59] Radin (1970 [1923]: 375).

[60] *See*, for examples, Radin (1970 [1923]: 343, 353, 361) and Lurie (1961b: 40-41).

[61] Radin (1970 [1923]: 375).

[62] It should be noted that Winnebago Peyotism had, in Aberle's terms (1962), a strong "redemptive" quality. The Peyote religion was more concerned with changing the Peyotists themselves—putting them on a path that would lead to health, psychological peace, and correct behavior—than with attempting to transform the institutions of white America that shaped their lives.

[63] *See* Hine (1974) and Gerlach (1974) for similar arguments in relation to Pentecostalism.

---

[64] Radin (1970 [1923]: 350). Also *see* Field Matron (1904), Hensley (1916), and Radin's comments concerning Oliver Lamere before he joined the Peyote relgion, Radin (1945: 36).

[65] Radin (1963 [1920]: 58).

[66] Oliver Lamere asserted in 1908 that "almost half the tribe belongs to our religion" Radin (1970 [1923]: 346). Albert Hensley writing in 1908 said that the "Mescal Winnebago" probably numbered three hundred (Hensley 1908). Superintendent Kneale estimated that "fully fifty per cent" used peyote (Kneale 1909b).

[67] Radin said: "It appears now as if the Peyote cult has run its course. Some of the members have recently returned to the old pagan customs, others have practically become Christians, and many have become indifferent" (Radin 1970 [1923]: 374). Although Radin's monograph was published in 1923, the manuscript was completed in 1913 (Radin 1970 [1923]: xvi). These developments may simply reflect the lessening of tensions between the Peyotists and "traditionalists" referred to in endnote 51 rather than a rejection of Peyotism as Radin implies. It is also clear that the Peyotists did not see a conflict between Peyotism and Christianity and that Christian elements were present in Winnebago Peyotism from the beginning, although the ceremony became more Christianized in the early 1900s; *see* Stewart (1948: 30-42; 1974; 1980a; 1987: 150-161); Page (1915: 206-208); and Radin (1970 [1923]: 348, 352).

[64] Peyote does not produce physical dependence; *see* Anderson (1996: 186-187, 199).

[69] Previously, he served as an educator at a day school at the Pine Ridge Agency, the Cheyenne and Arapaho Boarding School, the Wind River Boarding School, and the Crow Boarding School.

[70] Actually 94 names were on the list, but four names had been lined-out before signing.

[71] Kneale (1909a); Annual Report (1910); Valentine (1909a, 1909b); Winnebago Tribal Council (1909).

[72] Annual Reports (1911, 1912).

[73] Atkinson (1978) and Mandelbaum (1977).

[74] Roddy traded extensively with the Ho-Chunk and organized traveling Wild West shows which included Ho-Chunk performers (Jones et al. 2011: 12, 241). For a picture of Roddy taken about 1885 *see* Jones et al. (2011: 111).

[75] The statistical significance of these figures is difficult to determine because it depends upon which figure one accepts for the percentage of Peyotists in the general population. If Peyotists comprised 43% or less of the general population, the number of successful farmers who were Peyotists is statistically significant at the .05 level.

[76] But *see* endnote 38.

[77] I am not arguing that this pattern developed for the first time in the late 1800s; clearly many of its elements date from the days of the fur trade period (*see* Lurie's comments 1952: 285-286 and Mancall 1995a, especially 63-100).

[78] Compare my discussion with Lurie's (1952).

[79] Hampton Institute in Virginia, which was founded in 1868 for the education of freed slaves, began taking Indians in 1877. By 1895, 64 Omaha and 63 Winnebago had attended. The Winnebago students were not seen, however, as making good adjustments on their return home (Lindsey 1995: 20, 202). In 1890 Samuel Armstrong, the founder of Hampton, reported that 33% of the Winnebago students had done "bad" or "poor" on returning versus 7% from other tribes (Armstrong to Commissioner T. J. Morgan, April 14, 1890, *cited in* Lindsey 1995: 237).

Carlisle Institute, which was founded in 1879 in Carlisle, Pennsylvania by Richard Pratt and dedicated to Indian students, had accepted over 40 Winnebago by 1900, including as we saw, Albert Hensley and Oliver Lamere, although Lamere only stayed a little over two months (Carlisle 1906).

In 1898 Supervisor James Anderson identified 21 male and 18 female Winnebago who had returned from off-reservation schools like Hampton, Carlisle, and Genoa Indian School. Although we may be suspicious of the standards used to make the judgments, Anderson in consultation with several other local individuals including the Presbyterian missionary categorized 67% of the former students as making a "poor" or "bad" adjustment (Anderson 1898).

In contrast, Henry Roe Cloud, born around 1884, represents a case touted as a success by educators and Christian workers. Roe Cloud attended both the Genoa Indian School and the Santee Normal Training School before being accepted at Mount Herman in Northfield, Massachusetts. He became the first Native American to graduate from Yale University in 1910 (*see* Pfister 2009).

CHAPTER 9
THE PEYOTE RELIGION AS A NATIVE THERAPEUTIC SYSTEM[1]

> Strictly speaking, the question
> is not how to get cured, but
> how to live.
>
> Joseph Conrad

Introduction

What are the implications of the description and analysis offered in the preceding chapters for treatment and prevention? As I demonstrated earlier, problem drinking is not confined to a single type of drinker, life style, or phase of the life cycle and is not the result of a single "cause." Indeed, as we have seen, different episodes of problem drinking for a given individual can arise from a variety of circumstances. As a result, each problem drinker represents a unique case; that is, he has a distinctive personal history, health status, set of abilities and skills, biopsychological makeup, social network, and set of economic resources. In addition, as the last chapter demonstrated, when a given society is viewed diachronically, the extent of heavy and problem drinking can vary markedly over time, waxing and waning in response to a number of environmental, technological, and sociocultural forces. So when we examine a given instance of problem drinking by an individual, we confront many relevant factors that must be considered and dealt with in treating that behavior. When we look at the treatment procedures that have been applied to problem drinking, we discover a bewildering diversity, including Alcoholics Anonymous (AA); behavioral modification programs; use of pharmacological substances like disulfiram (Antabuse®), naltrexone, and acamprosate (Campral®); individual, family, and group therapies (with various brands of each); vocational counseling; detoxification; brief interventions; outpatient and inpatient programs; halfway houses; and a variety of spiritual approaches. Each major approach has its own rationale and set of procedures to bring about change in the problem drinker. Do the number of factors contributing to problem drinking and the diversity of the treatment regimens preclude meaningful generalizations about intervention? To explore the kinds of forces that can be brought to bear to effect successful control or treatment of problem drinking, I will examine in greater detail the manner in which the Peyote religion obtained the beneficial results described in the last chapter. Such a consideration will highlight some of the critical elements found in all effective interventions.

Peyotism and the Control of Heavy Drinking

The beneficial effects of the Peyote religion in controlling drinking have not been limited to the Winnebago. Many Peyotists have made such claims. Quanah Parker, one of the most influential Comanche Peyotists, said in 1908, "I do think piote beans have helped Indians to quit drinking" (Slotkin 1956: 140). Nor have Peyotists been alone in voicing this claim; many ethnologists have also commented on the relationship. Alanson Skinner noted in 1915 that "The effect of peyote eating on the Kansa has been to abolish drunkenness among its followers" (McGlothlin 1967: 13). Edgar Siskin (1983: 122) reported that among the Washo, "Even peyote's strongest antagonists admitted that most of the cultists stopped drinking." James Slotkin (1956: 41) observed that "In the post-frontier period two White disorders, tuberculosis and alcoholism, were the major health problems. Neither seemed curable by traditional means: the [Peyote] religion treated both."[2]

Although the relationship between Peyotism and abstinence has been widely noted, the causal connection has not been fully explicated. An early idea, since discredited, was that ingested peyote was pharmacologically incompatible with alcohol.[3] The conclusion reached by more recent analysts is that any beneficial effects obtained in controlling drinking are due primarily to the religion's social and psychological effects and that if the pharmacological properties are involved, they are more directly related to producing psychological insight, cathartic expression, or communicative openness than to adverse reactions with alcohol.[4]

How, then, did Winnebago participation in the Peyote religion during the early decades of the 1900s help control problem drinking? Certainly a critical element was the Peyote code's insistence on abstinence from alcohol. With the adoption of Peyotism, the requirement of avoiding alcohol was no longer merely a personal or secular call, it possessed a religious backing.[5] Followers believed that Earthmaker (God) decreed that it be this way. This new view of drinking was important because, as we have seen, heretofore, many Winnebago considered drinking, even forms of heavy drinking, to be acceptable behavior. By insisting that all alcohol use was wrong, the standards of Peyotism removed the gray area concerning drinking activities and made it easier for Peyotists to negotiate Winnebago life. That is, it was no longer an individual question of deciding how much alcohol to drink on a given occasion—any amount was too much. It also gave added justification and weight to one's refusal to join old drinking comrades: "I would like to share a bottle with you, but I am now a Peyotist and am no longer allowed to drink." In addition, through participation in Peyote meetings a member developed, or participated in, a social network of like-minded individuals who helped legitimize and enforce these standards. Since the religion spread along family lines, a newly converted drinker received social support from the individuals who were closest to him socially; all shared his new view of drinking and offered him social and psychological support in living up to it.

Participation in Peyote meetings and related religious affairs engaged members in activities that competed with the scheduling of old behavioral patterns. A person could not attend an all-night Peyote meeting Saturday night and at the same time be "chasing around" and drinking in the old haunts with his old acquaintances and friends. Indeed, during the early years when the members' enthusiasm was running particularly high, they sometimes had as many as four meetings a week. Later, it became the usual pattern to hold a meeting once a week, usually on Saturday night (Radin 1914: 2, 14; 1970

[1923]: 340). In any case, the restructuring of an individual's activities and social networks reduced the social pressures and opportunities to drink and developed competing activities that were at least as psychologically and socially rewarding as the old ones.

The public confession of past sins—including any excessive drinking—served a variety of functions. Through the public admission of past wrongs and the emotional abreaction associated with such an action, an individual helped rid himself of any ambivalence he felt regarding his excessive drinking. Depending on the level of emotional arousal achieved, confession could leave a member both physiologically and psychologically better adjusted.[6] The emotional nature of the act also helped develop a sense of a new beginning, a new psychological birth: "This is a new point in my life. I feel that things are going to be different from now on." Such emotional arousal strengthens the belief that it *is possible* for the individual to change his behavior. The public nature of the confession and the related promise to behave differently, particularly when esteemed figures were present, also helped bolster the inner resolve to live up to the new standards (Janis and Rodin 1979: 518). In addition, the descriptions of past, profligate behavior by members currently exemplifying the religion's ideals presented living proof that individuals could successfully change their lives by following the Peyote way.

The role that the psychoactive alkaloids played in helping to control heavy drinking is difficult to determine. Although there was a wave of psychiatric experimentation with the use of psychedelic drugs in the treatment of a variety of psychological problems during the 1950s and 1960s,[7] after a flurry of positive and enthusiastic reports, their use fell out of favor. More recently, interest in them has been rekindled.[8] Nonetheless, carefully controlled studies have not demonstrated that treatment regimens for heavy drinking that use mescaline or other psychedelic drugs are any more effective than treatment approaches without them.[9] Still, the treatment populations used in these studies had cultural traditions very different from traditional Winnebago, and the sociocultural contexts of treatment were also very dissimilar. This is of some importance because the effects of psychoactive substances depend not only on the dosage and pharmacological properties of the alkaloids, but also on such variables as the personality and psychological state of the person taking the substance, his previous experiences with the drug, and the setting for consumption. The setting and rituals of the Peyote meeting clearly reflected the serious and religious nature of the gathering. The fire, songs, drumming, speeches, and testimonials all united with the psychoactive elements to make the experience a vivid and memorable one. One would expect that the content of a vision in a meeting would depend to a great extent on the person's psychological state. If he has led a profligate life and has his guilt heightened in relation to his past behavior, his vision might be a highly dramatic and emotional one, focusing on sin, retribution, and salvation. An upright, clean-living, and relatively contented member's experience might be personally less troubling or stressful. Radin noted individual variations among the Winnebago in the effects of peyote, and although not all Peyotists claimed to have visions, Radin pointed out that they were frequent and often accompanied by vivid color sensations. Radin also said the visions fell into two basic types: those consisting of monsters chasing an individual and those composed of "more or less elaborate dreams" (Radin 1914: 19). Both types tended to be interpreted individually. Although Radin did not pursue the analysis further, it seems clear that the visions or states produced had a significant impact on the Winnebago Peyotists—if not because they provided new psychological insights into their personal problems, then because they raised their confidence in the power of peyote and heightened their expectations that, with its help, they could deal with their problems.

By developing a broad-based ethical code, the Peyote religion offered a workable model that could help individuals whose drinking problems stemmed from a variety of circumstances. It offered help for those who saw heavy drinking as acceptable behavior, but who nonetheless suffered from the effects of such views, by redefining that behavior. It offered help to those whose episodes of heavy drinking occurred in response to acute crises, such as the death of a close relative or the anxiety and pain associated with a flare-up of a chronic illness, by presenting an alternative mode of coping. It offered help to those whose drinking stemmed from feelings of guilt and low self-esteem due to past failures to live up to their ideal standards of behavior by exculpating their guilt and promising a new beginning. It offered help to those whose drinking was due to feelings of anxiety and self-doubt related to competing models of worth by endorsing a set of ideals that encouraged control, restraint, and responsibility rather than catharsis, self-indulgence, and the pursuit of physical pleasures. The religion was able to put a diverse set of converts on the "Peyote Road" that could lead to a more satisfying life style for them all.

Peyotism Compared to Other Forms of Therapy

When we compare alternative treatment approaches to alcohol-related problems, several fundamental questions arise. First, does any formal treatment program make a difference in the outcome? Second, are the procedures used for alcohol-related problems different from those used to deal with other psychological problems?

With respect to the first question, as we noted in Chapter Seven on problem drinking, epidemiological surveys in the past decades have documented that the majority of individuals who develop various types of problem drinking, including those who meet the criteria for "alcohol dependence," never receive formal treatment either with medical professionals or 12-step organizations like AA. Nonetheless, the majority of them resolve their problems. As we saw with reference to the Dawson et al. (2005) study, of the individuals who had been "alcohol dependent" prior to the previous year, but who were fully recovered during the year prior to the study, 72.4% achieved their recovery without formal help.[10] As we would expect, Carballo et al. (2007: 96) found in reviewing twenty-two natural-recovery studies from 1999 through 2005 "that the people who recover naturally have less serious substance abuse histories compared with those who seek treatment."[11] They also found for all the studies reviewed that the mean number of years the problems existed prior to recovery was 12.8 (standard deviation, S.D. 4.9), and the mean recovery length was 8.0 years (S.D. 2.7). The percentage of those whose recovery involved abstinence ranged in the different studies from 29.9% to 100% (mean, 56.6%), while those who continued to engage in low risk drinking ranged from 0.0% to 70.1% (mean, 43.4%). The mean number of years in recovery for the recovered drinkers in the studies reviewed was 8.0 years (S.D. 2.7).[12] The data show that in industrialized societies, at least, the majority of people suffering from problem drinking, or alcohol dependence, recover without formal treatment. Many of those with the more severe drinking problems do get formal treatment. How do these individuals fare?

The evidence indicates that many of these individuals do not have a quick path to recovery with up to 85% or more relapsing within a year of treatment.[13] For example, in a recent study of 878 patients treated at an addiction treatment center affiliated with Yale University using "state of the art, empirically based behavioral and pharmacologic therapies . . . less than 35% were abstinent from alcohol and opiates over the course of a one-year period" (Sinha 2011: 399).[14]

The percentage of patients improved for problem drinking is similar to the results obtained with other psychological problems treated by psychotherapists. Despite different theoretical approaches, the various psychotherapies produce about the same outcomes in terms of efficacy.[15] Some researchers argue that such a result suggests that despite apparent differences in psychotherapeutic approaches, all must include a common core which has roughly the same effect on the variables critical to treatment outcome. Torrey (1986), for example, in comparing psychotherapeutic techniques cross-culturally, argues that the effectiveness of all approaches is due to four basic components: 1) a similar world view being shared between the client and therapist, 2) the therapist's personal qualities, such as empathy, nonpossessive warmth, and genuineness, that interact with those of the client's to advance client improvement, 3) raising the client's expectations that his problems will improve, and 4) increasing the client's sense of mastery, giving him the knowledge and confidence that he needs to deal effectively with the problems confronting him. Although Torrey recognizes that the specific techniques of psychotherapy can, in themselves, have an impact on treatment outcome, he believes that their influence is negligible when compared to these four basic components and that the effectiveness of a specific regimen depends on the extent to which it incorporates these components. Jim Orford, who has critically examined treatment approaches to excessive behaviors, takes a similar view and claims "that most if not all 'treatments' for excessive appetites, whatever their form, work in the same way, principally by virtue of the commitment which the patient makes to entering and undergoing some form of 'therapeutic' procedures the purpose of which is to help control the excessive behavior."[16]

Such a perspective is appealing because it allows us to account for not only "professional" treatment regimens, but also for folk and non-Western curing approaches as well. With this view, the critical variables in successful treatment reinforce the problem drinker's belief that he needs to change his behavior, help him to become deeply committed to making those changes, and aid him in developing strategies and behavioral patterns that support his altered behavior.[17] As we have seen, the Peyote religion utilized a set of techniques that greatly increased the chances of effecting those changes in the Winnebago problem drinkers who attended peyote meetings.

However, the religion would be effective in controlling heavy drinking only to the extent, and only for the length of time, that it exerted a moral force on converts, provided strong social support, and offered a blueprint for behavior that led to a more successful life style. Individuals who tried Peyotism, but continued to believe that heavy drinking was acceptable behavior, or individuals who wished to change their drinking behavior, but remained with relatives and friends who did not support the new standards and behavior, might well continue to drink. Those who aspired to become successful farmers, but who were unable to acquire sufficient land due to the fractionalization of their allotments among many heirs, or who did not have sufficient funds to purchase draft teams or mechanized farming equipment, could become discouraged and turn to alcohol for consolation. And indeed, as the Winnebago moved further into the 20th century, the influence of Peyotism on the tribe lessened and heavy drinking again increased, even among those who claimed to be Peyotists. Radin noted "that as Rave's personal influence decreased and as the membership increased the number of people who drank liquor and ate peyote at the same time increased."[18] The relationship between Peyotism and abstinence continued to weaken, and by 1950, Nancy Lurie (1952: 232) found that "the peyote members who renounced alcohol are in a small minority." A similar situation prevailed among the Christian denominations. Among all groups (Christian and Peyote), there was a "small nucleus of earnest believers who [were] socially, economically and individually stable, along with the greater number of 'back sliders' and casual members" (Lurie 1952: 234).

When we examine the elements that made the Peyote religion successful in controlling problem drinking, we can identify the following:

1) The religion defined all forms of drinking as unacceptable and thus helped to counter the drinking standards held by many individuals in the population.

2) The religion pulled like-minded individuals into common social networks that helped reinforce and sustain the new drinking standards.

3) The religion engaged former heavy drinkers in new activities that made it difficult for them to participate in their old drinking-related activities.

4) The religion offered problem drinkers successful role models who had controlled their drinking and had achieved a satisfactory life style by following the "Peyote Road."

5) The religion provided a belief system and process through which existing guilt and dysphoric emotions could be dissipated.

6) The religion helped resolve underlying problems that in some cases led to heavy drinking as a coping mechanism with its comprehensive code for "right living."

7) The religion helped strengthen a set of values or identity ideals that were incompatible with those embodied in "chasing around" or "hell-raising" activities and encouraged individuals to make the transition from youthful hell-raising to adult responsibility.

8) The religion used ceremonial singing, drumming, meditating, testifying, and eating psychoactive peyote, which helped to set the stage for either psychological insight into converts' problems or a "conversion" experience, while at the same time demonstrated the "power" of the religion (or peyote), and thereby, raised the converts' expectations that they could quit drinking or otherwise deal with their personal problems.

Any movement or group capable of achieving these effects would be a potent force in controlling and preventing heavy drinking.

Implications for Treatment and Prevention

The early history of Winnebago Peyotism carries a number of implications for the design and implementation of treatment and prevention programs. If one accepts the view that a common set of factors underlies effective treatments, a therapist still faces the formidable task of correctly identifying the particular set of techniques or procedures that will, in fact, bring about the desired changes in a given sociocultural setting with a particular drinker. This means that each individual problem drinker must be examined carefully to determine the role that alcohol plays in his life, the strength of his motivation to change his behavior, the economic and social resources he has available, and his psychological (and possibly his genetic) makeup. Clearly, a "wino" on the street who has no relatives and few nondrinking acquaintances in Sioux City, suffers from poor health, and possesses little formal education will have a more difficult time changing his behavior than will a person like Frank Wolf who has a job and at least some relatives who do not wish to drink heavily. To be maximally effective, then, a treatment program needs to have the resources available to take a multi-pronged approach to problem drinkers. What this means in practice is that for some people the control of drinking will be related to solving, or at least dealing more effectively with, other problems in their lives. Treatment programs that are based solely on individual psychological therapy and that do not have the flexibility and resources to deal with different types of problem drinkers will not be as effective as they could be.

Second, in an environment in which forms of heavy drinking are widely viewed as acceptable behavior, an individual decision of — or even a more dramatic "peak" or "conversion" experience leading to — abstinence will be difficult to sustain without corresponding changes in the convert's sociocultural situation.[19] As we saw, one of the major reasons the Peyote religion had the impact it did was because it often effectively restructured the convert's social network to provide greater support and changed not only the convert's drinking standards, but those of his family and friends. As a result, any treatment program should try to incorporate as many individuals as possible from the client's family and social network to inform them about the treatment process and to enlist their aid in achieving the client's drinking goals. In many cases, to increase the chances of a client remaining abstinent or limiting his drinking, many of the family members will need to change their own drinking standards and alter their social networks, curtailing interaction with other heavy drinkers and developing new relationships with moderate drinkers or abstaining individuals. Although dealing with such issues presents additional challenges to the treatment staff, unless they are confronted, the chances of making lasting changes in the client's drinking patterns are decreased.

The question of whether a program should adopt the treatment goal of requiring total abstinence or moderation is a hotly debated one. I personally believe that it is best to use the concept of "problem drinking" (rather than "alcoholism" or "alcohol dependence") as the guiding concept and that an appropriate treatment goal for *some* drinkers is "controlled" or "low risk" drinking. However, I also feel that abstinence is a better strategy for other drinkers, particularly those who have experienced many episodes of heavy drinking and withdrawal. Abstinence may also be particularly appropriate for populations that view heavy drinking not only as acceptable, but also as desirable. That is, in populations that value drinking to the point of intoxication, a stance of abstinence may be easier to maintain than one which accepts drinking, but tries to limit the amount. As pointed out, the stronger the reason supporting the abstinence stance (such as *religion* or *health*), the more weight it carries as an acceptable excuse. In any case, the decision of abstinence or moderation should be reached through discussions with each client.[20]

Third, whenever possible, treatment and prevention programs should build on the existing standards and life-style transitions within the local community that initiate and support the desired changes. Among contemporary Sioux City Indians, as we saw, after young men and women marry and have children—even though they may have been heavy-drinking "hell-raisers" and women who "ran around"—they are now expected to "settle down" and become responsible "family men" and "homebodies." Although some drinking may be expected to continue, it ideally should not interfere with their roles as husbands, wives, and parents. Such a naturally occurring transition represents an ideal time to try to involve the community in treatment and prevention programs. Through the schools, hospitals, Indian-oriented agencies, and a general publicity campaign, attempts should be made to draw newly married individuals and pregnant women (and their families) into treatment and prevention programs. Such an approach has the advantage of engaging people in a program without forcing them to accept a stigmatized identity as either a "problem drinker" or an "alcoholic." The message should be: "given the new circumstance associated with your new status of family man, homebody, or pregnant mother, it is a good time to examine your family's drinking patterns to see if you should be more moderate or temperate." Indeed, one can argue that in at least some cases, the Peyote religion helped "formalize" or "ritualize" a rite of passage that already existed with Winnebago society.[21] For a variety of reasons, the ideal transition did not always successfully occur, but the belief system and ceremonies of the Peyote religion—through the procedures discussed—helped make that transition work.

For Native American youths in Sioux City, the alcohol-using issues should be developed and discussed in the context of their own tribal histories and their contemporary situation. To be effective, a prevention program cannot focus narrowly on the use of alcohol and other drugs, but must also help the students surmount the factors in their lives that both push and pull them toward poor academic performances, lowered educational and occupational aspirations, adoption of hell-raising values and ideals, and participation in peer networks of youthful hell-raisers. Although achieving such goals requires a major effort—particularly for children in disrupted families who are at the greatest risk—nothing less is likely to work.[22]

Role of Pharmacogenetics. As we saw in Chapter Seven, our growing knowledge of genetics and the development of an area called pharmacogenetics[23] may offer the possibility of designing treatment programs for specific individuals based on their genetic makeup. This is relevant because several drugs have been used in alcohol treatment programs to improve the outcomes, even though, as O'Malley and O'Connor found in a recent review, these agents "only have modest effects."[24] Currently, disulfiram (Antabuse®); acamprosate (Campral®); and naltrexone, in two forms, oral and extended-release (Vivitrol®) are approved by the FDA for use. Each drug has a different mechanism of action.

Disulfiram interferes with the second step in the metabolism of alcohol, the conversion of acetaldehyde to acetate, causing a buildup of acetaldehyde. The buildup, as we saw in Chapter 7, causes a variety of unpleasant symptoms like flushing, nausea, increased heart rate, hypotension, and headache. Because of these unpleasant reactions, an abstinent person taking disulfiram is not expected to drink alcohol. The treatment drawback is that the drug will only work if an individual takes the drug daily, and some studies have found a high rate of nonadherence.[25] Compliance is better in programs in which the administration of the drug is monitored by either family members or health personnel.

Acamprosate is believed to affect the gamma-aminobutyric acid (GABA) and glutamate neurotransmitter systems. Studies of its effectiveness have shown mixed results. Those studies conducted in Europe have indicated that patients who received the drug had greater abstinence rates at three, six, and twelve months than did those receiving placebo. However, U. S. studies have shown no significant differences between acamprosate and placebo groups. Differences in the study designs may account for the variant outcomes.[26]

Naltrexone is an opioid antagonist, blocking the actions of opioids on their receptors. The belief is that its actions decrease the rewarding effects of alcohol and the craving for it. It is administered in two forms: oral and extended-release (Vivitrol®, given through an intramuscular injection whose effects work for a month or longer). Although both oral and extended-release have reduced heavy drinking and increased abstinence, studies have shown the drug to be ineffective in individuals having a particular genetic makeup.[27] Individuals who carry the allele *OPRM1 118G* respond much better with naltrexone than people who are homozygous with the *OPRM1 118A* allele. The frequency of the *118G* allele varies across ethnic populations, occurring more often among Asians (56%), less frequently among Caucasians (around 30%), and in only about 10% of African Americans. The frequency among Native Americans is unknown. Once genotyping becomes readily available and its costs decrease, it will be possible to identify the individuals who are most likely to benefit from using naltrexone.

In addition to the drugs currently approved by the FDA, a number of others are under investigation for the treatment of alcohol dependence. These include dopamine antagonists, antipsychotics, anticonvulsants, mood-stablizers, and other agents (*see* Garbutt 2009, O'Malley and O'Connor 2011 for discussions).

Even as our abilities to match particular individuals to specific drugs improve with growing research, we must remember that at best the use of pharmacological agents will always be only an adjunct in treatment. They will not be silver bullets, solving a drinker's problems. The major goal will always be to keep the person committed to abstinence or low risk drinking while helping him to structure his life and sociocultural environments in such a fashion as to increase the likelihood of maintaining those changes.

Program Delivery. Although many institutional setups could deliver these services, an effective program might include an information and referral office, a detoxification center with related medical care, an intensive inpatient treatment facility, an intermediate care facility (a halfway house), and an outpatient follow-up team. Native Americans should help design and implement the entire set of programs. The program could offer a variety of alcohol education classes, assertiveness training, AA or other 12-step classes and weekly meetings, cultural heritage groups, and education classes. The outpatient program could help the client remain abstinent or in control of his drinking through brief interventions; group therapy; or individual, family, and marital counseling.

The advantage of having such an array of programs is that it offers a number of therapeutic options for meeting the needs of each individual. Some clients may only accept detoxification and have no interest in other intervention choices. Others may need substantial care for an extended period and would benefit from an inpatient facility and/or a halfway house environment. Still other may need only the services provided through an outpatient or outreach program. The theoretical underpinnings of the program could be based explicitly on a number of principles (such as cognitive-behavioral, motivational enhancement, relapse prevention, or 12-step facilitation)[28] but presented in terms of the issues and situations confronting local Indians. This is necessary because there are critical variations in the situations of different tribes whether urban, rural, or reservation, as well as in the cultural orientations and backgrounds of individual tribal members. Where appropriate, the treatment program should incorporate or make available traditional healing approaches to receptive individuals from the relevant tribal backgrounds such as the Native American Church, sweat lodge ceremony, Sun Dance, Spirit Quest/Winter Ceremony, Indian Shaker Church, Eskimo Spirit Movement, Wellbriety Movement, shamanic drumming, or a more general Aboriginal spirituality.[29] Whether a particular native approach is based on a specific tribal tradition, pan-Indian elements, or a newly developed ritual procedure is less important than the relevance and meaning of the ceremonies to the participants. For an example of the manner in which the pan-Indian Medicine Wheel icon and concept was used by a Canadian treatment center to integrate a variety of approaches including non-Aboriginal therapeutic talk and catharsis, *see* Gone (2011). Given the diversity in tribal backgrounds and the range of individual knowledge of, and interest in, "traditional" practices, it is a challenging task. For example, the Navajo have several religious options available to cure problem drinking, including Pentecostal Christianity, the Native American Church, and traditional healing. In discussing these approaches, Garrity (2000) described the case of a young woman who had two traditional ceremonies performed for her, but because she lacked knowledge of traditional culture and healing and was not fluent in Navajo, she did not relate to the rituals and healing symbols. She continued her substance abuse and suffering.

The programs need to be Indian-oriented for two basic reasons. First, as I indicated earlier and as we just saw in relation to the young Navajo woman, even though the general principles underlying effective approaches may be universal, unless they are presented in ways that make sense to the Indian clients and address their perceived needs, the programs are not likely to elicit the kind of commitment required from them to make successful changes in their lives. Second, if the programs are not perceived as being sensitive to Indian concerns and issues, they are not apt to take full advantage of them.

For example, Kathy Callahan, who examined the alcoholism treatment system available to Tohono O'odham (formerly called Papago) Indians in Tucson, Arizona, found such a problem:

> A comprehensive system of services does exist. However, many of the services in the system have been designed by and for Anglo populations and are not capable of dealing with problems specific to Indian populations. This discourages or in some cases prevents the use of these services by the Papago. Since the system is not being effectively utilized, it is not adequately providing care to the Papago population. It is the Indian designed and/or run services which appear to be best meeting Papago needs.[30]

In Seattle, the number of Indians entering a county treatment facility in 1980 decreased significantly after the Indian-specific components were integrated into other programs in such a way that they lost their distinctive Indian identity. The Indian participation decreased even though the effectiveness of the programs remained unchanged.[31]

Although I am endorsing an Indian orientation to treatment, I am not suggesting that the latest developments in neurobiological or treatment research be ignored. However, developing a program that combines both Indian cultural elements and effective science is not an easy task. Patricia Mail and George Menter,[32] who spent several years evaluating Indian alcoholism programs for the Indian Health Service, observed:

> The claim of uniqueness of the Indian culture, while often a valid consideration, should never-the-less not be allowed to interfere with or be substituted for demonstrably effective and tested treatment protocols. Many cultural supports may be an excellent adjunctive service or therapy to treatment, such as sweating [i.e., using a sweat lodge and related rituals] or participation in native ceremonials, but these are not substitutes for treatment planning and individual counseling.

Joan Weibel-Orlando also correctly pointed out, some twenty years ago, that the evidence supporting the effectiveness of traditional approaches is not particularly strong: "Anthropological enthusiasm for indigenous curing strategies as viable contemporary alcohol and drug interventions is based largely on anecdotal materials, short-term, synchronic observations of healing events and archival reviews. More systematic and observational investigations of the efficacy of such interventions are needed."[33] Although progress has been made, the situation has not changed dramatically.

A recent review of research on treatment approaches for American Indians (AIs) and Alaska Natives (ANs) comparing programs from 2000 to 2011 to earlier ones from 1968 to 1997 found that the recent programs included more traditional healing elements and that they generally reported reductions in substance use. Nonetheless, "attempts to incorporate AI/AN cultural traditions and worldviews into currently available treatment are difficult and still in their infancy . . . . Follow-up rates have remained variable and mostly low, and it is unclear if adding cultural components has improved outcomes."[34] In a review of substance abuse prevention programs, Whitbeck, Walls, and Welch noted that relevant publications were in the stage of focusing "on the process, theory, or description of interventions rather than documenting outcomes."[35]

A number of difficulties abound in integrating good science with native approaches. The challenges range from differing views of what the treatment goals should be, to the nature of the evidence to judge success, to methodological problems (such as randomizing treatment and control groups, small sample sizes, difficulties in following up participants), to outright rejection of science.[36] Nonetheless, these conflicts should not be irreconcilable if the programs are developed with true Indian collaboration and respect for native beliefs and values. Everyone shares the same ultimate goal of preventing and treating problem drinking and improving the quality of life for the people.

Concluding Comment

Problem drinking is the product of the complex interplay among genetic, neurobiological, psychological, sociocultural, and environmental factors. Each society aligns these forces into particular patterns that act on individuals over the course of their life cycles. When those forces develop, as they have among the Sioux City Indians, to create an environment conducive to heavy drinking, we should not be surprised to find that treating and preventing problem drinking are elusive goals not easily achieved. However, many of the same forces that conspire to create problem drinking can be manipulated at both the individual and societal level to decrease the likelihood of continued drinking. The early history of Winnebago Peyotism points the way, and if we combine the therapeutic insights embodied in the religion with programs that have been produced through research and clinical practice, we have a potent set of principles with which to proceed.

Endnotes to Chapter 9

[1] Parts of this chapter were originally published as "Peyotism and the Control of Heavy Drinking: The Nebraska Winnebago in the Early 1900s" in *Human Organization,* Vol. 49, No. 3, 1990, pages 255-265. It is published with permission of the Society for Applied Anthropology. An earlier version of this article was presented at the Annual Meeting of the American Anthropological Association, November 1988, Phoenix, Arizona. The research on which this chapter is based was supported by Summer Research Fellowships, University of Northern Iowa in 1977, 1980, 1981. I would like to thank Linda Bennett and Mac Marshall for organizing the session in Phoenix and Larry Gordon, Jay Noricks, Ron Roberts, Jerry Stockdale, and James Stokes for comments on an earlier draft of this chapter. I eliminated two sections of the original article that summarized the background history of the Winnebago and the nature of Winnebago Peyotism because they covered material presented in Chapter 8. I also made a number of changes to the remaining text and added new material.

[2] *See* Malouf (1942: 103), Maroukis (2010: 67, 231), Roy (1973: 330) for similar comments and Maroukis (2004: 78-79, 122-126) for the experience of Sam Necklace, an early Peyotist among the Yankton Sioux.

[3] Albaugh and Anderson (1974: 1248); La Barre (1975: 21, 63); Radin (1963 [1920]: 49); Siskin (1983: 121-122).

[4] Albaugh and Anderson (1974); Bergman (1971); La Barre (1975: 21, 147); Pascarosa and Futterman (1976); Pascarosa, Futterman, and Halsweig (1976).

[5] Or the religious support was regenerated with new vigor if one believes that the Shawnee Prophet's message from the 1800s still had a moral force (*see* endnote 38 in Chapter 8).

[6] *See* La Barre (1947) for a discussion of confession in Peyotism and as a widespread psychotherapeutic technique among aboriginal societies in the New World, Lex (1979) for a discussion of the role of arousal ("ritual catharsis") in attaining a new autonomic balance of the nervous system, Scheff (1977, 1979) for discussions of catharsis and abreaction, and Prince (1982) for a series of articles examining the role of endorphins in the body and in altered states of consciousness.

[7] *See* Dyck (2008: 58-78) for a discussion of the role of LSD and mescaline in the treatment of alcoholism during this period.

[8] *See,* for example, Fantegrossi, Murnane, and Reissig (2008); Sessa (2005); Vollenweider and Kometer (2010).

[9] *See,* for example, Ludwig et al. (1970), Mangini (1998), Smart et al. (1967); also *see* Grinspoon and Bakalar (1979: 192-237) and McCabe and Hanlon (1977) for reviews and critical discussions of therapeutic uses of psychedelics.

[10] D. A. Dawson, personal communication, cited in Rumpf et al. (2007: 75). Also, *see* Blomqvist (2007), Smart (2007), and Sobell (2007) for additional discussions of self-change and literature reviews.

[11] They cite the following studies: Bischof et al. (2002); Carbello et al. (under review); Chitwood and Morningstar (1985); Cunnigham et al. (2000); Sobell, Cunningham, and Sobell (1996); Sobell et al. (2000, 2001); Weisner, Matzger, and Kaskutas (2003).

[12] Carballo et al. (2007: 95).

[13] Brandon, Vidrine, and Litrin (2007); also, *see* Miller (1996). Clearly, as noted in the sources cited, the outcome of relapse studies will vary depending on how relapse is defined, the period covered, and the manner in which the treatment population is selected.

[14] And these relapse rates (i.e., 65%) were better than those for marijuana- and cocaine-dependent patients (75% relapse rate) only because the alcohol and opiate patients had been treated with "non-agonist medications for alcohol and opioids . . . in conjunction with behavioral relapse prevention approaches" Sinha (2011: 399).

[15] *See,* for example and discussion, Bergmark (2008), Bjornsson (2011), Frank (1973), Luborsky et al. (2002), Messer and Wampold (2002), Rosenzweig (1936), Wampold (1997), Wampold et al. (1997).

[16] Orford (1985: 299), also *see* Orford (2001: 339; 2008a, 2008b).

[17] Many researchers have tried to identify the elements of particular treatment approaches to problem drinking that make them effective. *See,* for example, Adler and Hammett (1973), Antze (1987), Brown (1985: 280-290), Galanter and Buckley (1978), Garrity (2000), Jilek (1974, 1994), Jilek and Todd (1974), Jilek-Aall (1981), Madsen (1974: 154-197 and 1979), Medicine (1983: 171-188; 2007: 95-103, 123-125), Miller (2003), Rodin (1985), Sadler (1977), Singer (1982), Singer and Borrero (1984), Slagle and Weibel-Orlando (1986), Sutro (1989), Wallace (1959), Weibel-Orlando (1989b), Westermeyer (1981).

[18] Radin (1963 [1920]: 49).

[19] McCabe and Hanlon (1977: 244), after reviewing the literature on the use of psychedelic drugs in psychotherapy, commented: "The limitations of the high-dose approach to psychedelic psychotherapy that relies on the

reintegration powers of a single peak experience have become increasingly apparent. Findings to date indicate that such an experience, albeit conversion-like on occasion, is not the sine qua non of personality reintegration, nor does it ensure freedom from symptoms or permanence of behavioral change."

[20] Because many of the Indians in the Sioux City area, including those professionals and para-professionals involved in alcoholism treatment programs, adopt the more traditional disease model and AA philosophy, an effort would be required to explain and generate support for this approach; otherwise, it would likely fail. See Levy and Kunitz (1981) for an insightful discussion of some of the difficulties involved in changing Indian alcoholism programs.

[21] See Weibel-Orlando (1984) for a discussion of Indian treatment programs as flawed "rites of passage."

[22] Oetting, Beauvais, and Edwards (1988: 99), after listing a number of prevention approaches that will not work with Indian youths, came to a similar conclusion: "What, then will work? Strong effective programs that 1) increase family strength, 2) lead to improved school adjustment, 3) create hope for the future, and 4) change peer clusters to discourage alcohol abuse." See Stigler, Neusel, and Perry (2011) for an overview of school-based prevention programs and Beauvais, et al. (2002); Hawken, Cummins, and Marlatt (2004); Henry et al. (2012); Moran and Bussey (2006); and Raghupathy and Go Forth (2012) for discussions of prevention programs for Indian and Alaska Native youths.

[23] Pharmacogenetics has been defined as the "study of the genetic basis for variation in drug response" (Relling and Giaomini 2011: 145). Some authors distinguish pharmacogentics from pharmacogenomics, which Meyer (2002: 3) defined as "the study of the entire spectrum of genes that determine drug response, including the assessment of the diversity of the human genome sequence and its clinical consequences." Other authors use both terms interchangeably (see Lucinio and Wong 2002).

[24] O'Malley and O'Connor (2011: 302).

[25] One study (Fuller et al. 1986) found a nonadherence rate as high as 80%.

[26] The patients had shorter periods of abstinence before beginning the acamprosate in the U.S. trials, and in Europe the vast majority of patients (90%) had received inpatient detoxification, while less than 8% of the U.S. patients had (see O'Malley and O'Connor 2011 and Garbutt 2009 for discussion and references).

[27] The *OPRM1* gene locus encodes for the mμ-opioid receptor (MOR, also called MOR1) active in dopamine neurotransmission in the corticomesolimbic system. Two human alleles (i.e., variants of the gene) have thus far been identified: *OPRM1 118G* and *OPRM1 118A*. In a study of patients using naltrexone, carrying a *118G* allele increased the proportion achieving a "good clinical outcome" from about 50% to about 90%. The drug had no effect on patients who were homozygous with *118A* alleles. Several lines of research involving rodents, monkeys, and humans, led Heilig et al. (2011: 674) to conclude that

> *118G* carriers activate dopaminergic reward circuitry in response to alcohol, and that this activation is mediated through actions of endogenous opioids. Activation of this cascade offers a target for naltrexone on the basis of the idea that naltrexone can inhibit alcohol-induced dopamine release by blocking the MOR upstream of the dopamine neurons. Conversely, the data indicate administration of alcohol is largely without influence on dopaminergic reward circuitry in *118A* homozygotes, and that there is therefore nothing for naltrexone to block in these subjects.

Although studies show that naltrexone helps block relapses caused by exposure to drinking cues and priming with alcohol, it does not appear to influence relapses caused by stress (Heilig et al. 2011: 677). As a result, researchers are investigating pharmacological agents that block corticotrophin-releasing factor (CRF1) receptors implicated in stress relapses. Some evidence suggests that variant alleles that encode for CRF1 receptors may influence responses to stress and alcohol use (*see* Heilig et al. 2011 for discussion of this research and other possible genetic loci relevant to stress-influenced reactions). A recent review and meta-analysis by Chamorro et al. (2012) also found individuals who carried the G allele and were treated with naltrexone had lower relapse rates than individuals who were homozygous for the A allele.

[28] *See* DiClemente et al. (2003), Fleming (2003), Galanter and Kleber (2011), Huebner and Kantor (2011), Humphreys (2003), Kadden (2003), Longabaugh (2003), McKay and Hiller-Strumhöfel (2011), Tucker and Simpson (2011), Witkiewtz and Marlatt (2011) for discussions of different psychosocial treatments.

[29] One study found that fewer than 20% of alcohol and other drug treatment programs nationwide offered specific services for Native Americans (Schmidt, Greenfield, Mulia 2006: 52). For overviews, discussions, and

bibliographies of prevention and treatment approaches for Indian alcohol problems, *see* Duran et al. (2005); Greenfield and Wenner (2012); Mail and Shelton (2002); Montag, et al. (2012); Moran (2002); Nebelkopf and Phillips (2004); Novins et al. (2012); Parker-Langley (2002); and Whitbeck, Walls, and Welch (2012) and the following for discussions of specific approaches: Bucko (1998); Colman and Merta (1999); Coyhis (1990); Coyhis and White (2006: 139-230); Duran and Duran (1995); Grobsmith (1994: 47-58); Hall (1985, 1986); Hornby (1995: 89-453); Jilek (1974, 1982, 1994: 233-241); Jilek and Todd (1974); Kelley (2008); Kulis et al. (2012); May and Hymbaugh (1989); Noe, Fleming, and Manson (2003); Ruby and Brown (1996); Slagle and Weibel-Orlando (1986); Waldram (1997); White Bison (2002); Winkelman (2004). *See* Grobsmith and Dam (1990) and Grobsmith (1994: 111-132) for discussions of the treatment programs available to Indian inmates and ex-offenders in the eastern Nebraska and Sioux City area.

[30] Callahan (1981: 179).

[31] Walker, Benjamin, Kivlahan, and Walker (1989: 304).

[32] Mail and Menter (1985: 17); also *see* Weibel-Orlando (1987).

[33] Weibel-Orlando (1989b: 152).

[34] Greenfield and Venner (2012: 488).

[35] Whitbeck, Walls, and Welch (2012: 431).

[36] *See* Castro et al. (2004); Gone (2012, 2011a, 2011b, and 2009); Hogue (2010); Levy and Kunitz (1981); O'Brien (2008); Orford (2008a, 2008b); Waldram (2000); Whitbeck, Walls, and Welch (2012) for discussions of these issues. For example, Waldram (1997: 201-221) is critical of efforts to determine the extent to which Aboriginal spiritual ceremonies like sweat lodge rituals are effective at healing. He sees science as the handmaiden of attempts to oppress and assimilate native peoples. Although the development and application of science does not occur independently of other sociocultural forces, the practice of science does generate its own set of values including independence, originality, dissent, freedom of thought, and tolerance (Bronowski 1965). Science is the best method we have developed to learn about the world and does produce knowledge that transcends individual cultures (Gellner 1992). I agree with Waldram that native healing procedures may achieve a variety of beneficial results and that many of these outcomes can be difficult to measure. Other outcomes, however, such as the length of time a person is abstinent or the number of times he engages in episodes of heavy drinking or low-risk drinking can be determined by both the participating individual and other observers. Many people come to these

ceremonies specifically looking for help in controlling their alcohol consumption. When claims are made that a particular approach can help people control their drinking, it is both appropriate and essential to see whether we can verify such assertions. The value of sweat lodge ceremonies specifically, or Aboriginal spirituality more generally, in a prison setting or elsewhere does not depend on their effectiveness in treating problem drinking. As Waldram argues, there are many potential, beneficial results that warrant their use even though it may be difficult to establish them empirically. Attempting to understand a particular religion's appeal using a biopsychosocial approach does not diminish the religion's value or exhaust all that the religion has to teach its participants or us. Nor does science limit its critical approach to only non-Western procedures: witness the evaluation of the psychiatric use of antidepressants (Kirsch 2009, Moncrieff 2009) and long-standing efforts to evaluate a series of biomedical practices such as tonsillectomies, radical mastectomies, and coronary by-pass surgeries (Glasser and Pelto 1980).

CHAPTER 10
HEAVY DRINKING, INTRASOCIETAL DIVERSITY, AND ALTERNATIVE PERSPECTIVES[1]

> [T]here is no way of seeing, hearing, or representing the world of others that is absolutely universally valid or correct. Ethnographies of any sort are always subject to multiple interpretations. They are never beyond controversy or debate.
>
> John Van Maanen

> Social science produces a multiple, contradictory truth for our time—that is, a set of diversified perspectives and diagnoses of our changing, tangled, and contradictory society. These truths live in the practices and understandings of a research community, not in particular laws, and when that community peters out, its truth passes into history along with the society it tried to understand.
>
> Paul Diesing

Introduction

In the preceding chapters, we examined alcohol use among Sioux City Indians from a number of perspectives. We looked at it from the perspective of the normative environment—how the people evaluated and responded to different types and levels of drinking both for themselves as well as for others. We also discussed other constraints such as jobs and health and the impact they had on drinking. We examined alcohol use from the perspective of drunken comportment—what the people actually did when they got drunk—and offered a model to help make sense of their behaviors. We examined drinking that had reached a point where the drinker himself and those around him considered it to be a problem. To understand the various types of problem drinking, I argued that we needed to use a biopsychosocial model to begin analyzing the various kinds of forces and factors that produce the patterns observed. We adopted a historical perspective to examine the ways in which alcohol use had changed over time for the Nebraska Winnebago and to understand the significance of the adoption of the Peyote religion. Finally, continuing our examination of the Peyote religion, we looked at alcohol use from the perspective of treatment and prevention—what can change drinking behaviors? As we saw, for every interpretation that I offered, alternative ones are also available. I suggested that such divergent views legitimately arise as researchers ask different kinds of questions and adopt different research strategies, methodologies, theoretical orientations, and modes of data presentation. In concluding this book, I would like to comment on one theoretical difference that I believe is central to adequately understanding alcohol use and to briefly discuss the significance of a micro perspective. This discussion explicates the theoretical orientation that guided my work and places my description and analysis in a broader theoretical context.

Intrasocietal Diversity

Although a number of methodological and theoretical weaknesses can be identified in studies of alcohol use, a major one has been the failure to adequately recognize and make sense of intrasocietal diversity.[2] As I noted in Chapter One, this limitation was an outgrowth of the approaches developed by early culture and personality researchers such as Ruth Benedict and Margaret Mead. Anthony F. C. Wallace, who helped reorient the field of psychological anthropology in the 1950s and 1960s,[3] labeled their approach to culture and personality "replication of uniformity." As we saw earlier, this position assumes that all, or at least most, individuals within a society share the same personality structure due to the shaping processes of enculturation or socialization. Since the 1950s, however, the amount of biological, psychological, and sociocultural diversity within a society has been shown to be much greater than early culture and personality researchers imagined.[4] A society is not a homogeneous collection of individuals sharing one or two personality types; instead, it is an *organization of diversity* (Wallace 1970b). The diversity is found not only among individuals, but behavioral patterns that earlier were taken to represent enduring personality traits of given individuals have been shown to be situationally influenced.[5] A person who is talkative and outgoing in one set of circumstances may be taciturn and withdrawn in another. A person's behavior does not occur apart from socioculturally defined situations. In the context of drinking studies, a replication-of-uniformity approach tends to wash out the diversity that occurs in the drinking behaviors, in the norms and sanctions applied to consumption, in the biopsychosocial factors influencing the behaviors, and in the functions served by the behaviors. Drinking episodes superficially treated as instances of the same type, such as "heavy drinking" or "alcohol dependence," on closer examination may represent a number of patterns, each having different origins and effects.

The Distribution and Nature of Culture

In dealing with the diversity encountered in drinking, a researcher is better served with some version of the organization-of-diversity model (or as it is also called, the distributive model of culture) and an ideational view of culture.[6] With the distributive approach:

> no population, within a stated cultural boundary, can be *assumed* to be uniform with respect to any variable or pattern. (For example, it cannot be *assumed* that males and females share the same values, the same role cognitions, the same emotional structure.) In every instance, a distribution will be found to characterize the sample [Wallace 1970b: 128; his emphasis].

An ideational conception defines culture in terms of cognition. It is seen as the knowledge, beliefs, and values of a people (or alternatively phrased, it is the learned distinctions, categories, and schemas of a people.[7] Observable behavior and material artifacts, therefore, are not defined as culture. As Ward Goodenough, an early proponent of an ideational view, put it:

> [C]ulture is not a material phenomenon; it does not consist of things, people, behavior, or emotions. It is rather an organization of these things. It is the form of things that people have in mind, their models for perceiving, relating, and otherwise interpreting them" [1964 (1957): 36].

> Culture . . . consists of standards for deciding what is, standards for deciding what can be, standards for deciding how one feels about it, standards for deciding what to do about it, and standards for deciding how to go about doing it [1963: 258-259].

With an ideational and distributive view of culture, a theorist is capable of making a number of distinctions relating to the use of the term culture that are analytically helpful in dealing with intrasocietal diversity. Although we do not need to review them all, Goodenough (1981) distinguishes seven different usages. An individual's own standards are called his *propriospect*[8] and include "both his cognitive and affective orderings of his experience" (Goodenough 1981: 98).[9] The set of standards that a person uses on a given occasion to interpret the behavior of others or to guide his own behavior is his *operating culture*. The *public culture* of a given group of people consists of all the versions that each individual of the group attributes to the group. For example, each man working on a hide gang in Sioux City (the crew of men who move and load cattle hides) has his own view of the understandings and rules that he thinks the other members of the hide gang use in performing their activities. The public culture of the hide gang consists of all these individual views. To the extent that identifiable groups within a society have unique sets of standards or public cultures relating to their activities, each group's public culture represents the subculture of that group. A *society's culture* is composed of all the public cultures relating to all the groups within the society. Finally, we need a term to distinguish the total contents of all the propriospects of all the members of a society; Goodenough calls this a society's *culture pool*.[10] For example, let us say only one elderly Winnebago in Sioux City remembers some of the rituals of the Medicine Lodge. Even if the man does not use that knowledge, it would be included in a description of his propriospect and in the description of the culture pool of the Sioux City Indians. Unique and idiosyncratic elements of a culture pool are particularly important in understanding the processes of culture change. The inventory of items in a society's culture pool forms the basis on which processes of change like innovative recombination operate. If circumstances warrant, the unused knowledge of the elderly man could form the basis of a new religious movement and spread throughout the population.

One of the benefits of this kind of approach is that it explicitly acknowledges the societal diversity (both at the individual level--the propriospects — and at the societal level — the society's culture pool), and yet also allows a researcher to identify a variety of subgroups or social networks and the subcultures related to their activities. Applying this perspective to Sioux City, it becomes apparent that Indians differentially participate in a variety of social networks with their related subcultures. As a result, knowledge of the subcultures is shared in varying degrees across the Indian population. For example, Frank Wolf's wife, Sharon, never participated in the activities of street life and so knows little about the subculture(s)[11] related to street life. The elderly father of one of my consultants had been both a self-described "periodic drunk" as well as a Peyotist, and as a result, knows the subcultures associated with street life and the Peyote religion. His son, however, knows little about the Peyote subculture but a great deal about the subculture of street life. With this perspective, any Sioux City Indian (and any individual in the U.S. for that matter) is clearly multi-(sub)cultural.

Many of the social networks in which Indians participate are not exclusively Indian. The activities and subculture of street life, for example, clearly are not limited to Indians, but rather are shared by a variety of whites, African Americans, Hispanics, and people of other ethnic backgrounds. The same is true of many of the networks associated with employment (such as jobs in the meat packing industries) or the city schools. In addition, although the social systems and subcultures of Sioux City Indians possess unique attributes, similar ones can be found in both the U.S. and other countries.[12] Some researchers, such as Bernard James[13] discussing Anishnabeg groups (also called Chippewa or Ojibwa in the literature), have focused on these factors and have emphasized the cultural components held in common with working-class or impoverished whites, arguing that contemporary Indian culture (in this case Chippewa culture) is essentially "working class" white culture. Others,[14] working with the same population, have stressed the relatively unique Indian elements that are not shared with whites (such as collecting wild rice, powwows, religious wakes and other ceremonies) to show that Chippewa culture is still a vibrant force.[15] The multiculturalism of Sioux City Indians allows them to perform as working-class or middle-class whites would in some contexts, such as on the job, but uniquely in other contexts, such as at a powwow.

Micro and Macro Perspectives

The social networks and related subcultures of the Sioux City Indians are obviously embedded in, and articulate with, the social systems of mainstream America. As a result, changes in the macro systems (the schools, social and legal agencies, medical facilities, political and economic institutions) directly affect the lives of Sioux City Indians. Some researchers feel that when social scientists study local populations they should focus on the linkages that exist between local systems and the macro systems, carrying the examination in some cases to the world system.[16] Handling these various linkages and the related macro versus micro perspectives in an ethnographic study is a challenging task. Often a researcher will adopt either the macro or micro perspective, placing the other in the background. Although both perspectives are required for a more complete understanding—each allows the researcher to ask different kinds of questions—in this work, the macro systems compose the background. My attempts to address the larger setting have taken three forms. In the first chapter, I briefly reviewed studies that dealt with the onslaught of Westernization and its impact on native peoples in terms of acculturation and drinking. In the Sioux City setting of the 1970s, I relied on brief descriptions and statistical data (such as the mean family income, percentage of families below the poverty line, years of education, and number of unemployed) to convey a sense of the larger systems and their influences on the Indians. In Chapter Eight, where I discussed the development of Winnebago drinking patterns from the mid-1800s into the early 1900s, I focused in greater detail on some of the institutions and forces external to Winnebago society. Even here, the description and analysis were confined to a limited time frame and to the major forces most relevant to the drinking practices

If valuable insights have been lost by concentrating on the micro perspective, I hope we have won insights that we would not otherwise have gained. Too frequently when a macro perspective is adopted, faulty and misleading descriptions and analyses of drinking behavior are produced. Some researchers, more from strongly felt ideological positions than relevant data, simply assert that the "real" cause of heavy drinking and other untoward behaviors of contemporary Indians is the disadvantaged positions they hold in the larger system.[17] Others, while offering data and analyses, are not as sensitive as they need to be to the social and biopsychological diversity that exists within the population. Consequently, they oversimplify and misconstrue the nature of Indian drinking.[18] We could describe the life of the everyday people in Sioux City as an oppressed subgroup within the larger society and treat hell-raising life styles exclusively as modes or rituals of resistance to the dominant order. However, by doing so, we would fail to give credence to the social and psychological diversity of the Indians. When individuals from the same family develop different life styles and drinking patterns, any approach that fails to take that diversity into account will lead neither to an accurate understanding of those life styles nor to effective intervention programs. The manner in which individuals experience and react to the larger sociocultural forces affecting them is more diverse than many researchers allow. The only way to fully explore that diversity is by retaining the individual as a critical unit of description and analysis.

Concluding Comments

The Sioux City Indian population suffers from a variety of social problems, one of which is heavy drinking. I have tried to accurately reflect the diversity that exists in relation to drinking activities and to make them understandable, both from my consultants' various perspectives and from my own, drawing not only on their views but on studies in other disciplines as well. In order to construct a holistic and richly-textured understanding of drinking, a biopsychosocial model is required. Such an approach, however, places a heavy burden on a single researcher because the knowledge and techniques generated by the relevant disciplines are growing exponentially. Anthropology, as a field of study, has historically held up the goal of integrating diverse perspectives. It matters less whether a single anthropologist, a team of researchers, or several investigators working independently produce those views, but the maintenance of the holistic ideal is essential for the discipline. Hopefully, the present study represents a step toward the development of such a multi-faceted understanding for the Sioux City Indians.

I wish I could feel optimistic that state and federal agencies will judiciously increase their support for educational, economic, and drug intervention programs designed to improve the lives of Sioux City Indians. Unfortunately, the political policies adopted over the past three decades give little reason for hope. To take just one example, funding for the Indian Health Service since the 1980s has fallen dramatically compared to the per capita spending for Medicare and Medicaid.[19] Over the same period, the wealthiest one percent of families have gotten vastly richer, while the poorest twenty percent of families have gained little, going from an average household income of $14,900 in 1979 to $16,500 in 2006.[20] In 1970, 38% of Indian families in Sioux City lived below the poverty line. In 1999 (the latest date for which we have data), 40% of Indian children in the Sioux City area lived in poverty (vs. 10% of non-Hispanic white children).[21] In Chapter Three, I indicated that the Sioux City school system was not serving Indian children adequately. According to a recent annual report of the Sioux City Community School District, the percentages of proficient Native American students for grades 6-7-8 were 53.1% in reading (vs. 69.9% for whites), 58.2% in math (vs. 73.3% for whites), and 69.4% in science (vs. 82.1% for whites). The percentages proficient in the 11th grade were 54.8% in reading (vs.78.6% for whites), 74.2% in math (vs. 76.6% for whites), and 74.2% in science (vs. 81.3% for whites).[22]

Given the current political climate, additional financial assistance from the government does not appear likely. Still, Sioux City Indians need not feel helpless in relation to drinking problems. Regardless of the other difficulties they face in their lives—discrimination, ineffective educational programs, limited job opportunities, reduced family supports, and poverty—they do not have to suffer the additional burdens of heavy drinking. Although, as I have argued, the sociocultural dice are loaded toward the development of heavy drinking for the population, the outcome for any individual is not foreordained. As the anthropologist Edward Sapir said many years ago in response to an argument concerning the nature and force of culture, it is still "always the individual that really thinks and acts and dreams and revolts" (1917: 442). Although it is difficult for a single individual or group of Sioux City Indians to radically alter the political and economic structures that condition their lives, they can change absolutely the standards that guide their own drinking, and with work and co-operation, they can also change the standards of their families and friends. Drinking standards are only one set of factors that influence drinking, but they are significant ones. As discussed in Chapters Six, Seven, and Eight, if people are passive and fatalistically believe they cannot change their drinking behaviors, chances are that they will not—even with the best treatment programs and facilities. Conversely, as many Indians like Albert Hensley and John Rave have demonstrated, with the appropriate motivation and vision, heavy drinking does not have to be added to their other problems.

Endnotes for Chapter 10

[1] I would like to thank Jay Noricks, Ron Roberts, Jerry Stockdale, and James Stokes for comments on an earlier version of this chapter.

[2] Other basic weaknesses include the failure to adopt an insider's perspective; an exclusive use of, and a reliance on, an equilibrium model of society that sees deviant behavior as rare or occurring only in response to forces outside the system; and a limited time frame.

[3] For overviews and discussions of the changes in psychological anthropology *see* Barnouw (1979); Bock (1980); Casey and Edgerton (2005); Schwartz, White, and Lutz (1992); Shweder (1991); Spindler (1978); Stigler, Shweder, and Herdt (1990); Wallace (1970b).

[4] Bergman, Thompson, and Affif (1984); Bock (1980: 131-138); Lewontin (1974); Lindesmith and Strauss (1950); Orlansky (1949); Pelto and Pelto (1975); Relling and Giacomini (2011); Runyan (1982); Wallace (1970b); Wilkins (2008); Williams (1956, 1974); Wong, Gottesman, and Petronis (2005); Wright (2008). Through advances in genetic and epigenetic studies, we now appreciate that even monozygotic twins can differ in significant ways, *see* Blickstein et al. (2011) and Haque, Gottesman, and Wong (2009).

[5] Mischel (1968, 1990); Shweder (1991: 269-312).

[6] Goodenough (1981), Schwartz (1978), Wallace (1970b).

[7] Theorists who adopt an ideational view of culture differ on a number of other issues, *see* for example, Blount (2011), D'Andrade (1995), Freilich (1989), Keesing (1974, 1994), Kronenfeld (2011), Geertz (1973), Quinn (2011), Schneider (1976), Shore (1996).

[8] As Goodenough (1981: 98) notes, this term is from the Latin *"proprio,* 'peculiar to the self,' and *spectus,* 'view' or 'outlook'."

[9] The propriospect is what Goodenough earlier (1963) referred to as "private culture" and corresponds to what Wallace calls "mazeway" and Schwartz labels "idioverse." Wallace defines a mazeway as "the entire set of cognitive maps of positive and negative goals that an individual maintains at a given time. This set includes goals of self, others, and material objects, and of their possible dynamic interrelations" (Wallace 1970b: 15). A person's idioverse consists of his total set of implicit constructs which are "simultaneously cognitive, evaluative, and affective mappings of the structure of events and classes of events, both past and possible, real and hypothetical" (Schwartz 1978: 425).

[10] Goodenough's culture pool corresponds to what Schwartz (1978: 430) defines as "a culture": "the total set of idioverses of the members of a society, including but not wholly comprised by, the structure and social structure of commonality. It includes all the experientially derived and transformed constructs held by any member of that society."

[11] Depending on the level of generality one adopts, the social networks that are involved in the activities of street life can be treated as one subgroup with a single subculture or, at a lower level, can be seen as being composed of a variety of subgroups each with its own subculture. For example, as indicated earlier, some Indians on the street work on hide gangs. The knowledge, values, and schemas the men use in relation to a hide gang represent a subculture. Many people on the street have not worked on a hide gang and do not know that subculture in any detail. In a similar fashion, the subgroup of individuals who regularly use the Salvation Army know its subculture. The police-court-jail subsystem operates with its own subculture, and the knowledge of that subculture also varies among the people on the street. Henceforth, I will use the singular form and refer to the subculture of life on the street, but with the understanding that at a lower level of specificity it is composed of many separate subcultures.

[12] Bahr (1973), Brody (1971), Hannerz (1969), Lang (1974), Liebow (1967), Singer (1986), Spradley (1970), White (1970), Wiseman (1970).

[13] James (1961, 1970, 1973, 1974).

[14] Paredes (1973); Pelto (1973); Roufs (1973, 1974).

[15] Lurie (1962: 829), in response to James's 1961 article, also argued that cultural differences are seen in the way similar activities are performed: "Their [Indian] humor is different; their decision-making processes are different; their religious attitudes are different, even if based on Christianity and church membership; their canons of politeness are different; their attitudes toward land and material wealth are different; and their expectations of one another are different."

[16] See Baer, Singer, and Susser (2003); Hind (1984); Leatherman and Goodman (2011); Nash (1981); Roseberry (1988) for overviews of this orientation and Baer, Singer, and Susser (2003: 97-141); Faiman-Silva (1997); Moore (1993); Pickering (2000); Singer (1986); Wolf (1982); Jorgensen (1971, 1978) for examples. In relation to drinking, Singer (1986: 116) feels that anthropologists have failed badly in framing their descriptions and analyses to adequately explore these linkages: "Has the holism of the discipline focused attention on the larger structure, patterns and processes that create

the settings, bring into being the social groups, produce and promote the intoxicants, and generate the motivations for prodigious consumption? Sad to say, it has not." Also *see* Baer, Singer, and Susser (2003: 97-141). *See* Fast (2002) for an explicit application of this perspective to drinking among an Athabascan group in Alaska.

[17] *See*, for example, Schlesier (1979) and the comments by Deloria (1980), DeMallie (1980), Hill (1980b), Washburn (1980), and Schlesier (1980).

[18] *See*, for example, Robert White's (1970) study of the Lakota in Rapid City, South Dakota. White argues that a subculture of deprivation among the Lakota he identifies as the "camp" and "lower-class transition" groups creates a personality structure that requires periodic discharges of tension and leads to a "culture of excitement." His description and analysis are inadequate on several points, but a critical weakness is his failure to note and handle the population's psychological and social diversity, basically adopting a replication-of-uniformity approach.

[19] Westmoreland and Watson (2006) and Forum (2010).

[20] Hacker and Pierson (2010: 22). Income inequality has grown dramatically in the U.S. since the end of the 1970s. The middle and working-class households, at best, made only modest gains during this period. Between 1979 and 2006 (the latest date for which data is available), the average, inflation-adjusted income of the bottom 20% of households, including government taxes and benefits and private employment-base benefits, increased 10%. The middle 20% of households gained 21%, which amounts to a 0.7% increase per year. Much of this increase, however, was due to the households working more hours today (and adding more women working outside the home) than in the late 1970s. The extra hours of work in 2000 amounted to ten additional full-time weeks per household. The top 1% of households between 1979 and 2006 experienced an increase in income of 256%. Their average, after-tax income was $1.2 million. Their average net worth in 2004 was nearly $15 million. In contrast, the bottom 40% of households had an average net worth of $2,200 in 2004, and 17% of households had zero or negative net worth (Hacker and Pierson 2010: 22, 32-33). In addition, both individual social mobility (Is an individual earning more now than two decades ago?) and intergenerational social mobility (Is an individual making more than his parents?) appear to have declined over this period. In a recent study, six affluent European countries and Australia and Canada had greater intergenerational mobility than the U.S. (Hacker and Pierson 2010: 29); also *see* Noah (2012) and Stiglitz (2012). *See* Wilkinson

and Pickett (2009) for an examination of the manner in which the extent of economic inequality relates to health and social problems among nations and among states within the U.S.; also *see* Hertzman and Boyce (2010), McEwen (2010), McEwen and Gianaros (2010), and Seeman et al. (2010). Kevin Phillips (1990) argues that our national public policy toward wealth and its distribution tends to oscillate between individual money-making and public-spirited reforms. One can only hope he is correct and that the political pendulum will start swinging in the other direction before we end up locked into a capitalist plutocracy.

[21] Sioux City, IA-NE-SD metropolitan area (http://www.diversitydata-archive.org).

[22] Sioux City Community Schools District (2010: 3, 6, 9). In general, African American and Hispanic students in these grades performed in a comparable fashion below white students. Asian American students, however, frequently scored better than white students on these tests.

REFERENCES CITED

The following abbreviations are used:

AA   Anthropological Archives of the Smithsonian Institution, Washington, D.C.

FA   Federal Archives and Record Center, Kansas City, Winnebago Agency, Subject File 1900-1929.

NA   National Archives, Record Group 75, Records of the Bureau of Indian Affairs, Washington, D.C.

Aberdeen Area Indian Health Service
    1990 Mortality Charts, May 1990. Aberdeen: Indian Health Service.
Aberle, David
    1982 The Peyote Religion Among the Navaho, 2nd Ed. Chicago: U Chicago Press.
Adams, R.
    1962 Ethnohistoric Research Methods: Some Latin American Features. Ethnohistory 9: 179-205.
Adesso, Vincent
    1985 Cognitive Factors in Alcohol and Drug Use. In Determinants of Substance Abuse: Biological, Psychological, and Environmental Factors. Mark Galizio and Stephen Maisto, Eds. NY: Plenum Press.
Adler, Herbert and Van Buren Hammett
    1973 Crisis, Conversion and Cult Formation: An Examination of a Common Psychosocial Sequence. American J of Psychiatry 130 (8): 861-864.
Agar, Michael
    1980 The Professional Stranger: An Informal Introduction to Ethnography. NY: Academic Press.
Agrawal, Arpana and Laura Bierut
    2012 Identifying Genetic Variation for Alcohol Dependence. Alcohol Research: Current Reviews 34 (3): 274-381.
Agrawal, Arpana and Michael Lynskey
    1991 The Role of Alcohol Metabolizing Enzymes in Alcohol Sensitivity, Alcohol Drinking Habits, and Incidence of Alcoholism in Orientals. In The Molecular Pathology of Alcoholism. T. Palmer, Ed. NY: Oxford U Press.
    2008 Are There Genentic Influences on Addiction: Evidence from Family, Adoption and Twin Studies. Addiction 103: 1069-1081.
Albaugh, Bernard and Philip Anderson
    1974 Peyote in the Treatment of Alcoholism Among the American Indians. American J of Psychiatry 131 (11): 1247-1250.
Allen, Arthur
    1927 Northwestern Iowa: Its History and Traditions. Volumes 1 and 2. Chicago: S. J. Clarke Publishing Company.
American Psychiatric Association
    1994 Diagnostic and Statistical Manual of Mental Disorders, 4th Ed. Washington, DC: APA Press.
Amoss, P.
    1978 Symbolic Substitution in the Indian Shaker Church. Ethnohistory 25: 225-249.

Anderson, Edward
    1996 Peyote the Divine Cactus, 2nd Ed. Tucson: U of Arizona Press.
Anderson, James
    1898 Letter to W. N. Hailman, January 6, 1898. NA, Letters Received.
Annual Report
    1910 NA, Winnebago Agency.
    1911 Narrative, Section IV. NA, Winnebago Agency.
    1912 Narrative, Section IV. NA, Winnebago Agency.
    1920 Narrative, Section IV. NA, Winnebago Agency.
Antze, Paul
    1987 Symbolic Action in Alcoholics Anonymous. In Constructive Drinking:
        Perspectives on Drink from Anthropology. Mary Douglas, Ed. NY: Cambridge U
        Press.
Arndt, Grant
    2012 Indigenous Autobiography en Abyme: Indigenous Reflections on Representational
        Agency in the Case of Crashing Thunder. Ethnohistory 59 (1): 27-49.
Ashford, John
    1904 Testimony at Winnebago. FA.
Ashford, Thomas, Jr.
    1904 Testimonry at Winnebago. FA.
Atkinson, R.
    1978 Knowledge and Explanation in History. Ithaca: Cornell U Press.
Axtell, J.
    1978 The Ethnohistory of Early America: A Review Essay. William and Mary Quarterly
        35: 110-144.
    1979 Ethnohistory: An Historian's Viewpoint. Ethnohistory 26: 1-13.
    1981 The European and the Indian: Essays in the Ethnohistory of Colonial North
        America. NY: Oxford U Press.
    1997 The Ethnohistory of Native America. In Rethinking American Indian History.
        Donald Fixico, Ed. Albuquerque: U New Mexico Press.
Bacon, M.
    1976 Alcohol Use in Tribal Societies. In The Biology of Alcoholism. Volume 4: Social
        Aspects of Alcoholism. B. Kissin and H. Begleiter, Eds. NY: Plenum Press.
Baer, Hans, Merrill Singer, and Ida Susser
    2003 Medical Anthropology and the World System, 2nd Ed. Westport: Praeger.
Baerreis, D.
    1961 The Ethnohistoric Approach and Archaeology. Ethnohistory 8: 49-77.
Bahr, Howard
    1973 Skid Row: An Introduction to Disaffiliation. NY: Oxford U Press.
Bailey, A.
    1969 The Conflict of European and Eastern Algonkian Cultures 1504-1700, 2nd Ed.
        Toronto: U Toronto Press.
Ballenger, J. and R. Post
    1978 Kindling as a Model for Alcohol Withdrawal Syndromes. British J of Psychiatry
        133: 1-14.
Bandura, Albert
    1986 Social Foundations of Thought and Action: A Social Cognitive Theory. Englewood
        Cliffs: Prentice-Hall, Inc.
    1997 Self-Efficacy: The Exercise of Control. NY: Worth Publishers.

2001 Social Cognitive Theory: An Agentic Perspective. Annual Review of Psychology 52: 1-26.

Bannister, D. and J. Mair

1968 The Evaluation of Personal Constructs. NY: Academic Press.

Barnett, H.

1957 Indian Shakers: A Messianic Cult of the Pacific Northwest. Carbondale: Southern Illinois U Press.

Barnouw, Victor

1979 Culture and Personality, 3rd Ed. Homewood, IL: Dorsey Press

Barrows, Susanna and Robin Room

1991 Introduction. *In* Drinking: Behavior and Belief in Modern History. S. Barrows and R. Room, Eds. Berkeley: U CA Press.

Barry, H.

1982 Cultural Variations in Alcohol Abuse. *In* Culture and Psychopathology, I. Al-Issa, Ed. Baltimore: U Park Press.

Beals, J., P. Spicer, C. Mitchell, et al.

2003 Racial Disparities in Alcohol Use: Comparison of Two American Reservation Populations with National Data. American J of Public Health 93 (10): 1683-1685.

Beauvais, Fred, P. Jumper-Thurman, H. Helm, B. Plested

2002 Prevention of Alcohol and Other Drug Abuse Among Indian Adolescents: An Examination of Current Assumptions. *In* Alcohol Use Among American Indians and Alaska Natives: Multiple Perspectives on a Complex Problem. P. Mail, et al., Eds. NIAAA Research Monograph No. 37. Bethesda: U.S. Dept of Health and Human Services.

Beauvais, Fred, P. Jumper-Thurman, H. Helm, B. Plested, and M. Burnside

2004 Surveillance of Drug Use Among American Indian Adolescents: Patterns Over 25 Years. J of Adolescent Health 34: 493-500.

Becker, Howard

1960 Notes on the Concept of Commitment. American J of Sociology 66: 32-40.

Becker, Howard C.

2008 Alcohol Dependence, Withdrawal and Relapse. Alcohol Research and Health 24: 348-361.

Beckett, Jeremy

1984 Comment. Current Anthropology 25 (2): 178-179.

Bee, R.

1974 Patterns and Processes. NY: The Free Press.

Beidelman, T.

1982 Colonial Evangelism: A Socio-Historical Study of an East African Mission at the Grassroots. Bloomington: Indiana U Press.

Belmont, F.

1952 History of Brandy in Canada. Mid-America 34: 42-63.

Benedict, Ruth

1930 Psychological Types in the Cultures of the Southwest. Proceedings of the Twenty-third International Congress of Americanists: 572-581.

1934a Anthropology and the Abnormal. J of General Psychiatry 10: 59-82.

1934b Patterns of Culture. Boston: Houghton Mifflin Co.

Bennett, John

1946 The Interpretation of Pueblo Culture. Southwestern J of Anthropology 4: 361-374.

Bennett, Linda
  1988 Alcohol in Context: Anthropological Perspectives. Drugs and Society 2: 89-131.
Bennett, Linda and Genevieve Ames, Eds.
  1985 The American Experience with Alcohol: Contrasting Cultural Perspectives. NY: Plenum Press.
Bennett, Linda and Paul Cook
  1990 Drug Studies. *In* Medical Anthropology: A Handbook of Theory and Method. T. Johnson and C. Sargent, Eds. Westport: Greenwood Press.
Bergman, Robert
  1971 Navaho Peyote Use: Its Apparent Safety. American J of Psychiatry 128 (6): 695-699.
Bergman, Ronald, Sue Thompson, and Adel Afifi
  1984 Catalog of Human Variation. Baltimore: Urban and Schwarzenberg, Inc.
Bergmark, Anders
  2008 On Treatment Mechanisms—What Can We Learn from the COMBINE Study? Addiction 103 (5): 703-705.
Berkhofer, Robert
  1965 Salvation and the Savage: An Analysis of Protestant Missions and American Indian Response, 1787-1862. NY: Atheneum.
  1978 The White Man's Indian. NY: Random House.
Berry, J.
  1980 Social and Cultural Change. *In* Handbook of Cross-Cultural Psychology. H. Triandis and R. Brislin, Eds. Boston: Allyn and Bacon.
Berthrong, D.
  1963 The Southern Cheyennes. Norman: U of Oklahoma Press.
Bierut, L., A. Goate, N. Breslasu, et al.
  2012 *ADH1B* Is Associated with Alcohol Dependence and Alcohol Consumption in Populations of European and African Ancestry. Molecular Psychiatry 17 (4): 445-450.
Biolsi, Thomas, Ed.
  2004 A Companion to the Anthropology of American Indians. Malden MA: Blackwell.
Biolsi, Thomas and I. Zimmerman, Eds.
  1997 Indians and Anthropologists. Tucson: U of Arizona Press.
Bischof , G., J. Rumpf, U. Hapke, C. Meyer, and U. John
  2002 Remission from Alcohol Dependence Without Help: How Restrictive Should Our Definition of Treatment Be? J of Studies on Alcohol 63: 229-236.
Bjornsson, Andri
  2011 Beyond the "Psychological Placebo": Specifying the Nonspecific in Psychotherapy. Clinical Psychology: Science and Practice 18: 113-118.
Black, M.
  1973 Belief Systems. *In* Handbook of Social and Cultural Anthropology. John Honigmann, Ed. Chicago: Rand McNally and Co.
Blair, E., Ed.
  1911 The Tribes of the Upper Mississippi Valley and Region of the Great Lakes, Vol. 2. Cleveland: Arthur Clark.
Blickstein, Isaac, Y. Martins, A. Matias, and S. Silva
  2011 Why Are Monozygotic Twins Different? J of Perinatal Medicine 39 (2): 195-208.

Blomqvist, Jan
2007 Self-Change from Alcohol and Drug Abuse: Often-Cited Classics. *In* Promoting Self-Change from Addictive Behaviors: Practical Implications for Policy, Prevention, and Treatment. H. Klingemann and L. Sobell, Eds. NY: Springer.

Blount, B. G.
2011 A History of Cognitive Anthropology. *In* A Companion to Cognitive Anthropology. D. Kronenfield, G. Bennardo, W. de Munch, and M. Fischer, Eds. NY: Wiley-Blackwell.

Blowsnake, Sam
1948 Application for a Patent Fee. November 10, 1948. NA, Accession Number 57A-185, Box 221.

Bock, P.
1980 Continuities in Psychological Anthropology. San Francisco: Freeman.

Borghese, Cecilia and R. Harris
2012 Alcohol Dependence and Genes Encoding $\alpha2$ and $\gamma1$ GABA$_A$ Receptor Subunits: Insights from Humans and Mice. Alcohol Research: Current Reviews 34 (3): 345-353.

Bosron, William, D. Rex, C. Harden, T-K. Li, and R. Akerson
1988 Alcohol and Aldehyde Isoenzymes in Sioux North American Indians. Alcoholism: Clinical and Experimental Research 12 (3): 454-455.

Brandon, T., J. Vidrine, and E. Litvin
2007 Relapse and Relapse Prevention. Annual Review of Clinical Psychology 3: 257-284.

Breese, G., D. Overstreet, and D. Knapp
2005 Conceptual Framework for the Etiology of Alcoholism: A "Kindling"/Stress Hypothesis. Psychopharmacology 178: 367-380.

Brody, Hugh
1971 Indians on Skid Row. Ottawa: Northern Science Research Group, Department of Indian Affairs and Northern Development.

Bronowski, J.
1965 Science and Human Values, Revised Ed. NY: Harper and Row.

Brown, D.
1980 Drinking as an Indicator of Community Disharmony: The People of Taos Pueblo. *In* Drinking Behavior Among Southwestern Indians. J. Waddell and M. Everett, Eds. Tucson: U of Arizona Press.

Brown, Stephanie
1985 Treating the Alcoholic: A Development Model of Recovery. NY: John Wiley and Sons.

Bruman, H.
1940 Aboriginal Drink Areas in New Spain. Unpublished Ph.D. Dissertation. U of CA at Berkeley.

Bruner, Jerome
1990 Acts of Meaning. Cambridge: Harvard U Press.

Bruner, Jerome, Jacqueline Goodnow and George Austin
1956 A Study of Thinking. NY: Wiley and Sons, Inc.

Buck, Karl, L. Milner, D. Denmark, et al.
2012 Discovering Genes Involved in Alcohol Dependence and Other Alcohol Responses: Role of Animals Models. Alcohol Research: Current Reviews 34 (3): 367-374.

Bucko, Raymond
    1998 The Lakota Ritual of the Sweat Lodge: History and Contemporary Practice.
        Lincoln: U of Nebraska Press.
Buell, R.
    1928 The Native Problem in Africa, Vol. 1. NY: Macmillan Co.
Bunzel, Ruth
    1940 The Role of Alcoholism in Two Central American Cultures. Psychiatry 3: 361-387.
    1976 Chamula and Chichicastenango: A Re-examination. *In* Cross-Cultural Approaches
        to the Study of Alcohol. M. Everett, J. Waddell, and D. Heath, Eds. The Hague:
        Mouton.
Bureau of Indian Affairs
    1970 Aberdeen Area Statistical Data. (Multilethed).
    1971a Winnebago Indian Reservation. (Multilethed).
    1971b Santee Indian Reservation. (Multilethed).
Cahalan, Don
    1970 Problem Drinkers. San Francisco: Jossey-Bass Inc., Publishers.
Callahan, Kathy
    1981 Intervention Strategies for the Treatment of Alcohol-Abusers and Alcoholics
        Among the Papago Indians: An Ethnographic Needs Assessment. Unpublished
        Ph.D. Dissertation. Purdue U.
Calloway, Colin
    2011 2008 Presidential Address: Indian History from the End of the Alphabet; And
        What Now? Ethnohistory 58 (2): 197-211.
Cantor, Nancy and John Kihlstrom
    1987 Personality and Social Intelligence. Englewood Cliffs, NJ: Prentice-Hall, Inc.
Carbello, J., J. Fernandez-Hermida, L. Sobell, et al.
    Under Review Process of Change Among Spanish Alcohol and Drug Abusers Who
        Recovered on Their Own and Through Treatment.
Carbello, J., J. Fernandez-Hermida, R. Secades-Villa, L. Sobell, et al.
    2007 Natural Recovery from Alcohol and Drug Problems: A Methodological Review of
        the Literature from 1999 through 2005. *In* Promoting Self-Change from Addictive
        Behaviors: Practical Implications for Policy, Prevention, and Treatment. Harald
        Klingemann and Linda Sobell, Eds. NY: Springer.
Carlisle
    1906 Records of the Carlisle Indian Industrial School. Registers of Pupils 1890-1906.
        Volume 1, 1890-1900. Volume 2, 1899-1906. NA. Hill entry 1324 [Hill 1965: 374].
Carmack, R.
    1972 Ethnohistory: A Review of Its Development, Definition, Methods, and Aims.
        Annual Review of Anthropology 1: 227-246.
Carpenter, E.
    1959 Alcohol in the Iroquois Dream Quest. American J of Psychiatry 116: 148-151.
Carpenter, John and Nicholas Armenti
    1972 Some Effects of Ethanol on Human Sexual and Aggressive Behavior. *In* The
        Biology of Alcoholism. Volume 2: Physiology and Behavior. B. K. Kissin and H.
        Begleiter, Eds. NY: Plenum Press.
Carr, L.
    1947 Native Drinks in the Southeast and their Values with Special Emphasis on
        Persimmon Beer. Proceedings of Delaware County Institute of Science 10 (2): 29-43.

Casey, Conerly and Robert Edgerton, Eds.
  2005 A Companion to Psychological Anthropology. Walden, MA: Blackwell.
Casson, Ronald, Ed.
  1981 Language, Culture, and Cognition: Anthropological Perspectives. NY: Macmillan
      Publishing Co.
Castro, F., M. Barrera, C. Martinez
  2004 The Cultural Adaptation of Preventive Interventions: Resolving Tensions between
      Fidelity and Fit. Prevention Science 5 (1): 41-45.
Cave, Alfred
  2006 Prophets of the Great Spirit: Native American Revitalization Movements in
      Eastern North America. Lincoln: U of Nebraska Press.
Chamorro, Antonio-Javier, M. Marcos, J-A. Miron-Canelo, et al.
  2012 Association of μ-opiod Receptor (OPREM1) Gene Polymorphism with Response
      to Naltrexone in Alcohol Dependence: A Systematic Review and Meta-Analysis.
      Addiction Biology 17 (3): 505-512.
Chance, N.
  1960 Culture Change and Integration: An Eskimo Example. American Anthropologist
      62: 1028-1044.
  1965 Acculturation, Self-identification and Personality Adjustment. American
      Anthropologist 67: 372-393.
  1966 The Eskimo of North Alaska. NY: Holt, Rinehart and Winston.
Chen, SH, M. Zhang, C. Scott
  1992 Gene Frequencies of Alcohol Dehydrogenase2 and Aldehyde Dehydrogenase2 in
      Northwest Coast Amerindians. Human Genetics 89 (3): 351-352.
Chitwood, D. and P. Morningstar
  1985 Factors Which Differentiate Cocaine Users in Treatment from Nontreatment
      Users. International J of Addiction 20: 449-459.
CIA-AR
  1860-1907 Annual Reports of the Commissioner of Indian Affairs. Washington, DC:
      Government Printing Office.
Clark, W., J. Norris, J. Hoskins, J. et al.
  1890-91 History of the Counties of Woodbury and Plymouth, Iowa, Including an
      Extended Sketch of Sioux City. Chicago: A. Warner and Company, Publishers.
Clifton, James, Ed.
  1990 The Invented Indian: Cultural Fictions and Government Policies. New Brunswick:
      Transaction Publishers.
Cloud, Henry Roe
  n.d. From Wigwam to Pulpit: A Red Man's Story of His Progress from Darkness to
      Light. NY: Woman's Board of Home Missions of the Presbyterian Church in the
      U.S.A. [1916 Southern Workman, July: 400-406.]
Cohen, E., R. Feinn, A. Arias, and H. Kranzler
  2007 Alcohol Treatment Utilization: Findings from the National Epidemiologic Survey
      on Alcohol and Related Conditions. Drug Alcohol Dependence 86: 214-221,
Cohn, B.
  1968 Ethnohistory. In International Encyclopedia of the Social Sciences, Vol. 6. D. Sills,
      Ed. NY: Macmillan and Free Press.
  1980 History and Anthropology: The State of Play. Comparative Studies in Social
      History 22: 198-221.

Coleman, J.
   1966 Equality of Educational Opportunity. Washington, DC: U.S. Gov. Printing Office.
Collins, James
   2009 Social Reproduction in Classrooms and Schools. Annual Review of Anthropology 38: 33-48.
Collins, James, Jr., Ed.
   1981 Drinking and Crime: Perspectives on the Relationships between Alcohol Consumption and Criminal Behavior. NY: Guilford Press.
Colmant, Stephen and Rod Merta
   1999 Using the Sweat Lodge Ceremony as Group Therapy for Navajo Youth. The J for Specialists in Group Work 24 (1): 55-73.
Commissioner of Indian Affairs
   1884-1920 Annual Reports. Washington, DC: Government Printing Office.
Cooper, J.
   1949 Stimulants and Narcotics. In Handbook of South Americans Indians. J. Steward, Ed. Washington, DC: Government Printing Office.
Coyhis, Don
   1990 Recovery from the Heart: A Journey through the Twelve Steps: A Workbook for Native Americans. Center City, MN: Hazelden.
Coyhis, Don and William White
   2006 Alcohol Problems in Native America: The Untold Story of Resistance and Recovery—The Truth About the Lie. Colorado Springs: White Bison Inc.
Crabbe, J., T. Phillips, R. Harris, M. Arends, G. Koob
   2006 Alcohol-Related Genes: Contributions from Studies with Genetically Engineered Mice. Addiction Biology 11: 195-269.
Crews, Fulton
   2012 Immune Function Genes, Genetics, and the Neurobiology of Addiction. Alcohol Research: Current Reviews 34 (3): 355-361.
Crozier, D.
   1965 History and Anthropology. International Social Science J 17: 561-570.
Cui, Wen-Yan, C. Seneviratne, J. Gu, M. Li
   2012 Genetics of GABAergic Signaling in Nicotine and Alcohol Dependence. Human Genetics 131: 843-855.
Cummings, C., J. Gordon, and G. Marlatt
   1980 Relapse: Prevention and Prediction. In The Addictive Behaviors: Treatment of Alcoholism, Drug Abuse, Smoking and Obesity. W. Miller, Ed. Oxford: Pergamon Press.
Cunnigham, John and F. Breslin
   2004 Only One in Three People with Alcohol Abuse or Dependence Ever Seek Treatment. Addictive Behavior 29: 221-223.
Cunnigham, John and Jim McCambridge
   2011 Is Alcohol Dependence Best View as a Chronic Relapsing Disorder? Addiction 107:6-12.
Cunnigham, John, E. Lin, H. Ross, G. Walsh
   2000 Factors Associated with Untreated Remissions from Alcohol Abuse or Dependence. Addictive Behavior 25: 317-321.
Curley, Richard
   1967 Drinking Patterns of the Mescalero Apache. Quarterly J of Studies on Alcohol 28: 116-131.

Dailey, R.
ms. Three Phases of Explosive Intoxication Among Northeastern Indians. Tallahassee: Florida State U.
1964 Alcohol and the Indians of Ontario: Past and Present. Project G-76, Substudy 1-20-64. Toronto: Addiction Research Foundation.
1968 The Role of Alcohol Among North American Indian Tribes as Reported in the Jesuit Relations. Anthropologica 10: 45-59.

Dam, Gitte, M. Sørensen, O. Munk, and S. Keiding
2009 Hepatic Ethanol Elimination Kinetics in Patients with Cirrhosis. Scandinavian J of Gastroenterology 44 (7): 867-871.

D'Andrade, Roy
1990 Some Propositions about the Relations Between Culture and Human Cognition. In Cultural Psychology: Essays on Comparative Human Development. James Stigler, Richard Shweder, and Gilbert Herdt, Eds. Chicago: U of Chicago Press.
1992 Schemas and Motivation. In Human Motives and Cultural Models. R. D'Andrade and C. Strauss, Eds. Cambridge: Cambridge U Press.
1995 The Development of Cognitive Anthropology. Cambridge: Cambridge U Press.

D'Andrade, Roy and C. Strauss, Eds.
1992 Human Motives and Cultural Models. Cambridge: Cambridge U Press.

Darnell, Regna
2011 2009 Presidential Address: What Is "History"? An Anthropologist's Eye View. Ethnohistory 58 (2): 213-227.

Dawson, D.
1996 Correlates of Past-Year Status Among Treated and Untreated Persons with Former Alcohol Dependence: United States, 1992. Alcoholism: Clinical and Experimental Research 20: 771-779.

Dawson, D., B. Grant, F. Stinson, P. Chou, B. Huang, W. Ruan, et al.
2005 Recovery from DSM-IV Alcohol Dependence: United States, 2001-2002. Addiction 100: 281-292.

Dawson, D., R. Goldstein, B. Grant
2007 Rates and Correlates of Relapse Among Individuals in Remission from DSM-IV Alcohol Dependence: A 3-Year Follow-up. Alcoholism: Clinical and Experimental Research 31: 2036-2045.

de Bruijn, C., W. van den Brink, R. de Graaf, W. Vollebergh
2006 The 3-Year Course of Alcohol Use Disorders in the General Population: DSM-IV, ICD-10 and the Craving Withdrawal Model. Addiction 101: 385-392.

Deitrich, R., M. Eagle Elk, K. Gill, and Y. Liu
1999 An Examination of ALDH2 Genotypes, Alcohol Metabolism and the Flushing Response in Native Americans. J of Studies on Alcohol 60 (2): 149-158.

Deloria, Philip
2002 Historiography. In A Companion to American Indian History. P. Deloria and N. Salisbury, Eds. Malden, MA: Blackwell Publishing.

Deloria, Vine, Jr.
1969 Custer Died for Your Sins: An Indian Manifesto. NY: Macmillan Company.
1980 Schlesier, Other Anthropologists, and Wounded Knee. American Anthropologist 82 (3): 560-561.

DeMallie, Raymond
1980 Comment on "Of Indians and Anthropologists." American Anthropologist 82 (3): 559-560.

Denman, H.
  1868a Letter to N. G. Taylor, February 12. NA, Letters Received, Winnebago Agency.
  1868b Letter to N. G. Taylor, July 21. NA, Letters Received, Winnebago Agency.
Deters, Pamela, D. Novins, A. Fickenscher, and J. Beals
  2006 Trauma and Posttraumatic Stress Symptomatology: Patterns Among American Indian Adolescents in Substance Abuse Treatment. American J of Orthopsychiatry 76 (3): 335-345.
Devereux, G.
  1942 The Mental Hygiene of the American Indian. Mental Hygiene 26: 71-91.
  1948 The Function of Alcohol in Mohave Society. Quarterly J of Studies on Alcohol 9: 207-251.
Devereux, G. and Edwin Loeb
  1943 Antagonistic Acculturation. American Sociological Review 8: 133-148.
Dewey, C.
  1915 Letter to the Commissioner of Indian Affairs, July 19. NA, Central Classified Files, Winnebago.
Dick, Danielle and K. Kendler
  2012 The Impact of Gene-Environment Interaction on Alcohol Use Disorders. Alcohol Research: Current Reviews 34 (3): 318-324.
Di Clemente, Carlo, N. Haug, L. Bellino, and S. Whyte
  2003 Psychotherapy and Motivation Enhancement. In Recent Developments in Alcoholism, Volume 16. Marc Galanter, Ed. NY: Plenum Press.
Diesing, Paul
  1990 How Does Social Science Work? Reflections on Practice. Pittsburgh: U of Pittsburgh Press.
Dietler, Michael
  2006 Alcohol: Anthropological/Archaeological Perspectives. Annual Review of Anthropology 35: 229-249.
Dobyns, H.
  1972 Ethnohistory and Contemporary United States Social Problems. Ethnohistory 19: 1-12.
  1978 Ethnohistory and Human Resources Development. Ethnohistory 25: 103-120.
Dorson, R.
  1961 Ethnohistory and Ethnic Folklore. Ethnohistory 8: 12-30.
Dougherty, Janet, Ed.
  1985 Directions in Cognitive Anthropology. Urbana: U of Illinois Press.
Douglas, Mary, Ed.
  1987 Constructive Drinking: Perspectives on Drink from Anthropology. Cambridge: Cambridge U Press.
Dowd, Gregory
  1992 A Spirited Resistance: The North American Indian Struggle for Unity, 1715-1815. Baltimore: Johns Hopkins U Press.
Dozier, Edward
  1966 Problem Drinking Among American Indians: The Role of Sociocultural Deprivation. Quarterly J of Studies on Alcohol 27: 72-87.
Dressler, David and Huntington Potter
  1991 Discovering Enzymes. NY: Scientific American Library.
Driver, H.
  1969 Indians of North America, 2nd Ed. Chicago: U of Chicago Press.

Dumett, R.
 1974 The Social Impact of the European Liquor Trade on the Akan of Ghana (Gold
     Coast and Asante), 1875-1910. J of Interdisciplinary History 1: 69-101.
Duran, Bonnie, J. Oetzel, J. Lucero, et al.
 2005 Obstacles for Rural American Indians Seeking Alcohol, Drug, or Mental Health
     Treatment. J of Consulting and Clinical Psychology 73 (5): 819-829.
Duran, Eduardo and Bonnie Duran
 1995 Native American Postcolonial Psychology. Albany: State U of NY Press.
Du Toit, B.
 1964 Substitution: A Process in Culture Change. Human Organization 23: 16-23.
Dyck, Erika
 2008 Psychedelic Psychiatry: LSD from Clinic to Campus. Baltimore: Johns Hopkins U
     Press.
Edenberg, Howard
 2007 The Genetics of Alcohol Metabolism: Role of Alcohol Dehydrogenase and
     Aldehyde Dehydrogenase Variants. Alcohol Research and Health 30 (1): 5-13.
 2011 Common and Rare Variants in Alcohol Dependence. Biological Psychiatry 70: 498-
     499
 2012 Genes Contributing to the Development of Alcoholism: An Overview. Alcohol
     Research: Current Reviews 34 (3): 336-338.
Edenberg, Howard and W. Bosron
 2010 Alcohol Dehydrogenases. In Comprehensive Toxicology, Volume 4,
     Biotransformation. Charlene McQueen, Ed. Boston: Elsevier.
Edenberg, Howard, D. Koller, X. Xuel, et al.
 2010 Genome-wide Association Study of Alcohol Dependence Implicates a Region on
     Chromosome 11. Alcoholism: Clinical and Experimental Research 34 (5): 840-52.
Edenberg, Howard, X. Xuel, H. Chen, et al.
 2006 Association of Alcohol Dehydrogenase Genes with Alcohol Dependence: A
     Comprehensive Analysis. Human Molecular Genetics 15 (9): 1539-1549.
Edgerton, R.
 1976 Deviance: A Cross-Cultural Perspective. Menlo Park, CA: Cummings.
 1978 The Study of Deviance—Marginal Man or Everyman? In The Making of
     Psychological Anthropology. G. Spindler, Ed. Berkeley: U of CA Press.
 1985 Rules, Exceptions, and Social Order. Berkeley: U CA Press.
Edmunds, David
 1983 The Shawnee Prophet. Lincoln: U of Nebraska Press.
 2008 Blazing New Trails or Burning Bridges: Native American History Comes of Age.
     Western Historical Quarterly 39: 5-15.
Eggan, F.
 1954 Social Anthropology and the Method of Controlled Comparison. American
     Anthropologist 56: 743-763.
 1961 Some Anthropological Approaches to the Understanding of Ethnological
     Cultures. Ethnohistory 8:1-11.
Ehlers, Cindy
 2007 Variations in ADH and ALDH in Southwest California Indians. Alcohol Research
     and Health 30 (1): 14-17.

Ehlers, Cindy, D. Gilder, L. Harris, L. Carr
2001 Association of the *ADH2*3* Allele with a Negative Family History of Alcoholism in African American Young Adults. Alcoholism: Clinical and Experimental Research 25 (12): 1773-7.
Ehlers, Cindy, K. Montane-Jaime, S. Moore, S. Shafe, R. Joseph, and L. Carr
2007 Association of the *ADH1B*3* Allele with Alcohol-Related Phenotypes in Trinidad. Alcoholism: Clinical and Experimental Research 31 (2): 216-220.
Ehlers, Cindy, T. Liang, and I. Gizer
2012 ADH and ALDH Polymorphisms and Alcohol Dependence in Mexican and Native Americans. American J of Drug and Alcohol Abuse 38 (5): 389-394.
Elkin, Henry
1940 The Northern Arapaho of Wyoming. *In* Acculturation in Seven Indian Tribes. R. Linton, Ed. NY: Appleton-Century-Crofts.
Eng, M., S. Luczak, and T. Wall
2007 *ALDH2, ADH1B,* and *ADH1C* Genotypes in Asians: A Literature Review. Alcohol Research and Health 30 (1): 22-27.
Enoch, Mary-Anne
2011 The Role of Early Life Stress as a Predictor for Alcohol and Drug Dependence. Psychopharmacology 214: 17-31.
2012 The Influence of Gene-Environment Interactions on the Development of Alcoholism and Drug Dependence. Current Psychiatry Reports 14: 150-158.
Erikson, Erik
1937 Observations on Sioux Education. J of Psychiatry 7: 101-156.
Euler, R.
1972 Ethnohistory in the United States. Ethnohistory 19: 201-207.
Evans-Pritchard, E.
1962 Social Anthropology: Past and Present. *In* Social Anthropology and Other Essays. NY: Free Press.
1962 Anthropology and History. *In* Social Anthropology and Other Essays. NY: Free Press.
Eveland, M.
1904 Testimony at Winnebago. FA.
Everett, M.
1980 Drinking as a Measure of Proper Behavior: The White Mountain Apaches. *In* Drinking Behavior Among Southwestern Indians. Tucson: U of Arizona Press.
Ewers, J.
1961 Symposium on the Concept of Ethnohistory—Comment. Ethnohistory 8: 262-270.
Factor, Roni, I. Kawachi, D. Williams
2011 Understanding High-Risk Behavior Among Non-dominant Minorities: A Social Resistance Framework. Social Science and Medicine 73: 1292-1301.
Fagan, Jeffrey
1990 Intoxication and Aggression. *In* Drugs and Crime. Michael Tonry and James Wilson, Eds. Chicago: U of Chicago Press.
Faiman-Silva, Sandra
1997 Choctaws at the Crossroads: The Political Economy of Class and Culture in the Oklahoma Timber Region. Lincoln: U of Nebraska Press.
Fantegrossi, William, K. Murnane, and C. Reissig
2008 The Behavioral Pharmacology of Hallucinogens. Biochemical Pharmacology 75: 17-33.

Fast, Phyllis
  2002 Northern Athabascan Survival: Women, Community, and the Future. Lincoln: U of Nebraska Press.
Feltenstein, M. and R. See
  2008 The Neurocircuitry of Addiction: An Overview. British J of Pharmacology 1545: 261-274.
Fenton, W.
  1952 The Training of Historical Ethnologists in America. American Anthropologist 54: 328-339.
  1962 Ethnohistory and Its Problems. Ethnohistory 9: 1-23.
  1966 Field Work, Museum Studies, and Ethnohistorical Research. Ethnohistory 13: 71-85.
Field Matron
  1904 Testimony at Winnebago. FA.
Fikes, Jay
  1996 Reuban Snake: Your Humble Serpent. Santa Fe: Clear Lights Publishers.
Fingarette, Herbert
  1988 Heavy Drinking: The Myth of Alcoholism as a Disease. Berkeley: U of CA Press.
Finn, D. and J. Crabbe
  1997 Exploring Alcohol Withdrawal Syndrome. Alcohol Health Research World 21: 149-156.
Fixico, Donald
  2000 The Urban Indian Experience in American. Albuquerque: U of New Mexico Press.
Fixico, Donald, Ed.
  1997 Rethinking American Indian History. Albuquerque: U of New Mexico Press.
Fleming, Michael
  2003 Brief Interventions and the Treatment of Alcohol Use Disorders: Current Evidence. In Recent Developments in Alcoholism, Volume 16. Marc Galanter, Ed. NY: Plenum Press.
Fogelson, Raymond
  1974 On the Varieties of Indian History: Sequoyah and Traveller Bird. J of Ethnic Studies 2: 105-112.
  1982 Person, Self, and Identity: Some Anthropological Retrospects, Circumspects, and Prospects. In Psychosocial Theories of the Self. B. Lee., Ed. NY: Plenum Press.
  1989 The Ethnohistory of Events and Nonevents. Ethnohistory 36 (2): 133-147.
Foley, Douglas
  1990 Learning Capitalist Culture: Deep in the Heart of Tejas. Philadelphia: U of Pennsylvania Press.
  1991 Reconsidering Anthropological Explanations of Ethnic School Failure. Anthropology and Education Quarterly 22 (1): 60-86.
  1995 The Heartland Chronicles. Philadelphia: U of Pennsylvania Press.
Folwell, William
  1921 A History of Minnesota, Vol. 1. Saint Paul: Minnesota Historical Society.
  1924 A History of Minnesota, Vol. 2. Saint Paul: Minnesota Historical Society.
Foran, Heather and K. O'Leary
  2008 Alcohol and Intimate Partner Violence: A Meta-analytic Review. Clinical Psychology Review 28: 1222-1234.

Foroud, T. and T. Phillips
    2012 Assessing the Genetic Risk for Alcohol Use Disorders. Alcohol Research: Current
        Reviews 34 (3): 266-272.
Forsyth, Thomas
    1911 The Shawee Prophet. *In* The Tribes of the Upper Mississippi Valley and Region of
        the Great Lakes, Vol. 2. E. Blair, Ed. Cleveland: Arthur Clark.
Forum, Open
    2010 A "Historic Failure": American Indian Health Care Suffers. Health and Human
        Rights: An International Journal [On line], 0 27 Aug.
Fox, Anne and Mike MacAvoy, Eds.
    2011 Expressions of Drunkenness (Four Hundred Rabbits). NY: Routledge.
Frank, Jerome
    1973 Persuasion and Healing: A Comparative Study of Psychotherapy. Baltimore:
        Johns Hopkins U Press.
Frederikson, Otto
    1932 The Liquor Question Among the Indian Tribes in Kansas, 1804-1881. Kansas
        Humanistic Studies Vol. 4, No. 4.
Freilich, Morris, Ed.
    1989 The Relevance of Culture. NY: Praeger.
Freund, P. and M. Marshall
    1977 Research Bibliography of Alcohol and Kava Studies in Oceania: Update and
        Additional Items. Micronesia 13: 313-317.
Frum, C.
    1904 Testimony at Winnebago. FA.
Fuller, R., L. Branchey, D. Brightwell, et al.
    1986 Disulfiram Treatment of Alcoholism. A Veterans Administration Cooperative
        Study. J of the American Medical Association 256: 1449-1455.
Furnas, R.
    1864 Letter to W. Dole, December 19. NA, Letters Received, Winnebago Agency.
Furst, Peter
    1976 Hallucinogens and Culture. San Francisco: Chandler and Sharp.
Galanter, Marc, Ed.
    1997 Recent Developments in Alcoholism, Volume 13: Alcoholism and Violence. NY:
        Plenum Press.
Galanter, Marc and Herbert Kleber, Eds.
    2011 Psychotherapy for the Treatment of Substance Abuse. Washington, DC: American
        Psychiatric Publishing, Inc.
Galanter, Marc and Peter Buckley
    1978 Evangelical Religion and Meditation: Psychotherapeutic Effects. J of Nervous and
        Mental Disease 166 (10): 685-691.
Galtung, Johan
    1967 Theory and Methods of Social Research. NY: Columbia U Press.
Gans, Herbert
    1962 The Urban Villagers: Group and Class in the Life of Italian Americans. NY: Free
        Press.
Garbutt, James
    2009 The State of Pharmacotherapy for the Treatment of Alcohol Dependence. J of
        Substance Abuse Treatment 36 (Suppl 1): S15-S23.

Gardner, Eliot
    2011 Addiction and Brain Reward and Antireward Pathways. Advances in
        Psychosomatic Medicine 30: 22-60.
Gardner, Eliot and Roy Wise
    2009 Animal Models of Addiction. *In* Neurobiology of Mental Illness. D. Charney and
        E. Nestler, Eds. NY: Oxford U Press.
Gardner, Howard
    1985 The Mind's New Science: A History of the Cognitive Revolution. NY: Basic Books.
Garrity, John
    2000 Jesus, Peyote, and the Holy People: Alcohol Abuse and the Ethos of Power in
        Navajo Healing. Medical Anthropology Quarterly 14 (4): 521-544.
Geertz, Clifford
    1973 The Interpretation of Cultures. NY: Basic Books, Inc.
    1977 "From the Native's Point of View": On the Nature of Anthropological
        Understanding. *In* Symbolic Anthropology. J.Dolgin, D. Kemnitzer and D.
        Schneider, Eds. NY: Columbia U Press.
Gellner, Ernest
    1992 Postmodernism, Reason and Religion. NY: Routledge.
Gerlach, Luther
    1974 Pentacostalism: Revolution or Counter-Revolution? *In* Religious Movements in
        Contemporary America. I. Zaretsby and M. Leone, Eds. Princeton: Princeton U
        Press.
Giancola, Peter
    2004 Executive Functioning and Alcohol-Related Aggression. J of Abnormal
        Psychology 113 (4): 541-555.
Gibbs, Jack
    1968 Norms. II. The Study of Norms. *In* International Encyclopedia of the Social
        Sciences. Volume II. David Sills, Ed. NY: Corowell, Collier, and Macmillian, Inc.
    1981 Norms, Deviance, and Social Control: Conceptual Matters. NY: Elsevier.
Gibson, C.
    1964 The Aztecs Under Spanish Rule. Stanford: Stanford U Press.
Gizer, Ian, H. Edenberg, D. Gilder, et al.
    2011 Association of Alcohol Dehydrogenase Genes with Alcohol-Related Phenotypes in
        a Native American Community Sample. Alcoholism: Clinical and Experimental
        Research 35 (11): 2008-2018.
Glaser, Barney and Anselm Strauss
    1967 The Discovery of Grounded Theory: Strategies for Qualitative Research. Chicago:
        Aldine.
Glasser, Morton and Gretel Pelto
    1980 The Medical Merry-Go-Round: A Plea for Reasonable Medicine. Pleasantville, NY:
        Redgrave Publishing Co.
Gluckman, Peter, A. Beedle, and M. Hanson
    2009 Principles of Evolutionary Medicine. NY: Oxford U Press.
Goedde, H., D. Agarwal, S. Harada, F. Rothhammer, J. Whittaker, and R. Lisker
    1986 Aldehyde Dehydrogenase Polymorphism in North American, South American,
        and Mexican Indian Populations. American J of Human Genetics 38:395-399.
Goffman, Erving
    1956 The Nature of Deference and Demeanor. American Anthropologist 58: 473-502.
    1959 The Presentation of Self in Everyday Life. Garden City, NY: Anchor Books.

1967 Interaction Ritual: Essays on Face to Face Behavior. Garden City, NY: Anchor Books.

1971 Relations in Public. NY: Basic Books, Inc.

1974 Frame Analysis: An Essay on the Organization of Experience. NY: Harper Colophon Books.

Goldfrank, Esther

1943 Historic Change and Social Character: A Study of the Teton Dakota. American Anthropologist 45: 67-83.

1945 Socialization, Personality, and the Structure of Pueblo Society (with Particular Reference to Hopi and Zuni). American Anthropologist 47: 516-539.

1978 Notes on an Undirected Life: As One Anthropologist Tells It. Queens College Publications in Anthropology 3.

Goldman, Aviel

2008 Neurobiology of Addiction: An Integrative View. Biochemical Pharmacology 75: 266-322.

Goldstein, Avram, Lewis Aronow, and Sumner Kalman

1968 Principles of Drug Action: The Basis of Pharmacology. NY: Harper and Row.

Goldstein, Dora

1983 Pharmacology of Alcohol. NY: Oxford University Press.

Gone, Joseph

2009 A Community-Based Treatment for Native American Historical Trauma: Prospects for Evidence-Based Practice. J of Consulting and Clinical Psychology 77 (4): 751-762.

2011a Is Psychology Science A-Cultural? Cultural Diversity and Ethnic Minority Psychology 17 (3): 234-242.

2011b The Red Road to Wellness: Cultural Reclamation in a Native First Nations Community Treatment Center. American J of Community Psychology 47: 187-202.

2012 Indigenous Traditional Knowledge and Substance Abuse Treatment Outcomes: The Problem of Efficacy Evaluation. American J of Drug and Alcohol Abuse 38 (5): 493-497.

Góngora, M.

1975 Studies in the Colonial History of Spanish America. Cambridge: Cambridge U Press.

Goodenough, Ward

1956 Residence Rules. Southwestern J of Anthropology 12: 22-37.

1963 Cooperation in Change. NY: Russell Sage Foundation.

1964 [1957] Cultural Anthropology and Linguistics. In Language in Culture and Society: A Reader in Linguistics and Anthropology. Dell Hymes, Ed. NY: Harper and Row, Publishers.

1970 Description and Comparison in Cultural Anthropology. Chicago: Aldine Publishing Company.

1971 Culture, Language, and Society. (MaCaleb Module in Anthropology.) Reading, MA: Addison-Weslely.

1981 Culture, Language, and Society, 2nd Ed. Menlo Park, CA: Benjamin/Cummings Publishing Company, Inc.

Gordon, Andrew

1984 Alcohol Use in the Perspective of Cultural Ecology. In Recent Developments in Alcoholism, Vol. 2. Marc Galanter, Ed. NY: Plenum Press.

Gorwood, Philip, Le Strat, N. Ramoz, et al.
    2012 Genetics of Dopamine Receptors and Drug Addiction. Human Genetics 131: 803-822.
Gottheil, Edward, Keith Druley, Thomas Skoloda, Howard Waxman, Eds.
    1983 Alcohol, Drug Abuse, and Aggression. Springfield: Charles Thomas Publisher.
Graff, G.
    1864a Letter to W. Dole, March 27. NA, Letters Received, Winnebago Agency.
    1864b Letter to W. Dole, April 8. NA, Letters Received, Winnebago Agency.
Graham, Kathryn, K. Leonard, R. Room, et al.
    1998 Current Directions in Research on Understanding and Preventing Intoxicated Aggression. Addiction 93 (5): 659-676.
Graves, Theodore
    1970 The Personal Adjustment of Navajo Indian Migrants to Denver, Colorado. American Anthropologist 72: 35-54.
Graves, Theodore and Minor Van Arsdale
    1966 Values, Expectations and Relocation: The Navaho Migrant to Denver. Human Organization 25: 300-307.
Greenberg, David
    1985 Age, Crime and Social Explanation. American J of Sociology 91: 1-21.
Greenfield, Brenna and K. Venner
    2012 Review of Substance Use Disorder Treatment Research in Indian Country: Future Directions to Strive toward Health Equity. American J of Drug and Alcohol Abuse 38 (5): 483-492.
Greenwald, Anthony and Anthony Pratkanis
    1984 The Self. In Handbook of Social Cognition, Volume 3. Robert Wyer, Jr. and Thomas Srull, Eds. Hillsdale, NJ: Lawrence Erlbaum Associates.
Griffith, D.
    1869 Letter to Eli Parker, August 3. NA, Letters Received, Winnebago Agency.
Grinspoon, Lester and James Bakalar
    1979 Psychedelic Drugs Reconsidered. NY: Basic Books, Inc.
Grobsmith, Elizabeth
    1989 The Relationship between Substance Abuse and Crime Among Native American Inmates in the Nebraska Department of Corrections. Human Organization 48: 285-298.
    1994 Indians in Prison: Incarcerated Native Americans in Nebraska. Lincoln: U of Nebraska Press.
Grobsmith, Elizabeth and Jennifer Dam
    1990 The Revolving Door: Substance Abuse Treatment and Criminal Sanctions for Native American Offenders. J of Substance Abuse 2: 405-425.
Gross, M. and E. Lewis
    1973 Observation on the Prevalence of the Signs and Symptoms Associated with Withdrawal during Continuous Observation of Experimental Intoxication and Withdrawal in Humans. In Alcohol Intoxication and Withdrawal: Experimental Studies. M. Gross, Ed. Advances in Experimental Medicine and Biology, Vol. 35. NY: Plenum Press.
Gross, M., E. Lewis, and J. Hastey
    1974 Acute Alcohol Withdrawal Syndrome. In The Biology of Alcoholism. Volume 3: Clinical Pathology. B. Kissin and H. Begleiter, Eds. NY: Plenum Press.

Gross, M., S. Rosenblatt, E. Lewis, S. Chartoff, and B. Malenowski
1972a Acute Alcoholic Psychoses and Related Syndromes—Psychosocial and Clinical Characteristics and Their Implications. British J of Addiction 67: 15-31.

Gross, M., et al.
1972b Classification of Acute Alcohol Withdrawal Syndromes. Quarterly J of Studies on Alcohol 33: 400-407.

Gross, M., et al.
1972c Sleep Disturbances in Alcohol Intoxication and Withdrawal. In Recent Advances in Studies of Alcoholism. N. Mello and J. Mendelson, Eds. Washington, D.C.: Government Printing Office.

Guengerich, F. Peter
2012 Cytochromes P450. In Metabolism of Drugs and Other Xenobiotics. P. Anzenbacher and U. Zanger, Eds. Weinheim, Germany: Wiley-VCH.

Gunson, N.
1966 On the Incidence of Alcoholism and Intemperance in Early Pacific Missions. J of Pacific History 1: 43-62.

Hacker, Jacob and Paul Pierson
2010 Winner-Take-All Politics: How Washington Made the Rich Richer—and Turned Its Back on the Middle Class. NY: Simon and Schuster.

Haggard H. and E. Jellinek
1942 Alcohol Explored. Garden City, NY: Doubleday, Doran and Co.

Hall, Robert
1962 The Archeology of Carajou Point. Volumes 1 and 2. Madison: U Wisconsin Press.

Hall, Roberta
1985 Distribution of the Sweat Lodge in Alcohol Treatment Programs. Current Anthropology 26: 134-135.
1986 Alcohol Treatment in American Indian Populations: An Indigenous Treatment Modality Compared with Traditional Approaches. Annals New York Academy of Sciences 472: 168-178.

Hallowell, A. I.
1946 Some Psychological Characteristics of the Northeastern Indians. In Man in Northeastern North America. F. Johnson, Ed. Andover, Mass.: R.S. Peabody Foundation for Archeology.
1950 Values, Acculturation, and Mental Health. American J of Orthopsychiatry 20: 732-743.
1955 Culture and Experience. Philadelphia: U of Pennsylvania Press.

Hammer, John
1965 Acculturation Stress and Functions of Alcohol Among the Forest Potawatomi. Quarterly J of Studies on Alcohol 26: 285-302.

Hanna, J.
1976 Ethnic Groups, Human Variation, and Alcohol Use. In Cross-Cultural Approaches to the Study of Alcohol. M. Everett, J. Waddell, and D. Heath, Eds. The Hague: Mouton.

Hannerz, Ulf
1969 Soulside: Inquiries into Ghetto Culture and Community. NY: Columbia U Press.

Haque, F., I. Gottesman, and A. Wong
2009 Not Really Identical: Epigenetic Differences in Monozygotic Twins and Implications for Twin Studies in Psychiatry. American J of Medical Genetics Part C, Seminar in Medical Genetics 151C:136-141.

Harada, S., D. Agarwal, H. Goedde
1981 Aldehyde Dehydrogenase Deficiency as Cause of Facial Flushing Reaction to Alcohol in Japanese. Lancet 31 (2): 982.
Harada, S., D. Agarwal, H. Goedde, and B. Ishikawa
1983 Aldehyde Dehydrogenase Isozyme Variation and Alcoholism in Japan. Pharmacology, Biochemistry, and Behavior 18, Suppl. 1: 151-153.
Harada, S., S. Misawa, D. Agarwal, and H. Goedde
1980 Liver Alcohol Dehydrogenase and Aldehyde Dehydrogenase in the Japanese: Isozyme Variation and Its Possible Role in Alcohol Intoxication. American J of Human Genetics 32 (1): 8-15.
Harrod, H.
1971 Mission Among the Blackfeet. Norman: U of Oklahoma Press.
Hart, E. S.
1903 Letter to Chas. Mathewson, July 31. NA, Letters Received.
Hasaeba, Takeshi and Y. Ohno
2010 A New View of Alcohol Metabolism and Alcoholism—Role of the High-Km Class III Alcohol Dehydrogenase (ADH3). International J of Environmental Research and Public Health 7: 1076-1092.
Hasaeba, Takeshi , G. Duester, A. Shimizu, I.Yamamoto, K. Kaneyama, and Y. Ohno
2005 In Vivo Contribution of Class III Alcohol Solution Hydrophobicity. Biochemica et Diophysica Acta 1762: 276-283.
Hasaeba, Takeshi, K. Kameyama, K. Mashimo, and Y. Ohno
2012 Dose-Dependent Change in Elimination Kinetics of Ethanol Due to Shift of Dominant Metabolizing Enzyme from ADH1 (Class I) to ADH3 (Class III) in Mouse. International J of Hepatology 207: 1-8.
Hasaeba, Takeshi, Y. Tomita, M. Kurosu, and Y. Ohno
2003 Dose and Time Changes in Liver Alcohol Dehydrogenase (ADH) Activity During Acute Alcohol Intoxication Involve Not Only Class I But Also Class III ADH and Govern Elimination Rate of Blood Ethanol. Legal Medicine 5: 202-211.
Hasin, D., E. Aharonovich, X. Liu, et al.
2002 Alcohol Dependence Symptoms and Alcohol Dehydrogenase 2 Polymorphism: Israeli Ashkenazis, Sephardics, and Recent Russian Immigrants. Alcoholism: Clinical and Experimental Research 26: 1315-1321.
Hawkins, E., L. Cummins, and G. Marlatt
2004 Preventing Substance Abuse in American Indian and Alaskan Native Youth: Promising Strategies for Healthier Communities. Psychological Bulletin 130 (2): 304-323.
Headland, Thomas, Kenneth Pike, and Marvin Harris, Eds.
1990 Emics and Etics: The Insider/Outsider Debate. Newbury Park, CA: Sage Publications, Inc.
Heath, Dwight
1975 A Critical Review of Ethnographic Studies of Alcohol Use. In Research Advances in Alcohol and Drug Problems, Vol. 2. R. Gibbins et al., Eds. NY: Wiley.
1976a Anthropological Perspectives on Alcohol: An Historical Review. In Cross-Cultural Approaches to the Study of Alcohol. M. Everett, J. Waddell, and D. Heath, Eds. The Hague: Mouton.
1976b Anthropological Perspectives on the Social Biology of Alcohol: An Introduction to the Literature. In The Biology of Alcoholism. Volume 4: Social Aspects of Alcoholism. B. Kissin and H. Begleiter, Eds. NY: Plenum Press.

1983 Alcohol Use Among North American Indians. *In* Alcohol and Drug Problems, Vol. 7. R. Smart, et al., Eds. NY: Plenum Press.

1984 Cross-Cultural Studies of Alcohol. *In* Recent Developments in Alcoholism, Volume 2. Marc Galanter, Ed. NY: Plenum Press.

1987a Anthropology and Alcohol Studies: Current Issues. *In* Annual Review of Anthropology, Vol. 16: 99-120.

1987b A Decade of Development in the Anthropological Study of Alcohol Use: 1970-1980. *In* Constructive Drinking: Perspectives on Drink from Anthropology. M. Douglas, Ed. NY: Cambridge U Press.

1988 Emerging Anthropological Theory and Models of Alcohol Use and Alcoholism. *In* Theories on Alcoholism. C. Chaudron and D. Wilkinson, Eds. Toronto: Addiction Research Foundation.

1989 American Indians and Alcohol: Epidemiological and Sociocultural Relevance. *In* Alcohol Use Among U.S. Ethnic Minorities. NIAAA Research Monograph 18. Washington, DC: U.S. Government Printing Office.

1992 Prohibition or Liberalization of Alcohol and Drugs? A Sociocultural Perspective. *In* Recent Developments in Alcoholism, Volume 10: Alcohol and Cocaine: Similarities and Differences. Marc Galanter, Ed. NY: Plenum Press.

1993 Anthropology. *In* Recent Developments in Alcoholism, Volume 11. Marc Galanter, Ed. NY: Plenum Press.

2000 Drinking Occasions: Comparative Perspectives on Alcohol and Culture. Philadelphia: Taylor and Francis.

2007 Why We Don't Know More about the Social Benefits of Moderate Drinking. Annals of Epidemiology 17: S71-S74.

Heath, Dwight and A. Cooper, Compls.
1981 Alcohol Use and World Cultures: A Comprehensive Bibliography of Anthropological Sources. Toronto: Addiction Research Foundation.

Hechter, Michael and Karl-Dieter Opp
2001 What Have We Learned about the Emergence of Social Norms? *In* Social Norms. Michael Hechter and Karl-Dieter Opp, Eds. NY: Russell Sage Foundation.

Heidenreich, C.
1976 Alcohol and Drug Use Among Indian-Americans: A Review of Issues and Sources. J of Drug Issues 6:256-272.

Heilig, Markus, A. Tahorsell, W. Sommer, A. Hanson, et al.
2010b Translating the Neuroscience of Alcoholism into Clinical Treatments: From Blocking the Buzz to Curing the Blues. Neuroscience and Biobehavioral Reviews 35: 334-344.

Heilig, Markus, D. Goldman, W. Berrettini, and C. O'Brien
2011 Pharmacogentic Approaches to the Treatment of Alcohol Addiction. Nature Reviews Neuroscience 12: 670-684.

Heilig, Markus, M. Egli, J. Crabbe, and H. Becker
2010a Acute Withdrawal, Protracted Abstinence and Negative Affect in Alcoholism: Are They Linked? Addiction Biology 15: 169-184.

Heinz, Adrienne, A. Beck, A. Meyer-Lindenberg, P. Sterzer, and A. Heinz
2011 Cognitive and Neurobiological Mechanisms of Alcohol-Related Aggression. Nature Reviews Neuroscience 12: 400-413.

Heinz, A., S. Lober, A. Georgi, et al.
2003 Reward Craving and Withdrawal Relief Craving: Assessment of Different Motivational Pathways to Alcohol Intake. Alcohol and Alcoholism 38: 35-39.

Helm, June
　　1961　The Lynx Point People: The Dynamics of a Northern Athapaskan Band. National Museum of Canada, Bulletin No. 176. Ottawa: Department of Northern Affairs and National Resources.
Helms, M.
　　1978　Time, History, and the Future of Anthropology: Observations on Some Unresolved Issues. Ethnohistory 25: 1-13.
Henderson, Eric
　　2000　Patterns of Alcohol Use. *In* Drinking, Conduct Disorder, and Social Change: Navajo Experiences. S. Kuntz and J. Levy, Eds. Oxford: Oxford U Press.
Henry, D., J. Allen, C. Ting Fok, et al.
　　2012　Patterns of Protective Factors in an Intervention for the Prevention of Suicide and Alcohol Abuse with Yup'ik Alaska Native Youth. American J of Drug and Alcohol Abuse 38 (5): 476-482.
Hensley, Albert
　　1908　Letter to the Commissioner of Indian Affairs, October 9. NA, Central Classified Files, Liquor Traffic.
　　1916　Letter to Mollier Gaither, February 22. NA, Records of the Carlisle Indian School.
Herring, Joseph
　　1988　Kenekuk, the Kickapoo Prophet. Lawrence: U Press of Kansas.
Herskovits, M.
　　1938　Acculturation: The Study of Culture Contact. NY: J. J. Augustin.
　　1960　The Ahistorical Approach to Afroamerican Studies: A Critique. American Anthropologist 62: 559-568.
Hertzberg, Hazel
　　1971　The Search for an American Indian Identity: Modern Pan-Indian Movements. Syracuse: Syracuse U Press.
Hertzman, Clyde and Tom Boyce
　　2010　How Experience Gets Under the Skin to Create Gradients in Developmental Health. Annual Review of Public Health 31: 329-347.
Hickerson, Harold
　　1970　The Chippewa and Their Neighbors: A Study in Ethnohistory. NY: Holt, Rinehart and Winston, Inc.
Higgins, E. Tory
　　1987　Self-Discrepancy: A Theory Relating Self and Affect. Psychological Review 94 (3): 319-340.
Hill, Edward
　　1965　Preliminary Inventory of the Records of the Bureau of Indian Affairs, Volume I. Record Group 75. National Archives. Washington, DC: General Services Administration.
Hill, Thomas
　　1974　From Hell-Raiser to Family Man. *In* Conformity and Conflict: Readings in Cultural Anthropology, 2nd Ed. James Spradley and David McCurdy, Eds. Boston: Little, Brown and Company.
　　1978　Drunken Compartment of Urban Indians: "Time-Out" Behavior? J of Anthropological Research 34 (3): 442-467.
　　1980a　Lifestyles and Drinking Patterns of Urban Indians. J of Drug Issues 10 (2): 257-272.
　　1980b　Grab the Children and Run: A Comment on Schlesier's "Of Indians and

Anthropologists." American Anthropologist 82 (3): 557-558.

1984 Ethnohistory and Alcohol Studies. *In* Recent Developments in Alcoholism, Volume 2. Marc Galanter, Ed. NY: Plenum Press.

1985 Alcohol Use Among the Nebraska Winnebago: An Ethnohistorical Study of Change and Adjustment. Contemporary Drug Problem 12 (2): 173-219.

1990 Peyotism and the Control of Heavy Drinking: The Nebraska Winnebago in the Early 1900s. Human Organization 49 (3): 255-265.

Hind, Robert

1984 The Internal Colonial Concept. Comparative Studies in Society and History 26 (3): 543-568.

Hine, Virginia

1974 The Deprivation and Disorganization Theories of Social Movements. *In* Religious Movements in Contemporary America. I. Zaretsky and M. Leone, Eds. Princeton: Princeton U Press.

Hinson, Riley

1985 Individual Differences in Tolerance and Relapse: A Pavlovian Conditioning Perspective. *In* Determinants of Substance Abuse: Biological, Psychological, and Environmental Factors. Mark Galizio and Stephen Maisto, Eds. NY: Plenum Press.

Hogue, Aaron

2010 When Technology Fails: Getting Back to Nature. Clinical Psychology Science and Practice 17: 77-81.

Holland, Dorothy and N. Quinn, Eds.

1987 Cultural Models in Language and Thought. Cambridge: Cambridge U Press.

Holland, Dorothy, W. Lachicotte, Jr., D. Skinner, and C. Cain

1998 Identity and Agency in Cultural Worlds. Cambridge: Harvard U Press.

Hollinger, David

1979 Historians and the Discourse of Intellectuals. *In* New Directions in American Intellectual History. J.Higham and P. Conkin, Eds. Baltimore: Johns Hopkins U Press.

Honigmann, John

1970 Sampling in Ethnographic Field Work. *In* A Handbook of Method in Cultural Anthropology. R. Naroll and R. Cohen, Eds. Garden City, NY: Natural History Press.

Honigmann, John and Irma Honigmann

1945 Drinking in an Indian-White Community. Quarterly J of Studies on Alcohol 5: 575-619.

1965 How Baffin Island Eskimos Have Learned to Use Alcohol. Social Forces 44: 73-83.

Hornby, Rodger, Ed.

1995 Alcohol and Native Americans. Mission, SD: Sinte Gleska U Press.

Horne, Chriarine

2001 Sociological Perspectives on the Emergence of Norms. *In* Social Norms. Michael Hechter and Karl-Dieter Opp, Eds. NY: Russell Sage Foundation.

Howay, F.

1942 The Introduction of Intoxicating Liquor Among the Indians of the Northwest Coast. British Columbia Historical Quarterly 6 (3): 157-169.

Howe, K.

1977 The Loyalty Islands: A History of Culture Contacts 1840-1900. Honolulu: U Press of Hawaii.

Hudson, Charles
 1973 The Historical Approach in Anthropology. *In* Handbook of Social and Cultural
   Anthropology. J. Honigmann, Ed. Chicago: Rand McNally.
 1976 The Southeastern Indians. Knoxville: U of Tennessee Press.
Huebner, Robert and Lori Kantor
 2011 Advances in Alcoholism Treatment. Alcohol Research and Health 33 (4): 295-299.
Hug, Carl
 1972 Characteristics and Theories Related to Acute and Chronic Tolerance
   Development. *In* Chemical and Biological Aspects of Drug Dependence. S. Mule
   and H. Brill, Eds. Cleveland: CRC Press.
Hultkranz, A.
 1967 Historical Approaches in American Ethnology: A Research Survey. Ethnol Eur 1:
   96-116.
Humphreys, Keith
 2003 Involvement of Support Networks in Treatment. *In* Recent Developments in
   Alcoholism, Volume 16. Marc Galanter, Ed. NY: Plenum Press.
Hunt, E.
 1903 Letter to Chas. Mathewson, July 31. NA, Letters Received, Winnebago Agency.
Hunter, Mark
 1904 Testimony at Winnebago. FA.
Hurley, Thomas and Howard Edenberg
 2012 Genes Encoding Enzymes Involved in Ethanol Metabolism. Alcohol Research:
   Current Reviews 34 (3): 339-344.
Hurley, Thomas, H. Edenberg, and T.K. Li
 2002 Pharmacogenomics of Alcoholism. *In* Pharamacogenomics: The Search for
   Individualized Therapies. J. Licinio and M.L. Wong, Eds. Weinheim, Germany:
   Wiley-VCH.
Hurt, Wesley
 1961-62 The Urbanization of the Yankton Indians. Human Organization 20: 226-231.
Hurt, Wesley and Richard Brown
 1965 Social Drinking Patterns of the Yankton Sioux. Human Organization 24: 222-230.
Hutchinson, B.
 1961 Alcohol as a Contributing Factor in Social Disorganization: The South African
   Bantu in the Nineteenth Century. Revista de Anthropologia 9: 1-13.
Hymes, Dell
 1977 Qualitative/Quantitative Research Methodologies in Education. Anthropology
   and Education Quarterly 8 (3): 165-176.
 1983 [1970] Linguistic Method in Ethnography. *In* Essays in the History of Linguistic
   Anthropology. Dell Hymes, Ed. Amsterdam/Philadelphia: John Benjamin
   Publishing Com.
Hymes, Dell, Ed.
 1969 Reinventing Anthropology. NY: Random House.
Indian Health Service
 2008 Indian Health Service Regional Differences in Indian Health 2002-2003 Edition.
   U.S. Department of Health and Human Services. Office of Public Health.
Inoue, K., M. Kufunaga, T. Kiriyama, and S. Komura
 1984 Accumulation of Acetaldehyde in Alcohol-Sensitive Japanese: Relation to Ethanol
   and Acetaldehyde Oxidizing Capacity. Alcoholism: Clinical and Experimental
   Research 8 (3): 319-322.

Iowa State Department of Public Instruction
    1971 An Advisory Report on Equal Educational Opportunities Sioux City Public
        Schools. Des Moines: Department of Public Instruction.
Ishii, Izumi
    2008 Bad Fruits of the Civilized Tree: Alcohol and the Sovereignty of the Cherokee
        Nation. Lincoln: U of Nebraska Press.
Jacob, Evelyn and Cathie Jordan, Eds.
    1987 Theme Issue: Explaining the School Performance of Minority Students.
        Anthropology and Education Quarterly 18 (4): 259-382.
Jacobs, W.
    1915 Letter to H. A. Larson, July 7. NA, Central Classified Files, Liquor Traffic.
Jacobs, Wilbur
    1950 Wilderness Politics and Indian Gifts. Lincoln: U of Nebraska Press.
    1972 Dispossessing the American Indian. NY: Charles Scribner's Sons.
Jaenen, J.
    1976 Friend and Foe. NY: Columbia U Press.
James, Bernard
    1961 Social-Psychological Dimensions of Ojibwa Acculturation. American
        Anthropologist 63: 721-746.
    1970 Continuity and Emergence in Indian Poverty Culture [and Comments and Reply].
        Current Anthropology 11 (4-5): 435-452.
    1973 Reply. Current Anthropology 14 (1-2): 166-167.
    1974 Reply. Current Anthropology 15 (3): 309-310.
Janis, Irving and Jeon Mann
    1977 Decision Making: A Psychological Analysis of Conflict, Choice, and Commitment.
        NY: The Free Press.
Janis, Irving and Judith Rodin
    1979 Attribution, Control, and Decision Making: Social Psychology and Health Care. In
        Health Psychology — Handbook. George Stone, Francis Cohen, and Nancy Adler,
        Eds. San Francisco: Jossey-Bass Publications.
Jellinek, E. M.
    1952 Phases of Alcohol Addiction. Quarterly J of Studies on Alcohol 13 (4): 673-684.
    1960 The Disease Concept of Alcoholism. New Haven: Hillhouse Press.
Jenness, D.
    1963 The Indians of Canada, 6th Ed. Bulletin 65. Anthropology Series No 15. Ottawa:
        National Museum of Canada.
Jessor, Richard, Theodore Graves, Robert Hanson, and Shirley Jessor
    1968 Society, Personality, and Deviant Behavior: A Study of a Tri-Ethnic Community.
        NY: Holt, Rinehart, and Winston, Inc.
Jilek, Wolfgang
    1974 Salish Indian Mental Health and Culture Change: Psychohygienic and
        Therapeutic Aspects of the Guardian Spirit Ceremonial. Toronto: Holt, Rinehart
        and Winston of Canada.
    1994 Traditional Healing in Prevention and Treatment of Alcohol and Drug Abuse.
        Transcultural Psychiatric Research Review 31: 219-258.
Jilek, Wolfgang and Norman Todd
    1974 Witchdoctors Succeed Where Doctors Fail: Psychotherapy Among Coast Salish
        Indians. Canadian Psychiatric Association J 19 (4): 351-356.

Jilek-Aall, Louise
    1981 Acculturation, Alcoholism and Indian-Style Alcoholics Anonymous. J of
        Studies on Alcohol, Suppl. 9: 143-158.
Jones, John
    1974 Winnebago Ethnology. [Before the Indian Claims Commission. An
        Anthropological Report on the Occupancy of Royce Areas 149, 174, and 245 . . .]
        NY: Garland Publishing.
Jones, Tom, M. Schmudlach, M. Mason, A. Lonetree, and G. Greendeer
    2011 People of the Big Voice: Photographs of Ho-Chunk Families by Charles Van
        Schaich, 1879-1942. Madison: Wisconsin Historical Society Press.
Jorgensen, Joseph
    1971 Indians and the Metropolis. In The American Indian in Urban Society. Jack
        Waddell and O. Michael Watson, Eds. Boston: Little, Brown and Company.
    1972 The Sun Dance Religion. Chicago: U of Chicago Press.
    1978 A Century of Political Economic Effects on American Indian Society, 1880-1980. J
        of Ethnic Studies 6 (3): 1-82.
Joseph, Alice, R. Spicer, and J. Chesky
    1949 The Desert People: A Study of the Papago Indians. Chicago: U of Chicago Press.
Julien, Robert, Claire Advokat, Joseph Comaty
    2011 A Primer of Drug Action., 12th Ed. NY: Worth Publishers.
Julius, Marvin
    1970 An Economic Base Study of Iowa's Sioux City Area. Ames, IA: IA State U
        Cooperative Extension Service.
Kadden, Ronald
    2003 Behavioral and Cognitive-Behavioral Treatments for Alcoholism: Research
        Opportunities. In Recent Developments in Alcoholism, Volume 16. Marc Galanter,
        Ed. NY: Plenum Press.
Kalant, Harold
    2009 What Neurobiology Cannot Tell Us about Addiction. Addiction 105: 780-789.
Kalant, Harold, Eugene LeBlanc, and Robert Gibbins
    1971 Tolerance to, and Dependence on, Ethanol. In Biological Basis of Alcoholism. Y.
        Israel and J. Mardones, Eds. NY: Wiley and Sons Inc.
Kaminshy, K. A. Petronis, et al.
    2008 Epigenetics of Personality Traits: An Illustrative Study of Identical Twins
        Discordant for Risk-Taking Behavior. Twins Research in Human Genetics 11 (1): 1-
        11.
Kappler, Charles, Compl. and Ed.
    1904 Indian Affairs, Laws and Treaties. Volumes 1 and 2. Washington, DC:
        Government Printing Office.
Karacki, L. and J. Toby
    1962 The Uncommitted Adolescent: Candidate for Gang Socialization. Sociological
        Inquiry 32: 203-215.
Kardiner, Abram
    1939 The Individual and His Society: The Psychodynamics of Primitive Social
        Organization. NY: Columbia U Press.
Keesing, Felix
    1953 Culture Change: An Analysis and Bibliography of Anthropological Sources to
        1952. Stanford: Stanford U Press.

Keesing, Roger
 1974 Theories of Culture. Annual Reviews of Anthropology 3: 73-97.
 1994 Theories of Culture Revisited. *In* Assessing Cultural Anthropology. Robert Borofsky, Ed. NY: McGraw-Hill.
Keiding, S. et al.
 1983 Ethanol Metabolism in Heavy Drinkers after Massive and Moderate Alcohol Intake. Biochemical Pharmacology 32 (920): 3097-102.
Kelbert, M. and L. Hale
 1965 The Introduction of Alcohol into Iroquois Society. Project G-19, Substudy 1-K and H-65. Toronto: Addiction Research Foundation.
Kelly, Dennis
 2008 Alcohol Abuse Recovery and Prevention as Spiritual Practice. *In* Religion and Healing in Native America: Pathways for Renewal. S. O'Brien, Ed. Westport: Greenwood Press.
Kelly, George
 1955 The Psychology of Personal Constructs. Volumes 1 and 2. NY: Norton.
Kelso, Dennis and William DuBay
 1989 Alaskan Natives and Alcohol: A Sociocultural and Epidemiological Review. In Alcohol Use Among U.S. Ethnic Minorities. NIAAA. Washington, DC: U.S. Government Printing Office.
Kimura, Mitsuru and S. Higuchi
 2011 Genetics of Alcohol Dependence. Psychiatry and Clinical Neurosciences 65: 213-225.
Kirsch, Irving
 2009 The Emperor's New Drugs: Exploding the Antidepressant Myth. NY: Basic Books.
Kluckhohn, Clyde
 1967 [1944] Navaho Witchcraft. Boston: Beacon Press.
Kluckhohn, Clyde and D. Leighton
 1946 The Navajo. Cambridge: Harvard U Press.
Kneale, Albert
 1909a Letter to the Commissioner of Indian Affairs, January 4. NA, Central Classified Files, Liquor Traffic.
 1909b Letter to William Johnson, March 24. NA, Central Classified Files, Liquor Traffic.
 1950 Indian Agent. Caldwell, Idaho: Caxton Printers, Ltd.
Ko, J., S. Martin, S. Kuramoto, H. Chilcoat
 2010 Patterns of Alcohol-Dependence Symptoms Using a Latent Empirical Approach: Associations with Treatment Usage and Other Correlates. J of Studies of Alcohol and Drugs 71: 870-878.
Koenig, Margaret
 1921 Tuberculosis Among the Nebraska Winnebago: A Social Study on an Indian Reservation. Lincoln: State Historical Society of Nebraska.
Koob, George and Michelle Le Moal
 2006 Neurobiology and Addiction. NY: Elsevier.
 2008 Addiction and the Brain Antireward System. *In* Annual Review of Psychology 59: 29-53.
Koob, George and Nora Volkow
 2010 Neurocircuitry of Addiction. Neuropsychopharmacology Reviews 35: 217-238.

Koss, M., N. Yuan, D. Dightman, et al.
    2003 Adverse Childhood Exposures and Alcohol Dependence Among Seven Native
        American Tribes. American J of Preventive Medicine 2: 238-244.
Krech, Shepard, III
    1991 The State of Ethnohistory. Annual Review of Anthropology 20: 345-75.
    2006 Bringing Linear Time Back In. Ethnohistory 53 (3): 567-593.
Kreek, Mary Jeanne
    2011 Extreme Marginalization: Addiction and Other Mental Health Disorders, Stigma,
        and Imprisonment. Annals of the New York Academy of Sciences 1231: 66-72.
Kronenfield, David
    2011 Afterword: One Cognitive View of Culture. In A Companion to
        Cognitive Anthropology. D. Kronenfield et al., Eds. NY: Wiley-Blackwell.
Kronenfield, Daivd, G. Bennardo, V. de Munch, and M. Fischer, Eds.
    2011 A Companion to Cognitive Anthropology. NY: Wiley-Blackwell.
Krupat, Arnold
    1985 For Those Who Come After: A Study of Native American Autobiography.
        Berkeley: U of CA Press.
Kulis, Stephen, D. Hodge, S. Ayers, et al.
    2012 Spirituality and Religion: Intertwined Protective Factors for Substance Use
        Among Urban American Indian Youth. American J of Drug and Alcohol Abuse 38
        (5): 444-449.
Kunitz, Stephen and Jerrold Levy
    1974 Changing Ideas of Alcohol Use Among Navaho Indians. Quarterly J of Studies on
        Alcohol 35: 243-259.
    1994 Drinking Careers: A Twenty-five-year Study of Three Navajo Populations. New
        Haven: Yale U Press.
    2000 Drinking, Conduct Disorder, and Social Change: Navajo Experiences. Oxford:
        Oxford U Press.
La Barre, Weston
    1947 Primitive Psychotherapy in Native American Cultures: Peyotism and Confession.
        J of Abnormal and Social Psychology 42 (3): 294-309.
    1975 The Peyote Cult, 4th Ed. New York: Schocken Books.
Labov, William
    1972 Language in the Inner City: Studies in the Black English Vernacular. Philadelphia:
        U of Pennsylvania Press.
Lang, Alan
    1983 Drinking and Disinhibition: Contributions From Psychological Research. In
        Alcohol and Disinhibition: Nature and Meaning of the Link. R. Room and G.
        Collins, Eds. NIAAA Research Monograph No. 12. Washington, DC: Government
        Printing Office.
Lass, W.
    1962-63 The Removal from Minnesota of the Sioux and Winnebago Indians. Minnesota
        History 38: 353-64.
Laudan, Larry
    1977 Progress and Its Problems: Towards a Theory of Scientific Growth. Berkeley: U of
        CA Press.
Leacock, Eleanor, Ed.
    1961 Symposium on the Concept of Ethnohistory—Comment. Ethnohistory 8: 256-261.

Leary, Mark
    2007 Motivational and Emotional Aspects of the Self. Annual Review of Psychology 58: 317-344.
Leatherman, Tom and Alan Goodman
    2011 Critical Biocultural Approaches in Medical Anthropology. In A Companion to Medical Anthropology. M. Singer and P. Erickson, Eds. Malden MA: Wiley-Blackwell.
Leenhardt, M.
    1937 Gens de la Grande Terre. Paris.
Leighton, Dorothea and C. Kluckhohn
    1948 Children of the People. Cambridge: Harvard U Press.
Leland, Joy
    1975 Drinking Styles in an Indian Settlement: A Numerical Folk Taxonomy. Unpublished Ph.D. Dissertation. U of California, Irvine.
    1976 Firewater Myths: North American Indian Drinking and Alcohol Addiction. Monographs of the Rutgers Center of Alcohol Studies, No. 11. New Brunswick: Rutgers Center of Alcohol Studies.
    1978 Women and Alcohol in an Indian Settlement. Medical Anthropology 2 (4): 85-119.
    1981 Native American Alcohol Use: A Review of the Literature. In Tulapai to Tokay. P. Mail and D. McDonald, Compls. New Haven: HRAF Press.
Lemert, Edwin
    1954a The Life and Death of an Indian State. Human Organization 13: 23-27.
    1954b Alcohol and the Northwest Coast Indians. U of California Publications in Culture and Society 2 (6): 303-406.
    1958 The Use of Alcohol in Three Salish Indian Tribes. Quarterly J of Studies on Alcohol 19: 90-107.
    1962 Alcohol Use in Polynesia. Trop Geo Med 14: 183-191.
Levine, H.
    1978 The Discovery of Addiction: Changing Conceptions of Habitual Drunkenness in American History. J of Studies on Alcohol 39 (1): 143-174.
Levran, Orna, V. Yuferov, and M. Kreek
    2012 The Genetics of the Opioid System and Specific Drug Addictions. Human Genetics 131: 823-842.
Levy, Jerrold
    1984 Comment. Current Anthropology 25 (2): 182-183.
Levy, Jerrold and Stephen Kunitz
    1971 Indian Reservations, Anomie and Social Pathology. Southwestern J of Anthropology 27: 97-128.
    1974 Indian Drinking: Navajo Practices and Anglo-American Theories. NY: John Wiley and Sons, Inc.
    1981 Economic and Political Factors Inhibiting the Use of Basic Research Findings in Indian Alcoholism Programs. In Cultural Factors in Alcohol Research and Treatment of Drinking Problems. D. Heath, J. Waddell, and M. Topper, Eds. J of Studies on Alcohol, Suppl. 9: 60-72.
Levy, R.
    1966 Ma'ohi Drinking Patterns in the Society Islands. J of Polynesian Society 75: 304-320.
    1973 Tahitians: Mind and Experience in the Society Islands. Chicago: U of Chicago Press.

Lewis, I.
    1968 Introduction. *In* History and Anthropology. I. Lewis, Ed. London: Tavistock Publications.
Lewis, Oscar
    1966a The Culture of Poverty. Scientific American 215 (4): 19-25.
    1966b La Vida: A Puerto Rican Family in the Culture of Poverty—San Juan and New York. NY: Random House.
Lewontin, R.
    1974 The Genetic Basis of Evolutionary Change. NY: Columbia U Press.
Lex, Barbara
    1979 The Neurobiology of Ritual Trance. *In* The Spectrum of Ritual: A Biogenetic Structural Analysis. Eugene d'Aquili, Charles Laughlin, Jr., and John McManus, Eds. NY: Columbia U Press.
    1985 Alcohol Problems in Special Populations. *In* The Diagnosis and Treatment of Alcoholism, 2nd Ed. J. Mendelson and N. Mello, Eds. NY: McGraw-Hill Book Company.
Li, An-Che
    1937 Zuni: Some Observations and Queries. American Anthropologist 39: 62-76.
Li, Dawei, H. Zhao, J. Gelernter
    2012a Strong Protective Effect of the Aldehyde Dehydrogenase Gene *(ALDH2)504lys(*2)* Allele Against Alcoholism and Alcohol-Induced Medical Diseases in Asians. Human Genetics 131: 725-737.
    2012b Further Clarification of the Contribution of the *ADH1C* Gene to Vulnerability of Alcoholism and Selected Liver Diseases. Human Genetics 131: 1361-1374.
Li, H., N. Mukherjee, U. Soundararajan, et al.
    2007 Geographically Separate Increases in the Frequency of the Derived *ADH1B*47His* Allele in Eastern and Western Asia. American J of Human Genetics 81 (4): 842-846.
Li, H., S. Borinskaya, K. Yoshimua, et al.
    2009 Refined Geographic Distribution of the Oriental *ALDH2*504Lys (nee 487Lys)* Variant. Annals of Human Genetics 73 (Pt. 3): 335-345.
Licinio, Julio and Ma-Li Wong, Eds.
    2002 Pharmacogenomics: The Search for Individualized Therapies. Weinheim: Wiley-VCH.
Lieber, Charles
    2005 Alcohol Metabolism: General Aspects. *In* Comprehensive Handbook of Alcohol Related Pathology, Volume 1. V. Preedy and R. Watson, Eds. NY: Elsevier Academic.
Liebow, Elliot
    1967 Tally's Corner: A Study of Negro Street Corner Men. Boston: Little, Brown and Company, Inc.
Lindesmith, A. and A. Strauss
    1950 A Critique of Culture-Personality Writings. American Sociological Review 15: 587-600.
Lindsey, Donald F.
    1995 Indians at Hampton Institute, 1877–1923. Urbana: U of Illinois Press.
Linger, Daniel
    2005 Identity. *In* A Companion to Psychological Anthropology. C. Casey and R. Edgerton, Eds. Malden, MA: Blackwell Publishing.

Linneberg, A., A. Gonzalea-Quintela, C. Vidal, et al.
2009 Genetic Determinants of Both Ethanol and Acetaldehyde Metabolism Influence Alcohol Hypersensitivity and Drinking Behavior Among Scandinavians. Clinical and Experimental Allergy 40: 123-130.

Linneberg, A., N. Berg, A. Gonzalez-Quintela, et al.
2007 Prevalence of Self-Reported Hypersensitivity Symptoms Following Intake of Alcoholic Drinks. Clinical and Experimental Allergy 38: 145-151.

Lithman, Yngve
1979 Feeling Good and Getting Smashed: On the Symbolism of Alcohol and Drunkenness Among Canadian Indians. Ethnos 1-2: 119-133.

Littman, Gerard
1970 Alcoholism, Illness, and Social Pathology Among American Indians in Transition. American J of Public Health 60 (9): 1769-1787.

Lloyd, D.
1968 Conflict Theory and Yoruba Kingdoms. In History and Social Anthropology. I. Lewis, Ed. London: Tavistock.

Lomnitz, L.
1976 Alcohol and Culture: The Historical Evolution of Drinking Patterns Among the Mapuche. In Cross-Cultural Approaches to the Study of Alcohol. M. Everett, J. Waddell, and D. Heath, Eds. The Hague: Mouton.

Long, Jeffrey, P. Mail, H. Thomasson
2002 Genetic Susceptibility and Alcoholism in American Indians. In Alcohol Use Among American Indians and Alaska Natives: Multiple Perspectives on a Complex Problem. P. Mail, et al., Eds. NIAAA Research Monograph 37.

Longabaugh, Richard
2003 Involvement of Support Networks in Treatment. In Recent Developments in Alcoholism, Volume 16. Marc Galanter, Ed. NY: Plenum Press.

Luborsky, L., R. Rosenthal, L. Diguer, T. Andrusyna, et al.
2002 The Dodo Bird Verdict Is Alive and Well—Mostly. Clinical Psychology: Science and Practice 9: 3-33.

Lucinio, Julio and Mal-Li Wong, Eds.
2002 Pharmacogenomics: The Search for Individualized Therapies. Weinheim: Wiley-VCH.

Luczak, S., S. Shea, L. Carr, et al.
2002 Binge Drinking in Jewish and Non-Jewish White College Students. Alcoholism: Clinical and Experimental Research 26 (12): 1773-1778.

Ludwig, Arnold, Jerome LeVine, and Louis Stark
1970 LSD and Alcoholism: A Clinical Study of Treatment Efficacy. Springfield, IL: Charles Thomas, Publisher.

Lugard, F.
1965 The Dual Mandate in British Tropical Africa, 5th Ed. Hamden: Archon Books.

Lurie, Nancy
1948 Trends of Change in Patterns of Child Care and Training Among the Wisconsin Winnebago. The Wisconsin Archeologist 29: 39-140.
1952 The Winnebago Indians: A Study in Culture Change. Unpublished Ph.D. Dissertation. Northwestern University.
1961a Ethnohistory: A Ethnological Point of View. Ethnohistory 8: 78-92.
1962 Comments on Bernard J. James's Analysis of Ojibwa Acculturation. American Anthropologist 64 (4): 826-833.

1971 The World's Oldest On-Going Protest Demonstration: North American Drinking Patterns. Pacific Historical Review 40 (3): 311-332.

1972 Two Dollars. *In* Crossing Cultural Boundaries: The Anthropological Experience. Solon Kinball and Jame Watson, Eds. San Francisco: Chandler Publishing Company.

1978 Winnebago. *In* Handbook of North American Indians, Vol. 15, Northeast. Bruce Trigger, Ed. Washington, DC: Smithsonian Institution.

Lurie, Nancy, Ed.

1961b Mountain Wolf Woman: Sister of Crashing Thunder. Ann Arbor: U Michigan Press.

Lurie, Nancy and Patrick Jung

2009 The Nicolet Corrigenda: New France Revisited. Long Grove: Waveland Press.

MacAndrew, Craig and Robert Edgerton

1969 Drunken Comportment: A Social Explanation. Chicago: Aldine Publishing Company.

McCabe, O. Lee and Thomas Hanlon

1977 The Use of LSD-Type Drugs in Psychotherapy: Progress and Promise. *In* Changing Human Behavior: Current Therapies and Future Directions. O. Lee McCabe, Ed. NY: Grune and Stratton.

McCall, George and J. L. Simmons, Eds.

1969 Issues in Participant Observation: A Text and Reader. Reading, MA: Addison Wesley Publishing Company.

McEwen, Bruce

2010 Stress, Sex, and Neural Adaptation to a Changing Environment: Mechanisms of Neuronal Remodeling. Annals of the New York Academy of Sciences1204: E38-E59.

McEwen, Bruce and Peter Gianaros

2010 Central Role of the Brain in Stress and Adaptation: Links to Socioeconomic Status, Health and Disease. Annals of the New York Academy of Sciences 1186: 190-222.

2011 Stress- and Allostatis-induced Brain Plasticity. Annual Review of Medicine 62: 431-445.

McGlothlin, William

1967 Social and Para-Medical Aspects of Hallucinogenic Drugs. *In* The Use of LSD in Psychotherapy and Alcoholism. Harold Abramson, Ed. Indianapolis: Bobbs-Merrill Company, Inc.

McGowan, Patrick

2012 Epigenetic Clues to the Biological Embedding of Early Life Adversity. Biological Psychiatry 72: 4-5.

MacGregor, Gordon

1946 Warriors Without Weapons: A Study of the Society and Personality Development of the Pine Ridge Sioux. Chicago: U of Chicago Press.

McKay, James and S. Hiller-Sturmhöfel

2011 Treating Alcoholism As a Chronic Disease: Approaches to Long-Term Continuing Care. Alcohol Research and Health 33 (4): 356-370.

Macleod, W.

1928 The American Indian Frontier. NY: Knopf.

Madsen, William

1974 The American Alcoholic: The Nature-Nurture Controversy in Alcoholic Research and Therapy. Springfield: Charles C. Thomas.

1979 Alcoholics Anonymous as a Crisis Cult. *In* Beliefs, Behaviors, and Alcoholic Beverages: A Cross-Cultural Survey. Mac Marshall, Ed. Ann Arbor: U of Michigan Press.

1988 Defending the Disease: From Facts to Fingarette. Akron: Wilson, Brown and Company.

Mail, Patricia

1985 Closing the Circle: A Prevention Model for Indian Communities with Alcohol Problems. HS Primary Care Provider 10: 2-5.

Mail, Patricia and C. Shelton

2002 Treating Indian Alcoholics. *In* Alcohol Use Among American Indians and Alaska Natives: Multiple Perspective on a Complex Problem. P. Mail, et al., Eds. NIAAA Research Monograph 37.

Mail, Patricia and D. McDonald, Compls.

1981 Tulapai To Tokay: A Bibliography of Alcohol Use and Abuse Among Native Americans of North American. New Haven: HRAF Press.

Mail, Patricia and George Menter

1985 Evaluation of Indian Alcoholism Programs: Lessons Learned over Three Years. Paper presented at the 20th Annual Meeting of the U.S. Public Health Service Professional Association.

Mail, Patricia and P. Walker

2002 Alcohol in the Lives of Indian Women. *In* Alcohol Use Among American Indians and Alaska Natives: Multiple Perspective on a Complex Problem. P. Mail, et al., Eds. NIAAA Research Monograph 37.

Mail, Patricia, S. Heurtin-Roberts, S. Martin, and J. Howard, Eds.

2002 Alcohol Use Among American Indians and Alaska Natives: Multiple Perspectives on a Complex Problem. NIAAA Research Monograph No. 37.

Malinowski, B.

1961 Argonauts of the Western Pacific. NY: Dutton.

Malouf, Carling

1942 Gosiute Peyotism. American Anthropologist 44: 93-103.

Mancall, Peter

1995a Deadly Medicine: Indians and Alcohol in Early America. Ithaca: Cornell U Press.

1995b Men, Women, and Alcohol in Indian Villages in the Great Lake Region in the Early Republic. J of the Early Republic 15 (3): 425-448.

Mandelbaum, M.

1977 The Anatomy of Historical Knowledge. Baltimore: John Hopkins U Press.

Mangini, Mariavittoria

1998 Treatment of Alcoholism Using Psychedelic Drugs: A Review of the Program of Research. J of Psychoactive Drugs 30 (4): 381-418.

Markus, Hazel and Ann Ruvolo

1989 Possible Selves: Personalized Representations of Goals. *In* Goal Concepts in Personality and Social Psychology. Lawrence Pervin, Ed. Hillsdale, NJ: Lawrence Erlbaum Associates, Publishers.

Markus, Hazel and Elissa Wurf

1986 The Dynamic Self-Concept: A Social Psychological Perspective. *In* Annual Review of Psychology 38: 299-337.

Markus, Hazel and Paula Nurius

1986 Possible Selves. American Psychologist 41 (9): 954-969.

Marlatt, G. Alan
  1978 Craving for Alcohol, Loss of Control, and Relapse: A Cognitive-Behavioral
     Approach. *In* Alcoholism: New Directions in Behavioral Research and Treatment. P.
     Nathan, G. Marlatt, and T. Loberg, Eds. NY: Plenum Press.
Marlatt, G. Alan and Dennis Donovan, Eds.
  2005 Relapse Prevention: Maintenance Strategies in the Treatment of Addictive
     Behaviors, 2nd Ed. NY: Guilford Press.
Marlatt, G. Alan and Judith Gordon, Eds.
  1985 Relapse Prevention: Maintenance Strategies in the Treatment of Addictive
     Behaviors. NY: Guilford Press.
Maroukis, Thomas
  2004 Peyote and the Yankton Sioux: The Life and Times of Sam Necklace. Norman: U
     of Oklahoma Press.
  2010 The Peyote Road: Religious Freedom and the Native American Church. Norman:
     U Oklahoma Press.
Marshall, Mac
  1974 Research Bibliography of Alcohol and Kava Studies in Oceania. Micronesia 10:
     299-306.
  1975 The Politics of Prohibition on Namoluk Atoll. J of Studies on Alcohol 36: 597-610.
  1976 A Review and Appraisal of Alcohol and Kava Studies in Oceania. *In* Cross-
     Cultural Approaches to the Study of Alcohol. M. Everett, J. Waddell, and D. Heath,
     Eds. The Hague: Mouton.
  1979 Weekend Warriors: Alcohol in Micronesian Culture. Palo Alto, CA: Mayfield.
  1980 A History of Prohibition and Liquor Legislation in Papua New Guinea, 1884-1963.
     JASER Discussion Paper No 33, Boroko, Papua New Guinea: Institute of Applied
     Social and Economic Research.
  1990a "Problem Deflation" and the Ethnographic Record: Interpretation and
     Introspection in Anthropological Studies of Alcohol. J of Substance Abuse 2: 353-
     367.
  1990b Combining Insights from Epidemiological and Ethnographic Data to Investigate
     Substance Use in Truk, Federated States of Micronesia. British of Addiction 85:
     1457-1468.
Marshall, Mac, Ed.
  1979 Beliefs, Behaviors, and Alcoholic Beverages: A Cross-Cultural Survey. Ann Arbor:
     U of Michigan Press.
Marshall, Mac and L. Marshall
  1975 Opening Pandora's Bottle: Reconstructing Micronesians' Early Contacts with
     Alcoholic Beverages. J of Polynesian Society 84: 441-465.
  1976 Holy and Unholy Spirits: The Effects of Missionization on Alcohol Use in Eastern
     Micronesia. J of Pacific History 11: 135-166.
  1980 Some Sober Reflections on Miller's Temperate Note on "Holy and Unholy
     Spirits." J of Pacific History 25: 232-234.
  1990 Silent Voices Speak: Women and Prohibition in Truk. Belmont, CA: Wadsworth.
Marshall, Mac, G. Ames, and L. Bennett
  2001 Anthropological Perspectives on Alcohol and Drugs at the Turn of the New
     Millennium. Social Science and Medicine 53: 153-164.
Martin, Calvin
  1987a Introduction: An Introduction Aboard the Fidèle. *In* The American Indian and
     the Problem of History. C. Martin, Ed. NY: Oxford U Press.

1987b The Metaphysics of Writing Indian-White History. *In* The American Indian and the Problem of History. C. Martin, Ed. NY: Oxford U Press.

1987c Epilogue: Time and the American Indian. *In* The American Indian and the Problem of History. C. Martin, Ed. NY: Oxford U Press.

Martin, Calvin, Ed.

1987 The American Indian and the Problem of History. NY: Oxford U Press.

Martin, Harry

1964 Correlates of Adjustment Among American Indians in an Urban Environment. Human Organization 23: 290-295.

Martin, J.

1911 Letter to F. H. Abbott, February. NA, Central Classified Files, Winnebago.

Masters, Susan

2009 The Alcohols. *In* Basic and Clinical Pharmacology, 11th Ed. Bertram Katzung, S. Masters, A. Trevor, Eds. NY: McGraw-Hill.

Mathewson, C.

1866 Letter to E. B. Taylor, November 19. NA, Letters Received, Winnebago Agency.

Matza, D. and G. Sykes

1961 Delinquency and Subterranean Values. American Sociological Review 26: 712-719.

May, Philip

1996 Overview of Alcohol Abuse Epidemiology for American Indian Populations. *In* Changing Numbers, Changing Needs: American Indian Demography and Public Health. G. Sandefur, et al. Eds. Washington, DC: National Academy Press.

May, Philip and J. Phillip Gossage

2001 New Data on the Epidemiology of Adult Drinking and Substance Use Among American Indians of the Northern States: Male and Female Data on Prevalence, Patterns, and Consequences. American Indian and Alaska Native Mental Health Research (Online). 2001, 10, 2: 1-2.

May, Philip and Karen Hymbaugh

1989 A Macro-Level Fetal Alcohol Syndrome Prevention Program for Native Americans and Alaska Natives: Description and Evaluation. J of Studies on Alcohol 50 (6): 508-518.

May, Philip, J. McCloskey, and J. Gossage

2002 Fetal Alcohol Syndrome Among American Indians: Epidemiology, Issues, and Research Issues. *In* Alcohol Use Among American Indians and Alaska Natives: Multiple Perspective on a Complex Problem. P. Mail, et al., Eds. NIAAA Research Monograph 37.

Mead, Margaret

1960 [1932] The Changing Culture of an Indian Tribe. NY: Capricorn Books.

1961 [1928] Coming of Age in Samoa. NY: William Morrow and Co.

1972 Blackberry Winter: My Earlier Years. NY: Morrow.

Mead, Margaret. Ed.

1959 An Anthropologist at Work: Writings of Ruth Benedict. Boston: Houghton Mifflin Co.

Medicine, Beatrice

1983 An Ethnography of Drinking and Sobriety Among the Lakota Sioux. Unpublished Ph.D. Dissertation. U of Wisconsin—Madison.

2007 Drinking and Sobriety Among the Lakota Sioux. Lanham, MD: Altamira Press.

Meeker, L.

1896 The Mescal Bean, no. 2537. AA.

1898 Letter to J. W. Powell, March 25th. AA.

Mekeel, H. Scudder
1937 A Social Science Approach to Case Work with the American Indian. The Family 18: 204-207.

Mello, Nancy
1972 Behavioral Studies of Alcoholism. In The Biology of Alcoholism. Volume 2: Physiology and Behavior. B. Kissin and H. Begleitor, Eds. NY: Plenum Press.

Mello, Nancy and Jack Mendelson
1970 Experimentally Induced Intoxication in Alcoholics: A Comparison Between Programmed and Spontaneous Drinking. J of Pharmacology and Experimental Therapeutics 173: 101-116.

Merton, Robert
1938 Social Structure and Anomie. American Sociological Review 3: 672-682.
1957 Social Theory and Social Structure, Rev. Ed. Glencoe, Ill: The Free Press.

Messer, S. and B. Wampold
2002 Let's Face Facts: Common Factors Are More Potent than Specific Therapy. Clinical Psychology: Science and Practice 9: 21-25.

Meyer, Urs
2002 Introduction to Pharmacogenomics: Promises, Opportunities, and Limitations. In Pharmacogenomics: The Search for Individualized Therapies. J. Licinio and Ma-Li Wong, Eds. Weinheim: Wiley-VCH.

Mielke, James, L. Konigsberg, and J. Relethford
2006 Human Biological Variation, 2nd Ed. NY: Oxford U Press.

Millar, C. and J. Leung
1971 Aboriginal Alcohol Consumption in South Australia: A Question of Choice. R. Brent, Ed. Nedlands: U of Western Australia Press.

Miller, C.
1979 A Temperate Note on "Holy and Unholy Spirits." J of Pacific History 24: 230-232.

Miller, George, Eugene Galanter and Karl Pribram
1960 Plans and the Structure of Behavior. NY: Holt, Rinehart and Winston, Inc.

Miller, Walter
1958 Lower Class Culture as a Generating Milieu of Gang Delinquency. J of Social Issues 14: 5-19.

Miller, William
1996 What Is Relapse? Fifty Ways to Leave the Wagon. Addiction 91: S15-S27.
2003 Spirituality, Treatment, and Recovery. In Recent Developments in Alcoholism, Volume 16. Marc Galanter, Ed. NY: Plenum Press.

Mischel, W.
1968 Personality and Assessment. NY: John Wiley.
1990 Personality Dispositions Revisited and Revised: A View After Three Decades. In Handbook of Personality: Theory and Research. Lawrence Pervin, Ed. NY: Guilford Press.

Mizoi, Y., I. Ijiri, Y. Tatsuno, T. Kijima, S. Fujiwara, and J. Adachi
1979 Relationship Between Facial Flushing and Blood Acetaldehyde Levels after Alcohol Intake. Pharmacology, Biochemistry and Behavior 10: 303-311.

Mizoi, Y. K. Yamamoto, Y. Ueno, et al.
1994 Involvement of Genetic Polymorphism of Alcohol and Aldeyde Dehydrogenase in Individual Variation of Alcohol Metabolism. Alcohol and Alcoholism 29 (6): 707-710.

Mizoi, Y., T. Fukunaga, and J. Adachi
    1989 The Flushing Syndrome in Orientals. *In* Human Metabolism of Alcohol, Vol. 2. Kathryn Crow and Richard Batt, Eds. Boca Raton: CRC Press, Inc.
Mizoi, Y., Y. Tatsuno, J. Adachi, et al.
    1983 Alcohol Sensitivity Related to Alcohol-Metabolizing Enzymes in Japanese. Pharmacology, Biochemistry and Behavior 18, Suppl. 1: 127-133.
Moffitt, T. E.
    1993 Adolescence-Limited and Life-Course-Persistent Antisocial Behavior: A Developmental Taxonomy. Psychological Review 100: 674-701.
Mohatt, G.
    1972 The Sacred Water: The Quest for Personal Power Through Drinking Among the Teton Sioux. *In* The Drinking Man. D. McClelland, et al., Eds. NY: The Free Press.
Moncrieff, Joanna
    2009 The Myth of the Chemical Cure: A Critique of Psychiatric Drug Treatment, Revised Ed. NY: Palgrave Macmillan.
Montag, Annika, J. Clapp, D. Calac, J. Gorman, and C. Chambers
    2012 A Review of Evidence-Based Approaches for Reduction of Alcohol Consumption in Native Women Who Are Pregnant or of Reproductive Age. American J of Drug and Alcohol Abuse 38 (5): 436-443.
Moore, D. A.
    1928 Letter to C. M. Ziebach, August 8. FA.
Moore, John, Ed.
    1993 The Political Economy of North American Indians. Norman: U of Oklahoma Press.
Moore, W.
    1974 Social Change, 2nd Ed. Englewood Cliffs, New Jersey: Prentice-Hall.
Moran, James
    2002 Urban Indians and Alcohol Problems: Research Findings on Alcohol Use, Treatment, Prevention, and Related Issues. *In* Alcohol Use Among American Indians and Alaska Natives: Multiple Perspective on a Complex Problem. P. Mail, et al., Eds. NIAAA Research Monograph 37.
Moran, James and M. Bussey
    2006 Results of an Alcohol Prevention Program with Urban American Indian Youth. Child and Adolescent Social Work J 24 (1): 1-21.
Morrell, W.
    1960 Britain in the Pacific Islands. London: Oxford U Press.
Mulligan, C., R. Robin, M. Osier, et al.
    2003 Allelic Variation at Alcohol Metabolism Genes (*ADH1B, ADH1C, ALDH2*) and Alcohol Dependence in an American Indian Population. Human Genetics 113 (4): 325-336.
Nabokov, Peter
    2002 A Forest of Time: American Indian Ways of History. NY: Cambridge U Press.
Nash, June
    1981 Ethnographic Aspects of the World Capitalist System. *In* Annual Review of Anthropology, Volume 10: 393-423.
Nebelkopf, Ethan and Mary Phillips, Eds.
    2004 Healing and Mental Health for Native Americans: Speaking in Red. Walnut Creek, CA: Altamira Press.

Neisser, Ulric
   1976 Cognition and Reality: Principles and Implications of Cognitive Psychology. San
      Francisco: Freeman and Company.
Nestler, Eric
   2009 Cellular and Molecular Mechanisms of Drug Addiction. *In* Neurobiology of
      Mental Illness, 3rd Ed. D. Charney and E. Nestler, Eds. NY: Oxford U Press.
Neumark, Yehuda, Y. Friedlander, R. Durst, et al.
   2004 Alcohol Dehydrogenase Polymorphisms Influence Alcohol-Elimination Rates in a
      Male Jewish Population. Alcoholism: Clinical and Experimental Research 28 (1): 10-
      14.
Noah, Timothy
   2012 The Great Divergence: America's Growing Inequality Crisis and What We Can Do
      About It. NY: Bloomsbury Press.
Noe, Tim, C. Fleming, and S. Manson
   2003 Healthy Nations: Reducing Substance Abuse in American Indian and Alaska
      Native Communities. J of Psychoactive Drugs 35 (1): 15-5.
Norton, T.
   1974 The Fur Trade in Colonial New York 1686-1776. Madison: U of Wisconsin Press.
Novins, Douglas, P. Spicer, A. Fickenscher, and B. Pescosolido
   2012 Pathways to Care: Narratives of American Indian Adolescents Entering Substance
      Abuse Treatment. Social Science and Medicine 74 (12): 2037-2045.
Novoradovsky, A., J. Kidd, K. Kidd, and D. Goldman
   1995 Apparent Monomorphism of ALDH2 in Seven American Indian Populations.
      Alcohol 12 (2): 163-167.
O'Brien, Charles
   2011 Drug Addiction. *In* Goodman and Gilman's The Pharmacological Basis of
      Therapeutics, 12th Ed. Laurence Brunton, et al., Eds. NY: McGraw-Hill.
O'Brien, Suzanne, Ed.
   2008 Religion and Healing in Native America: Pathways to Renewal. Westport, CT:
      Greenwood Press.
O'Connor, C.
   1904 Testimony at Winnebago. FA.
O'Dowd, Brian, Francisco Rothhammer, and Yedy Israel
   1990 Genotyping of Mitochondrial Aldehyde Dehydrogenase Locus of Native American
      Indians. Alcoholism: Clinical and Experimental Research 14 (4): 531-533.
Oetting, E. and Fred Beauvais
   1989 Epidemiology and Correlates of Alcohol Use Among Indian Adolescents Living
      on Reservations. *In* Alcohol Use Among U.S. Ethnic Minorities. NIAAA.
      Washington, DC: U.S. Government Printing Office.
Oetting, E., Fred Beauvais, and Ruth Edwards
   1988 Alcohol and Indian Youth: Social and Psychological Correlates and Prevention. J
      of Drug Issues 18 (1): 87-101.
Officer, James
   1971 The American Indian and Federal Policy. *In* The American Indian in Urban
      Society. Jack Waddell and O. Michael Watson, Eds. Boston: Little, Brown and Co.
Ogbu, John
   1990 Cultural Mode, Identity, and Literacy. *In* Cultural Psychology: Essays on
      Comparative Human Development. J. Stigler, R. Shweder, and G. Herdt, Eds. NY:
      Cambridge U Press.

O'Malley, Stephanie and Patrick O'Connor
    2011 Medications for Unhealthy Alcohol Use: Across the Spectrum. Alcohol Research
        and Health 33 (4): 300-312.
O'Nell, Theresa and C. Mitchell
    1996 Alcohol Use Among American Indian Adolescents: The Role of Culture in
        Pathological Drinking. Social Science and Medicine 42 (4): 565-578.
Oneta, C., C. Leiber, J. Li, et al.
    2002 Dynamics of Cytochrome P4502E1 Activity in Man: Induction by Ethanol and
        Disappearance During Withdrawal Phase. J of Hepatology 36: 47-52.
Orford, Jim
    1985 Excessive Appetites: A Psychological View of Addictions. NY: John Wiley and
        Sons.
    2001 Excessive Appetites: A Psychological View of Addictions, 2nd Ed. NY: John Willey
        and Sons.
    2008a Joining the Queue of Dissenters. Addiction 103 (5): 706-710.
    2008b Asking the Right Questions in the Right Way: The Need for a Shift in Research
        on Psychological Treatments for Addictions. Addiction 103 (6): 875-885.
Orlansky, Harold
    1949 Infant Care and Personality. Psychological Bulletin 46: 1-48.
Page, Elizabeth
    1915 In Camp and Tepee: American Indian Mission. NY: Fleming Revell.
Pan, L.
    1975 Alcohol in Colonial Africa. Helsinki: The Finnish Foundation for Alcohol Studies.
Paredes, J. Anthony
    1973 On James's "Continuity and Emergence in Indian Poverty Culture." Current
        Anthropology 14 (1-2): 158-162.
Parker-Langley, Linda
    2002 Alcohol Prevention Programs Among American Indians: Research Findings and
        Issues. In Alcohol Use Among American Indians and Alaska Natives: Multiple
        Perspective on a Complex Problem. P. Mail, et al., Eds. NIAAA Research
        Monograph 37.
Pascarosa, Paul and Sanford Futterman
    1976 Ethnopsychedelic Therapy for Alcoholics: Observations in the Peyote Ritual of the
        Native American Church. J of Psychedelic Drugs 8 (3): 215-221.
Pascarosa, Paul, Sanford Futterman and Mark Halswig
    1976 Observations of Alcoholics in the Peyote Ritual: A Pilot Study. Annals of the New
        York Academy of Sciences, Vol. 273: 518-524.
Pattison, E. Mansell, Mark Sobell, and Linda Sobell, Eds.
    1977 Emerging Concepts of Alcohol Dependence. NY: Springer Publishing Company.
Peele, Stanton
    1989 Diseasing of America: Addiction Treatment Out of Control. Boston: Houghton
        Mifflin Company.
    2007 Addiction as Disease: Policy, Epidemiology, and Treatment Consequences of a
        Bad Idea. In Addiction Treatment in the 21st Century: Science and Policy Issues. J.
        Henningfield, W. Bickel, and P. Santora, Eds. Baltimore: Johns Hopkins.
Peele, Stanton, Ed.
    1988 Visions of Addiction: Major Contemporary Perspectives on Addiction and
        Alcoholism. Lexington, MA.: Lexington Books.

Pelto, Gretel
    1973 On James's "Continuity and Emergence in Indian Poverty Culture." Current
        Anthropology 14 (1-2): 163-166.
Pelto, P. and G. Pelto
    1975 Intra-Cultural Diversity: Some Theoretical Issues. American Ethnologist 2: 1-18.
Pernanen, Kai
    1991 Alcohol in Human Violence. NY: Guilford Press.
    1993 Research Approaches in the Study of Alcohol-Related Violence. Alcohol Health
        and Research World 17: 101-107.
Pfister, Joel
    2009 The Yale Indian: The Education of Henry Roe Cloud. Durham: Duke U Press.
Phelan, J.
    1959 The Hispanization of the Philippines. Madison: U of Wisconsin Press.
Phillips, Kevin
    1990 The Politics of the Rich and Poor: Wealth and the American Electorate in the
        Reagan Aftermath. NY: Random House.
Phillips, P.
    1961 The Fur Trade. Volume 1. Norman: U of Oklahoma Press.
Pickering, Kathleen
    2000 Lakota Culture, World Economy. Lincoln: U of Nebraska Press.
Pike, Kenneth
    1990 On the Emics and Etics of Pike and Harris. In Emics and Etics: The
        Insider/Outsider Debate. T. Headland, K. Pike, and M. Harris, Eds. Newbury Park,
        CA: Sage Publications, Inc.
Plaut, T.
    1967 Alcohol Problems: A Report to the Nation by the Cooperative Commission on the
        Study of Alcoholism. NY: Oxford U Press.
Preedy, Victor and Ronald Watson, Eds.
    2005 Comprehensive Handbook of Alcohol Related Pathology, Vols. 1-3. New York:
        Academic Press.
Price, A.
    1950 White Settlers and Native Peoples. Westport: Greenwood Press.
Price, John
    1968 The Migration and Adaptation of American Indians to Los Angeles. Human
        Organization 27: 168-175.
Prince, Raymond, Ed.
    1982 Shamans and Endorphins. Special Issue of Ethos 10 (4): 299-423.
Prucha, Francis
    1984 The Great Father: The United States Government and the American Indians, 2
        Vols. Lincoln: U of Nebraska Press.
Quinn, Naomi
    2011 The History of the Cultural Models School Reconsidered: A Paradigm Shift in
        Cognitive Anthropology. In A Companion to Cognitive Anthropology. D.
        Kronenfeld, G. Bennardo, W. de Munch, and M. Fischer, Eds. NY: Wiley-Blackwell.
Quintero, Gilbert
    2000 "The Lizard in the Green Bottle": "Aging Out" of Problem Drinking Among
        Navajo Men. Social Science and Medicine 51: 1031-1945.

Radin, Paul
    1911 The Ritual and Significance of the Winnebago Medicine Dance. J of American
        Folklore 24: 148-208.
    1914 A Sketch of the Peyote Cult of the Winnebago: A Study in Borrowing. J of
        Religious Psychology 7: 1-22.
    1933 The Method and Theory of Ethnology. NY: Basic Books.
    1945 The Road of Life and Death: A Ritual Drama of the American Indians. NY:
        Panthean Books.
    1970 [1923] The Winnebago Tribe. Lincoln: U of Nebraska Press.
Radin, Paul, Ed.
    1963 [1920] The Autobiography of a Winnebago Indian. NY: Dover.
    1983 [1926] Crashing Thunder: The Autobiography of an American Indian. Lincoln: U
        of Nebraska Press.
Raghupathy, Shobana and April Lea Go Forth
    2002 The HAWK Program: A Computer-Based Drug Prevention Intervention for
        Native American Youth. American J of Drug and Alcohol Abuse 38 (5): 461-467.
Ramchandani, V., W. Bosron, T. K. Li
    2001 Research Advances in Ethanol Metabolism. Pathologie-biologie (Paris) 49 (9): 676-
        82.
Rattray, Richard
    n.d. Comprehensive Treatment Program for Indian Problem Drinkers. Des Moines:
        Office of the Governor, State of Iowa.
Ray, A.
    1974 Indians in the Fur Trade. Toronto: U of Toronto Press.
Ray, A. and D. Freedman
    1978 "Give Us Good Measure": An Economic Analysis of Relations Between the
        Indians and the Hudson's Bay Company Before 1763. Toronto: U of Toronto Press.
Ray, D.
    1975 The Eskimos of Bering Strait, 1650-1898. Seattle: U of Washington Press.
Redfield, R., R. Linton, M. Herskovits
    1936 Memorandum for the Study of Acculturation. American Anthropologist 38: 149-
        152.
Rehm, Jürgen
    2011 The Risks Associated with Alcohol Use and Alcoholism. Alcohol Research and
        Health 34 (2): 135-143.
Rehm, Jurgen, D. Bliunas, L. Guilherme, et al.
    2010 The Relation Between Different Dimensions of Alcohol Consumption and Burden
        of Disease: An Overview. Addiction 105: 817-843.
Relling, Mary and K. Giacomini
    2011 Pharmacogentics. In Goodman and Gilman's The Pharmacological Basis of
        Therapeutics, 12th Ed. L. Brunton, B. Chabner, and B. Knollman, Eds. NY: McGraw-
        Hill.
Rex, D., W. Bosron, J. Smialik, and T.-K. Li
    1985 Alcohol and Aldehyde Dehydrogenase Isoenzymes in North American Indians.
        Alcoholism: Clinical and Experimental Research 9 (2): 147-152.
Ricchiardi, Sherry
    1973 Alarming Dropout Rate of Indian Youths Prompts New Program. Des Moines
        Sunday Register, December 16: 5E.

Rieckmann, Traci, D. McCarty A. Kovas, et al.
  2012 American Indians with Substance Use Disorders: Treatment Needs and Comorbid Conditions. American J of Drug and Alcohol Abuse 38 (5): 498-504.
Robbins, Richard
  1973a Identity, Culture, and Behavior. *In* Handbook of Social and Cultural Anthropology. John Honigmann, Ed. Chicago: Rand McNally and Company.
  1973b Alcohol and the Identity Struggle: Some Effects of Economic Change on Interpersonal Relations. American Anthropologist 75: 99-122.
Robin, R., B. Chester, J. Rasmussen, et al.
  1997 Prevalence, Characteristics, and Impact of Childhood Sexual Abuse in a Southwestern American Indian tribe. Child Abuse and Neglect 21:760-787.
Robinson, Terry and Kent Berridge
  2003 Addiction. *In* Annual Review of Psychology 54: 25-53.
  2008 The Incentive Sensitization Theory of Addiction: Some Current Issues. Philosophical Transactions of the Royal Society 363: 3137-3146.
Rodin, Miriam
  1985 Getting on the Program: A Biocultural Analysis of Alcoholics Anonymous. *In* the American Experience with Alcohol: Contrasting Cultural Perspectives. Linda Bennett and Genieve Ames, Eds. NY: Plenum Press.
Romney, A. and R. D'Andrade
  1964 Cognitive Aspects of English Kin Terms. *In* Transcultural Studies in Cognition. A. Romney and R. D'Andrade, Eds. American Anthropologist 66, pt. 2: 146-170.
Ronda, J. and J. Axtell
  1978 Indian Missions: A Critical Bibliography. Bloomington: Indiana U Press.
Room, Robin
  1983 Sociological Aspects of the Disease Concept of Alcoholism. *In* Research Advances in Alcohol and Drug Problems, Vol. 7. Reginald Smart, et al., Eds. NY: Plenum Press.
  1984 Anthropology and Ethnography: A Case of Problem Deflation? Current Anthropology 25 (2): 169-178.
  2001 Intoxication and Bad Behavior: Understanding Cultural Differences in the Link. Social Science & Medicine 53: 189-198.
Room, Robin and Gary Collins, Eds.
  1983 Alcohol and Disinhibition: Nature and Meaning of the Link. NIAAA Research Monograph 12. Washington, DC: U.S. Government Printing Office.
Room, Robin and Wayne Hall
  2011 Population Approaches to Alcohol, Tobacco and Drugs: Effectiveness, Ethics and Interplay with Addiction Neuroscience. *In* Addiction Neuroethics: The Ethics of Addiction. Adrian Carter, W. Hall, and J. Illes, Eds. NY: Academic Press.
Rorabaugh, W. J.
  1979 The Alcoholic Republic: An American Tradition. NY: Oxford U Press.
Roseberry, William
  1988 Political Economy. Annual Review of Anthropology 17: 161-185.
Rosenberg, Morris
  1979 Conceiving the Self. NY: Basic Books, Inc.
Rosenzweig, S.
  1936 Some Implicit Common Factors in Diverse Methods of Psychotherapy. American J of Orthopsychistry 6: 412-415.

Roufs, Timothy
   1973 On James's "Continuity and Emergence in Indian Poverty Culture." Current Anthropology 14 (1-2): 162- 163.
   1974 Myth in Method: More on Ojibwa Culture. Current Anthropology 15 (3): 307-309.
Roy, Chunilal
   1973 Indian Peyotists and Alcohol. American J of Psychiatry 130 (3): 329-330.
Ruby, Robert and John Brown
   1996 John Slocum and the Indian Shaker Church. Norman: U of Oklahoma Press.
Rumpf, Hans-Jürger, G. Bischof, and U. John
   2007 Remission without Formal Help: New Directions in Studies Using Survey Data. In Promoting Self-Change from Addictive Behaviors: Practical Implications for Policy, Prevention, and Treatment. H. Klingemann and L. Sobell, Eds. NY: Springer.
Runyan, William
   1982 Life Histories and Psychobiography: Explorations in Theory and Method. NY: Oxford U Press.
Russo, Scott
   2012 GR-owing Up Stressed: Implications for Anxiety and Addiction. Biological Psychiatry 71: 182-183.
Sadler, Patricia
   1977 The "Crisis Cult" as a Voluntary Association: An Interactional Approach to Alcoholics Anonymous. Human Organization 36: 207-210.
Sahlins, Marshall
   1981 Historical Metaphors and Mythical Realities: Structure in the Early History of the Sandwich Islands Kingdom. Ann Arbor: U of Michigan Press.
   1985 Islands of History. Chicago: U of Chicago Press.
   2005 Preface. Ethnohistory 52 (1): 3-6.
Saitz, R.
   1998 Introduction to Alcohol Withdrawal. Alcohol Health and Research World 22: 5-12.
Santisteban, I., S. Povey, L. West, et al.
   1985 Chromosome Assignment, Biochemical and Immunological Studies on a Human Aldehyde Dehydrogenase, ALDH3. Annals of Human Genetics 49: 87-100.
Sapir, Edward
   1917 Do We Need a "Superorganic"? American Anthropologist 19: 441-447.
Sarkar, Dipak
   2012 Circadian Genes, the Stress Axis, and Alcoholism. Alcohol Research: Current Reviews 34 (3): 362-366.
Saum, L.
   1965 The Fur Trader and the Indian. Seattle: U of Washington Press.
Schaefer, J.
   1981 Firewater Myths Revisited. In Cultural Factors in Alcohol Research and Treatment of Drinking Problems. D. Heath, J. Waddell, and M. Topper, Eds. J of Studies on Alcohol, Suppl. 9: 99-117.
Scheff, Thomas
   1977 The Distancing of Emotion in Ritual. Current Anthropology 8: 483-505.
   1979 Catharsis in Healing, Ritual and Drama. Berkeley: U CA Press.
Schell, J.
   n.d. [1904] Testimony at Winnebago. FA.

Schlenker, Barry, Ed.

1985 The Self and Social Life. NY: McGraw-Hill.

Schlesier, K.

1979 Of Indians and Anthropologists. American Anthropologist 81: 325-330.

1980 Reply to Deloria, DeMallie, Hill, and Washburn. American Anthropologist 82 (3): 561-563.

Schmidt, L., T. Greenfield, and N. Mulia

2006 Unequal Treatment: Racial and Ethnic Disparities in Alcoholism Treatment Services. Alcohol Research and Health 29 (1): 49-54.

Schneider, David

1976 Notes Toward a Theory of Culture. In Meaning in Anthropology. K. Basso and H. Selby, Eds. Albuquerque: U of New Mexico Press.

Schuckit, Marc

2009 An Overview of Genetic Influences in Alcoholism. J of Substance Abuse Treatment 36 (Suppl 1): S1-S14.

2011 Ethanol and Methanol. In Goodman and Gilman's The Pharmacological Basis of Therapeutics, 12th Ed. L. Brunton, B. Chabner, and B. Knollman, Eds. NY: McGraw-Hill.

Schwappach, M., K. Spuhler, and R. Deitrich

1986 Aldehyde Dehydrogenase Polymorphism in American Indians (abstract). Clinical Research 34: 18a.

Schwartz, Theodore

1978 Where Is the Culture? Personality as the Distributive Locus of Culture. In The Making of Psychological Anthropology. George Spindler, Ed. Berkeley: U of CA Press.

Schwartz, Theodore, Geoffrey White, and Catherine Lutz, Eds.

1992 New Directions in Psychological Anthropology. NY: Cambridge U Press.

Schwerin, K.

1976 The Future of Ethnohistory. Ethnohistory 23: 323-341.

Scott, Marvin and Stanford Lyman

1968 Accounts. Sociological Review 22: 46-52.

Seeman, Teresa, E. Epel, T. Gruenewald, et al.

2010 Socio-economic Differentials in Peripheral Biology: Cumulative Allostatic Load. Annals of the New York Academy of Sciences 1186: 223-239.

Seitz, H and F. Strickel

2007 Molecular Mechanisms of Alcohol Mediated Carcinogenesis. National Review of Cancer 7: 599-612.

Seitz, H. and S. Mueller

2012 Metabolism of Alcohol and its Consequences. In Metabolism of Drugs and Other Xenobiotics. P. Anzenbacher and U. Zanger, Eds. Weinheim, Germany: Wiley-VCH.

Sellers, J., Ed.

1946 Diary of Dr. Joseph A. Paxson, Physician to the Winnebago Indians, 1869-1870. (Part 1). Nebraska History 27 (3): 143-204.

Sessa, Ben

2005 Can Psychedelics Have a Role in Psychiatry Once Again? British J of Psychiatry 186 (6): 457-458.

Shea, S., T.Wall, L. Carr, T-K. Li

2001 ADH2 and Alcohol-Related Phenotypes in Ashkenazic Jewish American College Students. Behavioral Genetics 31: 231-239.

Sheehan, B.
1973 Seeds of Extinction: Jeffersonian Philanthropy and the American Indian. Chapel Hill: U of North Carolina Press.

Sherman, Jack, Douglas Jorenby, and Timothy Baker
1988 Classical Conditioning with Alcohol: Acquired Preferences and Aversions, Tolerance, and Urges/Craving. In Theories on Alcoholism. C. Chaudron and D. Wilkinson, Eds. Toronto: Alcoholism and Drug Addiction Research Foundation.

Sherva, Richard, J. Rice, R. Neuman, et al.
2009 Associations and Interactions Between SNPs in the Alcohol Metabolizing Genes and Alcoholism Phenotypes in European Americans. Alcoholism: Clinical and Experimental Research 33 (5): 848-857.

Shkilnyk, Anastasia
1985 A Poison Stronger Than Love: The Destruction of an Ojibwa Community. New Haven: Yale U Press.

Shoemaker, Nancy, Ed.
2002 Clearing a Path: Theorizing the Past in Native American Studies. NY: Routledge.

Shore, Bradd
1996 Culture in Mind: Cognition, Culture, and the Problem of Meaning. NY: Oxford U Press.

Shweder, Richard
1991 Thinking Through Culture: Expeditions in Cultural Psychology. Cambridge: Harvard U Press.

Siegel, Larry and Joseph Senna
1988 Juvenile Delinquency Theory, Practice, and Law, 3rd Ed. NY: West Publishing Co.

Siegel, S.
1983 Classical Conditioning, Drug Tolerance, and Drug Dependence. In Research Advances in Alcohol and Drug Problems. Volume 7. R. Smart et al., Eds. NY: Plenum Press.

Simmel, Georg
1950 The Sociology of Georg Simmel. Kurt Wolff, Trans. and Ed. Glencoe, Ill: The Free Press.

Singer, Merrill
1982 Christian Science Healing and Alcoholism: An Anthropological Perspective. J of Operational Psychiatry 13: 2-12.
1986 Toward a Political-Economy of Alcoholism: The Missing Link in the Anthropology of Drinking. Social Science and Medicine 23 (2): 113-130.

Singer, Merrill and Maria Borrero
1984 Indigenous Treatment for Alcoholism: The Case of Puerto Rican Spiritism. Medical Anthropology 8: 246-273.

Sinha, Rajita
2011 New Findings on Biological Factors Predicting Addiction Relapse Vulnerability. Current Psychiatry Reports 13: 398-405.

Sinha, R. and C. S. Li
2007 Imaging Stress- and Cue-Induced Drug and Alcohol Craving: Association with Relapse and Clinical Implications. Drug and Alcohol Review 26: 25-31.

Sioux City Community Schools District
2010 Sioux City Community Schools. 2009-2010 Annual Progress Report. Sioux City, IA.

Sioux City Journal
  1973 Anderson Denies 100% Indian Drop Out Rate. June 22.
Siskin, Edgar
  1983 Washo Shamans and Peyotists: Religious Conflict in an American Indian Tribe.
    Salt Lake City: U of Utah Press.
Siverts, Henning, Ed.
  1973 Drinking Patterns in Highland Chiapas: A Teamwork Approach to the Study of
    Semantics through Ethnography. Bergen: Universitetsforlaget.
Slagle, A. Logan and Joan Weibel-Orlando
  1986 The Indian Shaker Church and Alcoholics Anonymous: Revitalistic Curing Cults.
    Human Organization 45 (4): 310-319.
Slotkin, James
  1953 Social Psychiatry of a Menomini Community. J of Abnormal Social Psychology 48:
    10-16.
  1956 The Peyote Religion: A Study in Indian-White Relations. NY: Octagon Books.
Smart, Reginald
  2007 Natural Recovery or Recovery without Treatment from Alcohol and Drug
    Problems as Seen from Survey Data. In Promoting Self-Change from Addictive
    Behaviors: Practical Implications for Policy, Prevention, and Treatment. Harald
    Klingemann and Linda Sobell, Eds. NY: Springer.
Smart, Reginald, T. Strom, E. Baker, and L. Solursh
  1967 Lysergic Acid Diethylamide (LSD) in the Treatment of Alcoholism. Toronto: U
    Toronto Press.
Smith, Alice
  1973 The History of Wisconsin. Volume 1: From Exploration to Statehood. Madison:
    State Historical Society of Wisconsin.
Smith, Huston and Reuben Snake, Eds.
  1996 One Nation Under God: The Triumph of the Native American Church. Santa Fe:
    Clear Lights Publishers.
Snyder, Peter
  1968 The Social Assimilation and Adjustment of Navaho Indian Migrants to Denver.
    Unpublished Ph.D. Dissertation. U of Colorado.
  1971 The Social Environment of the Urban Indian. In The American Indian in Urban
    Society. J. Waddell and O. M. Watson, Eds. Boston: Little, Brown and Company.
Sobell, Linda
  2007 The Phenomenon of Self-Change: Overview and Key Issues. In Promoting Self-
    Change from Addictive Behaviors: Practical Implications for Policy, Prevention, and
    Treatment. Harald Klingemann and Linda Sobell, Eds. NY: Springer.
Sobell, L., H. Klingemann, T. Toneatto, M. Sobell, et al.
  2001 Alcohol and Drug Abusers' Perceived Reasons for Self-Change in Canada and
    Switzerland: Computer-Assisted Content Analysis. Substance Use and Misuse 36:
    1467-1500.
Sobell, L., J. Cunningham, and M. Sobell
  1996 Recovery from Alcohol Problems with and without Treatment: Prevalence in Two
    Population Surveys. American J of Public Health 86: 966-972.
Sobell, L., T. Ellingstad, and M. Sobell
  2000 Natural Recovery from Alcohol and Drug Problems: Methodological Review of
    the Research with Suggestions for Future Directions. Addiction 95: 749-764.

Sobell, M. and L. Sobell
    1995 Controlled Drinking after 25 Years: How Important Was the Great Debate?
        Addiction 90: 1149-1153.
Sökefeld, Martin
    1999 Debating Self, Identity, and Culture in Anthropology. Current Anthropology 40
        (4): 417-447.
Spanagel, Rainer
    2009 Alcoholism: A Systems Approach From Molecular Physiology to Addictive
        Behavior. Physiological Review 89: 649-705.
Speck, Frank
    1933 Ethical Attributes of the Labrador Indians. American Anthropologist 35: 559-94.
Spector, Janet
    1974 Winnebago Indians, 1634-1829: An Archeological and Ethno-Historic
        Investigation. Unpublished Ph.D. Dissertation. U of Wisconsin—Madison.
Spicer, E.
    1961 Types of Contact and Processes of Change. In Perspectives in American Indian
        Culture Change. E. Spicer, Ed. Chicago: U of Chicago Press.
Spicer, P., J. Beals, C. Mitchell, et al.
    2003 American Indian Service Utilization, Psychiatric Epidemiology, Risk, and
        Protective Factors Project Team. The Prevalence of DSM-III-R Alcohol Dependence
        in Two American Indian Populations. Alcoholism: Clinical and Experimental
        Research 27 (11): 1785-1797.
Spindler, George, Ed.
    1978 The Making of Psychological Anthropology. Berkeley: U of CA Press.
Spindler, George and Louise Spindler
    1990 The American Cultural Dialogue and its Transmission. NY: Falmer Press.
Spores, R.
    1978 Ethnohistory in Middle Age: An Assessment and a Call for Action. Ethnohistory
        25: 199-205.
    1980 New World Ethnohistory and Archaeology, 1970-1980. Annual Review of
        Anthropology 9: 575-603.
Spradley, James
    1970 You Owe Yourself a Drunk: An Ethnography of Urban Nomads. Boston: Little,
        Brown and Company.
    1972a Adaptive Strategies of Urban Nomads. In The Anthropology of Urban
        Environments. T. Weaver and D. White, Eds. Society for Applied Anthropology,
        Monograph 11.
    1979 The Ethnographic Interview. NY: Holt, Rinehart and Winston.
Spradley, James, Ed.
    1972b Culture and Cognition: Rules, Maps, and Plans. San Francisco: Chandler.
Spradley, J. and D. McCurdy
    1975 Anthropology: The Cultural Perspective. NY: Wiley and Sons, Inc.
Starkman, Bela, A. Sakharkar, and S. Pandey
    2012 Epigenetics—Beyond the Genome in Alcoholism. Alcohol Research: Current
        Reviews 34 (3): 293-305.
Stein, G.
    1974 A Fearful Drunkenness: The Liquor Trade to the Western Indians as Seen by
        European Travelers in America, 1800-1860. Red River Valley Historical Review 1:
        109-121.

Steinmetz, Paul
    1990 Pipe, Bible, and Peyote Among the Oglala Lakota: A Study in Religious Identity. Knoxville: U Tennessee Press.
Stewart, Omer
    1948 Ute Peyotism: A Study of a Cultural Complex. Boulder: U of Colorado Press.
    1974 Origin of the Peyote Religion in the United States. Plains Anthropologist 19: 211-223.
    1980a The Native American Church. In Anthropology on the Great Plains. W. Woo and M. Liberty, Eds. Lincoln: U Nebraska Press.
    1980b Peyotism and Mescalism. Plains Anthropologist 25: 297-309.
    1987 Peyote Religion: A History. Norman: U of Oklahoma Press.
Stigler, James, R. Shweder, and G. Herdt, Eds.
    1990 Cultural Psychology: Essays on Comparative Human Development. Cambridge: Cambridge U Press.
Stigler, Melissa, E. Neusel, and C. Perry
    2011 School-Based Programs to Prevent and Reduce Alcohol Use Among Youth. Alcohol Research and Health 34 (2): 157-162.
Stiglitz, Joseph
    2012 The Price of Inequality: How Today's Divided Society Endangers Our Future. NY: W. W. Norton.
Stocking, George, Jr.
    1965 On the Limits of "Presentism" and "Historicism" in the Historiography of the Behavior Sciences. J of the History of Behavioral Science 1: 211-218.
Strong, Pauline
    2005 Recent Ethnographic Research on North American Indigenous Peoples. Annual Review of Anthropology 34: 253-268.
Sturtevant, W.
    1966 Anthropology, History, and Ethnohistory. Ethnohistory 13: 1-51.
Sutro, Livingston
    1989 Alcoholics Anonymous in a Mexican Peasant-Indian Village. Human Organization 48: 180- 186.
Tabakoff, Boris and Jeffrey Rothstein
    1983 The Biology of Tolerance and Dependence. In Medical and Social Aspects of Alcohol Abuse. B. Tabakoff, P. Sutker, and C. Randall, Eds. NY: Plenum Press.
Takeshita, Tatsuya and K. Morimoto
    1999 Self-Reported Alcohol-Associated Symptoms and Drinking Behavior in Three ALDH2 Genotypes Among Japanese University Students. Alcoholism: Clinical and Experimental Research 23 (6): 1065-1069.
Takeshita, Tatsuya, K. Mao, and K. Morimoto
    1996 The Contribution of Polymorphism in the Alcohol Dehydrogenase Beta Subunit to Alcohol Sensitivity in a Japanese Population. Human Genetics 97 (4): 409-413.
Takeshita, Tatsuya, X. Yang, and K. Morimoto
    2001 Association of the ADH2 Genotypes with Skin Responses after Ethanol Exposure in Japanese Male University Students. Alcoholism: Clinical and Experimental Research 25 (9): 1264-1269.
Taylor, W.
    1979 Drinking, Homicide, and Rebellion in Colonial Mexican Villages. Stanford: Stanford U Press.

Thompson, E. P.
> 1964 The Making of the English Working Class. NY: Pantheon.

Thompson, V. and R. Adloff
> 1971 The French Pacific Islands. Berkeley: U of CA Press.

Topper, M.
>> 1974 Drinking Patterns, Culture Change, Sociability and Navajo "Adolescents." Addictive Diseases 1: 98-116.
>> 1976 The Cultural Approach, Verbal Plans, and Alcohol Research. *In* Cross-Cultural Approaches to the Study of Alcohol. M. Everett, J. Waddell, and D. Heath, Eds. The Hague: Mouton.
>> 1980 Drinking as an Expression of Status: Navajo Male Adolescents. *In* Drinking Behavior Among Southwestern Indians. J. Waddell and M. Everett, Eds. Tucson: U of Arizona Press.
>> 1981 The Drinker's Story: An Important But Often Forgotten Source of Data. *In* Cultural Factors in Alcohol Research and Treatment of Drinking Problems. J of Studies on Alcohol, Suppl 9: 73-86.

Torrey, E. Fuller
>> 1986 Witchdoctors and Psychiatrists: The Common Roots of Psychotherapy and Its Future. NY: Harper and Row, Publishers, Inc.

Trelease, A.
>> 1960 Indian Affairs in Colonial New York: The Seventeenth Century. Ithaca, NY: Cornell U Press.

Trigger, Bruce
>> 1976 The Children of Aataentsic: A History of the Huron People to 1660, 2 Vols. Montreal: McGill-Queen's U Press.
>> 1982 Ethnohistory: Problems and Prospects. Ethnohistory 29 (1): 1-19.
>> 1985 Natives and Newcomers: Canada's "Heroic Age" Reconsidered. Kingston: McGill-Queen's U Press.

Trigger, Bruce, Ed.
>> 1978 Handbook of North American Indians, Vol. 15. Washington, DC: Smithsonian Institution.

Trueba, Henry
>> 1988 Culturally Based Explanations of Minority Students' Academic Achievement. Anthropology and Education Quarterly 19 (3): 270-287.

Trueba, Henry, George Spindler, and Louise Spindler, Eds.
>> 1989 What Do Anthropologists Have to Say About Dropouts? NY: Falmer Press.

Tucker, Jalie and C. Simpson
>> 2011 The Recovery Spectrum: From Self-Change to Seeking Treatment. Alcohol Research and Health 33 (4): 371-379.

Tyler, S., Ed.
>> 1969 Cognitive Anthropology. NY: Holt, Rinehart and Winston.

Unrau, William
>> 1996 White Man's Wicked Water: The Alcohol Trade and Prohibition in Indian Country, 1802-1892. Lawrence: U Press of Kansas.

U. S. Bureau of the Census
>> 1902 12th Census of the U.S. Taken in the Year 1900: Population, Part 1. Washington DC: Government Printing Office.
>> 1972 Census of Population: 1970. General Social and Economic Characteristics. Final Report PC (1)-C17 Iowa. Washington DC: Government Printing Office.

1973 Census of Population 1970. Volume 1: Characteristics of the Population, Part 17, Iowa. Washington DC: Government Printing Office.

1983a Census of Population 1980. Volume 1: Characteristics of the Population. Chapter C: General Social and Economic Characteristics. Part 29, Nebraska, PC80-1-C29. Washington, DC: Government Printing Office.

1983b Census of Population 1980. Volume 1: Characteristics of the Population. Chapter C: General Social and Economic Characteristics. Part 17, Iowa, PC80-1-C17. Washington DC: Government Printing Office.

1989 1980 Census of the Population. Volume 2: Subject Reports. Characteristics of American Indians by Tribes and Areas: 1980, PC80-2-1C. Washington, DC: Government Printing Office.

1992 1990 Census of the Population. General PopulationCharactertics. American Indian and Alaska Native Areas. 1990, CP-1-1A. Washington, DC: Government Printing Office.

n.d. Sioux City, Iowa: Statistical Profile. Computer Generated Profile Based on 1970 Census of Population and Housing. U. S. Department of Commerce.

U.S. Department of Commerce
1971 Federal and State Indian Reservations, An EDA Handbook. Washington, DC: Government Printing Office.

U.S. Department of Health and Human Services
2007 Substance Use and Substance Use Disorders Among American Indians and Alaskan Natives. The NSDUH Report, January 19, 2007.

U. S. Indian Health Service
1990 Regional Differences in Indian Health 1990. Washington, DC: Government Printing Office.

Valentine, Charles
1961 Symposium on the Concept of Ethnohistory — Comment. Ethnohistory 8: 271-280.
1968 Culture and Poverty: Critique and Counter-Proposals. Chicago: U Chicago Press.

Valentine, R.
1909a Letter to Albert Kneale, January. NA, Central Classified Files, Liquor Traffic.
1909b Letter to Secretary of the Interior, May 8. NA, Central Classified Files, Liquor Traffic.

Van Maanen, John
1988 Tales of the Field: On Writing Ethnography. Chicago: U of Chicago Press.

Vasiliou, V. and D. Petersen
2010 Aldehyde Dehyrogenases. In Comprehensive Toxicology, Volume 4, Biotransformation. Charlene McQueen, Ed. Boston: Elsevier.

Verhey, Jeffrey
1991 Sources for the Social History of Alcohol. In Drinking: Behavior and Belief in Modern History. S. Barrows and R. Room, Eds. Berkeley: U of CA Press.

Veysey, Lawrence
1979 Intellectual History and the New Social History. In New Directions in American Intellectual History. J. Higham and P. Conkin, Eds. Baltimore: Johns Hopkins U Press.

Vogt, Evon
1951 Navaho Veterans: A Study of Changing Values. Peabody Museum of American Archaeology and Ethnology Papers 41 (1).

Volkow, Nora, Gene-Jack Wang, Joanna Fowler, and Dardo Tomsi
    2012 Addiction Circuitry in the Human Brain. Annual Review of Pharmacology and
        Toxicology 52: 321-336.

Vollenweider, Franz and M. Kometer
    2010 The Neurobiology of Psychedelic Drugs: Implications for the Treatment of Mood
        Disorders. Nature Reviews Neuroscience 11: 642-651.

Waddell, Jack
    1975 For Individual Power and Social Credit: The Use of Alcohol Among Tucson
        Papagos. Human Organization 34: 9-15.
    1980a Drinking as a Means of Articulating Social and Cultural Values: Papagos in an
        Urban Setting. In Drinking Behavior Among Southwestern Indians. J. Waddell and
        M. Everett, Eds. Tucson: U of Arizona Press.
    1980b The Use of Intoxicating Beverages Among Native Peoples of the Aboriginal
        Greater Southwest. In Drinking Behavior Among Southwestern Indians. J. Waddell
        and M. Everett, Eds. Tucson: U of Arizona Press.
    1980c Similarities and Variations in Alcohol Use in Four Native American Societies in
        the Southwest. In Drinking Behavior Among Southwestern Indians. J. Waddell and
        M. Everett, Eds. Tucson: U of Arizona Press.
    1981 Cultural Relativity and Alcohol Use: Implications for Research and Treatment. In
        Cultural Factors in Alcohol Research and Treatment of Drinking Problems. D.
        Heath, J. Waddell, and M. Topper, Eds. J of Studies of Alcohol, Suppl. 9: 18-28.
    1985 Malhiot's Journal: An Ethnohistoric Assessment of Chippewa Alcohol Behavior in
        the Early Nineteenth Century. Ethnohistory 32 (3): 246-268.

Waldram, James
    1997 The Way of the Pipe: Aboriginal Spirituality and Symbolic Healing in Canadian
        Prisons. Peterborough: Broadview Press.
    2000 The Efficacy of Traditional Medicine: Current Theoretical and Methodological
        Issues. Medical Anthropology Quarterly 14 (4): 603-625.

Walker, D.
    1970 Ethnology and History. Idaho Yesterdays 14: 24-29.

Walker, R. Dale, G. Andrew Benjamin, D. Kivlahan, and P. Walker
    1989 American Indian Alcohol Misuse and Treatment Outcome. In Alcohol Use Among
        U.S. Ethnic Minorities. NIAAA Research Monograph 18. Washington, D.C.:
        Government Printing Office.

Wall, T., L. Carr, and C. Ehlers
    2003 Protective Association of Genetic Variation in Alcohol Dehydrogenase with
        Alcohol Dependence in Native American Mission Indians. American J of Psychiatry
        160 (1): 41-46.

Wallace, Anthony
    1951 Some Psychological Determinants of Culture Change in an Iroquoian Community.
        In Symposium of Local Diversity in Iroquois Culture. W. Fenton, Ed. Bureau of
        American Ethnology Bulletin 149.
    1956 Revitalization Movements: Some Theoretical Considerations for their
        Comparative Study. American Anthropologist 58: 264-81.
    1959 The Institutionalization of Cathartic and Control Strategies in Iroquois Religious
        Psychotherapy. In Culture and Mental Health: Cross-Cultural Studies. Marvin
        Opler, Ed. NY: Macmillian.
    1961 Culture and Personality, 1st Ed. NY: Random House.

1962 The New Culture-and-Personaltiy. *In* Anthropology and Human Behavior. T. Gladwin and W. Sturtevant, Eds. Washington, DC: Anthropological Society of Washington.

1967 Identity Processes in Personality and in Culture. *In* Cognition, Personality, and Clinical Psychology. R. Jessor and S. Feshbach, Eds. San Francisco: Jossey-Bass Inc., Publishers.

1970a The Death and Rebirth of the Seneca. NY: Alfred Knopf.

1970b Culture and Personality, 2nd Ed. NY: Random House.

1978 Origins of the Longhouse Religion. *In* Handbook of North American Indians, Vol. 15. B. Trigger, Ed. Washington, DC: Smithsonian Institution.

Wallace, Anthony and Raymond Fogelson

1965 The Identity Struggle. *In* Intensive Family Therapy: Theoretical and Practical Aspects. I. Boszormenyi-Nagy and J. Framo, Eds. NY: Harper and Row Publishers.

Walls, Melissa and L. Whitbeck

2012 Advantages of Stress Process Approaches for Measuring Historical Trauma. American J of Drug and Alcohol Abuse 38 (5): 416-420.

Wampold, B.

1997 Methodological Problems in Identifying Efficacious Psychotherapies. Psychotherapy Research 7: 21-43.

Wampold, B., G. Mondin, M. Moody, F. Stich, K. Benson, and H. Ahn

1997 A Meta-Analysis of Outcome Studies Comparing Bona Fide Psychotherapies: Empirically, "All Must Have Prizes." Psychological Bulletin 122 (3): 203-215.

Ward, J.

1978 Aborigines and Alcohol. *In* Alcohol in Australia: Problems and Programmes. A. Diehm, R. Seaborn, and G. Wilson, Eds. Sydney: McGraw-Hill.

Washburn, Wilcomb

1961 Ethnohistory: History "In the Round." Ethnohistory 8: 31-48.

1975 The Indian in America. NY: Harper and Row.

1980 "Of Indians and Anthropologists": A Response to Karl Schlesier. American Anthropologist 82 (3): 558-559.

Washburn, Wilcomb, Ed.

1988 Handbook of North American Indians, Vol. 4, History of Indian-White Relations. Washington, DC: Smithsonian Institution.

Washburn, Wilcomb and Bruce Trigger

1996 Native Peoples in Euro-American Historiography. *In* The Cambridge History of the Native Peoples of the Americas, Volume 1: North America. B. Trigger and W. Washburn, Eds. NY: Cambridge U Press.

Watermulder, G.

1910 Winnebago Mission. *In* 27th Annual Report. Women's Board of Domestic Missions of the Reformed Church in American. NY: Woman's Board of Home Missions of the Presbyterian Church in the U.S.A.

1912 The Past and Present of the Winnebagoes. Southern Workman 41: 270-81.

Wax, Rosalie

1967 The Warrior Dropouts. Trans-action, May: 40-46.

1971 Doing Fieldwork: Warnings and Advice. Chicago: U of Chicago Press.

Weibel-Orlando, Joan

1984 Indian Alcoholism Treatment Programs as Flawed Rites of Passage. Medical Anthropology Quarterly 15 (4): 62-67.

1987 Culture-Specific Treatment Modalities: Assessing Client-to-Treatment Fit in Indian Alcoholism Programs. *In* Treatment and Prevention of Alcohol Problems: Resource Manual. W. Cox, Ed. NY: Academic Press, Inc.

1989a Pass the Bottle, Bro!: A Comparison of Urban and Rural Indian Drinking Patterns. *In* Alcohol Use Among U.S. Ethnic Minorities. NIAAA Research Monograph 18. Washington, DC: U.S. Government Printing Office.

1989b Hooked on Healing: Anthropologists, Alcohol, and Intervention. Human Organization 48:148-155.

Weisner, C., H. Matzger, and L. Kaskutas

2003 How Important is Treatment? One-Year Outcomes of Treated and Untreated Alcohol-Dependent Individuals. Addiction 98: 901-911.

Welty, Thomas

2002 The Epidemiology of Alcohol Use and Alcohol-Related Health Problems Among American Indians. *In* Alcohol Use Among American Indians and Alaska Natives: Multiple Perspectives on a Complex Problem. P. Mail et al., Eds. NIAAA Research Monograph 37.

Weppner, Robert

1968 The Economic Absorption of Navajo Indian Migrants to Denver, Colorado. Unpublished Ph.D. Dissertation. U of Colorado.

1971 Urban Economic Opportunities: The Example of Denver. *In* The American Indian in Urban Society. J. Waddell and O.M. Watson, Eds. Boston: Little, Brown and Company.

Werner, O.

1972 Ethnoscience 1972. Annual Review of Anthropology 1: 271-308.

Werner, O. and J. Fenton

1970 Method and Theory in Ethnoscience or Ethnoepistemology. *In* A Handbook of Method in Cultural Anthropology. R. Naroll and R. Cohn, Eds. Garden City, NY: Natural History Press.

Westermeyer, Joseph

1981 Research on Treatment of Drinking Problems: Importance of Cultural Factors. J of Studies on Alcohol, Suppl. 9: 44-51.

Westmoreland, Timothy and K. Watson

2006 Redeeming Hollow Promises: The Case for Mandatory Spending on Health Care for American Indians and Alaska Natives. American J of Public Health 96 (4): 600-604.

Whitbeck, Les, M. Walls, and M. Welch

2012 Substance Abuse Prevention in American Indian and Alaska Native Communities. American J of Drug and Alcohol Abuse 38 (5): 428-435.

White, Barclay

n.d. Journal of Barclay White. Friends Historical Library, Swarthmore College.

White Bison, Inc.

2002 The Red Road to Wellbriety: In the Native American Way. Colorado Springs: White Bison, Inc.

White, Howard

1872 Letter to Barclay White, June 18. NA, Letters Received, Winnebago Agency.

White, Robert

1970 The Lower-Class "Culture of Excitement" Among the Contemporary Sioux. *In* The Modern Sioux: Social Systems and Reservation Culture. E. Nurge, Ed. Lincoln: U of Nebraska Press.

Whitesell, Nancy, C. Kasufman, E. Keane, et al.
    2012b Patterns of Substance Use Initiation Among Young Adolescents in a Northern
        Plains American Indian Tribe. J of Drug and Alcohol Abuse 38 (5): 383-388.
Whitesell, Nancy, J. Beals, C. Big Crow, et al.
    2012a Epidemiology and Etiology of Substance Use Among American Indians and
        Alaskan Natives: Risk, Protection, and Implications for Prevention. American J of
        Drug and Alcohol Abuse 38 (5): 376-382.
Whitesell, Nancy, J. Beals, C. Mitchell, et al.
    2007 Disparities in Drug Use and Disorder: Comparison of Two American Indian
        Reservation Communities and a National Sample. American J of Orthopsychiatry
        77 (1): 131-141.
Whitesell, Nancy, J. Beals, C. Mitchell, et al.
    2009 Childhood Exposure to Adversity and Risk of Substance-use Disorder in Two
        American Indian Populations: The Meditational Role of Early Substance-use
        Initiation. J of Studies on Alcohol and Drugs 70 (6): 971-981.
Whittaker, James
    1963 Alcohol and the Standing Rock Sioux Tribe. II. Psychodynamic and Cultural
        Factors in Drinking. Quarterly J of Studies on Alcohol 24: 80-90.
Wikler, Abraham
    1977 The Search for the Psyche in Drug Dependence. J of Nervous and Mental
        Disease 165 (1): 29-40.
Wilkins, Jon
    2008 Epigenetic Variation in Humans. In Handbook of Human Molecular Evolution,
        Volume 1. David Cooper and H. Kehrer-Sawatzki, Eds. Chichester: Wiley.
Wilkinson, Richard and Kate Pickett
    2009 The Spirit Level: Why Greater Equality Makes Societies Stronger. NY: Bloomsbury
        Press.
Williams, R.
    1956 Biochemical Individuality. NY: John Wiley.
    1974 Biology of Human Variation: Human Individuality. In Human Ecology. F.
        Sargent, Ed. NY: American Elsevier.
Willis, Paul
    1977 Learning to Labor: How Working Class Kids Get Working Class Jobs. NY:
        Columbia U Press.
Wilson, G. Terence
    1988 Alcohol Use and Abuse: A Social Learning Analysis. In Theories on Alcoholism.
        C. Chaudron and D. Wilkinson, Eds. Toronto: Alcoholism and Drug Addiction
        Research Foundation.
Winkelman, Michael
    2004 Spirituality and the Healing of Addictions: A Shamanic Drumming Approach. In
        Religion and Healing in America. Linda Barnes, Ed. NY: Oxford U Press.
Winnebago Tribal Council
    1909 Letter to Albert Kneale, April 21. NA, Central Classified Files, Liquor Traffic.
Winnebago Tribal Petitions
    1868a Petition to N. G. Taylor, August 7. NA, Letters Received, Winnebago Agency.
    1868b Petition to N. G. Taylor, October 31. NA, Letters Received, Winnebago Agency.
Winston, Ellen
    1934 The Alleged Lack of Mental Disease Among Primitive Groups. American
        Anthropologist 36: 234-238.

Wiseman, Jacqueline
    1970 Stations of the Lost: The Treatment of Skid Row Alcoholics. Chicago: U of Chicago
        Press.
Withiewitz, Katie and G. Marlatt
    2011 Behavioral Therapy Across the Spectrum. Alcohol Research and Health 33 (4):
        313-319.
Wolen, Aaron and M. Miles
    2012 Identifying Gene Networks Underlying the Neurobiology of Ethanol and
        Alcoholism. Alcohol Research: Current Reviews 34 (3): 306-317.
Wolf, Eric
    1982 Europe and the People Without History. Berkeley: U of CA Press.
Wolff, Peter
    1972 Ethnic Differences in Alcohol Sensitivity. Science 175: 449-450.
    1973 Vasomotor Sensitivity to Alcohol in Diverse Mongoloid Populations. American
        J of Human Genetics 25: 193-199.
Wong, A., II Gottesman, and A. Petronis
    2005 Phenotypic Differences in Genetically Identical Organisms: The Epigenetic
        Perspective. Human Molecular Genetics 14: R11-R18.
Woods, Stephen and James Mansfield
    1983 Ethanol and Disinhibition: Physiological and Behavioral Links. In Alcohol and
        Disinhibition: Nature and Meaning of the Link. R. Room and G. Collins, Eds.
        NIAAA Research Monograph No. 12. Washington, DC: Government Printing
        Office.
Wortham, S.
    2006 Learning Identity: The Mediation of Social Identity through Academic Learning.
        NY: Teachers College Press.
    2008 Linguistic Anthropology of Education. Annual Review of Anthropology 37: 37-51.
Wright, A.
    1904 Testimony at Winnebago. FA.
Wright, Alan
    2008 Genetic Variation: Polymorphism and Mutations. In Handbook of Human
        Molecular Evolution, Volume 1. D. Cooper and H. Kehrer-Sawatzki, Eds.
        Chichester: Wiley.
Wu, Li-Tzy, G. Woody, C. Yang, J-J Pan, D. Blazer
    2011 Racial/Ethnic Variations in Substance-Related Disorders Among Adolescents in
        the United States. Archives of General Psychiatry 68 (11): 1176-1185.
Wunder, John
    2007 Native American History, Ethnohistory, and Context. Ethnohistory 54 (4): 591-604.
Ying, S. J. and G. S. Peng
    2005 Overview of ALDH Polymorphism: Relation to Cardiovascular Effects of Alcohol.
        In Comprehensive Handbook of Alcohol Related Pathology, Volume 1. Victor
        Preedy and R. Watson, Eds. NY: Elsevier Academic.
Yin, S.-J., T.-C. Cheng, C.-P. Chang, et al.
    1988 Human Stomach Alcohol and Aldehyde Dehydrogenases (ALDH): A Genetic
        Model Proposed for ALDH III Isozymes. Biochemical Genetics 26 (5/6): 343-360.
Yosida, Akira
    1984 Determination of Aldehyde Dehydrogenase Phenotypes Using Hair Roots:
        Re-examination. Human Genetics 66: 296-299.

1991 Molecular Genetics of Alcohol-Metabolizing Enzymes. *In* The Molecular Pathology of Alcoholism. T. Palmer, Ed. NY: Oxford U Press.

Zahnd, Elaine, D. Klein, D. Crim, S. Holtby, and R. Bachman

2002 Alcohol-Related Violence Among American Indians. *In* Alcohol Use Among American Indians and Alaska Natives: Multiple Perspective on a Complex Problem. P. Mail, et al., Eds. NIAAA Research Monograph 37.

Zeiner, A., J. Girardot, N. Nichols, and D. Jones-Saumty

1984 Abstract. Second Congress of the International Society for Biomedical Reseach on Alcoholism. Alcoholism: Clinical and Experimental Research 8 (1): 129.

Zelditch, Morris

1962 Some Methodological Problems of Field Studies. American J of Sociology 67: 566-576.

INDEX

CPSIA information can be obtained at www.ICGtesting.com
Printed in the USA
LVOW07s0016171114

414026LV00001B/238/P